THE GENESIS OF BANGLADESH

THE GENESIS OF BANGLADESH

*A Study in International Legal Norms and
Permissive Conscience*

SUBRATA ROY CHOWDHURY

M.A. (CAL.), M.A. (CANTAB.)

*of Lincoln's Inn, Barrister-at-Law,
Senior Advocate, Supreme Court of India and High Court at Calcutta*

ASIA PUBLISHING HOUSE

NEW YORK

LIBRARY OF CONGRESS CATALOG CARD NUMBER 72-85069

ISBN O 210 40504 X

*First Published July 1972
2nd Printing December 1972*

MANUFACTURED IN THE UNITED STATES OF AMERICA

73- 18478

To the memory of my mother

LILABATY ROY CHOWDHURY

PREFACE

The events in Bangladesh at midnight of 25 March 1971 and in the subsequent months came as a rude shock to me, as they did to millions of others throughout the world. Since the creation of Pakistan many have been watching the developments in East Bengal with considerable disquiet, but it had never occurred to anybody that a repetition of the atrocities of Nazi Germany was possible under the regime of the United Nations Charter.

During my deep preoccupation with the Bangladesh issue the legal aspects naturally held my primary attention, and I came to realize that it was impossible to examine these in perspective independently of the relevant legal norms of the Charter regime. A persistent denial of the principle of equal rights and self-determination was the root cause of the problem. The political and constitutional history of Pakistan, and the social, cultural, racial and economic equations between her two erstwhile wings, examined in the first two chapters of the book, if viewed in the perspective of the legal norms formulated in the fifth chapter, reveal the startling paradox of a dependent people in a technically independent country. This is what Sheikh Mujibur Rahman meant by his familiar Bengali phrase *swadhin deshe paradhin nagarik*.

The lesson of Bangladesh is of perennial importance to the international community. The failure to reconcile the true content of self-determination with the territorial concept of independence not only was the crux of the problem in Bangladesh but, unfortunately, still is a major problem in many parts of the world. In contemporary law 'independence' is an attribute of the people, not of a physical territory. A status of subordination or colonial status is the inevitable outcome of the denial of the right of self-determination to the people even in a technically independent country.

In the last two chapters of the book I have drawn liberally from the American political tradition from Jefferson to Kennedy. I attach particular importance to the seven main points of difference between the American Civil War and the independence movement in Bangladesh. There is no parallel. On the contrary, the analogy applicable is that of the American War of Independence and Jefferson's famous declaration of 4 July 1776. In my attempt to reconcile the norms of recognition and self-determination I have been inspired by the immortal concepts formulated, in particular, by Jefferson, Lincoln and Wilson. But I regret that I have not been able to reconcile the precepts of the great American thinkers with the practice of the

Nixon-Kissinger Administration. It was left to Prime Minister Indira Gandhi to interpret the American principles in the light of the contemporary happenings and to apply this unhesitatingly to the case of Bangladesh. My study of the crisis of morals on the Bangladesh question inevitably led me to a modest research on the dichotomy between the two Americas—Lincoln's America and Nixon's America.

My investigations on the Bangladesh question also reveal the perfidious role of the United Nations in stifling a liberation movement and in giving succour to a military junta. Fortunately, the attempt did not succeed, but the experiment has reduced the credibility of the United Nations to a vanishing point.

Mrs Indira Gandhi's speech on 6 December 1971, granting recognition to Bangladesh, has raised the fundamental issue of the need for reconciling the contemporary norms of self-determination with the traditional norms of the law of recognition. This new bearing on the principle of recognition has been examined in the last chapter of my book. The principles which have evolved are now only of academic interest to Bangladesh, since a large number of countries have already extended her recognition, but these principles still remain valid for other situations in different parts of the world. For instance, the recent history of Argentina, Bolivia, Brazil, Burma, Burundi, Cambodia, Congo, the Dominican Republic, Ecuador, Greece, Indonesia, Iraq, Turkey, Libya, Mali, Nigeria, Somalia, Southern Yemen, Sudan, Togo and Pakistan—brings out the need for a reappraisal of the status of a non-representative government or a military junta in the law of recognition.

Bangladesh has won her independence without the international powers raising even a little finger to come to the help of her people and in spite of the permissive conscience of the international community. But she has had to pay a heavy price: over a million people have been exterminated, another two million were rendered homeless and ten million had to flee to India to live in conditions of unimaginable hardship in spite of India's best efforts. Atrocious war crimes, genocidal acts and other crimes against humanity were committed in Bangladesh by the Pakistani forces and their collaborators. One does not know when the horrifying discoveries of mass graves in different parts of Bangladesh will be completed. The imperative need for the trial of the criminals in the above context has currently assumed great importance. Chapter III of the book deals with this.

The emergence of Bangladesh as an independent sovereign state, her war of liberation, and the performance of her government during the last two weeks of December 1971 have been discussed in Chapter IV. This book appears shortly before the first anniversary of independence of the people of Bangladesh, while incidents of the immediate past are still fresh in the memory of her people. It may be argued that had the author waited longer more authentic facts regarding what happened after 25 March 1971 could have been established and the book's permanent value would have been enhanced. But the commentator on contemporary events must be reconciled to this inadequacy. He is not privileged to share the hindsight of his colleagues who might write a decade or two later. What he can do in the circumstances is to study what available material he has with discrimination, and this I have tried to do. I may add that in my examination of events in Bangladesh after 25 March 1971 I have greatly benefited from the discussions I have had with many of the political leaders of Bangladesh whom I had the opportunity of meeting, notably, Khondakar Moshtaque Ahmed, Abdus Samad Azad, A. H. M. Kamaruzzaman, Yusuf Ali, Abdul Mannan, Amirul Islam, K. M. Salauddin, Hossain Ali and Badal Rashid, and some of the important members of the Mukti Bahini whom I interviewed. I had the privilege of talking to some of the refugee intellectuals who came to Calcutta about their problems and aspirations. This qualified my ideas in many respects.

I have tried to follow the events in Bangladesh since 25 March 1971 with close attention. Since there was a complete news blackout in responsible public media and since Pakistan imposed an embargo on neutral observers, naturally the scope of the researcher was limited. For a judicious assessment of the happenings, political observers have had to rely mainly on what reports the international press could release. Following the precedent of Bertrand Russell in *War Crimes in Vietnam*, I have been careful to rely on only those sources which have been known to be balanced and impartial in their assessment. A remarkable feature of newspaper reporting on this particular case was, however, the unqualified condemnation of the brutality committed in Bangladesh by the repressive military junta of Pakistan.

Although a student of international law cannot hope to influence directly the decision-making coterie of big powers, yet a careful study of the issues involved in the struggle for liberation in Bangladesh may formulate certain firm principles and create a climate of sanity. It is with this end in view that my research was undertaken.

If I tried to express my sense of gratitude to all those who assisted me in the writing of this book my task would be enormous. Everybody with whom I have had discussions on the subject of my book contributed something useful, and often revealing, to the writing of it. My greatest debt of gratitude is to my friends, Dr. A. R. Mukherjea, Nirupam Chatterjee and Jatindra Chandra Ghosh, for going through every stage of the manuscript with care and discrimination, and to Professor John Broomfield of the University of Michigan, for reading the typescript and giving me valuable suggestions. Those who assisted me in collecting useful data for my book include such friends as Miss Basanti Mitra, Samaren Roy, P. N. Roy, A Huq, Dr. A. R. Mullick, Dr. Mazharul Islam, Abu'Jaffar, Dewan Ahmed, A. B. M. Khurshid, Dilip Chakravarty, Nitai Das Roy and Tapan Banerjee.

To my patient and long-suffering wife and family I cannot make a formal acknowledgement of gratitude, but I should like to record my sense of wonder at their charity. I am also grateful to those without whose devotion and untiring energy this book could not have materialized: Sri Nripen Gupta, my secretary and guide of the typing pool, and Sri G. Mukherjee, stenographer.

Asia Publishing House have taken great care in the production of this book, as they have been most generous in other respects. But, I am told, this is characteristic of them.

SUBRATA ROY CHOWDHURY

High Court, Calcutta
March 1972

CONTENTS

CHAPTER ONE

EAST BENGAL—A COLONIAL STATUS

Introduction

In August 1947, the Indian subcontinent, so long under the British rule, was split up into two sovereign nations, India and Pakistan. While India was able to maintain a geographical unity, Pakistan was constituted of two wings, the East and the West, separated by a distance of 1,200 miles of Indian territory. This physical separation was aggravated by a separation more profound, namely, a complete cultural dichotomy between the two parts of Pakistan. The East, fiercely jealous of its rich heritage of Bengali language and culture, had never really taken to Urdu, the official language of West Pakistan, nor could it find any Islamic identity in the culture of the West, for the simple reason that the West had little to offer.

From the beginning, the eastern wing remained distinctly apart from the western. The political and administrative leadership was centred in the West, while in trade and commerce, East Bengal, supplier of foreign exchange crops like jute and tea, was turned into a dumping ground for manufactured consumer goods of the West. If the whole of Pakistan was subjected to the bizarre experiments of political adventurists, it was the lot of the East Bengal people to play, in the name of Islam, the role of a loyal but subordinate colony.

The political initiation of the people of East Bengal in the system of responsible government had started in 1861 and matured with the nationalistic movement in the early twentieth century when its seat was the undivided Bengal. Most of what is now West Pakistan played a negligible role, if any at all, in national politics. In view of this it was the denial of basic democratic rights to East Bengal by West Pakistan, and the attempted deprivation of the Bengali language and culture since 1947 that made the eastern wing seethe with frustration and anger. The achieved self-determination of East Bengal (now Bangladesh), both cultural and political, was thus the *terminus ad quem* of historically inevitable processes. Between the two wings of Pakistan there had always been a systematic and deliberate attempt to exacerbate, not to reconcile, the racial, cultural, emotional and economic differences between the two peoples. Persistent denial of the principle of equal rights and self-determination, continuous economic exploitation of the East by the West, unalloyed racial chauvinism and linguistic fanaticism of the Punjabi-dominated Western wing not only made the fusion difficult but ultimately destroyed Pakistan as one nation. Any objective analysis of the racial, cultural, economic and political equations between the two wings during the last 24 years will lead to the inescapable inference that East Bengal was transformed into a colony of West Pakistan.

Struggle for Self-determination 1861-1971

To appreciate the movement for self-determination in East Bengal one must always keep in view three cardinal facts. First, the people of East Bengal always had been in a majority in the entire population of Pakistan: 65·7 per cent at the time of independence in 1947 and 54 per cent according to the 1961 census. In 1961, the total population of Pakistan was 93,720,613 of which 50,840,235 people were in East Bengal. The majority continued till 1971. Second, the people of East Bengal accepted a single Muslim state of Pakistan on the basis of the minimum self-determination provisions of the Lahore resolution of 1940, namely, equal and autonomous status of the two wings— East and West. Third, it is important for the international community to remember that in terms of political maturity and administrative experience, the struggle of the Bengali people for independence is qualitatively different from the struggle for self-determination in Southern Rhodesia or Portuguese Angola or South-West Africa or any other colonial or trust territory. For the transfer of power from the British rulers to the people of the subcontinent, it had taken 86 years of political exercise in the system of responsible government; but for the people of East Bengal, the struggle for self-determination was to continue for another 24 years. It is, therefore, the story of a people struggling for independence for a period of 110 years.

A brief reference to the pre-independence political and constitutional history will perhaps be relevant. As early as in 1861 'the seeds of representative institutions' were considered to have been sowed by the Indian Councils Act of 1861 (24 & 25 Vict. C. 67), because the Governor-General's executive council was required to include certain non-official members while transacting legislative business as a legislative council. The Indian Councils Act of 1909, implementing the Morley-Minto reforms, introduced an elected non-official majority into the Provincial Legislative Council; its deliberative functions were also increased to cover resolutions on the budget and in matters of public interest, save certain specific subjects, such as the armed forces, foreign affairs and the Indian States. As Coupland had observed: 'The Act of 1909 brought the constitutional advance begun by the Act of 1861 to the threshold of representative government.'[1]

[1] R. Coupland, *Constitutional Development in British India* (1942), p. 25.

The next landmark was the Montagu-Chelmsford Report which led to the enactment of the Government of India Act, 1919. In view of the growing demand for Home Rule, the British Government made a declaration on 20 August 1917 that the policy of His Majesty's Government was that of "increasing association of Indians in every branch of the administration and the gradual development of self-governing institutions with a view to progressive realization of responsible government in British India as an integral part of the British Empire."[2] The essential novelty of the Act of 1919 was the classification of subjects into 'Central' and 'Provincial' and the relaxation of the Central control over the Provinces not only in administrative but also in legislative and financial matters. The provincial subjects were sub-divided into 'transferred' and 'reserved' subjects. The foundation of responsible government was laid down in the sphere of 'transferred' subjects which were to be administered by the Governor with the aid of ministers responsible to the Legislative Council with 70 per cent elected members. In the context of the Act of 1919, the Royal Proclamation stated: "The Act of 1861 sowed the seeds of representative institutions; and the seed was quickened into life by the Act of 1909. The Act which has now become law entrusts the elected representatives of the people with a definite share in Government and points the way to full representative government hereafter."[3]

Next, the report of the Simon Commission was followed by the Government of India Act, 1935. As far as the provinces were concerned, the Act visualized the breaking up of the unitary state into a number of autonomous provinces and a federal structure in which both the federal and provincial governments should get definitely demarcated powers by direct delegation from the Crown. The Governor of the province was to act on the advice of ministers responsible to the legislature in all matters except those in which he had special statutory responsibility. Although the term 'provincial autonomy' was not defined in the Act of 1935, the principle was clearly stated in the recommendation of the Simon Commission: 'It is our intention that in future each province should be as far as possible mistress in her own house.'[4] Even earlier, the Montagu-Chelmsford Report of 1918 emphasized: 'The provinces are the domain in which the earlier steps towards the progressive realization of responsible government should be taken. Some measure of responsibility should be given at once, and our aim is to give complete responsibility as soon as conditions permit. This involves at once giving the provinces the

[2] D. Basu, *Constitutional Documents* (1969), Vol. I, p. V.
[3] *Ibid.* p. vi.
[4] *Ibid.* p. xv.

largest measure of independence—legislative, administrative and financial—of the Government of India, which is compatible with the due discharge by the latter of its own responsibilities.'[5]

The other feature of the Government of India Act, 1935, was the introduction of a separate electorate on communal basis—Muslim and non-Muslim. It had its origin in the pernicious Communal Award of Ramsay Macdonald. The statutory recognition of the communal policy in responsible democracy is an anachronism in any progressive society. It is a negation of human rights and fundamental freedoms. Yet, in this subcontinent, the familiar technique of *divide et impera* was employed by the British administration with responsive co-operation from a section of Muslim politicians. The guideline of the British policy can be traced back to 1860: 'Our endeavour should be to uphold in full force the (for us fortunate) separation which exists between the different religions and races, not to endeavour to amalgamate them. *Divide et impera* should be the principle of Indian government.' (Lieutenant-Colonel Coke, Commandant of Moradabad, 1860.)[6]

From the beginning of the twentieth century, when the movement for independence was gathering momentum all over India, especially in Bengal, it is ironical that a political conference on communal basis was held at Dacca in December 1906, attended by a section of Muslim religious leaders, landlords and professional men to form the All India Muslim League with its main objective resolution 'to foster a sense of loyalty to the British Government among the Muslims of India.'

The Muslim League grew up under British patronage. To allay the apprehension of a possible combined resistance to the British rule by the Hindu and Muslim politicians, the Governor of the United Province, as early as 1910, assured Lord Minto of the loyalty of the Muslim League: 'I have felt frightened lest the lawyer party, mainly consisting of young and irresponsible persons, would attain a predominant position, and that they might at some time coalesce with the advanced Hindu politicians against the government on one or more questions and later on rue the fact that they had done so. I think that the Aga Khan has put an effectual check to this, and that the League may be expected to be much more conservative and stable than it once promised to be.'[7] It is interesting to note that Winston Churchill, while resisting Roosevelt's plea for Indian independence during the last war, relied upon the report of the Governor of the Punjab: 'Responsible sections of Moslems, who are the majority, hold

---

[5] *Ibid.*

[6] Quoted by T. Ali, *Military Rule or People's Powers* (London, 1970), p. 25.

[7] Khalid bin Sayeed, *The Political System of Pakistan* (Oxford University Press, Pakistan, 1967) and quoted by T. Ali, op. cit., p. 27.

an unshakable view that until constitution for Moslem India is devised, Britain must continue to hold the ropes.'[8]

The Lahore Resolution and The Concept of Pakistan

The term 'Pakistan' appeared for the first time in a scheme outlined in the 1930s by Choudhuri Rehmat Ali. The scheme was for a Muslim state in North-West India; East Bengal was outside its ambit. When, in December 1930, Sir Mohammad Iqbal spoke about the need for creating a separate political entity consisting of Muslim-majority provinces in the North-West, East Bengal again had no place in it. Much later, in 1937, Rehmat Ali is said to have propounded his theory of two other Muslim states, viz. Bang-e-Islam for Bengal and Assam and 'Usmanistan' for Hyderabad (Deccan).[9] However, the definite foundation for the division of India on a two-nation theory was laid much later, in the Lahore Resolution of the Muslim League, in 1940. The resolution, moved by the Bengali Muslim League leader, A. K. Fazlul Haq, reiterated that the federal scheme embodied in the Government of India Act, 1935, was not acceptable to Muslim India. So it was: 'Resolved that it is the considered view of this session of the All India Muslim League that no constitutional plan would be workable in this country or acceptable to the Muslims unless it is designed on the following basic principle, viz. that geographically contiguous units are demarcated into regions which should be so constituted with such territorial readjustments as may be necessary that the areas in which the Muslims are numerically in a majority, as in the north-western and eastern zones of India, should be grouped to constitute 'independent States' in which the constituent units shall be autonomous and sovereign. . . . This session further authorizes the Working Committee to frame a scheme of constitution in accordance with these basic principles, providing for the assumption finally by the respective regions of all powers such as defence, external affairs, communications, customs and such other matters as may be necessary.'[10]

It is clear from the basic instrument that the constitutional plan of the Muslims in India visualized two independent states for the North-Western and the Eastern Zones of India where the Muslims were in a majority. This is the only interpretation which is consistent with the concluding part of the resolution, since it is inconceivable

---

[8] Winston Churchill, *The Second World War* (ed. Chartwell), Vol. IV, p. 163.

[9] *Bangla Desh—Background and Perspectives*, ed. Dr. Subhas C. Kashyap, Institute of Constitutional and Parliamentary Studies, New Delhi (National 1971), pp.5-7; D. N. Banerjee, *East Pakistan* (Vikas, 1969) pp. 26-7.

[10] C. H. Phillips, *The Evolution of India and Pakistan, 1858-1947 Selected Documents* (Oxford University Press, London), pp. 354-55.

that except on the basis of a completely independent status, either of the two regions could be expected to exercise such powers as defence, external affairs and customs.   The idea, therefore, was that the independent state in the North-Western Zone would comprise the Muslim majority provinces, each province to be an autonomous constituent unit; similarly if the independent state in the Eastern Zone consisted of two provinces, each province was to be an autonomous constituent unit.

It is true that subsequently Pakistan was mentioned as one state composed of two Zones, North-West and North-East, but even then reliance was always placed on the Lahore resolution.   One may refer in this connexion to Mr. M. A. Jinnah's letter to Mahatma Gandhi of 25 September 1944.[11]

The subcontinent was partitioned under the provisions of the Indian Independence Act, 1947, implementing the British Government Policy Statement of 3 June 1947. In the result, two independent Dominions, India and Pakistan, came into existence.   Although Pakistan emerged as a single state, the creation of the state can never be dissociated from the basic self-determination provisions of the Lahore resolution, namely, equal and autonomous status of its two wings in the East and West. It is only on this basis that the politically-conscious people of East Bengal accepted the partition of India and the creation of a single Muslim state.

Pakistan : Equations between East and West

The political and constitutional history of Pakistan during the last 24 years conclusively demonstrate not only a forcible denial by the West the autonomous status of the East, but the implementation of a deliberate policy of reducing the East to a status of subordination. The equations between the two wings of Pakistan—geographic, ethnic, linguistic, cultural, social, political, economic and administrative—seem to indicate that the status of the Eastern wing in relation to the Western wing was a colonial status according to the contemporary norms of international law discussed in Chapter V.   We shall now proceed to examine briefly the relevant facts.

The two erstwhile wings of Pakistan are in fact two different countries separated by 1,200 miles of Indian territory, 2,450 miles away by sea, and there is no direct land communication.   There is a popular belief that where West Pakistan ends, the Middle East begins, but where East Pakistan ends South-East Asia begins.   The West is mountainous, arid and desolate; but the East, with its lush green fields and luxuriant vegetation, is a deltaic land traversed by mighty

---

[11]*Ibid.* p. 357.

rivers and innumerable streams swollen by the monsoon rains. Geography, climate and the difference in fertility of soil not only account for the difference in density of population—922 people per square mile in the East, and only 138 per square mile in the West—but also explain the temperamental difference—the West is pragmatic, the East is emotional. Once the Bengalis come out of their shell, they are extremely friendly with non-Bengalis. Even President Ayub Khan had to concede: 'I found that once you got to know an East Pakistani he really accepted you, without reservation.'[12]

The people of East Bengal not only live in a compact and homogeneous atmosphere but speak only one language—Bengali, with its rich heritage of literary treasures. This has helped the creation of uniform cultural patterns throughout Bengal—in the traditional folk lores in rural areas as well as in the sophisticated but intensely humane creative works of the great writers like Madhusudan, Vidyasagar, Bankim Chandra Chatterjee, Mosarraf Hossain, Rabindranath Tagore, Sarat Chandra Chatterjee, Nazrul Islam, Jasimuddin, Jivanananda Das and many others. There can be no controversy that in art, literature and philosophy, in music, poetry and prose, the Bengali culture has attained a status which has hardly been paralled in West Pakistan.

In West Pakistan, on the other hand, there are four principal ethnic groups, each with its own language, in distinct geographical regions: Punjabis (20·8 million), Pakhtuns (5 million), Sindhis (3·9 million), and Baluchis (approximately one million), according to 1951 census. Urdu was in fact an imported language without any traditional or popular base in Pakistan. Thus, according to the census of 1951, Urdu was the mother tongue of 2·4 million inhabitants or only 3·3 per cent of the country's population—the bulk of these were immigrants from India who had mainly settled in West Punjab (1·07 million) and Karachi (565,000). Urdu was the mother tongue of only 268,000 inhabitants of East Pakistan or 0·63 per cent of the people living in the eastern wing. There was a slightly larger proportion of persons who could understand and speak Urdu. In 1951, in the whole of Pakistan, 5·4 million inhabitants or 7·3 per cent spoke Urdu. But in the eastern wing only 1·1 per cent of the population or 463,000 persons knew Urdu, while 98 per cent of the inhabitants spoke Bengali.[13]

[12] M. Ayub Khan, *Friends Not Masters* (Oxford University Press, Pakistan, 1967), p. 27.

[13] *Census of Pakistan, 1951*, Vol. I, Tables 7 and 7-A (Karachi, 1951); Y. V. Gankovsky & L. R. Gordon-Polonskay, *A History of Pakistan, 1947-1958* (U.S.S.R. Academy of Sciences, Institute of Asia, Nauka Publishing House, Moscow, 1964), pp. 98, 152 ; for brevity referred to hereafter as Gankovsky.

As early as in 1956, the insecure foundation of Pakistan, its under-
lying weakness, and future perspective, were, it seems correctly in
retrospect, analysed by Professor Morgenthau. He said:[14]

> But beneath these appearances of strength there is enormous and,
> so it seems, irremediable weakness. *Pakistan is not a nation
> and hardly a state.* It has no justification in history, ethnic ori-
> gin, language, civilization, or the consciousness of those who
> make up its population. They have no interest in common save
> one: fear of Hindu domination. It is to that fear, and to nothing
> else, that Pakistan owes its existence, and thus for its survival,
> as an independent state... These two regions, West Pakistan
> with the capital Karachi, and East Bengal, form the state of
> Pakistan. It is as if after the Civil War, Louisiana and Mary-
> land had decided to form a state of their own with the capital in
> Baton Rouge. In fact, it is worse than that. The two parts of
> Pakistan are separated not only by 1,200 miles of Indian terri-
> tory, but even more by language, ethnic composition, civilization
> and outlook. West Pakistan belongs essentially to Middle East
> and has more in common with Iran or Iraq than with East Bengal.
> East Bengal, in turn, with a population which is one-third Hindu
> is hardly distinguishable from West Bengal which belongs to
> India, and gravitates towards the latter's capital, Calcutta; the
> major labour unions in East Bengal, for instance, are run from
> Calcutta. The man in the street in West Pakistan speaks any
> one of four languages—none of which enables him to communicate
> with the Bengali-speaking inhabitants of East Bengal. A politi-
> cian in Karachi who is able to address an East Bengal audience in
> its own tongue has a rare political asset... Even Jinnah, the
> creator of this *strange state*, did not originally believe in its via-
> bility and there are few politicians in Karachi today who really
> believe in it. If there are solutions which could assure the *future
> of Pakistan*, only *extraordinary wisdom* and *political skill* will find
> them and put them into effect. If there is such wisdom and skill
> in Pakistan, it is not to be found among the politicians of Karachi.
> Thus it is hard to see how anything but a *miracle, or else a revival
> of religious fanaticism*, will assure Pakistan's future. (emphasis
> added).

The racial, temperamental and cultural differences between two
entirely different peoples, geographically wide apart, were sought to
be bridged only by the emotive symbol of Islam. The experiment did

[14] Hans J. Morgenthau, Military Illusions, *The New Republic* (Washington
D. C.), 19 March, 1956. pp. 14-16.

not succeed. Even though the technique is quite familiar in colonial administration, this was a novel experiment in the history of responsible democracy. It is inconceivable that a political experiment of this sort can ever succeed without implementation of the principle of equal rights and self-determination, without cultural and racial accommodation, without political freedom and economic justice, in the equation between the two wings. A total disregard of these essential requirements by the administering authority in the West eventually brought about the inevitable rupture between the two wings.

Policy of discrimination

A policy of discrimination has been consistently followed in every sphere of governmental and public activity—political, cultural, economic and administrative. To begin with, the movement for self-determination in East Bengal began, as we shall see later, as a revolt against the attempt of the West to impose Urdu as the only *lingua franca* on the whole of Pakistan by totally ignoring the status of the Bengali language. Eventually the West had to relent, being defeated by the Bengalis, but after much bloodshed and repression.

From a recent study by a group of scholars in Vienna,[15] it appears that in the field of education, the progress of 20 years (1947-48/1968-1969) indicates that, although the school-going population increased in East Pakistan, the number of primary schools decreased through a deliberate policy of neglect, whereas during the same period the number of schools in West Pakistan increased by 350% at a considerable cost to public exchequer. It has been said that there was a systematic plan for giving the West Pakistani children a better academic start so that their future career was firmly assured. The consequential disparity in the increase in the number of colleges and universities is as follows:

	West Pakistan		East Pakistan	
	1947-48	1968-69	1947-48	1968-69
Colleges—various types	40	271	50	162
	675% increase		320% increase	
Medical/Engineering/ Agricultural colleges	4	17	3	9
	425% increase		300% increase	
Universities	2	6	1	4
	(654 scholars)	(18,708 scholars)	(1,620 scholars)	(8,831 scholars)
Increase in scholars	30 times		5 times	

[15] *Why Bangla Desh*, the Paper of the Scholars in Vienna, which deals with

2

In East Pakistan, which had double the number of scholars in 1947, the number only increased by five times in 20 years, but in West Pakistan the corresponding increase is thirty times. In the field of research and development centres established for agricultural, medical, scientific and industrial research, out of 16 centres 13 are located in West Pakistan. The bulk of the scholarship and training grants for studies abroad under the Colombo Plan, Ford Foundation and Commonwealth Aid went to the West Pakistanis.

The disparity in the field of employment, and recruitment to civil, military and other services, appears from the following table in the *Vienna Paper*:

	West Pakistan	East Pakistan
Central Civil Service	84%	16%
Foreign Service	85%	15%
Foreign Heads of Missions (numbers)	60	9
Army	95%	5%
Army: Officers of General Rank (numbers)	16	1
Navy (technical)	81%	19%
Navy (non-technical)	91%	9%
Air Force Pilots	89%	11%
Armed Forces (numbers)	500,000	20,000
Pakistan Airlines (numbers)	7,000	280
P.I.A. Directors (numbers)	9	1
P.I.A. Area Managers (numbers)	5	none
Railway Board Directors (numbers)	7	1

The disparity in the field of social welfare is reflected from the following table:[16]

	West Pakistan	East Pakistan
Population	55 million	75 million
Total number of doctors	12,400	7,600
Total number of Hospital beds	26,000	6,000
Rural Health Centres	325	88
Urban Community Development Centres	81	52

The initial selection of Karachi as the capital of Pakistan gave the West a great impetus for development in different spheres. Rs. 200 million was spent on its development, and then it was handed over to the provincial government in the West. Thereafter another Rs. 200 million was allocated for the development of the capital at Islamabad. Only a sum of Rs. 20 million was provided for a second

educational, economic, industrial and administrative equations between the two wings of Pakistan, is based on statistics from official and other reliable sources. Our calculation is based on that. (For brevity, referred hereafter as the *Vienna Paper*): reproduced in *Bangla Desh Documents* (External Affairs Ministry, New Delhi, September 1971) pp. 15-22.

[16] *Ibid.*

capital at Dacca in East Pakistan. All the offices of the Central Government are located in the West including the headquarters of the army, navy, air force and the military academies. Head offices of the public and other important establishments, such as, State Bank of Pakistan, Pakistan International Airlines, National Bank of Pakistan, Insurance Companies, Pakistan Industrial Development Corporation, National Shipping Corporation, Foreign Missions and Agencies are situated in West Pakistan.[17]

Economic Subordination

In the economic field, the equation between the two wings of Pakistan discloses an unmistakable pattern of colonial exploitation of the East by the West. The basic objective has been so to regulate the economic and financial policies that not only should the West develop industrially at the expense of the East, but the East should remain a captive market for the industrial products of the West. The impact of this discriminatory policy is reflected in the disparities between the *per capita* income in the two wings. In 1959-60, the *per capita* income in the West was 32 per cent higher than in the East; but it was 61 per cent higher by 1969-70. Thus in ten years the income gap doubled in percentage terms; it increased even more in absolute terms.[18] In terms of rupees, the difference in *per capita* income between West and East was Rs. 86 in 1960; but it went up to Rs. 184 in 1970. The staple food is rice in East Bengal and wheat in West Pakistan. The market price of rice per maund (82 lbs.) is Rs. 18 in West Pakistan but Rs. 50 in East Pakistan; the market price of wheat per maund (82 lbs.) is Rs. 10 in West Pakistan but Rs. 35 in East Pakistan. The economic injustice therefore becomes clear when one compares the *per capita* income and the market price of staple food between the two wings.[19]

The widening gap of income between the two wings can be traced to three principal sources.

[17] *Ibid.*
[18] E. S. Mason, R. Dorfman and S. A. Marglin, *Conflict in East Pakistan: Background and Prospects*, Edward S. Mason, a Lamont University Professor Emeritus at Harvard University, and a former Dean of the Graduate School of Public Administration; Robert Dorfman, a Professor of Economics at Harvard University; and Stephen A Marglin, also a Professor of Economics at Harvard University (for brevity, hereafter referred to as the *Harvard Paper*): reproduced by the Department of Information, Government of Bangladesh, Mujibnagar ; reprinted by Calcutta University Bangladesh Sahayak Samity; for a summary, see *Cambridge Review*, 28 May 1971, pp. 1-4 ; *Bangla Desh Documents*, op. cit., pp. 9-15. This writer has drawn liberally from this excellent study and also from the *Vienna Paper* and gratefully acknowledges his debt.
[19] *Vienna Paper*, op. cit.

(1) Though East Bengal, less developed and more populated, deserved greater central assistance, the bulk of the development expenditure was diverted to West Pakistan. This will be clear from the following figures of the total development expenditure (public, private and outside plan) in the two wings.

Development Expenditure in East and West[20]

		West Pakistan	East Pakistan
Pre-plan	1950-51—1954-55	80%	20%
1st Plan	1955-56—1959-60	74%	26%
2nd Plan	1960-61—1964-65	68%	32%
3rd Plan	1965-66—1969-70	64%	36%

Another comparative study of the allocation of funds for development projects in the two wings of Pakistan reveals:[21]

Item	West Pakistan	East Pakistan
Foreign Exchange for various developments :	80%	20%
Foreign Aid (excluding U.S. Aid) :	96%	4%
U.S. Aid :	66%	34%
Pakistan Industrial Development Corporation :	58%	42%
Pakistan Industrial Credit & Investment Corpn. :	80%	20%
Industrial Development Bank :	76%	24%
House Building :	88%	12%
	77%	23%

During 1950-51-1954-55, 68·7% of all public sector investments were in West Pakistan alone; these went up to 70·2% during 1955-56-1959-60. During 1960-61-1964-65, West Pakistan's share came down to 55·2% from 68·7% and 70·2%, while East Bengal's share went up from 31·3% and 29·8% to 44·8%.[22] Although there was a marked upward trend in East Bengal's share of public development expenditure from a little over 25% in the pre-plan period to around 45% in the third plan period (over 50% of the expenditure on the Indus replacement works being excluded), the share of East Bengal in private investment continued to be low during the entire period and amounted only to a little over 25% in recent years.[23] Even this improvement of the position in public sector expenditure is more illusory than real since out of Rs. 1,600 crores allotted to East Bengal under the revised third plan, only Rs. 1,131 crores or 71% was actually spent. Further, the bulk of the defence expenditure (ranging around 50-55% of the revenue budget each year) as well as expenditure on

[20] Source: *Report of Advisory Panels for the Fourth Five-Year Plan*, Vol. I, Planning Commission, Government of Pakistan. July 1970; Table I of *Harvard Paper*.

[21] *Vienna Paper*, op. cit.

[22] *Bangla Desh* (National), p. 21.

[23] *Harvard Paper*, op. cit.

civil administration being concentrated in West Pakistan, the benefit to East Bengal was more nominal than what was really required.[24]

The bulk of foreign assistance including PL 480 was spent in West Pakistan. According to Sheikh Mujibur Rahman, 80% of the foreign aid received by Pakistan had been spent in the West and only 20% in the East.[25] The principal industrial enterprises financed by the Pakistan Industrial Development Corporation are located in the West. About 80% of foreign imports connected with industrialization went to the West. Even in those cases where industrial enterprises were set up in East Bengal, the beneficiaries were West Pakistani business-men. For example, jute mills in East Bengal were set up with a view to enabling West Pakistani capitalists to exploit the raw material resources of East Bengal.[26] By the middle of 1955 no less than Rs. 180 million were invested in the jute industry—47% of which was pro-vided by the Central Government through the Industrial Development Corporation and the rest came from leading West Pakistani mer-chants.[27]

A comparative study[28] of the industrial development shows the striking contrast between East and West in the growth of the established industries.

Established Industries in both wings	West Pakistan		East Pakistan	
	1947-48	1966-67	1947-48	1966-67
Cotton Textile production in million yards	350 1,853% increase	6,836	508 8.26% increase	550
Sugar production in thousand tons	10 2,940% increase	304	25 348% increase	112
Cement production in thousand tons	305 534% increase	1,934	46 63% increase	75

In the field of new industries the percentage of investments in West and East is roughly 75% and 25% respectively. The basic industry, steel, is produced in two mills situated in West and East Pakistan. Funds provided for these mills were £56 million for West Pakistan and £11 million for East Pakistan. Again, with regard to power development, West Pakistan generates by hydel, thermal and other

[24] *Bangla Desh—A Struggle for Nationhood* (Vikas Publications, 1971) pp. 17-8; *Economic Survey of East Pakistan, 1969-70; Pakistan Observer* (Dacca) July 1, 1970.
[25] *Dawn*, Karachi, 29 October 1970. For discrimination in disbursements of huge foreign aid received from China, USSR, U.K. and USA, see *Vienna Paper*, op. cit.
[26] Gankovsky, *A History of Pakistan 1947-1958*, p. 190.
[27] *Bangla Desh* (National), p. 21, f.n. 30.
[28] *Vienna Paper*, op. cit.

means a total of 838,000 KW (83% of the total) whereas East Pakistan generates 79,500 KW (17% of the total).[29]

Similar discrimination in favour of the West can be noticed in the field of agricultural development. Of the total funds allotted for agricultural development during the first 6 years, 79·6% went to West Pakistan. Of the total loans sanctioned by the Central Government between 1948 and 1953, the West was allotted Rs. 329,300,000 of which Rs. 277,700,000 or 83·9% was actually used; during the same period Rs. 164,100,000 was allotted to East Bengal but only Rs. 82,000,000 or 49·9% could be used. The loans could not be utilized because the development plans were not effectively carried out and also because the necessary machinery was not made available. On the other hand, the West not only received priority in the grant of loans but also had better opportunity of using them. Even in the West, the bulk went to Punjab. For instance, of Rs. 277,700,000 received by the West for agricultural development, Rs. 226,500,000 were allotted to Punjab, while Sind received only Rs. 6,000,000; NWFP Rs. 45,200,000 and Baluchistan not a single anna.[30]

Most of the large irrigation projects have been treated as federal projects, financed by the Central Government, and have been completed in West Pakistan. Although agricultural land in East Pakistan has more acreage and most lands produce two to three crops a year, while in the West the acreage is less and productivity per acre much smaller, yet discrimination has been in favour of West Pakistan. The following table is instructive[31]

	West Pakistan		East Pakistan	
Fertiliser distribution during 1964-68 in thousand nutrient tons	739	66%	371	33%
Improved seed distribution during 1964-69 in thousand tons	342	89%	40	11%
	1951-52	1966-67	1951-52	1966-67
Increase in fish production in thousand metric tons	56	153	175	259
	273% increase		48% increase	
Distribution of tractors :				
Wheel type (numbers)	20,069		1,825	
Other large (numbers)	2,000		350	
	91% increase		9% increase	

It is no wonder that while in Punjab there was a green revolution, in East Bengal there was stagnation in rice production. This, coupled with a decline in the world price of jute, led to a sharp increase in the ranks of landless labourers and a pronounced fall in

[29] *Ibid.*
[30] Gankovsky, op. cit., p. 191.
[31] *Vienna Paper*, op. cit.

the *per capita* income of the agricultural population in East Bengal. The average of rural *per capita* income in East Bengal at the 1959-60 price was Rs. 228 during the period 1949-50 to 1963-64 but it went down to Rs. 198 during the period 1964-65 to 1967-68.[32]

(2) There has been a systematic diversion of foreign trade earnings of East Bengal for financing the imports of West Pakistan. East Bengal, with its larger share of foreign export earnings, did not receive the corresponding benefit in foreign imports to help its industrial development. This will appear evident from the following table:[33]

Period		Percentage share of East Pakistan in foreign exports	Percentage share of East Pakistan in foreign imports
Pre-plan	1948/49—1954/55	50.1%	28.0%
1st Plan	1955/56—1959/60	61.4%	32.1%
2nd Plan	1960/61—1964/65	59.5%	30.6%
3rd Plan	1965/66—1969/70	49.8%	32.8%

From 1948 to 1953, the foreign trade balance was favourable to East Bengal to the tune of Rs. 2,900 million.[34] This huge surplus was used, not for developing the industrial potentials in East Bengal, but for offsetting the chronic unfavourable trade balance of West Pakistan which exported much less than the East and yet absorbed no less than 70% of the total imports of Pakistan every year.[35]

The pattern even during the third plan period remains the same although, as we expected due to the industrialization of the West and the neglect of the East, West Pakistan's share of total exports has shown some improvement.

(3) The general economic policy was formulated with a view to favouring West Pakistan at the expense of East Bengal making the latter a captive market for the West and by transfer of resources from the East to the West. Table 3 in the *Harvard Paper* shows that during 1957-58 and during 1961-62, exports to East Pakistan as a percentage of West Pakistan's total exports was often as high as 60%; even in recent years the figure varies between 40% to 50%; 42·8% (1964-65), 49·7% (1965-66), 49·4% (1966-67), 39·6% (1967-68), and 43·2% (1968-69).

[32] S. R. Bose, 'Trend of Real Income of the Rural Poor in East Pakistan, 1949-66', *Pakistan Development Review*, Vol. 8, 1968, pp. 452-88; Rehman Sobhan, 'The Rural Poor of East Pakistan', *Asian Review*, Vol. 2, No. 2, January 1969 pp. 136-47; *Bangla Desh* (Vikas), op. cit., pp. 21-2.

[33] Source: Table 2 *Harvard Paper; Monthly Statistical Bulletin*, various issues, Central Statistical Office, Government of Pakistan.

[34] *Bangla Desh* (National), op. cit., p. 17, calculated on the basis of the figures printed in *Statistical Bulletin*, Karachi, February, 1959.

[35] *Ibid.* p. 17.

In inter-wing trade relations, the East had a permanently unfavourable trade balance with the West.   During 1950-51/1954-55,
the annual average balance of trade of the East with the West was
adverse to the tune of Rs. 162·1 million and it went up to Rs. 283·7
million during 1955-56/1959-60 and to the alarming figure of Rs. 424·5
million during 1960-61/1964-65.   West Pakistan's annual average
exports to East Bengal during 1950-55 were in the order of Rs. 287·8
million as against imports of only Rs. 125·7 million.   During 1955-60
and 1960-65, the figures of West Pakistan's export to East Bengal
rose to Rs. 564·3 million and Rs. 881·5 million respectively, while its
corresponding imports from East Bengal during the same period were
only Rs. 280·6 million and Rs. 457 million.[36]

The general impact of the economic policy has been a considerable
transfer of resources from the East to the West.   As pointed out in
the *Harvard Paper*:

> An analysis of foreign trade data, coupled with the reasonable
> assumption that East Pakistan's fair share of foreign aid would
> have been a proportion equal to its proportion of Pakistan's
> population, 55%, indicates that a sizeable net transfer of re-
> sources has taken place from East to West Pakistan.   According
> to the official report referred to above, if allowance is made for
> the undervaluation of foreign exchange in terms of Pakistan's
> domestic currency, the total transfer from East to West over
> the period 1948/49-1968/69 was Rs. 31 billion.   Using a scarcity
> value of Rs. 11·90 to the dollar, this works out to $ 2·6 billion.

> The same conclusion was reached in another important paper:[37]
> The Central Government's instruments of tariffs, import con-
> trols, industrial licensing, foreign aid budgeting, and investment
> allocation have been used to direct investment and imports to
> develop high-cost industries in West Pakistan whose profitability
> is guaranteed by an East Pakistan market held captive behind
> tariff walls and import quotas.   Though 60% of all Pakistanis
> live in the East, its share of Central Government development
> expenditure has fluctuated between a low of 20% during 1950/51-
> 1954/55 and a high of 36% in the period 1965/66-1969/70. East
> Pakistan's share of private investment has averaged less than

[36] *Bangla Desh* (National), *Ibid.* p. 20.
[37] *History of Economic and Political Domination of East Pakistan*, a Paper
reviewed for The Ripon Society by J. Lee Auspitz, President, Ripon Society;
Stephen A. Marglin, Professor of Economics, Harvard University; and Gustav
F. Papenek, Lecturer in Economics and former Director, Development Advisory
Service, Harvard University: reproduced in *Bangla Desh Documents* (External
Affairs Ministry, New Delhi, September 1971), pp. 5-9.

25%. Historically, 50% to 70% of Pakistan's export earnings have been earned by East Pakistan's products, mainly jute, hides and skin. Yet its share of foreign imports (which are financed by export earnings and foreign aid) has remained between 25% and 30%. Basically, the East's balance of payments surplus has been used to help finance the West's deficit on foreign account leading to a net transfer of resources, estimated by an official report to be approximately 2·6 billion over the period 1948-49 to 1968-69.[38]

A recent research study by Dr. Hanna Papanek of the Centre for International Affairs at Harvard University shows that among the top 29 industrial houses in Pakistan only 2 belong to East Bengal. Most of these industrial houses are owned and controlled by West Pakistani Muslims of Punjab or West Indian origin and almost all of them have their headquarters in West Pakistan.[39] In the result, there has been a tremendous concentration of wealth in a few non-Bengali business families. It has been estimated by Mahbubul Haq, a leading official economist of Pakistan, that 20 such families control approximately 66% of industrial assets, 70% of the insurance funds

---

[38] This is also the view of American reporters on Bangladesh. *Time* Magazine of 2 August 1971 says: 'Even in less troubled times, Pakistanis were prone to observe that the only bonds between the diverse and distant wings of their Moslem nation were the Islamic faith and Pakistan International Airlines. Sharing neither borders nor cultures, separated by 1,100 miles of Indian territory (see map), Pakistan is an improbable wedding of the Middle East and Southeast Asia ... In 1940, Pakistan's founding father, Mohammed Ali Jinnah, called for a separate Islamic state. India hoped to prevent the split, but in self-determination elections in 1947, five predominantly Moslem provinces, including East Bengal, voted to break away. The result was a geographical curiosity and, as it sadly proved, a political absurdity... From the beginning, the East got the short end of the bargain in Pakistan. Though it has only one-sixth of the country's total land area, the East contains well over half the population (about 136 million), and in early years contributed as much as 70% of the foreign exchange earnings. But West Pakistan regularly devours three-quarters of all foreign aid and 60% of export earnings. With the Punjabi-Pathan power elite in control for two decades, East Pakistan has been left a deprived agricultural backwater. Before the civil war, Bengalis held only 15% of government jobs and accounted for only 5% of the 275,000-man army. Twenty multi-millionaire families, nearly all from the West, still control a shockingly disproportionate amount of the country's wealth (by an official study, two-thirds of the nation's industry and four-fifths of its banking and insurance assets). *Per capita* income is miserably low throughout Pakistan, but in the West ($ 48) it is more than half again that in the East ($ 30).' See also *Time*, 21.12.70, 15.3.71, 5.4.71; *Newsweek*, 5.4.71.

[39] *Bangla Desh* (National), pp. 22-3.

3

and 80% of the bank assets.[40] The growth of this monopolist capitalism confined to a few families in the West naturally indicates the necessity for protected markets in the East. It is in this field that the control of the West in the administration—civil and military—has been found particularly helpful to the West and harmful to the East. The *Harvard Paper* concludes:

> The economic domination of East Pakistan has been facilitated by West Pakistani dominance of the Central Government. The military regime in Pakistan has existed, with modifications, since 1958, and the decision-making authority rests with a well-entrenched civil service and their military bosses. All senior military members of the administration have been West Pakistani and of the senior officers in the Central civil service, 87% were West Pakistani in 1960, and the proportion has not changed much since. The Deputy Chairman of the Planning Commission and the Central Finance Minister, key individuals in resources allocation, have always been West Pakistanis.

To appreciate the magnitude of economic exploitation and its impact on the movement for self-determination in East Bengal, one must refer to a typical speech of Sheikh Mujibur Rahman before the national elections in December 1970. He said:[41]

> Today barely two dozen families have acquired control over 60 per cent of the nation's industrial assets, 80 per cent of its banking assets and 75 per cent of its insurance assets... To turn now to the appalling record of economic disparity it is seen that during the last 20 years, out of the total revenue expenditure of the Government, only about Rs. 1,500 crores (that is only one-fifth of the total) was spent in Bengal, as against over Rs. 5,000 crores in West Pakistan. Of the total development expenditure during the same period, Rs. 3,060 crores (that is only one-third

[40] *Bangladesh* (Vikas), pp. 20-1. This is supported by the Pakistani President Z. A. Bhutto's virtual branding of 22 rich families of West Pakistan and impounding their passports. The families are those of Khan, Adam, Adamji, Amin Bashir, Bawani, Dawood, Faucy, Gandhara, Habib, Habib (of Arag), Hoti, Hussein, Hyesons, Ispahani, Karim, Maula Baksh, Moonno, Rangoonwala, Saigol, Sheikh, Valika, and Wazir Ali. All these families had sent capital out of Pakistan which they refused to repatriate. (*The Statesman*, 24 December 1971).

[41] See *Bangladesh Documents*, op. cit., pp. 105-12. For a few other speeches in the same vein, see *The People* (Dacca), 10, 12, 18, 21 October 1970. In his speech of 20 October 1970, Sheikh Mujib said that if the people of Bengal failed to wrest their usurped rights they would continue to live like slaves in their own soil which had so long been treated as a virtual 'colony'.

of the total) was spent in Bengal, as against over Rs. 6,000 crores in West Pakistan. Over 20 years, West Pakistan has imported goods worth more than Rs. 3,000 crores as against its own foreign exchange earnings of barely Rs. 1,300 crores. Imports into West Pakistan have been three times the value of the imports into Bengal. It was made possible for West Pakistan to import goods worth Rs. 2,000 crores in excess of its export earnings by allocating to it Rs. 500 crores of the foreign exchange earnings of Bengal and allowing it to utilize over 80 per cent of all foreign aid... The record in the field of government services is just as deplorable after 22 years. Bengalis account for barely 15 per cent in Central Government services and less than 10 per cent in the defence service. . . The total economic impact of such discrimination has been that the economy of Bengal is today in a state of imminent collapse. Near famine conditions are prevailing in the majority of the villages. Some fifteen-lakh tons of rice had to be imported only to save the people from starvation... While inflation has been mounting, those who are worse hit are the poor people of Bengal. The price of essential commodities has been 50 to 100 per cent higher in Bengal than in West Pakistan. The average price of coarse rice in Bengal is Rs. 45 to 50 per maund as against Rs. 20 to 25 per maund in West Pakistan and that of wheat is Rs. 30 to 35 per maund in East Bengal as against Rs. 15 to 20 per maund in West Pakistan. Mustard oil sells in Bengal at Rs. 5 per seer as against Rs. 2·50 per seer in West Pakistan. The gold price is Rs. 135 to 140 per tola in Karachi as against Rs. 160 to 165 per tola at Dacca. Even a customs barrier has been imposed against carrying gold from West Pakistan to Bengal. This injustice is the product of the management of the economy for 22 years by the Central Government.

Racial Chauvinism

Economic exploitation and denial of political rights are of the essence of every race-oriented colonial administration. Once you pierce the veil, as Abraham Lincoln did, the picture is the same everywhere: 'Turn it in whatever way you will—whether it came from the mouth of a king, an excuse for enslaving the people of his country, or from the mouth of men of one race as a reason for enslaving the men of another race, it is the same old serpent that says: "You work and I eat, you toil and I will enjoy the fruits of it".'[42]

[42] Philip Van Doren Stern (ed.), *The Life and Writings of Abraham Lincoln* (Modern Library, New York, 1940), pp. 449-50; Lincoln's Chicago speech of 10 July, 1858.

Fundamentally, the policy of discrimination has to be explained by the attitude of the West to the people of East Bengal. It is an attitude of racial chauvinism. West Pakistan represents a 'conquering' race but in East Bengal the people belong to 'downtrodden races'. One can find a typical expression of this attitude of racial superiority in the observation of no less a person than President Ayub Khan himself. About the people of East Bengal, his comments are:

> As such they (East Bengalis) have all the inhibitions of down-trodden races and have not yet found it possible to adjust psycho-logically to the requirements of the new-born freedom.

But about the people in West Pakistan, his comments are:

> The population in West Pakistan, on the other hand, is probably the greatest mixture of races found anywhere in the world. Lying on the gateways to the Indian subcontinent, it was inevitable that each successive conquering race should have left its traces here. Consequently, this forced mixture of races has brought fusion of ideas, outlook and culture, despite the linguistic variety that obtained.[43]

With great contempt Malik Firoz Khan Noon, a Punjabi bureaucrat and Governor of East Bengal from 1950 to 1953, once bluntly declared that East Bengal Muslims were converted to Islam from low caste Hindus and they were not real Muslims.[44] The inevitable reaction of the Bengali people to this attitude of unalloyed racism was clearly expressed by Ataur Rahman Khan, a former Chief Minister of East Bengal, when he said: '. . . the leaders of Muslim League (Punjabi dominated) thought that we were a subject race and they belonged to the race of conquerors.'[45]

As will have been observed, the racial policy was scrupulously followed in every sphere of governmental and public activity. The manifest object was to keep the Bengali people in perpetual subjuga-tion. After the elections in December 1970, when it became clear that it would be impossible to resist the transfer of power to Sheikh Mujibur Rahman's Awami League, the military administration did not hesitate even to launch a war of genocide in East Bengal. Incon-trovertible evidence examined in Chapter III establishes that the

---

[43] M. Ayub Khan, *Friends Not Masters* (Oxford University Press, Pakistan, 1967), p. 187.

[44] Quoted by J. Sen Gupta, *Eclipse of East Pakistan* (Calcutta, 1963), p. 20.

[45] Quotation taken from K. Callard, *Pakistan: A Political Study* (London, 1957), pp. 72-3 and Gankovsky, *A History of Pakistan 1947-1958*, p. 192.

object of the army of occupation was to destroy substantially the Bengali people so that the colonial status of East Bengal might be perpetuated.

The United Nations was a silent spectator to the promotion, dissemination and ruthless implementation of the doctrine of racial superiority in spite of the provisions of the U.N. Charter, the Universal Declaration and the celebrated resolution 1904 (XVIII) of the General Assembly. The military administration of the West implemented its racial policies with impunity in spite of the declaration of the United Nations that 'any doctrine of racial differentiation or superiority is scientifically false, morally condemnable, socially unjust and dangerous, and that there is no justification for racial discrimination either in theory or in practice.'[46]

We shall see later that the racial and colonial policies were enforced with sophisticated weapons from America and other foreign countries. One cannot help recalling what Abraham Lincoln had said in the context of white supremacy and Negro slavery. He would prefer 'to emigrate to some country where they make no pretence of loving liberty . . . where despotism can be taken pure, without the base alloy of hypocrisy', if Jefferson's famous declaration meant that 'all men are created equal except Negroes, foreigners and Catholics'.[47] Lincoln had also threatened to tear out the declaration of independence from the statute book if it did not mean what it said, that without exceptions, all men were created equal.[48]

Having forcefully demolished the white supremacy theory of Judge Douglas, Abraham Lincoln observed: "He (Douglas) is satisfied with anything which does not endanger the nationalizing of Negro slavery. It may draw white men down, but it must not lift the Negroes up. Who shall say, 'I am the superior, you are the inferior'."[49] It seems that the military authorities in the West were equally bent upon implementing a racial policy which under no circumstances should lift the Bengalis up, even though in the process the image of Pakistan and the prosperity of its Punjabi-Pathan elite were to be recklessly destroyed.

The real cause of the rupture in Pakistan in March 1971 was the continuous exacerbation, and not progressive reconciliation, of the long-standing differences—racial, cultural, economic, political and administrative—between its two wings. This is now a generally accepted fact.

---

[46] For text of resolution 1904 (XVIII) see (1964) 58 *American Journal of International Law* (AJIL), p. 1081.

[47] *The Life and Writings of Abraham Lincoln*, op. cit., pp. 53-4.

[48] *Ibid.*, p. 449.

[49] *Ibid.*, p. 455.

CHAPTER TWO

THE POLITICAL AND CONSTITUTIONAL HISTORY OF PAKISTAN

The political and constitutional history of Pakistan since 1947 can be divided into 4 periods:

I   Erosion of Parliamentary Democracy: 14 August 1947 to 24 October 1954.

II   Advent of Military Oligarchy: 25 October 1954 to 27 October 1958.

III   Political Experiments of a Military Dictator: 27 October 1958 to 25 March 1969.

IV   The Strategy of Deception: 25 March 1969 to 25 March 1971.

I   *Erosion of Parliamentary Democracy*
14 August 1947 to 24 October 1954

During this period one finds the gradual erosion of parliamentary democracy, to which the people had been accustomed during the preceding 86 years under the British rule, and the emergence of a Punjabi-dominated bureaucracy as a decision-making authority. The constitutional experiment during this period was designed to deny the right of self-determination to the people of East Bengal.

In 1947 the Constituent Assembly of Pakistan which also functioned as the Central Legislative Assembly was composed of 72 members, of which 44 were from East Bengal and 28 were from the provinces in the West, on the basis of one member to one million people. The Government of India Act 1935 was adopted as the provisional constitution for the dominion of Pakistan. Mr. M. A. Jinnah, the creator of Pakistan, took office as its Governor-General.

Temperamentally it was difficult for Mr. Jinnah to reconcile himself to the role of a mere constitutional head in a representative democracy. His dominating personality, the historic role he played in the creation of the State, his political background and the position of patronage that he commanded among his followers did not prove very congenial to the growth of parliamentary democracy in Pakistan. In a sense Mr. Jinnah was not only the father of the state—*he was the state*—the fountain of all powers.   The position became quite confused after his premature death on 11 September 1948.

Where effective power is centralized in the Governor-General, not his Council of Ministers responsible to the legislature, such power can be exercised effectively only through an efficient bureaucracy.   This is what happened in Pakistan.   Instead of merely implementing the executive policy of a Council of Ministers responsible to the people, the bureaucracy itself became a policy-making authority.   As Mr H. F. Goodnow had observed: "The major participants in the governing of Pakistan fall into two principal categories: the selected and the elected or, in other words, the bureaucrats and the politicians."[1]

Since bureaucracy became an effective source of power, the regional character of the bureaucrats became an important factor in shaping governmental policies. The undisputed fact remains that East Bengal was practically unrepresented in the Pakistani bureaucracy—both civil and military.   Out of 86 I.C.S. Officers who were at the helm of the civil administration, there was only one from East Bengal. The role played by civil and military bureaucrats from the Western wing—Malik Firoz Khan Noon, Ghulam Mohammad, Chaudhri Mohammad Ali, M. Shoib, Aziz Ahmed, Iskander Mirza, Ayub Khan and Yahya Khan—has been far more significant in the history of Pakistan than that of its political leaders.   The politicians from East Bengal were no match against the bureaucracy from the West supported by the head of the state.   It is no wonder that the political leaders under a facade of parliamentary democracy in East Bengal often received an effective retort from Aziz Ahmed, the Chief Secretary of the province, who used to say "I am the Government."[2]

The movement for self-determination in East Bengal began as a revolt against an attempt in the West to culturally subjugate the former.   In other words, the struggle for cultural self-determination preceded, and inspired, the struggle for economic and political self-determination in East Bengal.   Within a few months of the birth of Pakistan came the cultural disillusionment of the Bengali people. The Bengali members of the Constituent Assembly were not allowed to speak in their mother tongue.   When a protest was made by an Opposition member, Mr. D. N. Dutta, in February, 1948, the first Prime Minister of Pakistan retorted: "Pakistan is a Muslim State and it must have as its *lingua franca* the language of a Muslim nation. . . It is necessary for a nation to have one language and that language can only be Urdu and no other language."[3] Next month, in March 1948, the father of the nation, Mr. M. A. Jinnah, told the

---

[1] Goodnow, *The Civil Services of Pakistan* (New Haven, 1964), p. 36.

[2] Quoted by J. Sen Gupta, *Eclipse of East Pakistan* (Calcutta, 1963), p. 28.

[3] Gankovsky, *A History of Pakistan, 1947-1958*.

students and the public in Dacca that "there could be only one *lingua franca* for Pakistan and that language should be Urdu."[4] The defiant students of Bengal rose in protest and thus began the historic language movement of East Bengal. After the Basic Principles Committee had declared that Urdu should be the only state language, the Bengali students held a mass demonstration in Dacca on 21 February 1952. They were dispersed by the police, who opened fire, killing 26 persons and wounding 400.[5] This massacre aggravated the situation and, what was initially a movement for recognition of Bengali as one of the state languages, soon developed into a national movement for the protection of civil liberties and the attainment of provincial autonomy. Every attempt was made by the Muslim League rulers to paralyse this popular movement and some of them went so far as to suggest that the defence of the Bengali language was both un-Islamic and anti-national. Further, vigorous efforts were aimed towards this drive for cultural subjugation in attempts to introduce the Arabic script for the Bengali language, an Urdu vocabulary in Bengali textbooks, and generally by the farcical invention of an Urduized Bengali with a view to making it Islamic. With the demand for recognition of Bengali as one of the national languages, the leaders of East Bengal also demanded as early as in February 1948 equality for Bengalis in the armed forces and civil administration. The response of the Prime Minister on 2 March 1948 was: "We must kill this provincialism for all times."[6]

The struggle of the Bengali people and the repressive policy of the Western rulers went on unabated until 7 May 1954 when the Constituent Assembly was compelled to recognize Bengali, along with Urdu, as a state language, and passed a resolution to that effect.

In the political field the movement for self-determination has to be examined both at the central and at the provincial level. The denial of provincial autonomy was the natural consequence of the unitary structure of governmental administration in which decisions taken at the central level had to be executed by the bureaucracy responsible to the centre, and naturally the popular ministry responsible to the legislature had little say in the matter. As early as on 24 February 1948, a Bengali member of the Constituent Assembly observed: "A feeling is growing among the Eastern Pakistanis that Eastern Pakistan is being neglected and treated merely as a 'Colony' of West Pakistan."[7]

[4] *Ibid.*

[5] *Ibid.*, p. 192.

[6] K. Callard, *Pakistan: A Political Study* (London, 1957), p. 174.

[7] *Constituent Assembly of Pakistan Debates*, II, No. 1, 24 February 1948, pp. 6-7.

Hamidul Haq Choudhury, a disillusioned Minister of Commerce and Industries in the Provincial Government, resigned from the Cabinet on 5 December 1949. Immediately proceedings were instituted against him under the repressive law popularly known as PRODA (Public and Representative Offices Disqualification Act)—a strong weapon in the armoury of the Central Government for punishing the non-conformist political leaders, by disqualifying them from public office for a period of up to ten years. The extent of economic exploitation of the East by the West was indicated by Mr. Choudhury in the proceedings before the court. Between him and the Central Government, there were nine points of difference:[8]

(1) He proposed to float a loan in East Bengal and this was not allowed by the Centre.

(2) He drew up schemes to set up mills but the Centre got the Constituent Assembly to pass legislation transferring industries to the jurisdiction of the Centre.

(3) He vainly opposed the taking away of Sales Tax from the province.

(4) He pressed for a share for the province in the Income-Tax but did not succeed.

(5) He protested against the levy of a cess by the Central Government on certain cloth.

(6) He asked permission to start a commercial bank, but the Centre opened the National Bank.

(7) The Centre proposed to take control of the Chittagong area when he and his colleagues protested against it.

(8) There were differences between him and the Central Government over the control of tea gardens, mining and oil, and the jute policy.

(9) He criticized the Central Government in his Budget speech of 1949-50.

The life of the Provincial Assembly in East Bengal was due to expire in 1953, but it was extended by a year by the Constituent Assembly. Elections to the Provincial Assembly in East Bengal, which took place in March 1954, became a turning point in the history of Pakistan.   The non-Muslim League opposition parties in East Bengal, including the Awami League, formed a United Front under the leadership of A. K. Fazlul Haq, H. S. Suhrawardy and Maulana Bhasani which approached the electorate with its 21-point manifesto. The recognition of Bengali as a state language, full provincial autonomy consistent with central responsibility for defence, foreign affairs and

[8] *Dawn*, 26 November 1951.

currency, industrialization of East Bengal, democratization of the administrative apparatus, safeguarding of the fundamental freedom, repeal of the repressive laws and release of political prisoners—those were some of the important provisions of the 21-point programme, popularly considered as the *magna carta* of Bengali aspirations. Implementation of this programme would have removed the discrimination between the two wings and secured the foundation of Pakistan. In fact, the election was a referendum for and against the demand for autonomy. The contest was between the United Front and the ruling Muslim League Party. To ensure its victory, the Muslim League Government in East Bengal, headed by Nurul Amin, launched a campaign of repression and terror, raised the familiar anti-Indian bogey, arrested 1,200 supporters of the United Front and tried to suppress the progressive press.[9] The electorate, however, was not misled. It voted overwhelmingly in favour of the United Front. The ruling Muslim League was completely routed: all the ministers were defeated and Chief Minister Nurul Amin himself lost to a student candidate of the United Front. The United Front captured 95% of the Muslim seats—winning 223 out of 237, whereas the Muslim League won only 10 seats. Of the 223 Muslim seats won by the United Front, the Awami League's share (142) was the largest. A United Front Government with Fazlul Haq as Chief Minister was formed on 3 April 1954. Fazlul Haq announced that the first measures of his government would be to declare Bengali as one of the state languages of Pakistan; to release political prisoners; to abolish the visa system that existed between East Bengal and the border regions of India since it disrupted the economy of the province; he also declared that he would take immediate steps to undertake a thorough investigation into the jute trade and industry with a view to exploring the possibility of ensuring fullest profit to jute cultivators.[10] The Centre was, however, determined to prevent the implementation of the 21-point programme. Taking advantage of an incorrect report published in a foreign newspaper alleging that Fazlul Haq was planning to proclaim an independent East Pakistan, the Central Government declared him a 'traitor' to Pakistan. Fazlul Haq's government refuted the charges and publicly announced: "East Pakistan and West Pakistan are integral parts of one component whole and it is one and indivisible and nothing shall part us. We are for the autonomy of provinces and not for their independence, nor for separation of each other."[11] The Haq

---

[9] Gankovsky, op. cit., p. 200. According to Sheikh Mujibur Rahman, over 3,000 Awami Leaguers were put behind bars by Nurul Amin's Government: *The People* (Dacca), 12 October 1970.

[10] *The Pakistan Times*, March 17 and 19, April 3, 1954.

[11] Gankovsky, p. 205; *Bangla Desh* (National), op. cit., p. 30.

Government further declared: "We want to make it clear once for all that we are true Pakistanis and stand for the unity and strength of Pakistan."[12]

The Central Government paid no attention to the public declaration of the Haq Ministry. Iskander Mirza, the Defence Secretary of the Central Government, became Governor of East Bengal on 29 May 1954. On 30 May 1954, he dissolved the Legislative Assembly, dismissed the United Front Government and proclaimed Governor's rule in the province. During the first week of Governor's rule, 659 active members of the United Front were arrested, including 13 members of the Legislative Assembly. By the middle of June over 1,000 persons were imprisoned. Fazlul Haq and several other members of his Cabinet were kept under house arrest. The offices of the United Front were closed, strict censorship introduced, meetings and demonstrations banned and groups of more than five persons not permitted to gather in the streets. Apart from several military units, 40,000 policemen were employed as instruments of terror and repression.[13] Thus ended the attempt to introduce provincial autonomy in East Bengal through democratic and constitutional means during the first period of Pakistan's history.

At the Central level, nearly two years after independence, on 12 March 1949, the first attempt was made at framing a constitution when the Basic Principles Committee of 25 members was appointed for the purpose. Successive attempts were made by the Committee to frame a constitution without conceding the democratic right of the Bengali people to representation proportionate to the population. The first report of the Committee, published in 1950, while providing for a lower house on a population basis, allotted seats in the upper house on the basis of equal representation among the five provinces; important decisions would only be taken at a joint session. The revised report of the Committee placed before the Constituent Assembly in December 1952 contemplated a parity of representation between East Bengal on the one hand and the four units of West Pakistan on the other. East Bengal was dissatisfied because of the denial of the principle of representation proportionate to population and because Urdu was recommended to be the only state language. Finally another revised draft was placed before the Constituent Assembly on 7 March 1953 on the basis of an agreement between the Chief Ministers of East Bengal and Punjab. In the two houses together East Bengal was given 50% seats and the four units of the West were to have another 50%. The amazing part of the scheme was that any deadlock had to be resolved at a joint sitting of the two houses by a majo-

[12] Keesings Contemporary Archives, 1954, p. 13746.
[13] Bangla Desh (National), p. 30.

rity vote which must include 30% of the members of each wing. The scheme was, however, adopted by the Constituent Assembly in September 1954. Although the representative character of the Assembly at the time was in serious doubt, particularly in the context of the elimination of the Muslim League as a political force in East Bengal, the acceptance of the scheme indicated a practical attempt to inaugurate a constitutional regime in Pakistan. The stage was set for the adoption of the Constitution on Mr. Jinnah's birthday, 25 December 1954.

The desire of the members of the Constituent Assembly was somehow to prevent further incursion of bureaucracy into the political arena. Their apprehension was justified by past experience. Ghulam Mohammed, Finance Minister, became Governor-General of Pakistan on 17 October 1951, when Mr. Nazimuddin stepped down and was appointed Prime Minister after the assassination of Liaquat Ali Khan. Ghulam Mohammed, formerly a member of the Indian Audit and Accounts Service, was an efficient Punjabi bureaucrat with immense political ambition who exercised autocratic powers. On 17 April 1953 he summarily dismissed Prime Minister Nazimuddin because the constitutional proposal envisaged by the latter was not conducive to the Punjabi domination. After the dismissal of Nazimuddin, Ghulam Mohammed brought back Mohammed Ali of Bogra, then serving as Pakistan's Ambassador to the United States, and made him Prime Minister. The ease with which Ghulam Mohammed could dismiss a Prime Minister enjoying the confidence of the legislature and then appoint a complete outsider to the highest political office is indeed a strange phenomenon in the history of parliamentary democracy.

About Ghulam Mohammed and other civil servants with political ambition President Ayub made some interesting comments:

> A civil servant who had become Finance Minister at the time of Independence elevated himself to the position of Governor-General. Another turned himself overnight from Secretary to Government (a civil service post) to Minister for Finance. All it required was rewriting the designation on the name-plates outside their offices. The politicians were naturally dependent on permanent services, but the more powerful among services had developed political ambitions of their own. Everyone seemed to have a group of his own and his sole occupation was to grind his own axe regardless of whether the country was ground to pieces in the process.[14]

[14] M. Ayub Khan, *Friends Not Masters* (Oxford University Press, Pakistan, 1967), p. 49.

With this background, in September 1954, the members of the Constituent Assembly decided to take certain elementary precautionary
measures.   The Law Minister, A. K. Brohi, introduced a bill with a
view to curtailing the powers of the Governor-General and making the
Constituent Assembly absolutely sovereign.   Two other bills were
introduced by M. H. Gazdar, Deputy President of the Assembly.   The
object of Mr. Gazdar's first bill was to provide that the Prime Minister
prior to his appointment by the Governor-General must be a member
of the Assembly; other ministers to be appointed on the Prime Minister's advice should also be its members; the Cabinet should be collectively responsible to the Assembly and the Governor-General should
function in accordance with the advice of the ministers.   The object
of the other bill was to repeal the repressive law popularly known as
PRODA which was recklessly used in the past to suppress political
opposition. All the three bills were passed by the Constituent Assembly
on 21 September 1954.[15]   Ghulam Mohammed was not in Karachi
when the above bills were approved by the Assembly.   His reaction
was prompt and surgical. He simply dissolved the Constituent Assembly on 24 October 1954.   The President of the Constituent Assembly
later challenged the constitutional validity of the Governor-General's
action in the Chief Court of Sind.   The Court declared the action of
the Governor-General invalid and *ultra vires* since the Assembly was
'subject to no agency or instrument outside itself to effect its dissolution or to give its laws validity except such as it itself chooses to
create.'[16]   Unfortunately the judgment was reversed by the Federal
Court on the technical ground that the legislation under which the
writ of mandamus was issued was not found to have been validly
enacted.[17]   Thus ended the efforts of the people of Pakistan to introduce a constitutional regime with a parliamentary form of government.

II   *Advent of Military Oligarchy*
25 October 1954 to 27 October 1958

While there was gradual erosion of the power of the legislature
during the earlier stage, the second period is significant for the total
eclipse of parliamentary democracy and the advent of military oligarchy in Pakistan.   During this period two bureaucrats—Ghulam
Mohammed and Iskander Mirza—were in absolute control of the

---

[15] G. S. Bhargava, *Pakistan in Crisis* (Vikas, 1969), pp. 65, 66; D. N. Banerjee,
East Pakistan (Vikas, 1969), pp. 72, 73.

[16] Quoted by Mushtaq Ahmed, *Government and Politics in Pakistan* (2nd
Edition, Karachi), p. 34.

[17] *Ibid.*, p. 35.

total power of the state.   They not only meddled in politics but controlled it completely by promoting endless intrigues.

After the dissolution of the Constituent Assembly the Ministry was reshuffled and a new cabinet was formed which was popularly known as the Governor-General's Council.   Mohammed Ali of Bogra continued to be the Prime Minister. General Ayub Khan, Commander-in-Chief of the Pakistan Army, became the Defence Minister. The members of the Council had no popular base whatsoever and they were only responsible to the Governor-General.

In May 1955, the state of emergency was called off and the scheme for a new Constituent Assembly was announced.   The Assembly was to consist of 80 members—40 from East Bengal and 40 from the Western provinces—to be elected indirectly by the members of the provincial assemblies.   On 5 August 1955 Ghulam Mohammad retired on grounds of health and Iskander Mirza became the Acting Governor-General.   On 19 September 1955, Mirza became the Governor-General.   On 7 August 1955 Mohammed Ali of Bogra resigned and Chaudhri Mohammad Ali, a former civil servant, became Prime Minister with a new cabinet.   It is significant that General Ayub Khan was dropped from the cabinet and A. K. Fazlul Haq was given the important portfolio of Home Affairs in the Central Cabinet.   It is worthwhile to note Ayub's reaction: "To provide a counter poise to Suhrawardy he (Mirza) started cultivating Fazlul Haq, forgetting that only a year before he had condemned him as a traitor.   The whole situation was becoming curiouser and curiouser. . .   Shrewd as he (Mirza) was, he could see how the Constitution could be used to promote political intrigues and bargaining.   No one knew any longer who belonged to which political party; it was all a question of swapping labels: a Muslim Leaguer today, a Republican tomorrow; and yesterday's traitors were tomorrow's Chief Ministers, indistinguishable as tweedledum and tweedledee."[18]

In September 1956, H. S. Suhrawardy replaced Chaudhri Mohammad Ali as Prime Minister; in October 1957 Suhrawardy was supplanted by Chundrigar, who stayed in office for a miserable 59 days and was replaced by Malik Firoz Khan Noon.[19]   At the provincial level, Fazlul Haq as Governor of East Bengal dismissed Ataur

---

[18] Ayub, op. cit., pp. 54-55.   About post-1954 election political events, in retrospect, Sheikh Mujibur Rahman had said: 'The people voted for Sher-e-Bangla, Fazlul Haq, but later he was termed as traitor; H. S. Suhrawardy, who was one of the founders of Pakistan, was also harassed and imprisoned. It is a misfortune for Bengal', he regretted. *The People* (Dacca) 1 November, 1970. Again, Sheikh Mujib observed that while Ayub Khan, after serving the British, claimed to be a patriot, those who fought for Pakistan were branded as traitors. *The People*, 26 October 1970.

[19] Ayub, op. cit, pp. 54-55.

Rahman Khan's cabinet on 31 March 1958. Later that night Fazlul Haq himself was dismissed by Iskander Mirza. Ataur Rahman was succeeded by Abu Hussain Sarkar, who was in turn dismissed within 12 hours of assuming office and Ataur Rahman's cabinet was again back in power. On 19 June 1958 the Ataur Rahman Government fell and Abu Hussain Sarkar came back to power on 20 June but had to leave within four days. The province remained under President's Rule for two months and thereafter Ataur Rahman was reinstated as Chief Minister.[20]

Apart from thriving in intrigues and corrupting political morals of a democratic people, Iskander Mirza's other contributions during the period were the formulation of his theory of controlled democracy, the introduction of an one-unit scheme in the West and the gift of a constitution to Pakistan. He was of the view, like his successor Ayub, that parliamentary democracy was not suited to the genius of the people of Pakistan and, therefore, he propounded as a substitute his theory of controlled democracy. In support of his theory he had declared that 'some underdeveloped countries have to learn democracy, and until they do so they have to be controlled. With so many illiterate people politicians can make a mess of things.'[21] This is reminiscent of the current argument of the South African Prime Minister John Vorster against the independence of the Africans in Namibia or South-West Africa, the only difference being that the people of Pakistan had a background of progressive realization of self-government since 1861.

It was during Mirza's period that the one-unit plan for Western Pakistan was implemented which aimed at perpetual domination of the Bengalis by the Punjabi dominated Western wing. The scheme was a Punjabi master plan carefully designed and skilfully implemented by Mian Daultana of Punjab. It meant the extinction of the identities and the aspirations of the people of Sind, NWFP, Baluchistan and Bhawalpur and the subordination of their democratic rights to the Punjabis comprising 60% of the population of the integrated Western unit. All opposition to the scheme was effectively eliminated. Daultana's famous document containing the scheme emphasized the need for a united West for effective 'confrontation with East Bengal'. To this Fazlur Rahman of East Bengal pointed out: 'It has been stated that the greatest merit of this bill is to do away with the distinction between Punjabis and Sindhis and Pathans and this and that but you do not realize that by dividing Pakistan into two, you are magnifying manifold (sic) that provincialism, by making it a local patriotism for the two regions. Then no longer the

[20] *Ibid.*, p. 56; Banerjee, op. cit., p. 100.
[21] Quoted by G. S. Bargava, *Pakistan in Crisis* (Vikas, 1969), p. 69.

cry will be Punjabis and Sindhis but the cry will be Bengalis and non-Bengalis.'[22]

The draft constitution was published on 8 January 1956. Eight days later the new Constituent Assembly took up the draft for consideration and by 29 February all the articles were debated and adopted. The debates were empty formalities because the members of the Assembly knew that the Governor-General had already assumed powers to frame a constitution under the Emergency Powers Ordinance which, *inter alia*, stated: "The Governor-General shall by order make such provision as appears to him to be necessary or expedient for the purpose of making provision as to the Constitution of Pakistan and for purposes connected therewith, and any such order may contain such incidental and consequential provisions as the Governor-General may deem necessary or expedient."[23]

The Constitution of 1956 was promulgated on 23 March 1956. Iskander Mirza was elected the first President of the Republic under the new Constitution. His Constitution was conspicuous for the denial of provisional autonomy to East Bengal and non-Punjabi units in the West, the introduction of the parity system instead of representation in the legislature on the basis of population, and the formation of an Islamic Republic instead of a secular democracy. The only merit of the Constitution was the recognition of Bengali along with Urdu as a state language of Pakistan under Article 214(1), although the identity of East Bengal was somewhat confused by the replacement of the expression 'East Pakistan' for the first time.

The Constitution did not satisfy the aspirations of the Bengali people, and opposition to Iskander Mirza's regime was mounting. Elections under the new Constitution were promised for November 1957. These were then postponed till 1958. Mirza never meant to implement his promise. As Ayub Khan had observed: "I do not think that he (Mirza) ever seriously wanted to hold general elections; he was looking for a suitable opportunity to abrogate the Constitution. Indeed, he was setting the stage for it."[24]

On 7 October 1958 at 8 p.m., Iskander Mirza in a dramatic sweep abrogated the Constitution, proclaimed martial law throughout Pakistan, dismissed the central and provincial governments, the national assemblies and provincial assemblies and appointed General Ayub Khan as the Chief Martial Law Administrator.[25] But within 20

---

[22] *Constituent Assembly of Pakistan Debates*, Official Report, 24 August 1955, p. 274.

[23] Quoted by Bhargava, op. cit., p. 69.

[24] M. Ayub Khan, *Friends Not Masters* (Oxford University Press, Pakistan, 1967), pp. 56-57.

[25] *Ibid.*, p. 71.

days three Generals of Pakistan saw Iskander Mirza and gave him an ultimatum to quit on behalf of Ayub Khan. Mirza was unceremoniously packed off to England and the military oligarchy assumed absolute power on the pretext that "all the politicians had been tried and found wanting; there was no one else left on the civil side."[26]

The military rule which thus commenced on 27 October 1958 in Pakistan is still continuing, for even though President Yahya Khan handed over power to Mr. Bhutto on 20 December 1971 Mr. Bhutto's authority is still being derived from the martial law of the military junta.

III   *Political Experiments of a Military Dictator*
       27 October 1958 to 25 March 1969

This is the regime of General Ayub Khan. He ruled like a dictator and did not pretend to have any faith in democracy. Having come to power through a military intrigue which he euphemistically described as a 'revolution', he frankly admitted that he had 'no sanction in law or constitution.'[27]   His regime was ushered in with a number of repressive laws by which every vestige of political freedom was ruthlessly suppressed. After silencing all opposition, Ayub made some experiments to implement his own political philosophy. He gave the country the institution of 'basic democracy' and also a constitution—the Constitution of 1962. His repressive measures did not succeed and the termination of his rule found him a bitterly disappointed man.

Ayub introduced a number of repressive laws through Presidential orders and ordinances and martial law regulations, such as the Elective Bodies (Disqualification) Ordinance 1959 (EBDO), the Public Offices (Disqualification) Order 1959, the Public and Representative Offices (Disqualification) Act Declaration Order 1960, the Public Conduct (Scrutiny) Ordinance 1959, the Security of Pakistan (Amendment) Ordinance 1959 etc.

When all political parties had been banned, meetings and demonstrations forbidden, and popular leaders imprisoned or disqualified or their movements restricted, the stage was set for Ayub to implement his political philosophy of basic democracy by the Basic Democracies Order, 1959 (PO No. 3 of 1959). Reminiscent of Soekarno's guided democracy and Mirza's controlled democracy, Ayub's philosophy was also inspired by a cynical and contemptuous disbelief in the efficacy of democratic institutions. To quote his own words: "Past experience had shown that the western type of parliamentary democracy could not be imposed on the people of Pakistan. . . It is too

[26] *Ibid.*, p. 75.
[27] Quoted by G. S. Bhargava, *Pakistan in Crisis* (Vikas, 1969), p. 30.

much to expect a man, sick and illiterate, and worried about his next meal, to think in terms of national policies. . . Unfortunately, we have no political parties worth the name; those that existed had no national programme.   To ask people to join in a mass ritual of voting for candidates whom they had never seen or known really meant robbing them of their vote by inducement or intimidation.   Such an arrangement suited only demagogues and charlatans."[28]   One is reminded of the familiar argument of a conqueror or colonizer—'inadequacy of political, economic, social or educational preparedness'—as a ground for delaying transfer of power to the people, which was so emphatically condemned by the United Nations in its famous resolution 1514 (XV). It will be interesting to recall the prophetic words of Abraham Lincoln from his Chicago speech of 10 July 1858.   "They are the arguments that kings have made for enslaving the people in all ages of the world.   You will find that all the arguments in favour of kingcraft were of this class; they always bestrode the necks of the people—not that they wanted to do it, but because the people were better off for being ridden."[29]

Since the elected representatives of the people could not be trusted with national policies or political power, the system of basic democracy provided for a local administration system.   80,000 basic democrats (40,000 in each province) were to be elected on adult franchise, approximately 1,000 voters to elect one basic democrat.   These single-member units in both rural and urban areas were then to be grouped together to form the tiers of the local administration system.   There were to be about 400 of these first stage groupings in each province. What was expected from the basic democrats was that "they should become the nerve centres of their areas where all local problems of development and civic responsibility could be studied at close range and their solutions discovered and applied with concentrated attention."[30]

Little enthusiasm was shown by the people of East Bengal, who were used to local self-government since the Bengal Local Self-Government Act of 1885. Increasing association of basic democrats with the bureaucracy at the expense of the politicians was one of the principal objectives of the system.   In practice the institution proved itself to be a fertile ground for recruiting supporters of the establishment by bribery, corruption and coercion.   It is common knowledge that many basic democrats were interested in contracts for rural work projects which were used as an inducement for political acquie-

[28] Ayub, op. cit., pp. 207-8.
[29] Philip Van Doren Stern (ed.), *The Life and Writings of Abraham Lincoln* (Modern Library, New York, 1940), p. 449.
[30] Ayub, op cit., p. 209.

scence. For those who were subservient to the regime, there was hardly any audit check into the expenditure of the allotted funds; but a charge of corruption would inevitably follow against those whose loyalty was in doubt.

While Z. A. Bhutto characterized 'basic democracy as only another name of fascism',[31] G. Tyson pointed out the reaction of the Bengali people: "But one of his (Ayub's) major problems is that the inhabitants of the East Wing wish to exercise their political genius a great deal more vigorously than the Basic Democracy will permit. The Bengali remains a highly political animal."[32]

After eliminating the possibility of any political opposition, and being assured of the loyalty of 80,000 basic democrats, Ayub announced on 7 January 1960 his decision to ask the basic democrats to indicate their confidence in his leadership by secret ballot. The ballot paper was marked 'yes' or 'no'. No wonder the so-called referendum on 14 February 1960 went in his favour. He then generously decided to give the country a constitution. The preamble to the Constitution of 1962, which was promulgated on 1 March 1962 and came into force on 8 June 1962 states: "Now, therefore, I, Field-Marshal Mohammad Ayub Khan, Hilal-i-Pakistan, Hilal-i-Jura'at, President of Pakistan, in exercise of the Mandate given to me on the Fourteenth day of February, One thousand nine hundred and sixty, by the people of Pakistan, and in the desire that the people of Pakistan may prosper and attain their rightful and honoured place amongst the nations of the World and make their full contribution towards international peace and progress and happiness of humanity, do hereby enact this Constitution."

The Constitution, in some of its important aspects, is a reproduction of Ayub's political philosophy which he had written down 'in a military fashion' on the night of 4 October 1954 at a hotel in London. It was 'a warmish night' and he 'could not sleep'; the document was prepared because he had a premonition that Governor-General Ghulam Mohammad might draw him into politics.[33]

The document shows Ayub's supreme distrust of the parliamentary form of Government. He had taken seriously the advice of the Aga

[31] Exclusive interview with *The Observer*, London, 6 July 1968: quoted by D. N. Banerjee, *East Pakistan* (Vikas, 1969), p. 163.

[32] G. Tyson, *Ayub Khan, the Reluctant Dictator*, quoted by Banerjee, op. cit., p. 154. Professor Hans J. Morgenthau has described the population of East Bengal as 'much more politically conscious and active than its western counterpart'. Military Illusions, *The New Republic*, 19 March 1956, pp. 14-16.

[33] Ayub, *Friends Not Masters* (Oxford University Press, 1969), pp. 186-91, for the text of the document; also see pp. 192-4. For text of the Constitution of 1962, see *Constitutions of Asian Countries* (Tripathi, 1968) p. 882.

Khan that 'if the parliamentary system is the one you are going to follow then you will lose Pakistan'. Instead, Ayub preferred a strong centre with a strong President. He said: "The intelligentsia of Pakistan had become accustomed to a sort of parliamentary democracy, but actual experience had shown that this form of government instead of serving the cause of the people had only encouraged divisive tendencies and brought the country to the verge of collapse. We had suffered enough in the past on account of it and could ill-afford to repeat the same mistake. The alternative form, and the one which seemed to meet our requirements, was the Presidential form of government."[34]

Accordingly, his terms of reference to the Constitution Commission contemplated a rejection of the parliamentary form of government to which the people were accustomed since 1909. The setting up of the Commission was really a farce, for he made it clear that he was prepared to 'accept the Commission's recommendations even if they were different from my ideas provided they were better than mine and good for the country'[35]—a controversy in which he was not only an interested party but also the sole judge. He gladly accepted the only recommendation that was expected from the Commission, i.e. Pakistan 'should have a form of government where there is only one person at the head of affairs.'[36] Distribution of power was alien to Ayub's political philosophy, for his main attack against the Constitution of 1956 was: "The Constitution, by distributing power between the President, the Prime Minister and his Cabinet, and the provinces, destroyed the focal point of power and left no one in a position of control."[37]

Ayub, however, did not accept the recommendation of the Commission that there should be a Vice-President to whom the President should delegate some of his functions and the occupants of the two offices should represent the two wings of Pakistan, because 'if he (President) were to be bracketed with a second-rate man the focus of elective decision might be blurred' and 'the supreme need would always be to find the best man for President, because so much would depend on him.'[38] In his Constitution the President was removable by not less than three-fourths of the total members of the National Assembly, but a novel deterrent was provided in Article 13(7) which, in his own words, meant: 'In order to check irresponsible and vindictive moves against the President it has been provided that if the resolution for the removal of the President fails to obtain one-half of the total votes in the

[34] *Ibid.*, pp. 204-5.
[35] *Ibid.*, p. 212.
[36] *Ibid.*
[37] *Ibid.*, p. 54.
[38] *Ibid.*, p. 215.

National Assembly, the movers of the impeachment resolution will cease to be members of the Assembly.'[39]

Under Ayub's Constitution, all effective powers, both at the centre and in the provinces, were vested in the President. The Council of Ministers at the centre was to be appointed by him and the ministers were not responsible to the legislature. The President's Council of Ministers might consist of outsiders or non-members of the National Assembly provided they 'are qualified to be elected as members of the National Assembly'. There were no effective safeguards against the President's power 'at any time to dissolve the Assembly'. The President had enormous powers to control the legislative functions of the Assembly. In the event of a conflict between him and the Assembly, the matter could be referred to a referendum only if 'the President considers that it is desirable'. The President would appoint the provincial Governors who would be 'subject to the directions of the President' and who would occupy the same position in relation to the provincial legislature as the President did in relation to the central legislature. The Governor could appoint his Council of Ministers only after the concurrence of the President. So large were the powers of the President that Chaudhri Mohammad Ali described the government of Pakistan under the 1962 Constitution as a 'Government of the President, by the President and for the President.'[40] In fact, Ayub did not seriously dispute, but tried to justify, his role as a dictator under his own constitution. To quote him:

> My opponents sometimes say: 'This man is a dictator; he has all the power in his hands'. How? I do not know. After all, there always has to be someone finally in charge whatever the system, be it parliamentary or presidential, a monarchy or a dictatorship. There are many to assist but, in the ultimate analysis, one man has to take the final decision. This has been the case throughout history, and it is so even today all the world over. If the man is chosen by the people and if he is a good man, he has to be trusted and given full co-operation.[41]

Is the President under Ayub's Constitution chosen by the people? The franchise question was left to the legislature (chosen by the basic democrats) which decided in April 1964 in favour of basic democrats serving as an electoral college for elections to the national and provincial assemblies and also to the office of the President. This was done

[39] *Ibid.*, p. 219.

[40] *Bangla Desh* (National), p. 39.

[41] Ayub, op. cit., p. 218.

in spite of the vehement protest of the All Party Action Committee and the observance of 'adult franchise and direct election day' on 18 and 19 March 1964. While popular leaders like Sheikh Mujibur Rahman and Maulana Bhasani were demanding adult franchise and direct elections, President Ayub pointed out that only indirect elections could ensure the stability of the government.[42]

Indirect election of a President and the members of the legislature by only 80,000 basic democrats in a population of over 100 million people is the most sweeping deprivation of the principle of popular representation. The form of the system of Presidential election in the United States, without its substance, was perhaps intended to be followed. Although in the United States the people vote for a President and Vice-President not directly but through the electoral college as an intermediary, the electoral area is the entire country and the people vote for Presidential electors who are in their turn usually pledged to vote for the respective party candidate for President and Vice-President. The American President stands at the head of a political party which has been able to capture a majority of the electoral votes.[43] The popular base of the American President is to be found amongst the ordinary voters throughout the country who have supported the Presidential electors voting for the winning candidate. On the other hand, the so-called popular base of the Pakistani President was the basic democrats elected earlier for the limited purpose of discharging the functions of local self-government. It is in this background that Ayub defeated his rival candidate Miss Fatima Jinnah and got himself elected as President in January 1965. *The Times*, London, commented on 2 January 1965: 'There is something unreal in the elections in Pakistan. Tomorrow 80,000 members of the Electoral College choose between two opposing systems of government but the excitement here is not open and public is suppressed, nervous and suspicious. The government had made it known that the Army would be standing by.' After Ayub's victory, *The New York Times* wrote on 5 January 1965: 'It may seem strange to Westerners to see a nation vote for virtual dictatorship over the possibility of internal liberty and parliamentary democracy—which was what the rival candidate, Miss Jinnah, offered—but this was understandable in Pakistan.' The purpose of keeping the Army ready at the time of the election is obvious. One can compare the free choice given to the basic democrats to a Napoleonic election in which Napoleon was supposed to have promised his soldiers that they could

---

[42] *The Pakistan Times*, 19 May 1964.

[43] C. B. Swisher, *The Theory and Practice of American National Government* (Houghton Mifflin Co, USA, 1951), pp. 150, 171, 336.

vote as freely as they pleased, but if they voted against him they would be shot.[44]

Ayub's Constitution is supposed to provide for a presidential form of government in a quasi-federal structure. In reality it is neither a presidential form nor is there any federal structure but it is a unitary form of government with the concentration of total power in the hands of one person. The President of Pakistan was given more powers than the American President without the obligations or the popular base of the latter. The American constitution provides for separation of powers in which the Congress makes the laws and the President is under a constitutional direction to 'take care that the laws be faithfully executed.' The idea of separation of powers is to prevent concentration in one organ since, as Montesquieu pointed out, there could be no liberty when legislative and executive powers were united in the same person and in the same group, or when the power of judging was not separated from legislative and executive powers.[45] The founding fathers knew that no drug and no beverage is more intoxicating than power over men and that intoxicated men are not to be trusted as unrestrained rulers.[46]

The American system therefore provides that the power and judgment of the executive head should be restrained by the power and the judgment of other men with proper checks and balances. After all, Lord Acton's formula still holds good that 'Power tends to corrupt and absolute power corrupts absolutely.' In spite of the vastness of his power, the American President is by no means a free agent. Notwithstanding his personal likes and dislikes, he must accept the body of federal law as he finds it, at least until he can persuade the Congress to make the desired changes. No doubt the President has the power of recommending measures for the consideration of the Congress and also the power of veto over all bills and joint resolutions passed by the two houses, but the Congress has the power to repass measures over the presidential veto by a two-thirds majority in each house. In such an eventuality the President of Pakistan could exercise the power of simply dissolving the National Assembly. It is true that a powerful President in America could exert a good deal of influence over the Congress. Lincoln's administration was characterized by some as a 'dictatorship' and Franklin D. Roosevelt was known to be a 'tough guy'; but they could wield such powers only because of their outstanding leadership and enormous popularity. It is therefore futile to compare the presidential system under the two respective constitutions.

[44] Philip Van Doren Stern (ed.), *The Life and Writings of Abraham Lincoln* (Modern Library, New York, 1940), p. 64.
[45] Montesquieu, *The Spirit of the Laws*, Book XI, Chapter VI.
[46] Swisher, op. cit., p. 62.

Ayub's political philosophy of a strong central government with one man in complete control of the affairs of the nation is a negation of a federal structure with two autonomous wings. In other words, Ayub's constitutional theory is completely destructive of the Lahore resolution with two independent states, or at least two equally sovereign autonomous wings in one independent state. It is a denial of the aspirations of the Bengali people. Having realized that dictatorial regime like the one visualized by him was inconsistent with the basic policy of the Lahore resolution, he got his Constitution Commission to put forward a case against the concept of Pakistan as reflected in that resolution. The reasoning of the Commission is as fallacious as it is grotesque. The Commission argued that the East Pakistan envisaged in the Lahore resolution was the whole of Bengal and Assam with their industries and large economic resources, but what Pakistan got as its eastern half as a result of the partition was 'the unindustrialized portion of Bengal'. Accordingly, the Commission concluded:

> If at the time of the Lahore Resolution, it could have been foreseen that ultimately a division would take place and that the present East Pakistan would be the only portion of Pakistan in the East, the Muslim League would not have thought of regarding it as an autonomous province because, without industrial development, it is impossible for East Pakistan to sustain itself as an independent unit. At the time the Lahore resolution was passed, partition of the subcontinent into two independent countries was not within the pale of practical politics. It seems to us extremely unwise and unrealistic to insist on a literal following of the said Resolution regardless of whether the present units of Pakistan can develop themselves, and manage their own affairs without a strong centre.[47]

At the time of independence East Bengal had all the potentialities of industrial development whereas West Pakistan was mainly an agriculture-based economy. Economically East Bengal was more viable than West Pakistan. Among others, jute, tea, sugar, paper, cotton, tobacco and leather industries had great possibilities in the East. The enormous water power resources of East Bengal, through well-planned hydro-electric projects, could have supported a variety of industries. Rural electrification could have promoted various small-scale industries. There had never been any serious attempt to survey or exploit the mineral resources of East Bengal. It is, therefore, unthinkable that the authors of the Lahore resolution, if they

[47] Quoted by Ayub Khan, *Friends Not Masters* (Oxford University Press, 1967), p. 213.

were to reconsider the matter in August 1947, would have agreed to a denial of a completely autonomous status for East Bengal. In retrospect, the real reason seems to be that East Bengal was deliberately deprived of the opportunity to develop its industrial potentials because it was intended to be kept as a protected market for Western products.[48]

The next remarkable feature of Ayub's Constitution was that the pretended gift of fundamental rights in Part II of the Constitution was neutralized by the sinister provision in Article 6(3)(ii)—'The provisions of this Article shall not apply to any of the laws specified in the Fourth Schedule as in force immediately before the coming into force of the Constitution (First Amendment) Act, 1963.' 31 Presidential Orders and Ordinances, Martial Law Regulations, Central and Provincial Acts and Governor's Ordinances specified in the Fourth Schedule were thus excluded from the scope of the fundamental rights. Among these, one can find many repressive laws comparable to those with which colonial rulers like Ian Smith had been suppressing the right of self-determination of the majority in Southern Rhodesia. To mention only a few: (i) The Public Offices (Disqualification) Order, 1959; (ii) The Basic Democracies Order, 1959; (iii) The Public and Representative Offices (Disqualification) Act Declaration Order, 1960; (iv) The Martial Law (Pending Proceedings and Protection) Order 1962; (v) The Public Conduct (Scrutiny) Ordinance, 1959; (vi) The Security of Pakistan (Amendment) Ordinance, 1961; (vii) The Political Parties Act, 1962.

Not only were the provisions of the protected laws rigorous in curtailing civil and political rights but they were being administered with the sole object of eliminating any effective political opposition to the authority of the military dictator. The objects of the repressive laws were *inter alia* to disqualify individually the political nonconformists, to control the activities of the political parties allowed to be revived after the repeal of the martial law of 8 June 1962, and to empower the executive to keep under detention political opponents without any effective judicial safeguards.

The worst victims of the repressive laws of the regime were collectively the people of East Bengal, individually the great Bengali political leader Sheikh Mujibur Rahman (popularly known as 'Bangabandhu'—the friend of Bengal), and politically the Awami League Party.

Born in 1920, Mujib entered the political scene as a young student

---

[48] Sheikh Mujib observed: 'Our flourishing weaving industry was made to suffer decay, salt industry destroyed and beedi industry dragged to ruination turning lakhs of people into virtual destitutes only to serve as a market to exploiters from West Wing.' *The People* (Dacca), 12 October 1970.

leader soon after independence. As early as in September 1947, he was disillusioned with the religious fanaticism of Muslim League leaders and organized a secular democratic youth movement at Dacca. He was a champion of the movement for the recognition of Bengali as a state language. Mujib was imprisoned in 1949 for his political activities. While behind bars, he was elected the joint secretary of the Awami Muslim League, the first political opposition to the ruling Muslim League. In September 1953 he succeeded in persuading his party to delete the word 'Muslim' from its name to make it thoroughly secular. He made great contributions to the success of the United Front in the provincial election in March 1954 and became a minister in the ill-fated Fazlul Haq cabinet. Mujib was elected to the Constituent Assembly in 1955 and gained considerable political experience as its member.

During ten years and five months of the Ayub regime, for a period of nearly nine years, Mujib was either in prison or under severe restrictive orders shadowed by intelligence people.

Soon after the promulgation of martial law, Mujib was arrested on 12 October 1958 under the East Pakistan Public Safety Ordinance. While under detention, the Ayub government instituted half a dozen criminal cases against Mujib but he was honourably acquitted in all of them. Though he was released from detention in December 1959, his movements were severely restricted. In 1962 he was again arrested under the Public Safety Ordinance. When in June 1962 Ayub allowed political parties to function again, Mujib revived the Awami League. At a meeting on 9 March 1964, the Awami League demanded full autonomy for East Bengal.

After the Indo-Pakistan war in 1965, Mujib appealed to President Ayub 'to give regional autonomy to East Pakistan and to make it self-sufficient in defence in the light of our experience during the war' when East Pakistan was completely disconnected from West Pakistan and the rest of the world.[49] After the Tashkent agreement of January 1966, when Ayub's Foreign Minister Z. A. Bhutto had resigned in protest and raised the cry of a 'thousand-year war' with India, Mujib supported the agreement because 'my people and I believe that all international disputes should be settled by peaceful means as we believe in world peace for progress.'[50] Early in 1966, when an all-Party Convention was held at Lahore to forge a united national opposition to the regime, Sheikh Mujib placed his now-famous six-point programme before the subjects committee, as a permanent constitu-

---

[49] Mujib's statement before a special tribunal in Agartala Conspiracy Case, see *Bangla Desh* (National), pp. 152-6.

[50] *Ibid.*

tional solution of the chronic problems between the two wings of Pakistan.

The six-point programme was accepted by the Awami League and was welcomed by the people of East Bengal from all walks of life. The spontaneous support of the programme made the military regime shaky. Ayub came to East Bengal in March 1966 and made an extensive tour of the province; in all his public speeches the attack was against the six-point programme and the Awami League. On 16 March 1966, while speaking at a public meeting at Rajshahi, President Ayub pointed out that the six-point programme was aimed at achieving their dream of 'greater sovereign Bengal', but warned that the 'fulfilment of this horrid dream would spell disaster for the country and turn the people of East Pakistan into slaves.'[51]   On 20 March 1966, while addressing the closing session of the Convention Muslim League at Dacca, of which he was the President, Ayub called upon his followers that 'they should be prepared to face even a civil war, if forced upon them, to protect the sovereignty and integrity of the country. . . . Civil war was a dangerous thing.   But if a nation faces disruption, it has to be accepted.'[52]

On the same day, 20 March 1966, at a public meeting held in support of the six-point programme, Mujibur Rahman called upon the people of East Bengal to prepare for 'a relentless peaceful democratic movement'.   He asked the Ayub government to explain[53] 'why East Pakistan could not be helped at the national crisis in September last? . . .   How was it that the Foreign Minister came out with a statement that East Pakistan was saved because of China?' He therefore suggested that both East and West should be self-sufficient in defence.

If by persuasion the people of East Bengal could not be won, by persecution they had to be suppressed.   This was the policy of the military oligarchy.   It was applied ruthlessly against Mujib and the workers of Awami League.[54]   On 7 April 1966, Mujib was arrested at Jessore and released on bail.   When he reached Dacca, he was

[51] *Dawn*, 17 March 1966.

[52] *Dawn*, 21 March 1966.

[53] D. N. Banerjee, *East Pakistan* (Vikas, 1969), p. 152.

[54] Sheikh Mujib said: 'When the six-point programme was launched four years back, we plunged into the struggle to save the people from exploitation knowing full well its consequences. Besides myself, hundreds of Awami Leaguers were immediately sent behind bars. . . . The offers for the Prime Ministership and other high positions in the Government were made to dissuade me from the movement but nothing could allure me because my mission has been to save the people from exploitation. I am not ready to make any compromise with my programme of demand for regional autonomy.' *The People* (Dacca), 12 October 1970.

again arrested and taken to Sylhet for an alleged prejudicial speech. Next day he was granted bail by the sessions judge of Sylhet but he was again arrested at the jail gate for an alleged prejudicial speech at Mymensingh. He was taken to Mymensingh jail and was granted bail on the following day by the sessions judge. He addressed a public meeting at Narayangunj on 8 May 1966 and was arrested at one o'clock at night under Rule 32 of the Defence of Pakistan Rules; he remained behind bars till February 1969. Many of his party leaders were simultaneously arrested. In protest the Awami League called a general strike on 7 June 1966. During the strike 11 persons were killed in Dacca and Narayangunj by police firing and about 800 workers were arrested. It was widely known that Mr. Monem Khan, Governor of East Pakistan, told his officers 'that so long as he (Monem Khan) was there, Sheikh Mujibur Rahman would have to be in jail.'[55]

In August 1966 a massive movement for autonomy was launched in East Bengal by the Awami League and the National Awami Party. The movement went on unabated in spite of the repressive policy of the government. Between December 1968 and February 1969, in East Bengal at least 117 persons were killed, 464 injured and 1,500 persons were arrested for participating in the movement. This was the general pattern of repression throughout the period.

In the meantime, on 6 January 1968, it was announced that 28 persons would be prosecuted for conspiring to bring about the secession of East Pakistan with India's help. Mujib was implicated as an accused 12 days later. This is known as the Agartala Conspiracy Case. The charge was based upon an alleged confession made by one Kamaluddin Ahmed. The confession was procured by inhuman torture.

A special tribunal was set up under the Criminal Law Amendment (Special Tribunal) Ordinance of 1968 promulgated on 21 April, 1968 for the trial of the case. The law of evidence was amended for the purpose of the trial by providing that confessions and statements made to the police would be admissible against the accused. Mujib exposed the design of the administration by declaring to the court: 'This is a conspiracy against me'.[56] In his statement to the court he stated,[57] *inter alia*: 'Ever since my detention I was facing a number

---

[55] Mujib's statement, op. cit.

[56] G. S. Bhargava, *Pakistan in Crisis* (Vikas, 1969), p. 36.

[57] Mujib's statement, op. cit., Later, Mujib said: 'I had no dispute with President Ayub—neither with property nor with business; yet sentence after sentence detained me in jail for long twenty-two months because I stood for Bengalees and spoke for Bangla Desh. That was the only offence. The matter went up to Agartala as a result of conspiracy against me. By the Grace of Allah, I came out in exchange of blood of my brethren and of the blessing of

of trials in Dacca Central Jail where the courts were being held. After about 21 months of detention on January 18, 1968, at one o'clock I was released from detention and from the jail gate some military personnel forcibly brought me to Dacca cantonment, where I was detained in a closed room. I was segregated and kept in solitary confinement and was not allowed to see anyone. I was not allowed to read newspapers. In fact, I was completely cut off from the rest of the world for five long months. During this period, I was subjected to inhuman mental torture and I was denied all physical amenities.'

Public protest against the farcical trial on a baseless charge was so great that eventually the Ayub government was compelled to withdraw the case and to release Sheikh Mujib unconditionally on 22 February 1969. The jubilation of the people of East Bengal was spontaneous and about 100,000 persons came to Paltan Maidan at Dacca to welcome their leader back.

In view of the persistent movement throughout Pakistan, particularly in East Bengal, for a constitutional regime based on adult franchise and direct elections, Ayub had no way out but to announce on 1 February 1969 that it was his intention to talk to 'responsible political leaders to solve the political crisis in Pakistan.'[58] At Ayub's invitation, a Round Table Conference of the political leaders was held for solving the crisis. Ayub had to concede to the demand for direct election based on adult franchise and a parliamentary system of government. No consensus was however arrived at on important questions like representation on the basis of population, dismemberment of one unit and regional autonomy for the provinces.

The movement for autonomy of East Bengal on the basis of the six-point programme under Mujib's leadership gathered so much momentum that it became impossible for Ayub Khan to resist it any longer. A frustrated man, in a broadcast to the nation on 25 March 1969, President Ayub announced that he was standing down as the President and handing over power to the Army Commander-in-Chief, General Agha Mohammad Yahya Khan, as the situation was no longer under the control of the government.[59] Thus ended the political experiments of a military dictator.

IV   *The Strategy of Deception*

25 March 1969 to 25 March 1971

The last cyclic breach of promise of the Government in power in

---

you all. And now give me a chance to save your blood from being sucked by others.' *The People* (Dacca), 16 November, 1970.

[58] Bannerjee, op. cit., p. 181.

[59] *The Pakistan Times*, 26 March 1969.

Pakistan to introduce a constitutional regime took place during the first two years of Yahya's regime. On assuming office as Chief Martial Law Administrator, Yahya dissolved the National and Provincial Assemblies and imposed martial law throughout the country. He appointed himself President on 31 March 1969, and banned all political activities. Ironically enough, in his first address to the nation on 26 March 1969, he pledged himself to strive to restore democratic institutions in the country and promised that he had no ambition 'other than the creation of conditions conducive to the establishment of a constitutional government.'[60]

On 3 April 1969, Yahya appointed a three-man Military Council of Administration and thereafter appointed two of his top military aides as Governors of the two wings of Pakistan. On 10 April he promised to hold elections on the basis of adult franchise. On 28 July Mr. Justice Abdus Sattar was appointed Chief Election Commissioner and was asked to reorganize the election machinery. A civilian cabinet of eight nominees was formed on 4 August, but the President kept Foreign Affairs, Defence and Planning for himself. In his address to the nation on 28 November Yahya reaffirmed his pledge to restore constitutional government and announced that polling for a general election to a national assembly of Pakistan would commence on 5 October 1970. The election was subsequently postponed till December 1970.

In his address to the nation on 28 March 1970 Yahya emphasized the achievements of his government and his plan for the peaceful transfer of power to the elected represenatives of the people. In the economic field, the need for removal of disparity between the two wings of Pakistan was clearly admitted by him and he promised: "I have given clear instructions that the Plan (Fourth Five Year Plan scheduled to be launched on 1 July 1970) should reflect a new strategy of development by placing greater emphasis on social justice, removal of disparity between the two wings of Pakistan, better distribution of income and accelerated development of the less developed region of the country. This is essential to ensure that the benefits of planned development are shared equitably by all Pakistanis wherever they may be living."[61]

Yahya also announced that a comprehensive programme would be undertaken for flood control in East Pakistan which was of crucial importance to its future and that the World Bank team had earlier identified 20 multipurpose projects for flood control and water resources development at a cost of about 800 million dollars. He

[60] Bhargava, op. cit., appendix VI, p. 211.
[61] Press Information Department, Government of Pakistan, Handout E. No. 684-R, Rawalpindi, 28.3.1970.

hoped to mobilize foreign assistance from all friendly countries to finance this programme.[62]

The ban on the activities of the political parties was lifted with effect from 1 January 1970, and Yahya admitted that except in a few cases there had been no abuse of the political freedom or of the freedom of the press. He said: "The Political Parties of the country were denied the freedom to propagate views and explain their programmes for many years and therefore when, on the 1st of January 1970, the ban on holding of public meetings and taking out of processions was lifted, an overenthusiastic use of this freedom was only to be expected. But unfortunately in some cases, people transgressed the limits of good order... It has been to me very gratifying that, by and large, our Press has acted in a most responsible manner."[63]

The Legal Framework Order (President's Order No. 2 of 1970) of 30 March 1970,[64] was intended to provide the guidelines for the National Assembly in its task of framing a constitution. In his address to the nation on 28 March 1970, the President announced that some of the salient features of the LFO had been formulated 'as a result of my assessment of the wishes of the people' and those guidelines were to be considered as 'certain basic principles for the future Constitution of Pakistan'. Some of these 'basic principles' were incorporated in paragraphs 20, 21, 22 and 23 of the LFO. For instance, the members of the National Assembly were directed to provide that 'Pakistan shall be a Federal Republic to be known as the Islamic Republic of Pakistan' in which 'Islamic ideology which is the basis for the creation of Pakistan shall be preserved; and the Head of the State shall be a Muslim'. It would follow that the elected representatives of the people were divested from their democratic right, in accordance with the Universal Declaration and the contemporary law of self-determination, to establish a secular Republic with a secular constitution without any discrimination on the ground of religion. This attempt on the part of a military ruler to dictate to the elected leaders of the people the contents of a future constitution is a strange exercise of the principle of responsible government.

Article 20, paragraphs 4 and 5 are, however, of great importance.

20(4): All powers including legislative, administrative and

---

[62] *Ibid.*

[63] *Ibid.*

[64] For text, see Press release, March 30, 1970, by Government of Pakistan, Press Information Department, Rawalpindi. Mujib said that he and his party had condemned the LFO but at the same time decided to participate in elections as they considered the election a referendum on regional autonomy on the basis of the six-point programme. He said, the election was the last chance of realizing their legitimate rights through constitutional way. *The Morning News* (Karachi & Dacca), 26 November 1970.

financial, shall be so distributed between the Federal Government and the Provinces that the Provinces shall have maximum autonomy, that is to say maximum legislative, administrative and financial powers, but the Federal Government shall also have adequate powers including legislative, administrative and financial powers, to discharge its responsibilities in relation to external and internal affairs and to preserve the independence and territorial integrity of the country.

20(5) : It shall be ensured that—
(a) the people of all areas in Pakistan shall be enabled to participate fully in all forms of national activities; and
(b) within a specified period, economic and all other disparities between the Provinces and between different areas in a Province are removed by the adoption of statutory and other measures.

The pith and substance of Yahya's guidelines for the future constitution of Pakistan are, therefore, three-fold:

(1) maximum autonomy for the Provinces;
(2) adequate powers for the Federal Government;
(3) removal of economic and all other disparities between the Provinces.

Yahya was so anxious to transfer power to the people that in Article 24 of the LFO he directed that the National Assembly should frame the constitution within a period of 120 days from the date of its first meeting or stand dissolved on its failure to do so. He however made it clear in Article 25 that if he did not approve of the constitution, there would be no constitution for Pakistan and the National Assembly would stand dissolved: 'The Constitution Bill, as passed by the National Assembly, shall be presented to the President for authentication. The National Assembly shall stand dissolved in the event that authentication is refused.'

In complete repudiation of Ayub's pet political theories of one unit for West Pakistan and the institution of basic democracy, Yahya on 1 April 1970 dissolved the artificially integrated Western unit and restored the four old Provinces of Punjab, Sind, Baluchistan and NWFP; on 22 April 1970, it was decided by his Governors that the basic democracy system would be replaced by local government at the union and district levels where the committees would be elected by the people directly on the basis of adult franchise and there would be no nominated members in the municipal bodies.

Some time prior to the national elections, East Bengal fell a victim to a massive cyclonic storm which has been described 'as the worst natural disaster of the 20th century—and one of the worst of all recorded history' and in which, at a conservative estimate, at least 500,000 people were killed.[65]   President Yahya who, as we have seen, waxed eloquent in his broadcast on 28 March 1970 about his comprehensive programme for flood control in East Bengal, however, displayed utter callousness when the worst cyclone of the century hit the province eight months later.[66]   A reasonable assessment of the attitude of Yahya's government to this devastating disaster was made by *Time* on 7 December 1970 in a leading article 'East Pakistan: The Politics of Catastrophe.'   There it was pointed out:

Yet, in the face of this, Pakistan's government proved shockingly inept and many of its people cruelly callous ...   Though people were still reported floating alive offshore three days after the cyclone, the Pakistani navy was never ordered to search for survivors.   Some 500,000 tons of grain were stock-piled in East Pakistan warehouses, but the 40-odd Pakistani army helicopters that could have airlifted them to the delta sat on their pads in West Pakistan.   India, the government explained—falsely— would not allow the craft to be ferried over 1,000 miles of its territory.   President Agha Mohammad Yahya Khan waited a total 13 days before making a formal visit to the Ganges area to see the toll for himself ...   In the world's fifth most populous nation (130 million) a group of '20 families'—nearly all in West Pakistan—control 66% of Pakistan's industry and 80% of its banking and insurance assets.   Only two of the enormously privileged 20 bothered to contribute to the disaster relief effort.

[65] *Time* Magazine, 30 November 1970, 15 March 1971; *The Sunday Times Magazine*, London, 6 June 1971.

[66] While deploring the apathy towards cyclone victims, Sheikh Mujibur observed: 'We have lived with floods and cyclones since independence. Today after 23 years of shared nationhood we are without even plans for flood control. Ten years after the cyclone and tidal bore which had ravaged these same areas, we have to live through the same disaster, magnified a thousand-fold. At that time plans were put forward for building permanent cyclone-proof shelters, for replanning our coastal villages, and improving communication facilities. A full decade later the plans remain buried among a pile of plans which have never been implemented. Rs. 20 crores could not be found in ten years for building these cyclone-proof shelters, yet over Rs. 200 crores could be found for building the monuments of luxury and waste in Islamabad. Before a plan for flood control could be prepared, over one million dollars could be allocated for building the Mangla and Tarbela dams in West Pakistan.' *The Morning News* (Karachi & Dacca), 27 November 1970.

The Awami League fought the election for a mandate on its six-point programme for autonomy for East Pakistan which was first enunciated by Sheikh Mujibur Rahman early in 1966. The six points were[67]:

(1) Establishment of a federation 'on the basis of the Lahore Resolution and the parliamentary framework of government with supremacy of legislature directly elected on the basis of adult franchise.'

(2) The federal government shall deal with only two subjects, that is, defence and foreign affairs, and all other residuary subjects should rest in the federating states.

(3) There should be two separate currencies mutually or freely convertible in each wing of each region, or in the alternative a single currency for the whole country, subject to the establishment of a 'Federal Reserve System' in which there will be regional Federal Reserve Banks which shall devise measures to prevent the transfer of resources and flight of capital from one region to another.

(4) The power of taxation and revenue collection shall be vested in the federating units. The federal government will receive a share to meet the federal expenses.

(5) Foreign trade: Five steps shall be taken:

   (i) There shall be two separate accounts for foreign exchange earnings.
   (ii) Earnings of East Pakistan shall be under the control of East Pakistan.
   (iii) Foreign exchange requirements of the federal government shall be met by the two wings either equally or in a ratio to be fixed.
   (iv) Indigenous products shall move free of duty within the two wings.
   (v) The Constitution shall empower the unit governments to establish trade and commercial relations with, set up trade missions in, and enter into agreements with foreign countries.

(6) A militia or para-military force, an ordnance factory, a military academy and the navy headquarters would be set up in East Pakistan.

[67] *Keesings Contemporary Archives*, January 30-February 6, 1971-72 p. 24413; *Bangla Desh* (National), p. 157; *Harvard Paper*, Note 13; *Awami League Manifesto*; *Bangla Desh Documents* (External Affairs Ministry, New Delhi, September 1971), pp. 66-82.

The six points of the Awami League are not a new innovation. Except in respect of currency, simliar demands for the realization of provincial autonomy were made as early as in 1954. The twenty-one-point programme on the basis of which the United Front fought and won overwhelmingly the provincial elections in East Bengal in March 1954, included:

"19. In accordance with the historic Lahore Resolution, to secure full and complete autonomy and bring all subjects under the jurisdiction of East Pakistan, leaving only Defence, Foreign Affairs and Currency under the jurisdiction of the Centre. Even in the matter of Defence, arrangements shall be such as to have headquarters of the Army in West Pakistan and the headquarters of the Navy in East Pakistan and to establish ordnance factories in East Pakistan with a view to making East Pakistan self-sufficient in the matter of Defence, and to convert the present Ansars into full-fledged militia."[68]

Again, on 2 April 1957 the Provincial Assembly adopted a motion to grant full autonomy to East Bengal without delay, leaving only defence, foreign affairs and currency in the hands of the Centre.[69]

As early as in March 1966, Sheikh Mujibur Rahman had explained the *raison d'etre* of the six-point programme.[70] The first point which provides for the Federation of Pakistan has seven ingredients viz: (i) Pakistan shall be a Federation, (ii) it shall be based on the Lahore Resolution, (iii) its Government shall be of a Parliamentary form, (iv) it must be responsible to the Legislature, (v) the Legislature must be supreme, (vi) it must be directly elected and (vii) election must be on the basis of universal adult franchise. The Sheikh said:

Those who are unitarists are definitely against Lahore Resolution. Conversely, those who are opposed to Lahore Resolution are definitely unitarists. So let it be decided once for all who own and who do not own the Lahore Resolution by which Pakistan was created and is rightly called the Pakistan Resolution. The people who disown Lahore Resolution disown Pakistan itself... It will be sheer political dishonesty to deviate from Lahore Resolution after Pakistan was created by people's votes obtained on the basis of that Resolution. If it is now found necessary to so deviate for the sake of stability and integrity of

[68] J. Sen Gupta, *Eclipse of East Pakistan* (1963), p. 166.
[69] *Dawn*, 4 April 1957.
[70] 'Six-Point Formula—Our Right to Live', by Sheikh Mujibur Rahman, President of the Awami League, 23 March 1966. For further discussion on the Six Points, see *Awami League Manifesto*, op. cit., Sheikh Mujib's address to the Round Table Conference: *Dawn* (Karachi), 14 March 1969.

Pakistan itself, the people will certainly agree to such changes or even complete reversal. But in any event it is the people who will decide and not anybody else. As far as the people of East Pakistan are concerned they in the 1954 general election overwhelmingly voted for a constitution based on the Lahore Resolution. If, however, anybody has any doubt about their present attitude due to lapse of long twelve years, we are prepared to face another referendum on the issue. Until that is done by a specific referendum on universal adult suffrage, the Lahore Resolution and all its corollaries remain the *magna carta* of the people of Pakistan, and the rulers and the leaders are bound to give them a Constitution based on the Resolution.

Regarding the second point, Sheikh Mujib felt that a two-subject Centre would be sufficiently strong to become a respectable Federation. He referred to the proposal of the British Cabinet Mission in 1946 for an Indian Federation with only three subjects, viz: Defence, Foreign Affairs and Communication. In the case of an undivided Indian Federation, Communication would really have been a federal subject because of the geographical contiguity. An unbroken railway line and a non-stop through railway could have run from Khyber to Chittagong. But the geographical separation of the two wings of Pakistan makes it impossible for Communication to become a federal subject.

By transferring the railways to the provinces the Pakistan Government has reluctantly admitted the hard fact of geography. The same procedure would have to be followed in the case of Posts and Telegraphs and all other branches of Communication.

With regard to the third point, if the second alternative be accepted, Currency would remain a Central subject. The only difference in that event would be the provision for separate Reserve Banks for the two wings in a Federal Reserve System as obtained in the USA. The State Bank of Pakistan would have two Reserve Banks for the two wings. The currency for East Pakistan would be issued through the East Pakistan Reserve Bank and marked 'East Pakistan' or simply 'Dacca' and a similar procedure would be followed for the West Pakistan currency. This was the only way East Pakistan could be saved from economic ruination by effectively stopping the flight of capital from East to West.

The economic consequences of the flight of capital from East Bengal were explained by Sheikh Mujib:

We are supposed to belong to one indivisible economy. We have one currency. There is no distinguishing mark to show the currency circulation wingwise. We are under only one Finance Ministry situated in and operating from West Pakistan presided over always by a West Pakistani Minister formulating financial, fiscal and monetary policies through one single Central Bank, that is, the State Bank of Pakistan, also located in West Pakistan, issuing money minted, coined and printed in West Pakistan. This money after travelling and meandering in circulation throughout the country journeys back to and rests in accumulation in West Pakistan. Along with the head office of the Government Central Bank the head offices of all the joint-stock banks, except one or two small ones of very recent origin, are also located in West Pakistan. The seat of the Government being located in West Pakistan, head offices of the three Armed Forces, all Foreign Missions and almost all foreign and national trades and industries organizations are situated in that wing. As a result, all money transactions done in East Pakistan are instantaneously transferred to West Pakistan. All share money of joint-stock companies, all deposits of banks, their security money, all Government reserves, all earnings, profits and savings of trade and industry operating in East Pakistan move in a matter of seconds to West Pakistan. Anyone conversant with banking operation knows well that only barely ten per cent of the entire deposit need be kept for payment and the rest can be and generally is invested. Savings when invested become capital. This investment is naturally done in West Pakistan as West Pakistan's capital. This is how capital formation in West Pakistan has become so rapid. This again is how there has been total absence of capital formation in East Pakistan. As investment means employment, this incident has meant the employment in West Pakistan only. As capital formation is followed by rapid industrialization, this has meant industrialization of West Pakistan alone. This process will continue unless and until the prevailing one-way traffic of finance is effectively checked by stopping this flight of capital. This can be done and capital investment can be generated in East Pakistan only by creating a Reserve Bank for East Pakistan as suggested by me. It is the only way to save East Pakistan from economic extinction. This reform in our currency system while saving East Pakistan from economic collapse will keep currency a Central subject as a symbol of our unity and oneness.

If, however, the first alternative is to be accepted then currency would become a provincial subject but one which would not weaken the Centre nor would it affect the oneness of Pakistan.

The fourth point provides that the power of taxation and revenue collection should vest in the federating units and the federal Centre would have no such power. The Centre, however, would have a share in the State taxes for meeting its expenditure. The proposal visualized that the Constitution would provide that a certain percentage of the revenue collections on all heads should automatically be credited to the Federal Fund by the Reserve Banks on which amount the unit governments should have no control. "If a Central Government is constitutionally assured of the required amount, why should it bother about the actual collection? In the case of a Federation it is only the fiscal taxation in which it is interested. The rest of the purposes of taxation, viz: protective, social, commercial and moral, are the responsibility of the federating units. This is what is done in USA and some other Federations. In USSR even the fiscal taxation is not done by the Union. There is no Finance Minister and Finance Ministry in the Union Government of the Soviet Union. The Finance Ministries and Ministers are all with the Federating Republics. They meet the requirements and serve the purposes of the Union Government. Have these arrangements weakened the Central authorities of USA and USSR? It was with the knowledge and experience of the working of a Federation that the Cabinet Mission offered an Indian Federation without the power of taxation and it was for the same reason that the Congress and the Muslim League accepted the offer." If the scheme be implemented, the federal Centre would have more time to devote to matters of defence and external relations and to act as a unifying force, and tax and revenue collection would be cheaper and easier.

The need for implementing the fifth point clearly arises from the economic history of Pakistan which reveals that East Pakistan has earned the bulk of the annual foreign exchange of Pakistan; East Pakistan's earnings have been spent in West Pakistan in industrializing that wing and earnings from those industries have been reinvested in West Pakistan as the earnings of the West; East Pakistan's earnings are not being spent in East Pakistan on the pretext of its inability to absorb them owing to the absence of capital formation; imports to East Pakistan are less than her exports whereas imports to West Pakistan are more than her exports; two-thirds of Pakistan's foreign exchange is earned by jute but that earning is utilized neither for the benefit of the jute growers nor for East Pakistan; almost all foreign aids and loans are secured against foreign exchange earned by East Pakistan but they are spent in West Pakistan on the same plea of the non-absorbing capacity of East Pakistan; but the irony is that the interest on these loans and their instalments are being borne by East Pakistan.

The cumulative effects of these economic incidents were: (i) East Pakistan had not been industrialized sufficiently; (ii) the little industrialization that had been done by West Pakistanis or by people other than East Pakistanis with all the characteristics of foreign investments both in the matter of employment and profit earning; (iii) there was chronic inflation causing soaring high prices of commodities with all its concomitants like blackmarketing and profiteering bringing untold miseries to the people; (iv) jute-growers were not only being denied the economic price of their produce, but even the cost of production resulting in the inevitable evils of injustice—perpetual indebtedness and impoverishment. Consequently Sheikh Mujib felt that the acceptance of his proposals would help remedy these man-made inequities.

About the sixth point, Sheikh Mujib had said: "East Pakistan is the home of the majority of Pakistanis.   To defend it is the political obligation as well as moral duty of the Government of Pakistan. Why then should it be necessary for East Pakistanis to demand it?   Why do they not do it on their own initiative?   How and with what conscience do they say that defence of East Pakistan lies in West Pakistan?   Does it not tantamount to saying that the mouth, the belly and the stomach of East Pakistan lie in West Pakistan?   How will the arms, ammunition and wealth in West Pakistan help East Pakistan when transport between the wings can be snapped in a matter of seconds?   Has not the recent 17-day war proved our utter helplessness?   How can one brag that some event in Warsaw saved East Pakistan?   It is the defence policy of our Government that has reduced us to this position.   In spite of all this we want a united Defence of the country and to retain it as a Central subject.   But at the same time we want that East Pakistan be made self-sufficient in the matter of Defence; that an Ordnance Factory, a Military Academy and the Navy Headquarter must be set up in East Pakistan.   These things were actually demanded in 1954."

During the election campaign in 1970, Sheikh Mujib again dealt at length with his six-point formula and pointed out that the constitutional structure envisaged therein would provide a just federal balance and make Pakistan stronger. For instance, he said: "The only feasible solution is the re-ordering of the constitutional structure by giving full regional autonomy to the federating units on the basis of our six-point formula.   Such autonomy in order to be effective must include the power of managing the economy.   This is why we insist upon the federating units having control over monetary and fiscal policy and foreign exchange earnings and other powers to negotiate foreign trade and aid, by giving to the federating units full control over its economic destiny, while entrusting to the federal government responsibility over foreign affairs and defence and, subject to certain safeguards, currency. We believe a just federal balance will be attained... This scheme will understandably be opposed by those in one region who would like to treat another region as a colony or a market. We believe, however, that this scheme will have the full support of the common people of Bengal and West Pakistan. Within this constitutional framework, we believe it will be possible to bring about a social revolution through the democratic process and to create a socialist economic order, free from exploitation."[71]

The Awami League also advocated the nationalization of banks, insurance companies, heavy industries, foreign trade, transport, shipping and other key industries; development of co-operative enterprises; workers' participation in the management of industry; exemption from land revenue tax of holdings up to $8\frac{1}{2}$ acres; and cancellation of tax arrears on such holdings. Fundamental rights should be guaranteed by the Constitution and should be limited only in wartime. Pakistan should pursue an independent foreign policy, and should withdraw from SEATO, CENTO and other military pacts. Mr. Z. A. Bhutto of the Pakistan People's Party (PPP) fought in West Pakistan on the basis of a programme which was in common with the Awami League's in several respects particularly with regard to the pattern of domestic economy. Mr. Bhutto described himself on 11 December 1970 as 'a democratic socialist who believes in socialism on the Willy Brandt or British pattern.' In his election campaign he advocated nationalization of banking and basic industries, including gas, natural resources, shipping, paper and cement; limitation of land holdings; distribution of state lands to landless peasants; and the introduction of co-operative farming on a voluntary basis. In foreign policy he advocated withdrawal from SEATO and CENTO. His policy differed in two fundamental respects from that of Sheikh Mujib: (i) he supported the establishment of a strong central government and (ii) demanded the intensification of the confrontation with India over the Kashmir question, calling for "a 1000-year war", if necessary.[72]

No constitutional lawyer can help observing that Mujib's six points were fully in conformity with the LFO formula of maximum autonomy for the provinces and adequate powers for the federal gov-

---

[71] *Bangla Desh Documents* (External Affairs Ministry, New Delhi, September 1971), pp. 107-8. For other important election speeches of Shiekh Mujib see: *The People* (Dacca), 10, 11, 12, 18, 21, 26 October; 1, 6, 10, 13, 14, 15, 16, 19 November 1970. *The Morning News* (Karachi and Dacca), 26, 28 October, 27 November 1970.

[72] *Keesings Contemporary Archives,* January 30-February 6, 1971-72 p. 24413.

ernment. President Yahya never objected to the six points and, in fact, had shown his acquiescence by permitting the Awami League to contest the election on the basis thereof and to propagate the same through State-owned radio and television centres. Yahya must have thought that Mujib's programme was the only possible means of curing the chronic imbalances between the two wings and thereby to preserve the swiftly eroding image of Pakistan as one nation. It is difficult to conceive that a military dictator in possession of total power would have otherwise permitted the Awami League to fight the election on the basis of the six-point programme.

In fact, one can find a clear justification of the six-point programme, and an admission that its implementation would not have meant the separation of the East from the West, in the remarks made by President Yahya at a press conference in Dacca on 27 November 1970.[73] The President said that he would not stand in the way of maximum autonomy for the people of East Pakistan; he would rather encourage it so that the people of East Pakistan could have 'full charge of their destiny, planning and utilization of its resources' within 'the concept of Pakistan.' He said that although East Pakistan was one of the five provinces, because of its geographical distance of over a thousand miles from the other wing, it must have maximum autonomy to run her own affairs within the overall framework of one Pakistan. When asked to comment on the six-point programme, and whether it would finally lead to separation between the two wings, the President said he was not concerned with six or any other points, but it was imperative that the people of East Pakistan should have a lot more say in their affairs than they had so far. He also said that he did not believe that there was any tendency of separatism in East Pakistan. According to him: *'They are the majority. How can a majority separate from a minority?'* (emphasis added).

Mr. Bhutto's PPP avoided raising directly the issue of Mujib's six-point programme in its election campaign and it was under no obligation to its electorate to resist it. In Baluchistan and NWFP the dominant National Awami Party (NAP) was committed to the principle of provincial autonomy as reflected in Mujib's six points.

In the national elections held on 7 December 1970, the Awami League emerged victorious with an absolute majority in the National Assembly. Out of 162 seats allotted to East Bengal in an Assembly of 300 elected members, Mujib's party captured 160. The remaining two seats went to Nurul Amin of the Pakistan Democratic Party and to an independent, Raja Tridib Roy of Chittagong Hill areas, respec-

---

[73] *The Morning News* (Karachi & Dacca), 28 November, 1970.

tively. Both of them subsequently extended their full support to Mujib's six points. It is therefore an outstanding feature in the history of modern democracy that all the elected members to the National Assembly from East Bengal were committed to a specific programme advocated by the Awami League.

Out of the remaining 138 seats distributed in the four provinces of the West, Bhutto's PPP secured 81, Qayyum Muslim League (QML) 9, Muslim League (Council) 7, National Awami Party (NAP) 6, Nizam-i-Islam 7, Jamaat-i-Islam 4, Jamiat-ul-Ulema Pakistan 7, Muslim League (Convention) 2, and Independent 15.[74]

In the Provincial Assembly, the Awami League captured 288 seats out of 300 in East Bengal but Bhutto's PPP gained an absolute majority in only two provinces in the West, capturing 113 and 34 seats out of 180 and 60 seats respectively in Punjab and Sind. NAP emerged as the dominant party in Baluchistan and NWFP although no party could obtain an absolute majority there.[75]

The net result of the elections both at the centre and in the provinces, therefore, were:

(a) Sheikh Mujib's Awami League captured in its own right 98·4% elected seats allotted to East Bengal in the National Assembly, whereas out of 138 elected seats allotted to West Pakistan in the National Assembly, Bhutto's PPP got only 81 seats, i.e., 58·7%.

(b) In the Provincial Assemblies, Mujib's Awami League captured 96% of the total number of seats allotted to East Bengal, but received the support of 99·3% on its basic six-point programme because NAP, PDP and the Independents were with the Awami League on this issue. In the West, Bhutto's PPP won only 151 seats out of 300 seats allotted to the four Provinces, without however winning a single seat in the Province of Baluchistan and winning only 4 out of 40 seats in NWFP, thereby capturing only 50% of the total number of seats allotted to the Western wing.

After the landslide victory of the Awami League, Sheikh Mujib said: "I am overwhelmed by a deep sense of gratitute to Almighty Allah and to my beloved countrymen—the students, workers and peasants—for the unprecedented victory of the Awami League, both in the National and Provincipal elections. I warmly thank the people for having given a historic verdict in favour of our six-point programme. We pledge to implement this verdict. There can be no constitution except one which is based on the six-point programme."[76]

President Yahya congratulated the nation on its peaceful elections. He said: 'You have set an example in the world. You have shown

[74] The Pakistan Times, 20 January 1971.
[75] The Pakistan Observer, 19 December 1970.
[76] Dawn (Karachi), 20 December 1970

great maturity.'[77] Describing the conduct of the elections, *Keesings Contemporary Archives* comment: "Apart from a few incidents, the election campaign and the voting took place in a peaceful atmosphere, and all parties, including those which were defeated, agreed that the elections were both free and fair. There was a heavy poll which surpassed 90 per cent in some areas. Women, who were voting for the first time, turned out in large numbers."[78]

Apart from the striking feature of an absolute majority secured by Mujibur Rahman, international comments on the results of the election reveal four points: (i) The voters decisively repudiated Field-Marshal Ayub Khan's regime, as was shown by the overwhelming defeat of the Convention Muslim League and by the victory of Sheikh Mujibur Rahman and Z. A. Bhutto, both of whom had been imprisoned by Ayub. (ii) The older parties, apart from the Awami League, and established politicians, including many former ministers, were generally rejected by the electorate. (iii) Right-wing religious parties such as the Jamaat-i-Islami received little support, suggesting that the influence of the Mullahs, even in the rural areas, was much less than had been believed. (iv) Candidates from the armed forces were also generally unsuccessful; it was suggested that this reflected a popular reaction against military intervention in politics.[79]

Bhutto said on 15 December 1970 that he would do everything possible to frame an agreed constitution, but not at the cost of Pakistan's unity, although he was prepared to negotiate on certain adjustments here and there. He added that he was ready to meet Mujib at any time to work out an agreed constitution. On 20 December Sheikh Mujib declared that the future constitution would be based on the six-point formula and there could be no compromise on that issue. Surprisingly enough, on 20 December, the minority leader Bhutto declared that no constitution could be framed nor could any government at the Centre be run without his party's cooperation; and his party (PPP) was not prepared to occupy the Opposition Benches in the National Assembly. While he had all regard for Mujibur Rahman who had returned with a great majority of the Awami League in the National Assembly, Bhutto added: 'Majority alone doesn't count in national politics.' To this the rejoinder of Tajuddin Ahmed of the Awami League on 22 December was that the people had voted for a real democracy in which power was vested in the people and the legislature constituted on the basis of one man, one vote. 'In such a system', he added, 'a party enjoying a comfortable and indeed an absolute majority—as the Awami League has, with a clear electoral

[77] *Dawn*, 12 January 1971.
[78] *Keesings Contemporary Archives*, January 30-February 6, 1971-72, p. 24413.
[79] *Ibid*.

mandate—is quite competent to frame a constitution and to form a central government.' On 27 December Bhutto said at a press conference that if the majority party insisted on making a constitution to its own liking, he would step aside, but in such an event his PPP would not be responsible for the consequences that would ensue. Bhutto reiterated that his party would resist any intrigue or conspiracy to make it sit in the Opposition. Addressing a vast crowd estimated at 2,000,000 people in Dacca on 3 January 1971, Sheikh Mujib declared that the people of East Pakistan had given a clear verdict on the six-point programme and the future constitution would be framed on the basis of those points alone. The people were ready to accept a constitution which would be prepared by their elected representatives, and would launch a strong mass movement if any one opposed the framing of the constitution. He added, however, that his party would not frame the constitution alone, even though it was in a majority in the Assembly.[80]

In the background of this impressive and overwhelming electoral mandate behind Mujib's Awami League, General Yahya conceded, apparently graciously, Mujib's demand for holding the session of the National Assembly at Dacca; equally graciously the President referred to Sheikh Mujib as the future Prime Minister of the country at a press conference on 14 January 1971.[81] During the first major talks over Pakistan's future constitution with Sheikh Mujib in mid-January 1971 'General Yahya gave the impression of not finding anything seriously objectionable in the six points but emphasizing the need for coming to an understanding with the PPP in West Pakistan.'[82] The next round of talks between Mujib and Bhutto took place in Dacca on and from 27 January 1971. The object was to arrive at a consensus about the future constitution. Mr. Bhutto, however, had no positive suggestion. His approach was 'essentially negative.' The important fact to remember is that when he left Dacca 'there was no indication from their (PPP) part that a deadlock had been reached with the Awami League.... Rather they confirmed that all doors were open and that following a round of talks with the West Pakistani leaders, the PPP would either have a second or more substantive round of talks with the Awami League or would meet in

[80] Ibid., p. 24414. Also see, The Pakistan Times, 21 December 1970; The Pakistan Observer, 22 December 1970; Dawn, 28 December; The Pakistan Observer, 4 January 1971.

[81] The Pakistan Observer, 15 January 1971.

[82] Statement by Mr. Tajuddin Ahmed, Prime Minister of Bangladesh on 17.4.71, released by the Government of Bangladesh. Also see Bangla Desh Documents (External Affairs Ministry, New Delhi, September 1971), pp. 291-98. The statement was issued after the inauguration of the Government of the People's Republic of Bangladesh.

the National Assembly whose committees provided ample opportunity for detailed discussions on the constitution.'[83]

On 13 February 1971 General Yahya fixed 3 March for the National Assembly session at Dacca. When, therefore, Bhutto suddenly announced on 15 February his surprising decision to boycott the National Assembly session if Sheikh Mujib did not accommodate the views of his party on the making of a constitution, it came as a rude shock to the majority party. The obstructionist attitude of the PPP was being gradually revealed. Bhutto first put forward his astounding proposal for a separate Prime Minister for each of the two wings, forgetting that there was no West wing because the West has already been broken up into four separate provinces. On 28 February Bhutto, pampered by the military junta, came out with another startling and unreasonable demand for the postponement of the inaugural session of the National Assembly to facilitate talks between his party and the Awami League.[84] Without consulting the majority party leader Sheikh Mujib, and the other political parties in the West representing 42% of the members in the National Assembly and 50% of the members of the Provincial Assemblies, President Yahya on 1 March suddenly announced his decision to postpone the inaugural session of the National Assembly fixed for 3 March;[85] simultaneously, Vice-Admiral S. M. Ashan, Governor of East Pakistan, a reputed liberal amongst the ruthless army bureaucrats from the West, was sacked. Mujib called for a general strike in protest against the postponement of the National Assembly session and Yahya responded by ordering his troops to move in and by imposing a curfew.[86] The Awami League launched its non-violent

[83] *Ibid.* This is fully supported by Bhutto's press statement in Dacca on 30 January; see *The Pakistan Times* (Lahore), 31 January 1971.

[84] Bhutto warned if any session of the National Assembly was held on 3 March without the PPP's participation he would launch a popular agitation from one end of Pakistan to the other. Yet he made it clear that he had never opposed the six points although the programme was not acceptable to him. Personally, in fact, he narrowed down his disagreement to foreign trade and foreign aid. *The Pakistan Times*, 1 March 1971.

[85] *The Morning News* (Karachi & Dacca), 2 March, 1971. It is clear from the President's statement that he had put off the session of the National Assembly only because of Bhutto's opposition; he did not specify any other political party which opposed it.

[86] On 1 March 1971 Sheikh Mujib said: 'Only for the sake of a minority party's disagreement the democratic process of constitution-making has been obstructed and the National Assembly session has been postponed *sine die*. This is most unfortunate as far as we are concerned. We are representatives of the majority people and we cannot allow it to go unchallenged... We are ready for any consequences. I have mentioned many times the fact that a conspiracy is going on in this country. There was a General Election and the people have elected

non-cooperation movement against the decision of the military junta. Several civilians and Awami League volunteers were killed by Yahya's army. Sheikh Mujib strongly condemned the killing of unarmed persons and urged the Government to desist forthwith from this reckless course. He said that the Bengalis could not be suppressed any more and they would no longer tolerate exploitation as a colony or as a market. On 6 March Yahya announced his decision to convene the National Assembly on 25 March. On 7 March Mujib asked Government servants to take orders from him and also asked his people not to pay taxes until the demands of his people were accepted, and declared that his party would consider attending the National Assembly session on 25 March only if his four demands were conceded. He was addressing a public meeting at Dacca attended by over a million people from all over East Bengal. His four demands were: (i) martial law be lifted immediately, (ii) power be transferred to the elected representatives, (iii) the troops should be recalled to their barracks, and (iv) an inquiry be held into the killings of civilians by the army. The Sheikh announced the closure of all Government and semi-Government offices.[87]

The performance of the military enraged the people of East Bengal. They were convinced that Yahya would never transfer power to the people. The disillusionment was total. The rupture between the two wings appeared to have become irrevocable, and the popular demand for independence of East Bengal became overwhelmingly strong. Yet, Sheikh Mujib, even at the risk of his political career, advised his people to be calm and restrained while he tried for a political settlement with a view to preserving the integrity of Pakistan. *The Guardian* of London in a leading article on 5 June 1971 recorded:

---

us to serve them and we have a responsibility towards them. But in spite of the clear verdict in our favour, the conspiracy has struck its root. The majority of the elected representatives of the people are from Bangla Desh and in collaboration with the elected representatives from West Pakistan with the exception of Bhutto's and Qayyum's Parties, we were quite capable of framing the Constitution... But the Chairman of the Pakistan People's Party has threatened the members of the National Assembly from West Pakistan who were willing to come to East Pakistan to attend the session that they would be liquidated if they come to East Pakistan to attend the National Assembly Session. Mr. Bhutto has taken Law in his own hands. Is the Law and Order situation only meant for the poor Bengalees?' The Sheikh announced a programme of struggle for the next six days which included observance of a complete strike in Dacca on 1 March and a countrywide strike on 3 March. *The People* (Dacca), 2 March 1971.

   [87] *The People* (Dacca), 3 March, 1971; *Dawn* (Karachi), 4, 5, 6, 7 and 8 March, 1971; *The Morning News* (Karachi & Dacca), 7 March, 1971.

Confronted with this mood Mujib staked his political life, first in his public meeting on March 3, then before a million people on March 7, when he deflected the demand for independence towards a negotiated demand for full autonomy. On March 7, the army in Dacca was prepared for unleashing a bloodbath if Mujib declared independence. Heavy machine-gun emplacement had been prepared on the cantonment perimeter. Tanks were ready and the air force was alerted. Denied an open provocation by Mujib, and faced with a complete erosion of central authority in the East Wing, Yahya appeared to opt for compromise in talks with Mujib. He flew to Dacca on March 15 with a clutch of generals, several of whom secreted themselves in the cantonment to finalize their battle plan for March 25.

On 15 March Mujib issued 35 directives[88] to the people of East Bengal, in aid of his non-violent, non-cooperation movement, a recognized political weapon for achieving self-determination.

The response of the entire people in East Bengal to the call of their leader was spontaneous, complete and overwhelming. Since in contemporary international law the effectiveness of an authority is to be measured by the popular support it commands, the authority of Mujib and his Awami League in East Bengal was conclusively proved by the success of the movement between 1 and 25 of March. One can get an estimate of the success from Tajuddin Ahmed's statement of 17 April 1971,[89] an estimate which is fully corroborated by all published reports. Mr. Ahmed observed:

The course of the non-cooperation movement is now a part of history. Never in the course of any liberation struggle has non-cooperation been carried to the limits attained within Bangladesh between 1st and 25th March. Non-cooperation was total. No judge of the High Court could be found to administer the oath of office to the new Governor, Lt.-General Tikka Khan. The entire civil administration, including the police and the civil service of Pakistan, refused to attend office. The people stopped supply of food to the army. Even the civilian employees of the Defence establishment joined the boycott. Non-cooperation did not stop at abstention from work. The civilian administration and police positively pledged their support to Sheikh Mujibur Rahman and put themselves under his orders. In this situation the Awami League without being a formally consti-

[88] *Dawn*, 16 March 1971.
[89] Tajuddin Ahmed's statement on 17.4.71, released by the Government of Bangladesh.

tuted Government was forced to take on the responsibility of keeping the economy and administration running whilst non-cooperation lasted. In this task they had the unqualified support not only of the people but the administration and business community. The latter two subordinated themselves to the directive of the Awami League and accepted them as the sole authority to solve their various problems. In this unique circumstance economy and administration were kept going in spite of the formidable problems arising out of the power vacuum which had suddenly emerged in Bangladesh. In spite of the lack of any formal authority, Awami League volunteers in co-operation with the police maintained a level of law and order which was a considerable improvement on normal times.

In the meantime, there was a gradual erosion of Bhutto's influence in West Pakistan and a growing criticism of his policies. It can safely be shown that 210 out of 300 elected representatives of the National Assembly supported the four-point demands of Mujib and wanted him to form an interim central government preparatory to the framing of a new constitution. At a meeting held at Lahore on 10 March 1971, participated in by all the political parties in the West (except Bhutto's PPP and Qayyum's Muslim League), representatives of lawyers and trade unions, the four-point demands of Mujib were fully endorsed and the obstinate stand of Bhutto severely criticized.[90] Another meeting was held at Lahore on 13 March which was convened and presided over by Maulana Mufti Mahmud of Jamait-e-Ulema-e-Islam. The meeting was attended by the elected members of the National Assembly (MNA) including independents and represented the views of all the political parties in the West except the PPP and QML. The meeting demanded immediate acceptance of Mujib's demands for the withdrawal of the army to the barracks and judicial inquiry into the firings by the army in East Bengal. The other points regarding the lifting of martial law and the transfer of power to the elected representatives were considered to be the 'unanimous demands of the entire nation.' An important resolution was adopted which, *inter alia*, provided: 'Whatever the solution arrived at in this respect, we feel that Sheikh Mujibur Rahman as the leader of the majority in the National Assembly should be called upon to form a government interim to the framing and promulgation of a new constitution. All these steps must be expeditiously taken so that the National Assembly session duly takes place on 25 March 1971 as scheduled.'[91] It will thus appear that out of 300 elected re-

[90] *Dawn*, 11 March 1971.
[91] *Dawn*, 14 March 1971.

presentatives of the National Assembly, 210, i.e. more than a two-thirds majority, supported the immediate transfer of power to a government headed by Sheikh Mujib. Only 90 MNAs were not in favour of this proposal—81 of Bhutto's PPP and 9 of QML.

At a Press conference at Lahore on 12 March, Bhutto said that he supported Mujib's demands for a judicial probe and the return of the army to the barracks;[92] about the other two demands he said: 'We are not opposed in principle but it is a question of choosing the forum.' On 14 March at a public meeting in Karachi Bhutto came out with the startling suggestion that power should be transferred to the Awami League and the PPP, the two majority parties in the two wings.[93] A champion of democratic socialism of the British or West European pattern, Bhutto, a minority leader in the National Assembly, when cornered even in the West, declared bluntly that the 'rule of majority does not apply in Pakistan. PPP cannot be ignored in the country's governance.'[94]

Bhutto's attitude and his policies were severely criticized by the political leaders in the West. Khawaja Mohammed Refique, General Secretary of PDP (Punjab), pointed out that Bhutto's 'fascist tendencies' were responsible for creating an atmosphere of disunity in the country and he called upon the political leaders to save the country from disintegration.[95] Mufti Mahmud, General Secretary of the Jamaiat-e-Ulema-e-Islam, said that 'the demand of Bhutto was incomprehensible. How power could be transferred to two majority parties?' He wanted the President to call upon Mujibur Rahman to form the Central Government. 'There could be only one majority party in the Assembly and that was the Pakistan Awami League. After the break up of one unit, there are four provinces in West Pakistan, Bhutto could claim to be the leader of the majority party of West Punjab and Sind.'[96] The Baluch political leader, Nawab A. R. Bagti, blamed Bhutto for the deadlock. Begum Tahina Masood of the Bahwalpur United Party administered an ominous warning that 'history will never forgive Bhutto'. She assured Sheikh Mujib of the complete support of the 32-lakh people of Bahwalpur.[97] The Karachi Bar Association supported Mujib's four points. Even in Punjab, the citadel of Bhutto's PPP, the students of Lahore went on a hunger-strike in support of Mujib's four points.[98] Bhutto's hostile and pro-

---

[92] *Dawn*, 13 March 1971.
[93] *Ibid.*, 15 March 1971.
[94] *Ibid.*, 16 March 1971.
[95] *Ibid.*, 13 March 1971.
[96] *Ibid.*, 15 March 1971.
[97] *Ibid.*, 15 March 1971.
[98] *Ibid.*, 18 March 1971.

vocative attitude was criticized at a meeting at Karachi attended by the representatives of all political parties except PPP and QML. Nurul Amin, the veteran PDP leader, declared at Dacca that the Awami League was the only majority party and Bhutto's suggestion was impractical; there could not be two majority parties in one National Assembly. Maulana Ghulam Ghaus Hazarvi, General Secretary of Jamait-ul-Ulema-e-Pakistan, which had seven representatives in the National Assembly, while criticizing Bhutto, pointed out that 'a number of leaders from West Pakistan considered the six-point programme of the Awami League as against their interest. But parliamentary traditions do not envisage that a minority should decide to attend the National Assembly session only after bringing the majority party to agree to its terms... It is sad that a party tries to create crisis in the country when it does not have a share in the governance of the country.'[99] Thus, even in the West, while Bhutto's authority was shrinking, Mujib's image was growing fast. Important men in public life such as Nawab Nasurallah Khan, the retired Air Marshal Asghar Khan, a former Judge of the Supreme Court and many others praised Mujib for the courage and restraint that he had displayed at the hour of crisis and described him 'as the last link in the rapidly loosening chain of East-West unity.'[100]

It is with the background of three important facts—the effectiveness of the authority of Sheikh Mujib in East Bengal, the growing demand in the West for the immediate transfer of power to a government led by Sheikh Mujib and the swiftly eroding foundation of Bhutto's political base in the West—that President Yahya pretended to adopt a conciliatory attitude in his talks with Mujib during the crucial period from 16 March to 25 March. Tajuddin Ahmed had described Yahya's policy as a 'strategy of deception'. The deception is without a parallel in modern history. As it now appears, the strategy of Yahya was to keep an unsuspecting Mujib engaged in talks for a pretended political settlement while his army, under his secret directions, was surreptitiously making final preparation for a reign of terror and calculated genocide in East Bengal. As The Guardian comments: "While he (Yahya) negotiataed with Mujib, his generals planned carnage. His vaunted bluff sincerity (and sincerity of Pakistan's brief return to democracy) lies tattered. Henceforth, the country must be regarded as particularly brutal insensitive military dictatorship, its elected leadership in prison, majority party obliterated by decree."[101]

[99] Dawn, 17 March 1971.
[100] Dawn, 12 March 1971.
[101] The Guardian, London, 31 March 1971.

In his talks beginning on 16 March, Yahya expressed his regrets for what had happened and a desire for a political settlement.[102] To Mujib he indicated that there were no serious objections to the four-point proposals and that an interim constitution could be worked out by the respective advisers accordingly. The basic points on which an agreement was reached were: (i) lifting of martial law and transfer of power to a civilian government by a presidential proclamation; (ii) transfer of power in the provinces to the majority parties; (iii) Yahya to remain the President and in control of the Central Government; and (iv) separate sittings of the National Assembly members from East and West Pakistan preparatory to a joint session of the house to finalize the constitution. The last suggestion in fact came from Yahya to accommodate Bhutto.

The only question that remained was to define the powers of East Bengal vis-a-vis the Centre during the interim period. It was again jointly agreed that the distribution of power should as far as possible approximate to the final constitution to be approved by the National Assembly which, it was expected, would be based on the six points. For giving effect to this interim settlement, M. M. Ahmed, the Economic Adviser to the President, was specially flown in. In his talks with Awami League leaders, Ahmed made it clear that provided a political settlement had been reached there were no insuperable problems in working out some compromise on the 6-point programme even in the interim period. He suggested three amendments to the Awami League draft. At a meeting on 24 March the amendments were accepted by the Awami League with certain minor changes of language. There was nothing to prevent the framing of an interim constitution at a final drafting session. There was at no stage any breakdown of talks or any indication to that effect by Yahya or his advisers.

Contemporary reports in the press support Tajuddin Ahmed's contention that at no stage was there any breakdown of talks or any indication to the effect. On 22 March, President Yahya said[103] that "the stage is now set for our elected representatives to work together for the common goal which would accommodate both East and West Wings in a smoothly working harmonious system... I have no doubt that we shall succeed in dissolving the current political crisis." A brief announcement from the President's House stated: "In consultation with leaders of both the wings of Pakistan and with a view to facilitating the process of enlarging areas of agreement among the

---

[102] This version of the talks since 16 March is largely based on Tajuddin Ahmed's statement of 17 April 1971, released by the Government of Bangladesh and is supported by contemporary reports in the Press.

[103] The Pakistan Times (Lahore), 23 March 1971.

political parties, the President has decided to postpone the meeting of the National Assembly called on March 25.''[104] (emphasis added)

There is clear evidence that a broad agreement had been reached between the President and Sheikh Mujibur Rahman. On 22 March Mr. Bhutto said that he was examining the *broad agreement reached between* the President and the Awami League chief and assured that his party would make every effort to reach an understanding to end the present crisis. He also said: 'I had a fruitful and satisfactory meeting with Sheikh Mujibur Rahman this morning. I would welcome another meeting.'[105] On 24 March there were hectic political parleys, and the various leaders held a series of meetings 'in the light of the *agreement reached* between the President and the Awami League chief, Sheikh Mujibur Rahman, to end the present crisis.' Mian Mumtaz Daultana said he was 'hopeful about the talk.'[106] On 24 March Bhutto had a talk with the President and thereafter he said: 'We are making *some progress*'; he was examining the terms 'of the broad *agreement and understanding reached* between President Yahya Khan and Sheikh Mujibur Rahman to end the present political crisis in the country.'[107] On 25 March Bhutto said at a press conference in Dacca that while he supported in principle the *four-point* preconditions of Sheikh Mujibur Rahman, his party was trying to come close to the six points. He believed that since the Awami League had concluded its discussions with the President and his advisers, the PPP must continue their bit now.[108] There was not even a whisper from Bhutto about the breakdown of talks. When reports of military action from Saidpur, Chittagong and other places resulting in numerous 'casualties in firings' reached Dacca, a bewildered Tajuddin Ahmed regretted: 'It is unfortunate that while a *political solution is being pursued* in talks with President Yahya, the atmosphere is being vitiated by these untoward incidents.'[109] In his last statement to the press before the military action commenced Sheikh Mujibur Rahman was under the impression that a political solution on the basis of the agreement reached between him and the President, though regrettably delayed, was still possible. He said:

> The arrival of the President in Dacca and his subsequent talks led the people to expect that there was a realisation that this grave crisis engulfing the country could only be resolved

[104] *Ibid.*
[105] *Dawn* (Karachi), 23 March 1971.
[106] *The Morning News*, 25 March 1971.
[107] *Dawn*, 25 March 1971.
[108] *The Pakistan Times*, 26 March 1971
[109] *Ibid.*

politically. It was for this reason that I met the President. The President affirmed that there could only be a *political solution* of the crisis. Upon that promise, *certain fundamental principles* on which such a solution would be based were *accepted by the President*. Subsequently my colleagues sat with the President's advisers to work out those principles. We have thus done our duty and contributed our utmost efforts towards the attainment of a political solution. There is *no reason or justification for any delay*. If a political solution is desired by those concerned they should realise that it is for them to take matters immediately to a conclusion, and that to delay this would expose the country and its people to grave hazards. It is, therefore, unfortunate that there is a regrettable delay in resolving the crisis politically. Indeed the critical situation already prevailing is being aggravated by *renewed military activities,* the pace of which, according to reports from different parts of Bangladesh, is being *stepped up*. This is all the more regrettable at a time when the President is in Dacca for the *declared purpose of resolving the crisis politically*. After last week's firing at Joydevpur, reports of atrocities are pouring in from Rangpur, Saidpur, where curfew has been imposed. From Chittagong, there are reports of heavy firing on the civilian population. (emphasis added) [110]

While Awami League leaders were anxiously awaiting a call from General Peerzada for the final session which never materialized, it was learnt that Ahmed had suddenly left for Karachi on the morning of 25 March without any warning to the Awami League. No one knew what transpired in the private meetings between Yahya and Bhutto at Dacca, but a consensus between the two must have been reached. [111] Yahya suddenly left Dacca on the night of 25 March and Bhutto followed next morning. The President made a broadcast to the nation on the evening of 26 March and announced his policy of banning the Awami League, the imposition of military rule in East Bengal and complete censorship throughout Pakistan. The reaction of Bhutto on his arrival at Karachi airport on the evening of 26

[110] *Dawn* (Karachi), 26 March 1971.

[111] According to Peter Hazelhurst, Yahya and Mujib had agreed to an interim settlement providing (*i*) immediate withdrawal of martial law by a Presidential proclamation, (*ii*) immediate restoration of power at the provincial level, and (*iii*) the interim central government to be administered by the President until the Constitution was framed. Bhutto opposed the scheme stating that if martial law was withdrawn, and power transferred to the provinces, Pakistan would be broken up into five sovereign states. 'It was Bhutto who finally brought the President to take the decision which set East Bengal on fire . . . Taking events to their logical conclusion there is no doubt that the present holocaust was pre-

March was: 'By the Grace of Almighty God, Pakistan has at last been saved.'[112]

Let us now examine the reasons given by President Yahya in his broadcast on 26 March for the failure of the political talks and for military action in East Bengal.[113] The main grounds advanced by Yahya were: First, the Awami League wanted, during the interim period, the withdrawal of martial law and transfer of power by a presidential proclamation prior to the meeting of the National Assembly. To this Yahya's reaction was: "Despite some serious flaws in the scheme in its legal as well as other aspects, I was prepared to agree in principle to this plan in the interest of peaceful transfer of power but on one condition. The condition which I clearly explained to Sheikh Mujibur Rahman was that I must first have unequivocal agreement of all the political leaders to the scheme. I thereupon discussed the proposal with other political leaders. I found them unanimously of the view that the proposed proclamation by me would have no legal sanction. It will neither have the cover of the Martial Law, nor could it claim to be based on the will of the people. Thus a vacuum would be created and chaotic conditions will ensue."

While giving his version of the talks, Tajuddin Ahmed in his statement of 17 April said: "The question of legal cover for the transfer of power is merely another belated fabrication by Yahya to cover his genocide. He and his team had agreed that, in line with the precedent of the Indian Independence Act of 1947, power could be transferred by presidential proclamation. The notion that there would be no legal cover to the agreement raised subsequently by Mr. Bhutto and endorsed by General Yahya was never a bone of contention between Sheikh Mujib and Yahya."

It is for readers to judge which version is more plausible. A military dictator who came to power as martial law administrator under a presidential proclamation, and later appointed himself President by his own proclamation, contends that he was not legally competent to transfer power to the elected representatives of the people by another presidential proclamation. The technical argument is as flimsy as it is grotesque. No one would seriously suggest that if there was a will to transfer power to the leader of the majority party duly chosen in free and fair elections, a technical argument of this sort could stand in the way. It, therefore, seems reasonable to accept

---

cipitated by President Yahya Khan when he postponed the Assembly without consulting the Bengalis, but even more so by Mr. Bhutto's deliberate decision to boycott the Assembly on 3 March.' *The Manila Chronicle*, 5 July 1971.

[112] *Dawn*, 27 March 1971.

[113] *Dawn*, 27 March 1971.

Tajuddin Ahmed's version and to reject Yahya's explanation as completely fabricated.

Secondly, Yahya argued that the transfer of power during the interim period was not in accordance with the will of the people because he found that the leaders of the other political parties were opposed to Mujib's scheme. He said: "They (the leaders of other political parties) therefore expressed the opinion that if it is intended to lift Martial Law and transfer power in the interim period, the National Assembly should meet, pass an appropriate interim Constitution Bill and present it for my assent. I entirely agreed with their view and requested them to tell Sheikh Mujibur Rahman to take a reasonable attitude on this issue. I told the leaders to explain their views to him that a scheme whereby, on the one hand, you extinguish all sources of power, namely, Martial Law, and on the other fail to replace it by the will of the people through a proper session of the National Assembly, will merely result in chaos. They agreed to meet Sheik Mujibur Rahman, explain the position and try to obtain his agreement to the interim arrangement for transfer of power to emanate from the National Assembly. The political leaders were also very much perturbed over Sheikh Mujib's idea of dividing the National Assembly into two parts right from the start. Such a move, they felt, would be totally against the interest of Pakistan's integrity. The chairman of the Pakistan People's Party, during the meeting between myself, Sheikh Mujibur Rahman and him, had also expressed similar views to Mujib. On the evening of 23rd March the political leaders, who had gone to talk to Mujib on this issue, called on me and informed me that he was not agreeable to any changes in his scheme. All he really wanted was for me to make a proclamation, whereby I should withdraw Martial Law and transfer power."

What transpired during the talks between 16 and 24 March has been mentioned earlier. It will be interesting in this connexion to refer to the observations of Tajuddin Ahmed: "Contrary to the distortions now put out by both Yahya and Bhutto, the proposal for separate sittings of the Assembly was suggested by Yahya to accommodate Mr. Bhutto. He cited the practical advantage that whilst the six points provided a viable blueprint to regulate relations between Bangladesh and the Centre, its application raised serious difficulties in the West Wing. For this reason West Wing MNAs must be permitted to get together to work out a new pattern of relationships in the context of a six-point constitution and the dissolution of One Unit... There is not the slightest doubt that had Yahya indicated that a meeting of the National Assembly was essential to transfer power, the Awami League would not have broken up the talks on such a minor legal technicality. After all as the majority party it had nothing to fear from such a meeting and its acceptance of the decision for a separate sitting was designed to accommodate Mr. Bhutto rather than a fundamental stand for the party."

Here again, Tajuddin's version seems more plausible than Yahya's. It is difficult to conceive that Mujib would insist upon dividing the National Assembly into two parts, since he had nothing to gain from such separate sittings—a suggestion which could only emanate from Bhutto and Yahya because of the growing opposition in the West against the authority of the PPP. A separate sitting of the Western wing of the Assembly would naturally permit Bhutto with his majority to have a greater voice in formulating the constitutional pattern in the context of Mujib's six points. The other suggestion that Mujib was opposed to the idea of an interim constitution emanating from an undivided National Assembly is equally, if not more, inconceivable. The interim settlement is based on Mujib's four points. It will have been observed that on this issue the political parties representing at least 210 out of 300 elected members of the National Assembly had declared their support for the Awami League and wanted immediate transfer of power to a government led by Sheikh Mujib. The only political parties in the West which could conceivably oppose transfer of power to an interim government led by Mujib are Bhutto's PPP and QML with a combined strength of only 90 MNAs. In these circumstances, why should Mujib refuse to accept the transfer of power from a session of an undivided National Assembly?

In his broadcast the President also gave his reason for his drastic action in East Bengal: "Sheikh Mujibur Rahman's action of starting his non-cooperation movement is an act of treason. He and his party have defied the lawful authority for over three weeks... They have tried to run a parallel government. I have ordered them (armed forces) to do their duty and fully restore the authority of the Government. In view of the grave situation that exists in the country today, I have decided to ban all political activities throughout the country. As for the Awami League it is completely banned as a political party. I have also decided to impose complete Press censorship. Martial Law regulations will very shortly be issued in pursuance of these decisions."

By admitting the total success of the non-cooperation movement Yahya had admitted the forfeiture of his lawful authority to administer the country. It was the writ of Mujib alone which ran throughout East Bengal during the three weeks of peaceful non-cooperation movement. There was no one to carry out the orders of the military junta. If Mujib could run a parallel government in East Bengal, it was only because he had the unstinted loyalty of 75 million people.

If Yahya's authority was ignored during the three weeks of March 1971, it only proved the truth of the immortal Lincoln concept that 'bullets can never successfully replace ballots'.   The minimum right of the people in East Bengal to launch a peaceful non-cooperation movement for achieving self-determination can never be in dispute. This is an acknowledged right of the people.   The people of East Bengal would have been within their legal rights to declare independence early in March 1971 if they were satisfied that on the basis of the six-point programme a constitutional regime would be frustrated by the brutal force of military oligarchy.   This legal position will be examined in Chapter V.

President Yahya accused Sheikh Mujib of treason.   The simple answer is that under no system of jurisprudence in a civilized country, nor under the municipal law of Pakistan as on 25 March 1971, can a non-violent non-cooperation movement for transfer of power from a non-representative military oligarchy to the elected representatives of the people be considered an act of treason.   It is one of the most important recognized rights of a democratic people.   As Thoreau had observed in a memorable passage in his *Civil Disobedience*,[114]

> ... If a thousand men were not to pay their tax-bills this year, that would not be a violent and bloody measure, as it would be to pay them, and enable the State to commit violence and shed innocent blood.   This is, in fact, the definition of a peaceable revolution, if any such is possible.   If the tax-gatherer, or any other public officer asks me, as one has done, 'But what shall I do?' my answer is, 'If you really wish to do anything, resign your office.' When the subject has refused allegiance, and the officer has resigned his office, then the revolution is accomplished.   But even suppose blood should flow.   Is there not a sort of blood shed when the conscience is wounded?   Through this wound a man's real manhood and immortality flow out, and he bleeds to an everlasting death.   I see this blood flowing now...

Let us assume that Sheikh Mujib had inspired the movement for independence of East Bengal and the consequent dismemberment of Pakistan.   Is that an offence under international Law?   When a majority is denied its democratic right to bring about a constitutional regime—as the Awami League was denied in Pakistan—the revolutionary right of the majority to the dismemberment or division of a State can never be in dispute in international law.   Such a right was conceded even by Abraham Lincoln.   It is one of the legitimate and

[114] *Living Ideas In America*, edited by Henry Steele Commager (Harper, New York, 1951), p. 383.

10

permissible modes of implementing self-determination according to the contemporary norms of international law.

Much later, on 5 August 1971, on second thoughts, Yahya's government published yet another version for the failure of the political talks in March. The new version is contained in a White Paper[115] on the political events in the country since the general election in December last. The main allegations are that Sheikh Mujibur Rahman and the Awami League attempted to secure effective independence for East Bengal by constitutional negotiations and, when this failed, planned to launch an armed rebellion to take independence by force. As *The Guardian* rightly comments: 'The White Paper produces little fresh evidence to support the first contention and none at all to support the second.'

In support of the first contention, the White Paper alleged that President Yahya as far as he possibly could tried to help create conditions for transferring power to elected representatives by evolving a consensus among the various parties; Sheikh Mujib however progressively escalated his demands with complete disregard for the fact that his mandate was autonomy within a federation even in the terms of the Awami League's six points. Towards the concluding phase of talks, the Awami League's draft proclamation spoke of 'a confederation' and included 'other unmistakable indications of their resolve to break up the country.'

In view of Yahya's contemporaneous version of 26 March and Tajuddin Ahmed's statement of 17 April, and the reports in the Press already discussed, no further comment is necessary. It is impossible to disbelieve the cogent evidence that Sheikh Mujib staked his political life with a view to preserving the integrity of Pakistan. In any event, 'confederation' is a perfectly legitimate modality for achieving self-determination.

In support of the second contention, it was alleged in the White Paper that in collusion with India, 'an operational plan with meticulous details' was prepared which provided that East Bengal Regiment troops would occupy Dacca and Chittagong to prevent a landing by the Pakistani army by air or sea. It was further alleged that the troops of the East Bengal Regiment, helped by East Pakistan Rifles, police and armed volunteers would eliminate the armed forces of Pakistan on various bases and occupy all key border posts to keep open the frontier for aid from India. Indian troops would come to the assistance of the Awami League forces after the first phase. As *The Guardian* points out, the White Paper 'gives no source for the claim that the Awami League had a worked-out plan of rebellion for

[115] *The Guardian, The Daily Telegraph, The Statesman,* Calcutta, 6 August 1971.

March 26.' This is a fabricated charge and clearly an afterthought. It is strange that no such allegation was made in Yahya's earlier version of 26 March.[116]

There is a third charge in the White Paper that various atrocities and acts of lawlessness were committed by the Awami League in East Bengal from 1 March till the Pakistani army restored control, resulting in 100,000 victims. If this allegation were true, it is surprising that there was not even a whisper of protest from Yahya or Bhutto during the month of March nor was it mentioned in Yahya's broadcast on 26 March. On the other hand, a number of unarmed Bengali civilians were killed by Yahya's army early in March for which Mujib demanded a judicial inquiry. Yahya's government had to order an official inquiry. The document is, therefore, another attempt to confuse world opinion.

President Yahya concluded his broadcast on 26 March with the usual promise: 'In the end let me assure you that my main aim remains the same, namely, transfer of power to the elected representatives of the people. As soon as the situation permits I will take fresh steps towards the achievement of this objective.' The people of East Bengal had no longer any illusion about the familiar assurances of a military dictator in Pakistan.

---

[116] A Foreign Office spokesman of the Bangladesh Government, describing the White Paper as a 'Bunch of White Lies' comments: 'We want to tell the world that if Sheikh Mujibur Rahman had planned any armed struggle he would not have faced the possibility of arrest in the hand of the junta against whom his own army would be waging a war' (see Bangla Desh Documents op. cit., p. 341).

CHAPTER THREE

CRIMES OF A SOULLESS REGIME

Introduction

There is no double standard for war crimes and crimes against humanity. The standard is uniform as declared by Chief Prosecutor Justice Jackson of the United States Supreme Court at the Nuremberg War Crimes trials:

> If certain acts and violations of treaties are crimes, they are crimes whether the United States does them or whether Germany does them. We are not prepared to lay down a rule of criminal conduct against others which we would not be willing to have invoked against us.[1]

Much of the happenings in East Bengal (now Bangladesh) between 25 March and 16 December 1971 is now a matter of common knowledge. These acts of commission and omission by the Government of Pakistan were generally condemned by responsible international public opinion throughout the period as amounting to crimes against humanity. For instance, the Catholic daily, *Religion*, of Caracas (Venezuela) in an editorial on 3 July, 1971 said:

> Before this grim tragedy, this gruesome Dante-like spectacle, other tragedies like Hungary, Biafra, Congo, Vietnam, become insignificant. To find a parallel one has to look towards the extermination camps of Hitler or perhaps towards the days of Chengiz Khan or Temerlene. Its best sons, its intellectuals, writers, journalists, professors, the youth are being hunted like rats—this repression, massacre, the reign of terror must cease. This nightmare, this hell must come to an immediate end.[2]

The editorial further said that "Jesus would have trembled in horror 'at the nightmare and hell' let loose by Pakistan on the people of Bangladesh. It would be insulting to human intelligence to call the

---

[1] Quoted by Bertrand Russell in *War Crimes in Vietnam* (Allen & Unwin, 1967), p. 125.

[2] Reproduced in *The Statesman*, Calcutta, 9 July 1971 quoting UNI Report.

repression by Pakistan an internal affair. The problem was of international dimensions and a challenge to human conscience."

The *Washington Post* in an editorial on 31 July pointed out that in Pakistan the world was witnessing the holocaust unmatched since Hitler. Mr. Cornelius Gallagher, member of the U.S. House of Representatives Foreign Affairs Committee, who had toured the Indian border, said on 4 June 1971 that he was convinced that 'genocide of no small magnitude' had been committed in East Bengal.[3] Again, Senator Edward Kennedy after an extensive tour of the evacuee camps, said in New Delhi on 16 August that he had no hesitation in describing the mass killing of unarmed civilians by the West Pakistan Army as genocide.[4] The caption of *Newsweek's* cover story of 2 August 1971 reads, 'Bengal: The Murder of a People'. Dr. H. E. Jahm, member of Parliament of the Federal Republic of Germany, described the recent happenings in East Bengal as a 'crime against humanity' and a 'gross violation of the UN Charter.'[5] Again on 7 December 1971, Mr. Anthony Lewis wrote in the *New York Times:* 'Yahya is not a man with a racist mission but a spokesman for xenophobic forces in West Pakistan. But in terms of results—in terms of human beings killed, brutalized or made refugees—Yahya's record compares quite favourably with Hitler's early years. The West Pakistanis have killed several hundred thousand civilians in the East, and an estimated ten million have fled to India. The oppression has been specifically on lines of race or religion. The victims are Bengalis or Hindus, not Czechs or Poles or Jews, and perhaps therefore less meaningful to us in the West. But to the victims the crime is the same.' The opinions so expressed represent a reasonable assessment of international public opinion in relation to the impugned acts of West Pakistan authorities in East Bengal.

The purpose of this Chapter is to examine some of the happenings in East Bengal in the light of the relevant norms in contemporary international law. The armed conflict in East Bengal since 25 March 1971 was editorially described by the *Daily Mail*, London, on 7 June 1971 as a 'civil and racial war' unleashed in March by President Yahya Khan when he sent in his Punjabi troops from the West to crush the Bengali movement in East Bengal. Whether one describes it as a revolt or revolution, a civil war, racial war, a war of liberation or a resistance movement against illegal use of force, it represented in reality a situation of armed conflict. The United Nations has recently emphasized that fundamental human rights, as accepted in international law and laid down in international instruments, conti-

---

[3] *The Times*, London, 5 June, 1971.
[4] *The Statesman*, Calcutta, 17 August 1971.
[5] *The Statesman*, Calcutta, 9 August 1971.

nue to apply fully in situations of armed conflicts and has further reaffirmed the well-recognized priciple of the immunity of the civilian population from the military attack. Ever since the law of the Nuremberg Charter and the judgment of the Nuremberg Tribunal, international law recognizes that war crimes and crimes against humanity cover a wide common area and accordingly several common norms become relevant. Many of these norms are based essentially on humanitarian principles accepted by the international community long prior to the Charter regime. Various Conventions (e.g. the Genocide Convention and the Geneva Convention) and resolutions of the United Nations (e.g. 9 December and 15 December 1970) have progressively expanded the scope of these principles and imposed stricter liabilities on public authorities for any breach thereof. For instance, the resolution of 15 December 1970 urged the importance of a thorough investigation into war crimes and crimes against humanity and for the punishment of the criminals wherever they might have been committed. It has been recognized that these crimes are frequently committed as a result of policies of racism and colonialism.

In order to appreciate whether the Government of Pakistan has in fact committed, and if so, to what extent, any transgressions against international norms in East Bengal, it will perhaps be useful to examine the status of some relevant norms in contemporary law.

Law of the Nuremberg Charter and Judgment

The massive violations of certain fundamental norms by Adolf Hitler during the Second World War induced the international community not only to condemn what Hitler did but to formulate stricter measures than hitherto existing for the protection of the individual. In the common areas of war crimes and crimes against humanity, criminal liability is imposed as a matter of international public policy irrespective of any contractual or conventional obligation. 'For the laws of humanity, which are not dependent upon positive enactment, are binding, by their very nature, upon human beings as such.'[6]

Article 6 of the Nuremberg Charter[7] provided that there 'shall be individual responsibility' for 'crimes against peace', 'war crimes' and 'crimes against humanity'. Article 6 has defined, inter alia, war crimes and crimes against humanity. Under Article 6(b), war crimes are: 'Violations of the laws or customs of war. Such violations shall include, but not be limited to, murder, ill-treatment or deportation to slave labour or for any other purpose of civilian

[6] Oppenheim's International Law, Vol. 1 (8th ed.), pp. 341-2.

[7] (1945) 39 AJIL. Suppl. p. 259; Cmd. 6668 (1945)—see also the Indictment of 18 October 1945. Cmd. 6696 (1945).

population of or in occupied territory, murder or ill-treatment of prisoners of war or persons on the seas, killing of hostages, plunder of public or private property, wanton destruction of cities, towns or villages, or devastation not justified by military necessity.' These crimes are covered, among others, by Articles 46, 50, 52 and 56 of the Hague Convention (IV) of 1907, and Articles 2, 3, 4, 46 and 51 of the Geneva Convention of 1929. By 1939, the rules laid down in the Hague Convention 'were recognized by all civilized nations, and were recognized as being declaratory of the laws and customs of war which are referred to in Article 6(b).'[8]

In the present context it will be necessary to refer to following provisions of the Hague Convention IV:[9]

> Article 46: Family honour and rights, the lives of persons, and private property, as well as religious convictions and practice, must be respected. Private property cannot be confiscated.
> Article 47: Pillage is formally forbidden.
> Article 50: No general penalty, pecuniary or otherwise, shall be inflicted upon the population on account of the acts of individuals for which they cannot be regarded as jointly and severally responsible.
> Article 56: The property of municipalities, that of institutions dedicated to religion, charity and education, the arts and science, even when State property, shall be treated as private property. All seizure of, destruction or wilful damage done to institutions of this character, historic monuments, works of art and science, is forbidden, and should be made the subject of legal proceedings.

Article 6(c) of the Nuremberg Charter defined crimes against humanity as follows:

> Crimes against humanity: namely, murder, extermination, enslavement, deportation, and other inhumane acts committed against any civilian population, before or during the war, or persecution on political or religious grounds in execution of or in connection with any crime within the jurisdiction of the Tribunal, whether or not in violation of the domestic law of the country where perpetrated.

All the three categories of crimes (namely, crimes against peace, war crimes and crimes against humanity) within the jurisdiction of the Nuremberg Tribunal were covered by the following common provision: 'Leaders, organizers, instigators and accomplices parti-

---

[8] L. C. Green, *International Law Through Cases* (Stevens, 2nd ed.). ch. 33, p. 689; *Oppenheim's International Law* (7th ed.), Vol. II, p. 578.

[9] Herbert W. Briggs, *The Law of Nations* (Stevens, 1953), pp. 1022-24.

cipating in the formulation or execution of a common plan or conspiracy to commit any of the foregoing crimes are responsible for
all acts performed by any person in execution of such plan.'

As early as in the eighteenth century it became a universally recognized customary rule of the law of nations that private enemy individuals should not be killed or attacked; in so far as they do not take
part in the fighting, they should not be directly attacked, killed or
wounded.[10] The immunity of non-combatants from direct attack is
one of the fundamental rules of international law of war—a rule
which before the last war applied equally to warfare on land, at sea
and in the air.   Article 25 of the Hague Convention IV categorically
enacted: 'The attack or bombardment, by whatever means, of towns,
villages, dwellings or buildings which are undefended is prohibited.'
The customary rules of air warfare in relation to the immunity of
civilians was restated by the British Prime Minister in a statement
to the House of Commons in 1938, following upon the operations of
German and Italian air forces in the course of the Spanish civil war
and similar Japanese action in China, and the position was accepted
as correct by the Assembly of the League of Nations. He laid down
three main principles:[11] (i) Any deliberate attack upon the civilian
population is an undoubted violation of international law; (ii) targets
which are aimed at from the air must be legitimate military objectives
and must be capable of identification; (iii) reasonable care must be
taken in attacking the military objectives so that by carelessness
a civilian population in the neighbourhood is not bombarded. It will
be recalled that during the last war, while Hitler, in breach of his
promise to spare the civilian population, had ordered indiscriminate
aerial bombing, unrelated to any direct military objective, in War-
shaw, Norway, Rotterdam, Belgrade etc., the British aircraft, at
an early stage, often returned to their base with their bombs being
unable to identify specified military objectives.

These were binding principles of international law at the time
Hitler committed his atrocities and today they apply with still greater
force because of the developments since 1946 in the common areas
of war crimes and crimes against humanity.

In the sequence of time, a brief reminder to readers about some
of the atrocities committed by Hitler during the last War will perhaps be useful in order that they may have a better appreciation of
the happenings in occupied East Bengal since 25 March 1971. Apart
from the war crime of indiscriminate bombing of civilian populations
for the purpose of terrorization, in areas under German occupation,
particularly in Eastern Europe, Germany was found guilty of un-

---

[10] *Oppenheim's International Law*, Vol. II (7th ed.), p. 346.
[11] *Ibid.*, p. 523; *House of Commons Debates*, Vol. 337, Col. 937.

precedented violation of practically all the laws of belligerent occupation; the suspension of local laws subjecting private and public property to a planned policy of exploitation in the interest of Germany, suppression of the civil and political rights of the population and promotion of Nazi ideas; and deportation of millions for forced labour in Germany. The population was subjected to a policy of terror with a view to stifling all resistance against the occupant. It was particularly in that respect, and in relation to Article 46 of the Hague Convention IV, that the Nuremberg Tribunal found that 'the territories occupied by Germany were administered in violation of the laws of war' and that 'the evidence is quite overwhelming of a systematic rule of violence, brutality and terror'. In Eastern Europe, a policy was put into effect for reducing the number of intelligentsia and of political opponents. Concentration camps were set up in Germany and elsewhere for persons from occupied territories and according to the Nuremberg Tribunal, 'they were conveyed to the camps in many cases without any care whatever being taken for them, and great numbers died on the way. Those who arrived at camps were subjected to systematic cruelty. They were given hard physical labour, inadequate food, clothes and shelter, and were subjected at all times to the rigours of a soulless regime, and the private whims of individual guards.' Special detachments of the German army were used for destroying in planned and periodic raids part of the population. Concentration camps were the main instrument of extermination, in pursuance of the racial policy of the German Government, of six million Jews from occupied territories—mostly in gas chambers established in these camps. The other means included starvation effected by the issue of purely nominal food rations. Prior to extermination, the Jewish citizens of these countries were exposed to wholesale deprivation of political and civil rights and to segregation in ghettos. In the words of the International Military Tribunal at Nuremberg, the persecution and extermination of the Jews 'is a record of consistent and systematic inhumanity on the greatest scale.' The following passage from the judgment gives a picture of the treatment, in the concentration camps, of the victims of that policy:

> Evidence was given of the treatment of the inmates before and after their extermination. There is testimony that the hair of women victims was cut off before they were killed, and shipped to Germany, there to be used in the manufacture of mattresses. The clothes, money, and valuables of the inmates were also salvaged and sent to the appropriate agencies for disposition. After the extermination, the gold teeth and fittings were taken from the heads of the corpses and sent to the Reichsbank. After

cremation, the ashes were used for fertiliser, and in some instances attempts were made to utilize the fat from the bodies of
the victims in the commercial manufacture of soap.   Special
groups travelled through Europe to find Jews and subject them
to the 'final solution'.   German missions were sent to such satel-
lite countries as Hungary and Bulgaria, to arrange for the shipment of Jews to extermination camps, and it is known that by
the end of 1944, 400,000 Jews from Hungary had been murdered
at Auschwitz.[12]

In short, the Nuremberg Tribunal found that the systematic
plunder of public and private property and the ruthless exploitation
of the resources in the occupied territories without consideration of
the local economy amounted to war crimes within the meaning of
Article 6(b) of the Charter. It was also held that the ill-treatment
of the civilian population, and the deportation of the civilians from
occupied territory amounted to war crimes within the meaning of
Article 6(b). With regard to the treatment of prisoners of war the
Tribunal accepted as correct the following legal position: Since the
eighteenth century the principle of international law has been that
war captivity is neither revenge nor punishment but solely protective
custody, the only purpose of which is to prevent the prisoners of war
from further participation in the war.   This principle was developed
in accordance with the view held by all armies that it is contrary to
military tradition to kill or injure helpless people.[13]

With regard to Crimes against Humanity by the Germans, the
Tribunal concluded:

> With regard to Crimes against Humanity, there is no doubt what-
> ever that political opponents were murdered in Germany before
> the war, and that many of them were kept in concentration camps
> in circumstances of great horror and cruelty. The policy of
> terror was certainly carried out on a vast scale, and in many
> cases was organised and systematic. The policy of persecution,
> repression and murder of civilians in Germany before the war
> of 1939, who were likely to be hostile to the Government, was most
> ruthlessly carried out. The persecution of Jews during the same
> period is established beyond all doubt. To constitute Crimes

---

[12] *Oppenheim's International Law*, Vol. II, p. 448-51. For Nuremberg Judgment: 1946 Cmd. 6964 (1946), 22 H.M.S.O. *Trial of German Major War
Criminals*, p. 411. Also see, L. C. Green, op cit., Ch. 33; (1947) 41 AJIL,
pp. 172-333 at p. 247.

[13] L. C. Green, *International Law Through Cases* (Stevens. 2nd ed.), Ch. 33,
pp. 687-9.

against Humanity, the acts relied on before the outbreak of war must have been in execution of, or in connection with, any crime within the jurisdiction of the Tribunal. The Tribunal is of the opinion that revolting and horrible as many of these crimes were, it has not been satisfactorily proved that they were done in execution of, or in connection with, any such crime. The Tribunal therefore cannot make a general declaration that the acts before 1939 were Crimes against Humanity within the meaning of the Charter, but from the beginning of the war in 1939, War Crimes were committed on a vast scale, which were also Crimes against Humanity; and in so far as the inhumane acts charged in the Indictment, and committed after the beginning of the war, did not constitute War Crimes, they were all committed in execution of, or in connection with, the aggressive war, and therefore constituted Crimes against Humanity.[14]

The judgment further pronounced that the provisions relating to individual responsibility for war crimes and crimes against humanity were declaratory of an inescapable principle of international law:

It was submitted that international law is concerned with the actions of sovereign States, and provides no punishment for individuals; and further, that where the act in question is an act of State, those who carry it out are not personally responsible, but are protected by the doctrine of the sovereignty of the State. In the opinion of the Tribunal, both these submissions must be rejected... Crimes against international law are committed by men, not by abstract entities, and only by punishing individuals who commit such crimes can the provisions of international law be enforced.[15]

Genocide Convention of 1948

Hitler's pogrom consisting of an organized massacre of helpless people in Europe prompted the United Nations to recognize that genocide under the international law is a crime which has, at all periods of history, inflicted great losses on humanity. To liberate mankind from such an odious scourge condemned by the civilized world, the General Assembly of the United Nations approved the Genocide Convention of 3 December 1948. The popular meaning of 'genocide' is 'the deliberate and systematic destruction of a racial, political or cultural group.'[16] In Article II of the Genocide Convention,[17] the

[14] *Ibid.*, pp. 689-90; (1947) 41 AJIL, p. 249.
[15] (1947) 41 AJIL p. 220, Oppenheim, Vol. I, op. cit., p. 342.
[16] Webster's Seventh *New Collegiate Dictionary*, p. 348.
[17] For text, *International Organization* (1949), Vol. III, p. 206.

term 'genocide' means any of the following acts, committed with intent to destroy, in whole or in part, a national, ethnical, racial or religious group, as such: (a) killing members of the group; (b) causing serious bodily or mental harm to members of the group; (c) deliberately inflicting on the group conditions of life calculated to bring about its physical destruction in whole or in part; (d) imposing measures intended to prevent births within the group; (e) forcibly transferring children of the group to another group.

Article III makes punishable not only an act of genocide but also conspiracy to commit genocide, direct and public incitement to commit genocide, attempt to commit genocide and complicity in genocide. Under Article IV persons committing genocide or any of the other acts enumerated in Article III shall be punished, whether they are constitutionally responsible rulers, public officials or private individuals. Article V contemplates the enactment of appropriate national legislation by a contracting party with a view to making the Convention effective, and particularly to provide effective penalties for persons guilty of genocide or any of the other acts enumerated in Article III. Persons charged with the impugned acts should be tried by 'a competent tribunal of the State in the territory of which the act was committed, or by such international penal tribunal as may have jurisdiction with respect to those contracting parties which shall have accepted its jurisdiction': (Article VI). The acts covered by the Convention 'shall not be considered as political crimes for the purpose of extradition': (Article VII). Article VIII provides: 'Any contracting party may call upon the competent organs of the United Nations to take such action under the Charter of the United Nations as they consider appropriate for the prevention and suppression of acts of genocide or any other acts enumerated in Article III.' Article IX deals with disputes between the contracting parties relating to the interpretation, application or fulfilment of the Convention, including those with regard to the responsibility of a State for genocide or any other acts enumerated in Article III. Such disputes shall be submitted to the International Court of Justice at the request of any of the parties to the dispute.

The Genocide Convention is one of those instruments based on essential values of civilized nations which imposes absolute obligations upon a state without granting them any rights in this regard. This was so held by the International Court of Justice in its advisory opinion on reservations to the Genocide Convention. The advisory opinion was given pursuant to the General Assembly's request as contained in resolution 478(V) of 16 December 1950. By its resolution 598(VI) of 12 January 1952 the General Assembly recommended that in regard to the Convention all states should be guided by the advisory opinion. The International Court observed: "The Convention was manifestly adopted for a purely humanitarian and civilizing purpose... In such a Convention the contracting States *do not have any interest of their own*; they merely have, one and all, a *common interest*, namely, the accomplishment of those high purposes which are *raison d'etre* of the Convention. Consequently, in a Convention of this type one cannot speak of individual advantages or disadvantages of States, or of the maintenance of a perfect contractual balance between rights and duties." (emphasis added) [18]

The Judgment constitutes a clear affirmation of the existence in international law of an international public policy in matters connected with genocide and the limitation it imposes on the contractual freedom of states.[19] All fundamental humanitarian rules prohibiting genocidal acts or inhumane acts of cruelty, either in war or in peace, it is submitted, have the character of *jus cogens*, i.e. norms with which treaties must not conflict. The rules are 'absolute' because they 'do not exist to satisfy the needs of the individual states but the higher interest of the whole international community.'[20]

Geneva Convention of 1949 and Civil Wars

By the four Geneva Conventions of 1949, three of the earlier conventions were revised and a new convention for the protection of civilians was established. The earlier conventions which were revised are: The Geneva Convention of 1929 relating to the wounded and sick in armies in the field, the Hague Convention (X) of 1907 relating to maritime warfare, and the Geneva Convention of 1929 relating to prisoners of war. The four Conventions of 1949 relate to: (a) the wounded and sick in the armed forces in the field; (b) wounded, sick and shipwrecked members of the armed forces at sea; (c) the treatment of prisoners of war, and (d) the protection of civilian persons. One of the results of the cruelties of the German occupation forces in Europe prompted the international community to supplement and to make more precise the provisions of the Hague Regulations through the Convention of 1949 relating to civilian persons. All the four Conventions were concluded at Geneva on 12 August 1949.[21]

Pakistan is a party to the Geneva Conventions of 1949. The Con-

---

[18] (1951) I.C.J. Rep. p. 23.

[19] For the correlation between the Genocide Convention and International Public Policy, see Ralph Zacklin, 'Challenge of Rhodesia—Toward an International Public Policy', *International Conciliation*, Nov. 1961.

[20] Alfred Verdross *Jus Dispositivum And Jus Cogens in International Law* (1966) 60 AJIL 54, 58, 59, for Genocide Convention And Jus Cogens.

[21] For text, see (1950) Vol. 75 United Nations Treaty Series, 1. Nos. 970-973.

ventions impose a number of obligations upon a contracting party not only in respect of its own civilian population in a situation of armed conflict but also with regard to the members 'of organised resistance movements, belonging to a party to the conflict and operating in or outside their own territory.'[22]

According to Oppenheim: "It has already been stated that an armed contention between a Federal State and its member-States ought to be considered as war because both parties are real States, although the Federal State may correctly designate it as rebellion. Such armed contentions may be called civil wars in a wider sense of the term. In the proper sense of the term a civil war exists when two opposing parties within a State have recourse to arms for the purpose of obtaining power in the State, or when a large portion of the population of a State rises in arms against the legitimate Government. As war is an armed contention between States, such a civil war need not be war from the beginning, nor become war at all, in the technical sense of the term. But it may become war through the recognition of the contending parties, or of the insurgents, as a belligerent power. Through such recognition a body of individuals receives an international position, in so far as it is for some purposes treated as though it were a subject of International Law."[23]

One may contend that prior to the recognition of Bangladesh by India on 6 December 1971, the armed conflict in East Bengal between the West Pakistani troops and the Mukti Bahini (Liberation Forces) of the Government of Bagladesh was not an international war. But there are certain provisions of the Geneva Convention which are fully operative even in the situation of a civil war or an armed conflict not of an international character. These provisions were at all material times applicable in the Bangladesh conflict. All the provisions of the Geneva Convention, however, became fully applicable from 6 December. The recognition of Bangladesh by India and Bhutan was enough to make all the provisions of the Convention operative even though the Government of Pakistan treated it as an internal revolt.[24]

For the purpose of the present discussion, we shall proceed on the basis that the armed conflict in East Bengal was not of an international character and it amounted to a civil war. All the four Geneva

[22] Article IV of the Geneva Convention of 1949 relating to Prisoners of War.

[23] *Oppenheim's International Law*, Vol. II, p. 209.

[24] This view, according to Professor Lauterpacht, is probably accurate. He has referred to the American Civil War when the Confederate States were treated as belligerents by Great Britain and some other states but not by the United States; Oppenheim's Vol II, op cit., p. 370, f.n. 1.

Conventions of 1949 uniformly provide that in such a situation a state which is a party to the Conventions shall be bound to apply, as a minimum, certain humanitarian provisions of a fundamental character. These provisions are to be found in Article 3 which is common to all the four Conventions.

Article 3: In the case of armed conflict not of an international character occurring in the territory of one of the High Contracting Parties, each Party to the conflict shall be bound to apply, as a minimum, the following provisions:

(1) Persons taking no active part in the hostilities, including members of armed forces who have laid down their arms and those placed *hors de combat* by sickness, wounds, detention, or any other cause, shall in all circumstances be treated humanely, without any adverse distinction founded on race, colour, religion or faith, sex, birth or wealth, or any other similar criteria.

To this end, the following acts are and shall remain prohibited at any time and in any place whatsoever with respect to the above-mentioned persons:

(a) violence to life and person, in particular murder of all kinds, mutilation, cruel treatment and torture;

(b) taking of hostages;

(c) outrages upon personal dignity, in particular humiliating and degrading treatment;

(d) the passing of sentences and the carrying out of executions without previous judgment pronounced by a regularly constituted court, affording all the judicial guarantees which are recognized as indispensable by civilised peoples.

(2) The wounded and sick shall be collected and cared for.

An impartial humanitarian body, such as the International Committee of the Red Cross, may offer its services to the Parties to the conflict. The Parties to the conflict should further endeavour to bring into force, by means of special agreements, all or part of the other provisions of the present Convention. The application of the preceding provisions shall not affect the legal status of the Parties to the conflict.

Article 3 treats individuals as entities entitled to certain minimum humanitarian rights and the state to which they belong is under an international duty to respect those rights. This is because the observance of fundamental humanitarian rights is not dependent upon the recognition of a specific status and 'neither is it affected by the circumstance that the insurgents have risen in rebellion against the legitimate authority.'[25]   Article 3 primarily applies to civil wars in cases in which there has been no recognition of belligerency. But where, in a civil war, belligerency has been recognized and the conflict is therefore of an international character, 'the Convention applies in full in respect of States which are bound by it provided that the other belligerent accepts and applies the Convention.'[26]

As we will examine later, all parties to any armed conflict were called upon by the General Assembly by its resolution 2677 (XXV) of 9 December 1970 to observe the rules laid down *inter alia* in the Geneva Conventions of 1949 and other humanitarian rules applicable in an armed conflict.

It will have been observed that the ambit of Article 3 is very wide indeed and, it is submitted, covers many of the specific humanitarian principles laid down in the other provisions of the four Conventions. Inhumane acts—killings, ghastly tortures and cruelties, outrages on women, despoiling the dead, ill-treatment of helpless civilians, and similar offences, constitute crimes against humanity according to binding principles and precedents of international law. Many of these international norms, it is submitted, have the character of *jus cogens* and provide the basis of the modern principle of international public policy. We will therefore examine some of those humanitarian principles in the Geneva Conventions which are applicable to the armed conflict in East Bengal for two reasons: first, they come within the wide ambit of Article 3; second, they are attracted independently on humanitarian principles and by reason of the resolutions of 9 December 1970 of the General Assembly, notwithstanding the technical ground that the people of East Bengal were not 'protected persons' and Pakistan was not an 'occupying power'.

Among others, the following humanitarian principles under the Geneva Conventions relating to the protection of civilian persons seem to be relevant. Article 5 recognizes the elementary principle of the law of nations that an individual person, even though 'definitely suspected of or engaged in activities hostile to the security of the State' or 'detained as a spy or saboteur', must be treated with humanity and must not be deprived of the rights of a fair and regular trial as provided by the Convention. The procedure for a fair trial can be found *inter alia* in Articles 64 to 73 which will, we submit, apply *mutatis mutandis* in respect of persons protected by Article 3 of the Convention. Under Article 27 the civilians are entitled to respect for their persons, their honour, their family rights, their religious convictions and practices and their manners and customs. They shall at all times be treated humanely and shall be protected specially

---

[25] *Oppenheim's International Law*. Vol. II. p. 211. f.n. 3.
[26] *Ibid.*, pp. 370-1.

CRIMES OF A SOULLESS REGIME

against all acts of violence and threats thereof. 'Women shall be specially protected against any attack on their honour, in particular against rape, enforced prostitution or any form of indecent assault.' Under Article 31 there should be no physical or moral coercion against civilians, in particular to obtain information from them or from third parties. Article 32 prohibits any measure which would cause physical suffering or extermination of civilians and this prohi-- bition applies 'not only to murder, torture, corporal punishment, mutilation, medical or scientific experiments' but also 'to any other measures of brutality whether applied by civilian or military agents'. Under Article 33 'collective penalties and likewise all measures of intimidation or of terrorism are prohibited'. Article 49 prohibits individual or mass forcible transfers as well as deportation of civilians. The occupying power shall not transfer parts of its own civilian population into the territory it occupies. This is intended to prevent transfer of nationals with a view to displacing the local population. Article 53 prohibits any destruction of real or personal property belonging individually or collectively to private persons or to the state or to other public authorities or to co-operative organisations except when military operations render such destruction absolutely necessary. Article 54 forbids measures of coercion or discrimination against public officials or alteration of their status.

According to a well-recognized customary rule of international law, dead bodies shall not be multilated but shall be collected and buried or cremated. The Geneva Convention relating to 'wounded and sick in the armies in the field' has made adequate provisions in respect of wounded, sick and dead persons. Under Article 15, there is an obligation to collect the wounded and sick, to ensure their adequate care, and to search for the dead and prevent their being despoiled. Under Article 17 burial or cremation of the dead must be ensured and should be preceded by a careful examination in order to make sure that life is extinct. It must also be ensured that 'the dead are honourably interred, if possible according to the rites of the religion to which they belonged, that their graves are respected ... properly maintained and marked so that they may always be found.' It is submitted that these principles would apply a *fortiori*, on humanitarian grounds, to civilians wounded or killed in the armed conflict in East Bengal.

Prohibition of Chemical Warfare

Apart from the Geneva Conventions, the rules of chemical warfare may also become relevant in the context of the events in East Bengal. Pakistan was one of the sponsors of the draft resolution of L. 489 which was adopted by the General Assembly in resolution

2603A (XXIV) on 16 December 1969,[27] regarding the question of chemical and bacteriological (biological) weapons. After confirming the position that the Geneva Protocol of 17 June 1925 embodies the generally recognized rules of international law regarding the prohibition of the use of asphyxiating, poisonous and other gases, the resolution reiterated the prohibition against the use of (a) any chemical agents of warfare—chemical substances, whether gaseous, liquid or solid—which might be employed because of their direct toxic effects on man, animals or plants; (b) any biological agents of warfare—living organisms, whatever their nature, or infective material derived from them—which are intended to cause disease or death in man, animals or plants, and which depend for their effects on their ability to multiply in the person, animal or plant attacked.

Different Kinds of War Crimes

Oppenheim states: '251. In contradistinction to hostile acts of soldiers by which the latter do not lose their privilege of being treated as lawful members of armed forces, war crimes are such hostile or other acts of soldiers or other individuals as may be punished by the enemy on capture of the offenders. They include acts contrary to International Law perpetrated in violation of the law of the criminal's own State, such as killing or plunder for satisfying private lust and gain, as well as criminal acts contrary to the laws of war committed by order and on behalf of the enemy State. To that extent the notion of war crimes is based on the view that States and their organs are subject to criminal responsibility under International Law... 252. In spite of the uniform designation of these acts as war crimes, four different kinds of war crimes must be distinguished on account of the essentially different character of the acts, namely, (1) violations of recognised rules regarding warfare committed by members of the armed forces, (2) all hostilities in arms committed by individuals who are not members of the enemy armed forces, (3) espionage and war treason, (4) all marauding acts.' Professor Lauterpacht has mentioned 20 examples of more important violations of rules of warfare. Among them the following are relevant in the present context: (1) Making use of poisoned, or otherwise forbidden, arms and ammunition, including asphyxiating, poisonous and similar gases; (2) Assassination, and hiring of assassins; (3) Ill-treatment of prisoners of war, or of the wounded and sick. Appropriation of such of their money and valuables as are not public property; (4) Killing or attacking harmless private enemy individuals. Unjustified appropriation and destruction of their private property, and especially pillaging. Compelling the population of occupied territory

[27] (1970) 64 AJIL 393.

to furnish information about the army of the other belligerent, or about his means of defence; (5) Disgraceful treatment of dead bodies on battlefields; (6) Appropriation and destruction of property belonging to museums, hospitals, churches, schools and the like; (7) Assault, siege, and bombardment of undefended open towns and other habitations. Unjustified bombardment of undefended places by naval forces. Aerial bombardment for the sole purpose of terrorising or attacking the civilian population; (8) Unnecessary bombardment of historical monuments, and of such hospitals and buildings devoted to religion, art, science, and charity as are indicated by particular signs notified to the besiegers bombarding a defended town; (9) Violations of the Geneva Conventions.[27a]

Punishment of Criminals: Recent Trends

It is regrettable that in spite of the growing international concern for war crimes and crimes against humanity, no effective international forum for adjudication of such crimes has yet been devised. As early as in 1950, proposals were put forward for the establishment of an international criminal court.[28] Still earlier, the Genocide Convention itself contemplated the setting up of an international penal tribunal. On the recommendation of the Human Rights Commission, the Economic and Social Council of the United Nations in 1964 urged all states to continue their efforts to ensure that in accordance with international law and national laws, the criminals responsible for such crimes should be traced, apprehended and equitably punished by competent courts. The Commission on Human Rights at its 21st session had recommended the establishment of the principle in international law that there was no period of limitation for the prosecution and punishment of such crimes.[29]

Thereafter, the Convention on Non-Applicability of Statutory Limitations to War Crimes and Crimes against Humanity was adopted at the 23rd session of the UN General Assembly on 26 November 1968 and it entered into force on 11 November 1970 having been ratified by the required minimum of ten countries.[30]

Pakistan is not as yet a party to the Convention. The principles however seem to be applicable on humanitarian grounds. Article I of the Convention has defined war crimes and crimes against humanity.

[27a] *Oppenheim's International Law*, Vol. II, pp. 566-7.

[28] Oppenheim, Vol. I, op. cit., p. 342.

[29] Extracts of the UN Report on the Economic and Social Council (16.8.64-31.7.65), Chapter XIII, Sec. VI: *Bangla Desh* (National), pp. 101-2.

[30] For the text of the Convention, see *Keesings Contemporary Archives*, 1969-70, page 23196. The Convention was adopted by 58 votes to 7 with 36 abstentions. The dissenting votes were cast, among others, by Australia, Portugal, South Africa, UK and USA. The ratifying states are all Communist.

Article I: No statutory limitation shall apply to the following crimes, irrespective of the date of their commission:

(a) War crimes as they are defined in the Charter of the International Military Tribunal, Nurnberg, of August 8, 1945 and confirmed by resolutions February 13, 1946, and December 11, 1946, of the U.N. General Assembly, particularly the 'grave breaches' enumerated in the Geneva Conventions of August 12, 1949, for the protection of war victims.

(b) Crimes against humanity whether committed in time of war or in time of peace as they are defined in the Charter of the International Military Tribunal, Nurnberg, and confirmed by the (abovementioned) resolutions of the General Assembly, eviction by armed attack or occupation and inhuman acts resulting from the policy of apartheid, and the crime of genocide as defined in the 1948 Convention on the prevention and punishment of the crime of genocide, even if such acts do not constitute a violation of the domestic law of the country in which they were committed.

Article II of the Convention provides: 'If any of the crimes mentioned in Article I is committed, the provisions of this Convention shall apply to the representatives of the State authority and private individuals who, as principals or accomplices, participate in or who directly incite others to the commission of those crimes or who conspire to commit them, irrespective of the degree of completion, and to representatives of the State authority who tolerate their commission.'

The 'grave breaches' of the Geneva Conventions for the protection of war victims, mentioned in Article I, can be found, for instance, in Article 51 of the Convention relating to armed forces at sea: viz. breaches involving any of the following acts, if committed against persons or property protected by the Convention: wilful killing, torture or inhuman treatment, including biological experiments, wilfully causing great suffering or serious injury to body or health, and extensive destruction and appropriation of property, not justified by military necessity and carried out unlawfully and wantonly.

In an important resolution 2712 (XXV) adopted on 15 December 1970,[31] on the question of the punishment of war criminals and of persons who have committed crimes against humanity, the General Assembly expressed its deep concern at the fact that in present day conditions, as a result of aggressive wars and the policies and practices of racism, apartheid and colonialism and other similar ideologies

[31] United Nations Press Services, N.Y., *Resolutions of Legal Interest*, 15 September-17 December, 1970, p. 57.

and practices, war crimes and crimes against humanity are being committed in various parts of the world. The Assembly was convinced that a thorough investigation of war crimes and crimes against humanity, as also the arrest, extradition and punishment of persons guilty of such crimes—*wherever they may have been committed*—and the establishment of criteria for determining compensation to the victims of such crimes, are important elements in the prevention of similar crimes now and in the future, and also in the protection of human rights and fundamental freedoms, the strengthening of confidence and the development of co-operation between people and the safeguarding of international peace and security. The Assembly condemned the war crimes and crimes against humanity at present being committed as a result of aggressive wars and the policies of racism, apartheid and colonialism and called upon the states concerned to bring to trial persons guilty of such crimes. A request was made for the punishment of the persons guilty of such crimes. All states were requested to become parties to the Convention of 1968 and to refrain from taking any action running counter to the main purpose of that Convention. The Secretary-General was asked to study the question of punishment of war crimes and crimes against humanity as well as the question of compensation to the victims of such crimes.

Human Rights in Armed Conflicts: Recent Trends

The United Nations has always been concerned with the need for protection of civilian populations and the respect of human rights in all armed conflicts *however characterized*. In this regard three important[32] resolutions were adopted by the General Assembly of the United Nations on 9 December 1970 to which Pakistan was a party. The resolutions are applicable to the current situation in East Bengal.

Resolution 2675 (XXV) affirmed eight basic principles for the protection of civilian populations in armed conflicts of all types. The principles are:

1. Fundamental human rights, as accepted in international law and laid down in international instruments, continue to apply fully in situations of armed conflicts.

2. In the conduct of military operations during armed conflicts, a distinction must be made at all times between persons actively taking part in the hostilities and civilian populations.

3. In the conduct of military operations, every effort should be made to spare civilian populations from the ravages of war, and all necessary precautions should be taken to avoid injury, loss or damage to the civilian populations.

[32] *Ibid.*, pp. 49-56, for text of the Resolution Nos. 2675 (XXV), 2676 (XXV) and 2677 (XXV).

4. Civilian populations as such should not be the object of military operations.

5. Dwellings and other installations that are used only by civilian populations should not be the object of military operations.

6. Places or areas designated for the sole protection of civilians, such as hospital zones or similar refuges, should not be the object of military operations.

7. Civilian populations, or individual members thereof, should not be the object of reprisals, forcible transfers or other assaults on their integrity.

8. The provision of international relief to civilian populations is in conformity with the humanitarian principles of the Charter of the United Nations, the Universal Declaration of Human Rights and other international instruments in the field of human rights. The Declaration of principles for international humanitarian relief, as laid down in resolution XXVI, adopted by the twenty-first International Conference of the Red Cross, shall apply in situations of armed conflict, and all parties to a conflict should make every effort to facilitate this application.

In resolution 2676 (XXV) in relation to human rights in armed conflicts, it was reiterated by the General Assembly that the treatment accorded to victims of war and armed aggression is the concern of the United Nations, and all parties to an armed conflict, *no matter how characterized,* were called upon to comply with the terms and provisions of the Geneva Convention of 12 August 1949, relating to the prisoners of war so as to ensure humane treatment of all persons entitled to the protection of the Convention. The Secretary-General was requested to exert all efforts to obtain humane treatment for prisoners of war, especially for the victims of armed aggression and colonial suppression. Combatants in armed conflicts not covered by Article 4 of the said Convention was to be accorded the same humane treatment defined by the principles of international law applied to prisoners of war. The resolution also asked for strict compliance with the provisions of the existing international instruments concerning human rights in armed conflicts.

By resolution 2677 (XXV), the General Assembly, while realizing that the existing humanitarian rules do not adequately meet all contemporary situations of armed conflicts, and accordingly, it was necessary to develop the substance of these rules and procedures for their implementation, called upon all parties to any armed conflict to observe the rules laid down in the Hague Conventions of 1899 and 1907, the Geneva Protocol of 1925, the Geneva Conventions of 1949 and other humanitarian rules applicable to armed conflicts.

With this legal background of international norms relating to war crimes and crimes against humanity, an attempt will be made to analyse the relevant facts between 25 March and the liberation of Dacca on 16 December 1971.

Analysis of Facts

We propose to examine the objective, as well as the nature and extent, of the operations of the West Pakistani Army in East Bengal since 25 March 1971. There is evidence to indicate that a contingency battle plan had been worked out over the last two years for making effective 'the operation genocide' and the decision to put the plan into action was probably taken some time between 1 and 6 March 1971, and was symbolized by the replacement of Lt.-General Yakub on 7 March by Lt.-General Tikka Khan, 'regarded as the fiercest of the Punjabi hawks.' The troops were being flown in plain clothes on PIA commercial flights and by 25 March, a full division, with support equipment, had reinforced the existing force. A fleet had been mobilized and a special plainclothes commando unit had been infiltrated into selected urban areas to create trouble as a cover for military action.[33]

Mens Rea to Commit Genocide

What was the objective of the military action in East Bengal? Reliable evidence has come to light that the main objective was to ensure the status of subordination of East Bengal to West Pakistan by employing military force and introducing a reign of terror and persecution. To achieve the result the military authorities were determined to eliminate the leaders and sympathisers of Sheikh Mujib's Awami League in general and the Hindu community in particular. 'That means virtually everyone, as 98.5 per cent of the Bengali people voted for the Sheikh in last December's national elections.'[34]

The operation has in fact covered a substantial part of the Bengali population. Although earlier estimates of the death toll varied between 200,000 and a million,[35] recent indications are more

[33] "Prelude to an Order for Genocide", *The Guardian*, London, 5 June 1971.
[34] *Daily Mirror*, 16 June 1971.
[35] *Time*, 2 August 1971: Estimates of the death toll in the army crackdown range from 200,000 all the way up to a million. The lower figure is more widely accepted, but the number may never be known. For one thing, countless corpses have been dumped in rivers, wells and mass graves. *Time*, 25 October 1971: No one knows how many have died in the seven-month-old civil war. But in Karachi, a source with close connections to Yahya's military regime concedes: 'The generals say the figure is at least 1,000,000;'. For other estimates of huge death toll: see the *New York Times*, 14 July 1971; *The Baltimore Sun*, 14 May 1971; *Wall Street Journal*, New York, 23 July 1971.

precise: 'Yahya's response was brutal. He loosed the Punjabi army on the East in a terror campaign that eventually took the lives of more than 1 million Bengalis and drove 9·8 million into exile in India. And, however unwittingly, he brought his country and India to the brink of war.' (*Newsweek*, 6 December 1971). In January 1972, Sheikh Mujib estimated a death toll of about 3 million. The extent of the havoc is a convincing proof of the objective of the military operations.

Genocidal acts forbidden by Article II of the Genocide Convention were reported to have been committed with a view to attaining the army objectives. There is independent evidence of the *mens rea* or the guilty intention to commit genocidal acts. This is fully supported by the overt acts of the army of occupation.

In a revealing article 'Genocide' published in the *Sunday Times* on 13 June 1971, the correspondent Anthony Mascarenhas had disclosed:

> The Government's policy for East Bengal was spelled out to me in the Eastern Command headquarters at Dacca. It has three elements: (1) The Bengalis have proved themselves 'unreliable' and must be ruled by West Pakistanis; (2) The Bengalis will have to be re-educated along proper Islamic lines. The 'Islamisation of the masses'—this is the official jargon—is intended to eliminate secessionist tendencies and provide a strong religious bond with West Pakistan; (3) When the Hindus have been eliminated by death and flight, their property will be used as a golden carrot to win over the under-privileged Muslim middle class. This will provide the base for erecting administrative and political structures in the future. This policy is being pursued with utmost blatancy.
>
> 'We are determined to cleanse East Pakistan once and for all of the threat of secession, even if it means killing of two million people and ruling the province as a colony for 30 years' I was repeatedly told by senior military and civil officers in Dacca and Comilla. The West Pakistani army in East Bengal is doing exactly that with a terrifying thoroughness.

Major-General Shaukat Raza, one of the three divisional commanders in the field, informed the *Sunday Times* correspondent: 'You must be absolutely sure that we have not undertaken such a drastic and expensive operation—expensive both in men and money— for nothing. We've undertaken a job. We are going to finish it, not hand it over half done to the politicians so that they can mess it up again. The army can't keep coming back like this every three or four years. It has a more important task. I assure you that when we have got through with what we are doing there will never be need again for such an operation.' Mascarenhas confirms: 'Significantly, General Shaukat Raza's ideas were echoed by every military officer I talked to during my 10 days in East Bengal. And President Yahya Khan knows that the men who lead the troops on the ground are the *de facto* arbiters of Pakistan's destiny.' Yahya Khan was not only aware of what his army did in East Bengal but it seems that he was in complete agreement with his field officers. In an interview published in the daily, *Le Figaro* of Paris, on 1 September 1971, President Yahya Khan had said: 'What happened in Dacca was no football match... When my soldiers kill they do it cleanly... My Army is a professional Army and it is well trained.'[36] This must sound strange in view of the Nuremberg judgment that it is contrary to military tradition to kill or injure helpless people.

At the initial phase a decision was taken that outright killing of a large number of Bengalis was a preferable *modus operandi* for terrorizing the rest of the population into submission. At an early stage, Peter Hazelhurst of *The Times*, London, had disclosed:[37] 'Evidence has become available which appears to confirm that the Pakistani Army's operations in Dacca on March 26 were part of a well-organized plan devised to terrorize the inhabitants into submission. Certainly it disproved the claim of the Pakistan Government that its troops only attacked rebels who offered armed resistance.' The evidence relied upon was a transcript of monitored radio messages passed between the Pakistani army units during the early hours of attack on 26 March. Some excerpts from the messages reveal that instead of capturing or wounding the university students, the Army Control preferred outright killing because: "That's (killing) much easier. Nothing asked nothing done. You don't have to explain anything. Once again, well done."

The Pakistani Army policies are reminiscent of the notorious Barbarossa Jurisdiction Order issued in 1941 by Hitler's army of occupation in Eastern Europe, which was criminal in its design and execution and was branded as such by various war crimes tribunals. The common feature of both is to leave it to the officers in the field to decide whether the suspected persons were to be shot at sight and to eliminate all resistance by spreading terror. Summary execution was preferable to legal prosecution. Hitler's order directed ruthless

---

[36] Reuter's report of the interview published in *Le Figaro*: *Hindusthan Standard*, 2 September, 1971.

[37] *The Times*, London, 2 June 1971. Also see Dan Coggin in *Time*, 3 May 1971: 'We can kill anyone for anything,' a Punjabi captain told a relative. 'We are accountable to no one.'

13

liquidation of enemy civilians, suppression on the spot of the enemy registers and the military officer was given the discretion to decide whether the suspected persons were to be shot. It provided for punishment 'not by legal prosecution of the guilty but by the spreading of such terror by the armed force as is alone appropriate to eradicate every inclination to resist among the population.'[38]

Overt acts in execution of the plan: (*Initial phase*)

The well-planned military operation which commenced on the midnight of 25 March was intended to exterminate the political leaders of the Awami League, the intelligentsia and student community, the organized labour forces in Dacca and other major cities, and the Hindu minority. An eye-witness account states: 'The soldiers would fire a flare and the informer would point out the houses of staunch Awami League supporters. The house would then be destroyed—either with direct tank or recoilless rifle fire or with a can of petrol.'[39] Sheikh Mujib was taken into the custody by the army and many of the top members of his Awami League party were also arrested.[40]

The 14th Punjab Regiment went to Pabna town on 25 March and sorted out Mr. Aminuddin, an Awami League MPA along with seven others and left them killed and huddled in a bath room of the Staff Quarters club.   In Jessore soldiers surrounded the house of Mashier Rahman, an Awami League MNA, and non-Bengali civilians went in killing everyone.   A ten-year-old boy jumped from the first-floor window and was shot in the mid-air by a sepoy.[41] This was the general pattern for exterminating the political leaders of the majority party which won a stunning victory in the December elections.

To effectively spread terror, the Pakistani army killed between 7,000 and 10,000 civilians within the first 34 hours of the army attack in Dacca alone.[42] The victims included innocent university professors and students, journalists, members of the police force, the Hindu minority community and the organized labour forces in areas such as New Market, Islampur, Zinjira, Kamalpur within Dacca city and several places in the suburbs of Dacca.   The sophisticated weapons employed included American-supplied M-24 World War II tanks,[43]

[38] *Oppenheim's International Law*, Vol. II (7th ed.), pp. 215-6.

[39] Simon Dring in *Daily Telegraph*, London, 30 March 1971.

[40] *Ibid.*

[41] 'Pogrom in Pakistan', *Sunday Times*, 20 June 1971.

[42] Simon Dring of the *Daily Telegraph* estimates 7,000 dead in 24 hours in Dacca alone and he puts the figure in the region of 15,000 dead taking into account Chittagong, Comilla and Jessore as well: *Daily Telegraph*, 30 March 1971.   Dan Coggin of *Time* magazine estimates more than 10,000 were killed in Dacca alone during the first 34 hours of wanton slaughter: *Time*, 3 May 1971.

[43] *Daily Telegraph*, 30 March 1971.

and six Chinese-made I-54 light tanks.[44] Machine-guns and rifles, flame-throwers and petrol were used liberally for burning and destroying property.

The eye-witness account of an American national[45] gives a chilling picture of the events at the initial phase. Describing the events as 'one of the history's most massive examples of genocide', the American author points out that there was a simultaneous attack by the Army on the midnight of March 25-26 at five main points: New Market, Old Dacca, Dacca University, the Cantonment of East Pakistan Rifles and the house of Sheikh Mujib. Rifles, machine-guns and Chinese tanks were used. By 1 a.m. 'the sky was aglow in all directions but the bigger fires were in the old city.' By 3 a.m. 'the frequent flashes and air-splitting reports of the tank cannon would momentarily drive out the almost steady chatter of machine-guns and rifle fire.' At about 4·30 a.m., after some amplified orders calling upon the students to surrender, the shooting was promptly resumed. The next night was a repetition of the previous one. On the morning of 27 March, apart from the physical destruction of the University buildings, the author noticed that 'the University's record of students' accomplishment past and present was reduced to ashes inches deep.' Most of the bodies of those killed at Iqbal Hall, Jagannath Hall and Rokya Hall had been removed; even then the author came across a pile of bodies, one or two deep and about 40 ft. long. The leading brains of the institution including 32 professors and departmental heads were executed during curfew. About New Market in smoking ruins, the report states that 'hundreds of families who lived with their goods had been killed on their mat beds during the surprise attack of Thursday night... the soldiers had looted the shops after the indiscriminate killings.' Between 27 March and 4 April 1971, 'the Dacca Police force has been effectively wiped out.' The estimate of the number killed varied between 4,000 and 10,000. 'The Rajarbagh Special Police barracks had been sprayed with liquid fire and possibly hit by incendiary shells from tanks... A staggering but unknown number of police and their wives and children fell victim to the flame-throwing tanks, rockets and machine-guns. This happened more or less in similar circumstances at several police stations throughout the city.'

[44] Loren Jenkins in *Newsweek*, 5 April 1971.

[45] The author of the 24-page report was in Dacca till 4 April 1971. The report was distributed to his Senator and other prominent personalities in the USA for giving a true picture of the events in East Pakistan. The author preferred to remain anonymous in order not to jeopardize the possibility of his return to East Bengal. Excerpts from the report were published in *The Statesman*, Calcutta, on 21 July 1971 in an article captioned 'Carnage in Dacca: An American's Account' by V. M. Nair.

There has been a good deal of reliable corroboration from other disinterested international sources. Mr. Jon E. Rohde, an American official who spent three years in Dacca, was an eye-witness to the mass killings of unarmed civilians. His report, which was made public by the U.S. Senate Foreign Relations Committee, states:[46] 'It is clear that the law of the jungle prevails in East Bengal, where the mass killing of unarmed civilians, the systematic elimination of the intelligentsia and the annihilation of the Hindu population is in progress.' At Dacca University, Mr. Rohde saw 'two of the student dormitories which had been shelled by army tanks. All residents are slaughtered.' The report states: 'We saw the breach in the wall where a tank broke through, the mass grave in front of the wall where one man, who was forced by the enemy to drag the bodies outside, counted 103 of the Hindu students buried there... The two ensuing weeks have documented a planned killing of much of the intellectual community, including a majority of the professors at Dacca University. Many families of these professors were shot as well.'

Simon Dring's report in the *Daily Telegraph* of 30 March confirms:

Only the horror of military action can be properly gauged—the students dead in their beds, the butchers in the market killed behind their stalls, the women and children roasted alive in their houses, the Pakistanis of Hindu religion taken out and shot *en masse*, the bazaars and shopping areas razed by fire and the Pakistani flag that now flies over every building in the capital... Seven teachers died in their quarters and a family of 12 were gunned down as they hid in an outhouse. The military removed many of the bodies, but the 30 still there could never have accounted for all the blood in the corridors of Iqbal Hall. At another hall, the dead were buried by the soldiers in a hastily dug mass grave and then bulldozed over by tanks... One of the biggest massacres of the entire operation in Dacca took place in the Hindu area of the old town. There the soldiers made the people come out of their houses and then just shot them in groups... One of the latest targets was the Bengali language

---

[46] AP report from Washington published in *Times of India*, 2 May 1971. Letter dated 17 April 1971 from Jon E. Rohde, M. D. to Senator William B. Saxbe, was printed in the RECORD: See Senator Saxbe's speech in the U.S. Senate on 29 April 1971. Numerous other reports in the same vein have appeared in the press: to wit, Sydney H. Schanberg in *New York Times*, 28 March, 7 April, 1971. Schanberg describes the military operation as 'an incredible drama.' *The Guardian*, London, in its editorial on 31 March described the operation 'a massacre in Pakistan.'.. *The Times*, London, in its editorial on 3 April considered 'the slaughter of students' as 'well attested'.

daily newspaper *Ittefaq*. Over 400 people had taken shelter in its offices when the fighting started. At 4 o'clock on the after-noon of 26 March four tanks appeared in the road outside. By 4·40 p.m. only the charred remains of the corpses were left.'

Extended Operations :
Shelling and Bombing of Civilian Targets

The magnitude and the severity of the army operations at the initial phase failed to produce the expected result. Instead of sub-mitting to the military junta, disorganized but spontaneous resistance grew up throughout East Bengal. The army operations were accor-dingly extended to all the major cities including Chittagong, Khulna, Comilla, Jessore, Rangpur, Rajshahi, Mymensingh and Sylhet. The story everywhere was the same. Sophisticated weapons of mass des-truction were indiscriminately used. Cities and towns which were thriving centres were reduced to rubble, villages were destroyed wholesale and murder, rape, looting and arson went on unabated for months.

During the second phase, warships, gunboats and jet planes were employed for killing people and destroying properties with a view to attaining the army objectives. Continuous heavy shelling of Chitta-gong port by Pakistani naval ships 'Babar' and 'Jehangir' was wit-nessed by many. Similarly, gunboats were used for shelling and burning villages on either side of Mongla and Chalna Channels and also villages on the banks of the Madhumati river in Barisal.[47] A member of the crew of a foreign cargo ship was a witness to razing fires all over Chalna and adjoining areas in Khulna resulting from continuous shelling from three Pakistani gunboats on 3 and 4 April 1971.[48] Dr. Mazharul Islam, Head of the Department of Bengali, Rajshahi University, had informed this writer that he was an eye-witness to a savage shelling from gunboats on 26 May on four villages—Deghulia, Bonwarinagar, Sonarahara and Natungram—on the banks of the river Atrai in Pabna. The villages were burnt to ashes and there were many victims.

In the month of April there were frequent bombings of undefended cities, towns and villages. Even napalm was reported to have been used against villagers in Nurnagar. Again, napalm bombs were reported to have been dropped by Pakistan air force to wipe out seve-ral civilian targets in Sylhet resulting in considerable damage to life and property.[49] A PTI report of 16 April 1971 states: 'West Pakis-

---

[47] *The Statesman*, Calcutta, 8, 14 and 27 April 1971.
[48] *The Statesman*, Calcutta, 9 April 1971.
[49] Contemporary reports in the press, particularly *The Statesman*, Calcutta, 1, 4, 9 April. Also see *The Statesman* of 16 September 1971: 'Pakistanis Using

tani Airforce planes have been dropping chemical bombs on paddy
jute plantations in East Bengal in a bid to destroy food production
for the next season ... chemical bombing has been so extensive that
paddy fields in several areas have been completely destroyed.' Sabre
jets were used for bombing Rajshahi, Khulna and several other places.
Massive PAF bombing of Bogra, Khulna, Rangpur, Dinajpur, Rajshahi, Kusthia, Chuadanga, Jessore and several areas of Brahmanbaria took place early in April. Chuadanga was extensively strafed
by four Sabre jets.[50] The crowded Nayabati Bazar near Laksam was
bombed by Pakistani aircraft on 6 April, killing 200 civilians and
injuring many others.[51] Many instances of indiscriminate air attacks
and random bombing by PAF on the innocent civilian population in
cities, towns and villages have been reported by the terror-stricken
evacuees. The planes flew over a wide area in search of fleeing Bengalis
and when spotted, they swept down and showered bullets. There
was indiscriminate, merciless and continuous strafing in Comilla,
Rangpur, Dinajpur, Rajshahi, Kusthia and some small towns in
Chittagong on 7 April.[52] 700 villagers were killed as a result of PAF
bombing of large areas around Jamalpur in Mymenshing district.[53]
The telling picture in *Time* magazine of 26 April depicts '*East Pakistan Bombing Victims in Pedicabs*'. The victims were unsuspected
poor rickshaw pullers. *The Statesman* carried a report of its correspondent on 24 October which states that even as late as 22 October,
four PAF planes strafed and bombed a large civilian area in Comilla,
and in ten villages near Kasba and Mandabhag. There were several
civilian victims. The U.S. State Department admitted on 5 May that
American tanks and jets sent to West Pakistan originally meant as
protection against attacks from China were used to help crush the
freedom movement in East Bengal.[54]

The extent of shelling, bombing and killing was wholly disproportionate to the threat of resistance presented by the liberation forces

---

Napalm Bombs Again.' The report states: 'The Pakistanis have been using
napalm bombs on innocent civilians and villages in the Tangail—Kishoreganj
area for a month now. They had used napalm bombs in the past in Bangladesh
but such a long and continuous spell underlines the terrorizing of villages in
roughly the operational area of the now famous Tangail group, the farthest
guerrilla group of the Mukti Fouj in Mymensingh District under the command
of the young and energetic Siddique.'

[50] *The Statesman*, Calcutta, 1 and 4 April 1971. Also see Press reports
throughout the month of April.

[51] *The Statesman*, Calcutta, 7 April 1971.

[52] *The Statesman*, Calcutta, 8 April 1971.

[53] *The Satesman*, Calcutta, 21 April 1971.

[54] AP Report from Washington published in *The Statesman*, Calcutta, 6 May
1971.

of Bangladesh. As *Time* magazine of 26 April 1971 reports: 'The Bangladesh forces are critically short of gasoline and diesel fuel and lack of field-communication equipment necessary for organized military activity. They have avoided any full-scale engagements, in which they would undoubtedly sustain heavy losses. Some observers believe, in fact, that the long guerrilla phase of the civil war has already began, with the army holding most of the towns and rebels controlling much of the countryside.'

Even in an international war, the employment of armed force in self-defence must be commensurate with the threat presented. Apparently the main object of the devastating operations of the Pakistani army was to kill or terrorize the ordinary civilian populations in execution of a war of genocide. The civilian targets aimed at were totally unconnected with the operations of the forces of resistance. One is reminded of the destruction on 6 April 1941 of the larger part of Belgrade in the Operation 'Punishment' (as designated by the German High Command), following upon the refusal of Yugoslavia to ally herself with Germany.

Patterns of Slaughter and Atrocities

Some severe and brutal methods of slaughter were devised by the Pakistani soldiers. I have interviewed numerous evacuees who have fled in terror of their lives. Their stories are amply corroborated by international observers. In many cases the option of the Bengali people was to choose between death by being roasted alive in houses in flames or to face death by running into Pakistani gunfire. The *modus operandi* of the army was to surround a particular area all of a sudden, pour gasoline around the entire block of houses and ignite them with flame-throwers, and then mow down people trying to escape the cordons of fire.Confirming this brutal method practised in Dacca, Dan Coggin of *Time* magazine concludes:[55] 'If they escaped the bullets and tried to reach a safety zone across the border, if caught, were killed by bullets or the thrusts of bayonets.' The pattern was implemented with ruthless efficiency in cities, towns and villages. Residential buildings and slums, clay-thatched cottages, tin-shed dwellings and hovels, and peasants' hamlets were all treated alike. Mort Rosemblum of the Associated Press reported that in Chittagong area 'entire blocks of Bengali homes and shops were blasted and burned to the ground as a revenging Pakistani Army settled the score.' At Jessore, 'with mortars and heavy guns, the three-block markets of two-storey brick buildings were pounded to rubble. Homes were blasted off their foundations. Soldiers asked Bengalis to come out of their houses and then machinegunned them.'

[55] *Time* magazine, 3 May 1971.

Mr. Rosemblum concludes: 'When the Army regained control, they shelled towns and fired at anything that moved. Evidence shows Army action far more brutal than anything seen in the Nigerian civil war. European likened the damage and terror to that of the hardest hit theatres of World War II.'[56]

A senior journalist from Dacca who left East Bengal on 7 June described the army killings in and around Dacca as 'slightly more sophisticated' compared to the crude mass murders in villages particularly in districts like Barisal, Faridpur and Dacca. Whole villages were being wiped out and millions of destitutes and homeless Bengalis were being forced to take shelter in India. The villages in which the army had earlier faced stiff resistance were being completely wiped out.[57] A labourer from Kusthia told a correspondent of *The Times* that from their hiding places in the fields, he and other villagers saw troops burning down all their houses.[58] Dr. Mazharul Islam who reached India on 9 June told me that he was an eye-witness to an indiscriminate and savage burning of at least 300 villages in the districts of Dacca, Tangail, Pabna, Bogra, Rajshahi and Kusthia between April and the first week of June. Thousands lost their lives either in blazing houses or from the bullets fired by the army. Valuable properties were looted and cattle slaughtered. A harrowing incident narrated by him took place when the Pakistani troops set the Shantinagar Bazar on fire on 30 March at 9·30 p.m. Those who tried to escape from the flames were shot down or died at the point of bayonets. Those who were wounded were physically thrown into the flames by the soldiers, crying piteously for help. On another occasion, Dr. Islam and his pupils counted 1,251 dead bodies of the fairly educated inhabitants of the village Kenai in Pabna district. Besides there were numerous dead bodies found in the river Atrai adjacent to the village.

[56] The eye-witness report written on 12 May, 1971 at Dacca was filed by Associated Press correspondent, Mr. Mort Rosemblum from Bangkok and published in *The Statesman*, Calcutta, 13 May 1971.

[57] *The Statesman*, Calcutta, 12 June 1971.

[58] *The Times*, London, 5 June 1971. Besides numerous incidents of atrocities in villages have been published and reported by evacuees. For instance, many houses in Maherpur area were set on fire resulting in the death of hundreds. A teacher was burned alive in a Sylhet village and the members of his family machinegunned.Dhaleswar and other villages in Comilla have been destroyed by fire by the army. 9 villages in Manickganj sub-division were burned in the second week of May and an estimated 300 people were killed. The survivors of the Rajshahi carnage during the middle of April were eye-witnesses to the use of flame-throwers for burning people alive and the use of gunfire against those who tried to escape from the blazing houses. In late May, a number of villages opposite Lankakura and Fakiratua in Tripura were burned down by the army and many villagers were killed: *The Statesman*, Calcutta, 26 April 1971; 20 May and 23 May, 1971.

The incident took place in the early hours of 14 May when about 70 Pakistani soldiers committed atrocities and went back with country boats full of booty collected by looting. Another village on the bank of the river was spattered with human blood. Many old women and children were roasted alive.

Bengali people had been slaughtered *en masse,* in groups and individually. The patterns of slaughter and atrocities perhaps have no precedent in modern history. In a letter to *The Guardian* published on 27 May, Rev. John Hastings and Rev. John Clapham wrote: "Villages have been surrounded, at any time of day or night, and the frightened villagers have fled where they could, or been slaughtered where they have been found, or enticed out to the fields and mown down in heaps. Women have been raped, girls carried off to barracks, unarmed peasants battered or bayoneted by the thousands." Mr. John Horgan after visiting the evacuee camps recorded his impression in *The Irish Times* of 7 June 1971: "In English or in Bengali, their story is essentially the same: the soldiers arrived: there was killing and destruction: they fled... One well-corroborated story, for instance, tells of the occasion when the troops separated about 2,000 men from their wives and children and attempted to machine-gun them all to death. About 800 died in the fusillade: the others shammed death, hoping that the soldiers would go away. But the soldiers piled the bodies of the dead and living alike, like children building a house of matches, poured petrol over them and set them alight. Luckily, it was dusk, and some of the men managed to escape with the petrol on their skins still alight—into the forest. There is another story of how a priest watched helplessly from a rooftop as the soldiers took out school children and shot them in cold blood." There are many other stories of the massacre of school children. For instance, several students of St. Francis Xavier School in Jessore town were machine-gunned to death·by the Pakistani army. An Italian missionary who was the parish priest of Jessore was also reported to have been shot dead.[59]

It defies human imagination to visualize the patterns of killings, ghastly tortures and cruel atrocities stated to have been perpetrated by the Pakistani troops in East Bengal. 'With the passing of time, the magnitude of the slaughter has diminished, but there has been no lessening in the brutality of the Pakistani Army.'[60] Yahya's troops behaved in a manner no civilized troops would behave. We have already seen a few samples of such behaviour. From the numerous incidents of unbridled cruelties reported in the international press, a few more samples will be cited. Many others have been reported

[59] *The Statesman*, Calcutta, 15 April 1971.
[60] *Newsweek*, 2 August 1971.

by eye-witnesses or victims of such atrocities, and there is sufficient intrinsic evidence to support their versions.

From the letter of Rev. John Hastings and Rev. John Clapham in *The Guardian*, London, of 27 May, the following instances are cited:

(i) babies thrown up to be caught on bayonets;

(ii) women stripped and bayoneted vertically;

(iii) children sliced up like meat;

(iv) gangrene in a mother's arm and child's foot from bullet wounds, necessitating amputation;

(v) many refugees saw their daughters raped and the heads of their children smashed in;

(vi) some women refugees watched their husbands, sons and grandsons tied up at the wrists and shot in more selected male elimination.

Mr. John Pilger, the correspondent of *The Daily Mirror* (16 June) reported the following information collected from within East Bengal:

(i) an old man lifted his shirt revealing a neat lattice work of bayonet cuts on his stomach;

(ii) a small boy's ear is caked with blood, the lobs shot away at close range;

(iii) a woman sits in a field grieving for her husband who had been buried alive two days before;

(iv) each of a dozen families that Mr. Pilger spoke to at random reported that a son or a husband had been shot and thrown in the river and wives and daughters had been outraged;

(v) on 24 May Pakistani troops put the two boys of Kasimuddin in a trench and filled it with mud that came up past their noses and the crows did the rest.

Mr. Pilger concludes: "They are typical and they are evidence that the military government of West Pakistan, under General Yahya Khan, is waging *a war of selected genocide* and of starvation *against two per cent of the human race:* 75,000,000 Bengali people of Bangladesh, or East Pakistan as it was called after partition of the subcontinent. The pattern of atrocities is the same in village after village. The Punjabi and Pathan troops of the Pakistan army arrive in a region with orders to 'live off the land'—to loot—and to seek out those who supported Sheikh Mujibur Rahman's Awami League Party." (italics **added**).

Tony Clifton of *Newsweek* reported several incidents and patterns of atrocities with the following introductory remarks:[61]

"Anyone who comes to the camps and hospitals along India's borders with Pakistan comes away believing the Punjabi army capable of any atrocity. I have seen babies who've been shot, men who have had their backs whipped raw. I've seen people literally struck dumb by the horror of seeing their children murdered in front of them or their daughters dragged off into sexual slavery. I have no doubt at all that there have been a hundred My Lais and Lidices in East Pakistan—and I think there will be more."

The atrocities reported by him include:

(i) Ismatar, a shy little girl, the daughter of the late Ishague Ali, a businessman in Kusthia, told her sad story. One day her father went to his shop but was never seen again. Two months later Punjabi soldiers came to their house at night, killed her mother, four sisters and a brother who was a bachelor of science. She was stabbed by a soldier, fell to the floor and played dead. There was a livid scar on her neck where a Pakistani soldier had cut her throat with his bayonet.

(ii) There was a boy of four at Agartala hospital who survived a bullet through his stomach.

(iii) A woman related how the soldiers murdered two of her children in front of her eyes and then shot her. As she held her youngest child in her arms, the bullet passed through the baby's buttocks and then through her left arm.

(iv) There was another woman, with the bones in her upper leg shattered by bullets, with an infant in her arms. She was shot.

(v) A village was burned and everyone in it was killed except two small boys. They were lying on the floor of the Agartala Hospital 'clinging to each other like monkeys' and 'so terrified that they are unable to speak.'

Another atrocious method of killing by draining blood from their bodies has been reported. *Newsweek* of 2 August 1971 states:

It seemed a routine enough request. Assembling young men of the village of Haluaghat in East Pakistan, a Pakistani Army major informed them that his wounded soldiers needed blood.

---

[61] *Newsweek*, 28 June 1971.

Would they be donors? The young men lay down on makeshift cots, needles were inserted in their veins and then slowly the blood was drained from the bodies until they died.

The Daily Mirror of 16 June 1971 reports the following version of Mr. Iqbalan Waral Islam, who was elected to the National Assembly of Pakistan in December with a majority of 40,000 votes: "My son who is sixteen was one of the sixty boys who were picked up and taken away to give blood for the Punjabi soldiers. Almost all their blood was drained from them, and only thirteen managed to survive for a few days."

That this was a routine affair will appear from an earlier report stating that the Pakistani army had extracted all the blood from about 5,000 civilians in the wake of the sudden guerrilla offensive in Dacca city on Monday, 17 May. According to reliable reports from across the border, a large number of Pakistani troops cordoned off the entire Dacca city and took about 5,000 people into custody. The army thereafter blind-folded them, tied their hands and feet and extracted their blood allegedly required for transfusion to injured soldiers. The people were thrown almost dead into the Buriganga.[62]

Newsweek's Tony Clifton concludes:[63] "I collect a notebook of horror—rape and murder and kidnapping. They tell me how they saw their children stabbed, their husbands or brothers executed, their wives collapsed with fatigue or sickness. The stories are all new, and all the same. And I remember Luthra's plaintive question, 'How can we think that human race is evolving to a higher level when it lets this go on'?"

After interviewing refugees avalanching into India, Alvin Toffler reported in *The New York Times* of 5 August 1971: "Part of the time I travelled with a Canadian parliamentary delegation. We saw babies' skin stretched tight, bones protruding, weeping women who told us they would rather die today in India than return to East Pakistan after the tragedies they had witnessed. . ."

[62] PTI report in *The Statesman*, Calcutta, 23 May 1971.
[63] *Newsweek*, 2 August 1971, page 13. *The Hongkong Standard*, 25 June, 1971: 'For hundreds of years, the name of Genghis Khan has echoed through history as a byword for Cruelty and Butchery. In the 20th century, it seems a Pakistani namesake of the great killer is determined to outdo his grisly predecessor.' The *Dagens Nyheter*, Stockholm, 27 June 1971: 'The reign of terror in East Bengal is now in its fourth month. The fleeing and hunted people are still streaming across the border into India. There is no limit to the brutality of the Pakistani military dictatorship; very few of the terror victims belong to the Bengali group of leaders whom the aggressors are trying to eradicate.' *Vecernje Novosti*, Yugoslavia, 8 July 1971: 'The capital Dacca is still in the shadow of fear, violence and terror.'

Outrages on Women

Apart from what we have already noticed, there had been numerous incidents of outrages on women and children. The patterns disclose continuous raping, raping to death, killing the girls raped, keeping the girls from respectable families for the entertainment of the officers and using ordinary Bengali women for prostitution, sterilization of women, deportation of women to West Pakistan and forced marriages. Only a few typical cases will be mentioned. *Time* magazine of 21 June 1971 states:

> In the refugee camp at Patrapole on the West Bengal-East Pakistan border, a 16-year-old Bengali girl recalled how she and her parents were in bed 'when we heard the tread of feet outside. The door burst open and several soldiers entered. They pointed their bayonets at the three of us and before my eyes killed my mother and father—battering them to death with the butts of their rifles. They flung me on the floor, and three of them raped me.' Another teen-age girl in a Tripura camp told she was raped by 13 West Pakistani soldiers before escaping. Other girls have reportedly been taken from fleeing families to be sold as prostitutes to the soldiers, particularly if their fathers could not pay a ransom for them.

The *Sunday Times* of 20 June 1971 points out: "The Razakars have now extended their operations from murder and extortion to prostitution. In Agrabad in Chittagong, they run a camp of young girls who are allocated nightly to senior officers. They have also kidnapped girls for their parties. Some have not returned."

The *Amrita Bazar Patrika* of 5 June 1971 carried an eye-witness account of a professor from East Bengal about the conditions in Chittagong. Many unmarried girls and newly married young brides were abducted by the Pakistani troops from different parts of Chittagong district. In Aburkhil area one of the young girls was abducted by the army and two of her sisters committed suicide to escape from the indignity. One truckload of young girls was sent to Chittagong cantonment from Mireswari village during the end of May. Threatening directives to prepare lists of all young girls in their respective areas were issued to the members of the Muslim League and Peace Committees.

There are many reports of sterilization of Bengali women carried away by the troops to the military camps so that they could bear no children. In some cases the sterilized girls were returned to the parents and new girls taken away to fill their places. Pakistani troops in Rajshahi were reported to have said that they did not want Bengali girls to beget children for 'more Bengalis will mean more trouble for Pakistan.' Many orphaned children were taken away to West Pakistan or committed to the custody of the supporters of the military regime in order to make them immune from the influence of Bengali culture.[64] There have been many reports of forced marriages of Bengali girls to West Pakistanis.

A gruesome pattern was recorded in *Time* magazine of 25 October 1971: 'One of the more horrible revelations concerns 563 young Bengali women, some only 18, who have been held captive inside Dacca's dingy military cantonment since the first days of the fighting. Seized from Dacca University and private homes and forced into military brothels, the girls are all three to five months pregnant. The army is reported to have enlisted Bengali gynecologists to abort girls held at military installations. But for those at the Dacca cantonment it is too late for abortion. The military has begun freeing the girls a few at a time, still carrying the babies of Pakistani soldiers.'

Violations of Religious Practices and Despoiling the Dead

Even the religious convictions and practices of the Moslems were not immune from the military attack. The Imam of Kachahary mosque and Samed Molla, while accompanying a funeral procession at Gobindapara, were shot down by the Army. A mosque at Feni was destroyed by PAF bombing on 19 April. Another Imam, while coming out of a mosque at Jhenidah, was shot down by the Army on 19 April. A mosque at Potya in Chittagong was substantially destroyed in April by PAF bombing and 10 Moslems were killed.[65] *Time* correspondent, Dan Coggin, records: "An old man who decided that Friday prayers were more important than a curfew was shot to death as he walked into a mosque."[66]

Not only were the minimum funeral requirements according to religious rites denied to the Bengali victims, but the dead were despoiled, and dead bodies treated contrary to all canons of civilized society. For a period of three weeks, the dead bodies of students were lying rotting on the roof of Iqbal Hall in Dacca University.[67] At another students' hall the dead were buried by soldiers in a hastily dug mass-grave and then bulldozed over by tanks.[68] To frighten survivors, soldiers refused to allow the removal of decomposing bodies for three days despite the Moslem belief in prompt burial, preferably

[64] These facts were narrated by Dr. Mazharul Islam, Head of the Department of Bengali, Rajshahi University: *Amrita Bazar Patrika*, 23 June, 10 July 1971.

[65] Among other contemporary reports, see *The Statesman*, Calcutta, 10, 20 and 26 April, 1971.

[66] *Time*, 3 May, 1971, page 22.

[67] *Sunday Times*, 13 June, 1971.

[68] *Daily Telegraph*, 30 March 1971.

within 24 hours, to free the soul.[69] Dead bodies were dumped into rivers, wells and ponds. 'From a well at Natore, fetid gases rise up around bones and rotting flesh. A tiny child gazes at a break in the lavender carpet of water hyacinths in a nearby pond where his parents' bodies were dumped.'[70] The bodies of the victims were flung into huge pits dug in the Golf Course ground next to the Signals' Mess of Dacca Cantonment and also those of several others were seen floating in the river Buriganga.[71] The bodies of patriotic Bengalis killed in the freedom struggle were reported to have been used by the Pakistani army to erect road barricades in Comilla, Chittagong, Dacca and thereafter burned with flame-throwers and the remnants thrown into ditches.[72]

Treatment of Minorities

Although the Nehru-Liaquat Ali Agreement of 8 April 1950 guarantees to the Hindu minority in Pakistan 'a full sense of security in respect of life, culture, property and personal honour, freedom of movement... freedom of occupation, speech and worship', it will have been observed that the declared policy of the Pakistani army was to eliminate the Hindu minority consisting of nearly 10 million people. The plan was executed by killing indiscriminately as many Hindus as possible and terrorizing others to leave the country. The Hindu community was the major target but other minorities like Buddhists and Christians were not totally spared. Apart from the ghastly killings and barbaric cruelties, the properties of the minorities were destroyed and looted, and Hindu temples, Buddhist monastaries and Christian churches were also attacked.

A volume of evidence has come to light about the initial phase of the attack on the Hindu minority.[73] The eye-witness account of the American national in his 24-page report mentioned before gives an authentic picture of the atrocities. In the old city of Dacca the Hindus were killed indiscriminately. 'One was the fairly well-confirmed report that Father Paul Gomes (R. C.) had been killed with some 800 plus, mostly Hindu converts who had sought sanctuary on the parish ground.' Two ancient Hindu temples were in ruins and the walls breached apparently by the work of a tank. There was a pit

[69] *Time*, 3 May 1971, page 22.
[70] Mort Rosemblum of AP; *The Statesman*, Calcutta, 13 May, 1971.
[71] *The Statesman*, Calcutta, 12 June, 1971.
[72] *The Statesman*, Calcutta, 9 April 1971.
[73] Every version is corroborated by many impartial observers: *Daily Telegraph*, 30 March: *Time*, 3 May: *Times of India*, 2 May, 1971 for the AP report of the American official John Rohde's version: *The Times*, London on 11 June published contents of some of the letters received from Britons resident in East Bengal. The report says: An eye-witness account of the atrocities in East Pakistan

filled with bodies and covered, after the attack, with earth bush but 'hungry dogs had uncovered some arms and legs—a sickening sight.' An eye-witness had estimated several hundreds of dead bodies inside the pit... 'By cross checking with other refugees during and after evacuation i learned that the mass killing at St. Gregory's was only a part of the fate of the Hindus in Old Dacca. The whole area, largely inhabited by the Hindu community, was cordoned off and burned and its inhabitants machine-gunned in the streets. The destruction of many small industries seen by me in ruins and the elimination of the Hindu community was not enough of a tragedy in the Old City for the unrestrained Punjabi soldiers. On the afternoon of April 4 (Sunday) while we were waiting for the long overdue PIA plane to evacuate us, all remaining men and boys residing on a certain street off Nawabpore Road as it enters Old Dacca were rounded up and shot. This came to me by an eyewitness account of unquestioned reliability who was evacuated later.'

After the random killings at the initial phase the army officers proceeded in a calculated manner to execute what has been characterized as 'kill and burn mission'. The pattern has been described by Anthony Mascarenhas in the *Sunday Times* of 13 June. Take the case of Major Iftikhar who said: 'We got an old one. The bastard had grown a beard and was posing as a devout Muslim. Even called himself Abdul Manan, but we gave him a medical inspection and the game was up. I wanted to finish him there and then, but my men told me such a bastard deserved three shots. So I gave him one in the balls, then one in the stomach. Then I finished him off with a shot in the head.' At Hajiganj, Major Iftikhar discovered 12 Hindus hiding in a house on the outskirts of a town on 17 April. They were all 'disposed of'. He then went on with the second part of his mission.

---

says that Hindu men 'are being slaughtered wherever they are found and the women and children left to go as refugees to India. Groups of 30 or 40 refugees have been lined up by graves and shot...' Another letter states: "The basic situation is that there is genocide and colonialism. With regard to the former there are 'Sharpevilles' and 'My Lais' everywhere. The Hindus are taken out and shot. The women and children are not shot (they are so humane!). But you can imagine what their future will be." The writer adds: "Until March I reckoned that Pakistan had a better record than India in the treatment of minorities. But now it is genocide: Killing of Hindus only because they are Hindus." Sydney H. Schanberg reports in the *New York Times* (14 July 1971): "Foreign missionaries who are posted even in the remotest parts of East Pakistan report new massacres almost daily. One missionary said that the army recently killed over 1,000 Hindus in a day in a section of Barisal District in the south. Another reported that in the Sylhet District, in the north-west, a 'peace committee' called a meeting of all the residents of one area, ostensibly to work out a reconciliation. When everyone had gathered troops arrived, picked out the 300 Hindus in the crowd, led them away and shot them."

The Medical Store of a Hindu, A. N. Bose, was broken open and Iftikhar set it on fire. He threw burning jute bags into one corner of the shop and it began to blaze. The next day, Major Iftikhar ruefully told the *Sunday Times* correspondent: 'I burned only sixty houses. If it hadn't rained I would have got the whole bloody lot.'

The ghastly performance was repeated throughout East Bengal. The Hindu and Moslem refugees have both narrated stories of unspeakable atrocities inflicted upon the Hindus in Chittagong, Faridpur, Khulna, Jessore, Mymensingh, Comilla, Sylhet, Pabna, Rangpur and Dinajpur.[74] Peter Hazelhurst has narrated in *The Times*, London, (5 June) the story of Hindu migrants who had fled from the Kusthia district, 'that the army swept through their villages burning the houses of Hindus. These people are simple peasants, too unsophisticated to concoct propaganda stories.' *The Times*, London,[75] carried the story of Michael Hornsby from Sinduri (East Bengal) about the atrocities in predominantly Hindu villages like Sinduri, Boliadi, Chapair, Radhanagar, Attabha, Tekerbari, Bhringraj and Sewratali. The usual pattern was for the troops, guided by Muslim informers, to enter the villages and destroy systematically almost every dwelling and hut. The villagers would be killed, the girls raped and money, gold and ornaments looted or stolen. Hornsby concludes: 'The fate of Sinduri and other villages is incontrovertible proof of a continuing, calculated persecution of the Hindu community in East Pakistan by the armed forces. There is absolutely no evidence that any of the villages offered provocation of any kind to the Army. No conceivable strategy or security reasons can be found to justify what it did.' *Time* magazine of 2 August sums up the position: "The Hindus, who account for three-fourths of the refugees and a majority of the dead, have borne the brunt of the Moslem military's hatred. Even now, Moslem soldiers in East Pakistan will snatch away a man's lungi (sarong) to see if he is circumcised, obligatory for Moslems; if he is not, it usually means death. Others are simply rounded up and shot. Commented one high U.S. official last week: 'It is the most incredible, calculated thing since the days of the Nazis in Poland'."

[74] From many evacuee students and professors of East Bengal this writer has collected a considerable volume of evidence about atrocities on the Hindu community. To cite only a few incidents in Chittagong: Between April and May, 15 villages in Chittagong mainly inhabited by the Hindus were attacked by the army and hundreds of Hindus were massacred. Between 10 and 30 April, 25 Hindus were rounded up at Noapara, and they did not return. At Kanungopara, a Hindu village, 7 persons including a professor were killed, 25 women violated and a Hindu temple demolished. Another Hindu temple was demolished in village Mohra in Bowalkhali.

[75] Reproduced in *The Statesman*, Calcutta, 4 July 1971.

15

Other minority communities like Christians and Buddhists have had their share of atrocities although in a lesser degree. One Kshitish Halder, a Bengali Christian, was among the twelve victims of a firing squad at Rangpur burning ghat. He was found dead with pins in his stomach and legs severed. The tenements of a Christian Mission Hospital premises in the Meherpur area were set on fire by the troops on 23 April.[76] The Pakistani army destroyed three Christian villages of Loodaria, Nalchata and Laripara near Dacca, burning down and flattening houses of purely Christian communities. Between 3,000 and 4,000 Christians were homeless, and a few hundreds were taken away by the army for questioning.[77] Many Buddhists were tortured and killed and their monasteries destroyed, particularly in the Chittagong area. An old monastery at the village of Pahartali, Chaumuhani, was burned down and its valuable and sacred possessions stolen by the Pakistani troops. More recently, Mr. Dharma Viryu, General Secretary of the South-East Asia Buddhist Association, made serious charges of persecution of the Buddhists by the military regime for the refusal of the Buddhists to send a delegation to South-East Asia to advocate the military junta's case. The charges include: (a) the killing of D. P. Barua, General Secretary of the Pakistan unit of the World Fellowship of Buddhists, his wife and two children, (b) the desecration of the Buddhist temple at Satparia, Chittagong; the pillage of a Buddha statue, scriptures and other valuable articles by the soldiers; (c) Abayatissa Mahathero, 100-year-old head of the Buddhist community of Pakistan, had been beaten up by the soldiers.[78]

Extent of Devastation

The impact of the military operations in terms of devastation to property and the uprooting of population is almost incredible. Many impartial observers who took part in the conducted tour of East Bengal under the observation of the military regime have recorded their impressions. For instance, Mr. Henrik van der Heijden, an economic member of the World Bank special mission which toured East Bengal from 4 May to 11 June, gave his personal account of the places he visited in the western part of East Bengal. 90 per cent of the houses, shops, banks and other buildings were totally destroyed in Kusthia and the population came down from 40,000 to 5,000. Kusthia looked 'like a German town in the Second World War after the Allied strategic bomb attacks.' 'There must have been strong resistance. When the insurgents withdrew the Army punitive action

---

[76] *The Statesman*, Calcutta, 20, 26 April, 1971.
[77] Clare Hollingworth in *Sunday Telegraph*, London, 1 August, 1971.
[78] UNI report: *The Statesman*, Calcutta, 4 October, 1971.

started and it lasted 23 days, leaving Kusthia virtually deserted and destroyed.'

As a result of severe Army punitive action at Jessore, some 20,000 people were killed. From the air totally destroyed villages were visible. Many houses and buildings, including 50 per cent of the shops in the city, were destroyed. Whenever any incident occurred by way of resistance to the army, indiscriminate punitive action was immediately taken. 'A number of these incidents took place in the week I arrived, and the Army is reacting to these incidents by burning down the villages from which these shots are being fired. Generally, the Army terrorizes the population, particularly aiming at Hindus and suspected members of the Awami League.' The town of Mangla, where the labour for Chalna anchorage lived, was virtually obliterated by naval shelling. The population was, therefore, down from 22,000 to 1,000. Extensive damages included the total destruction of houses, the market place, the telephone exchanges, and the power distribution lines. It was at the Thana level that the shock waves of the Army action hit the hardest. 20,000 out of a total population of 42,000 of Phultala Thana, mostly Hindus, had fled. Khulna city was substantially damaged and the population of greater Khulna was down from 400,000 to 150,000.[79]

Excerpts from the World Bank Report as published in the *New York Times* and reproduced in *The Statesman* of 24 July 1971 contains: "There is also no question that punitive measures by the military are continuing, as considered necessary by the Martial Law administration, and whether directed at the general populace or at particular elements these have the effect of fostering fear among the population at large."[80]

Two-fold Objectives of Military Operations

The two-fold objectives of military operations were outlined by Anthony Mascarenhas in the *Sunday Times* of 13 June, 1971: 'The bone-crushing military operation has two distinctive features. One is what the authorities like to call the "cleansing process", a euphemism for massacre. The other is "rehabilitation effort." This is a way of describing the methods of turning East Bengal into a docile colony of West Pakistan. These commonly used expressions and

---

[79] *Hindusthan Standard*, 14 July 1971 quoting a report from New York, 13 July, about the eyewitness account of Mr. Hendrik van der Heijden.

[80] On 14 July 1971, the *New York Times* comments: 'The report of a World Bank Mission to East Pakistan last month is a devastating indictment of the West Pakistani military crackdown in Bengal. It strongly challenges the Administration's policy of continuing both military and economic support for the Yahya regime in Islamabad... The official confirmation of earlier widespread

the repeated official references to "miscreants" and "infiltrators" are part of the charade which is being enacted for the benefit of the world. Strip away the propaganda, and the reality is colonialism—and killing.'

The follow-up action of the military government in East Bengal after the initial defeat of the liberation forces reveals a ruthless attempt to implement the above objectives. All supporters or sympathizers of the Awami League along with others were listed as suspects and were classified into three categories—white, grey and black. The white would be given clearance; the grey would lose their jobs and might be imprisoned and the black would be shot. 'A new element in the regime of terror is the Gestapo-style pick-up. Some of those wanted for questioning are arrested openly. Others are carried to the army cantonment for questioning. Most of them do not return. Those who do are often picked up again by secret agents, known as Razakars... By night and day, parts of Dacca are sealed off by troops, searchring for Hindus, Awami Leaguers and students.'[81]

Civil servants on the grey list were transferred to West Pakistan. Abu Awal, the District Magistrate at Bhola, known for his loyalty to Islamabad, went to receive the Army on 1 May. The Brigadier asked him to resume his post. 'He had hardly turned his back on the officer, when a sepoy shot him with a rifle.' About a dozen Bengali

---

reports of barbaric action in East Pakistan renders inexcusable any further shipment of American military equipment to the Pakistani armed forces. Military supplies already en route to Pakistan can and should be promptly diverted, just as food shipments were diverted from Chittagong soon after the outbreak of fighting. There are clear grounds for suspending all further military and economic aid to the Pakistani Government, excepting relief supplies, until the reign of terror in East Pakistan is ended and steps are taken to restore power to elected representatives of the people who are currently in prison or in hiding. The World Bank also offers strong practical grounds for a moratorium on development assistance... Continuation of American development assistance to Pakistan is incomprehensible in the face of that international consensus and of the damning evidence contained in the World Bank report.' Also see *Time*, 2 August 1971: 'World Bank President Robert McNamara classified the report on the grounds that it might worsen an already difficult diplomatic situation. The report spoke bluntly of widespread fear of the Pakistani army and devastation on a scale reminiscent of World War II. It described Kusthia, which was 90% destroyed, as "the My Lai of the West Pakistan army."' (P. 32)

[81] *Sunday Times*, 20 June, 1971. Also see the report of Peter R. Kann in *Wall Street Journal* (New York), 23 July 1971: 'The student, a girl, has a room in a house that overlooks an army interrogation centre. "All day the students, young boys, are brought in and beaten", she says. "Three soldiers walk on them with boots. All night we hear the screams. I cannot sleep. We cannot stand to see and hear these things".'

officers were transferred to West Pakistan and reported at Dacca airport to board a PIA flight to Karachi. When their families inquired at army headquarters, they were told that the officers had deserted. 'The mutilated body of a major was delivered to his family with a letter of regret that he had committed suicide.' The whereabouts of Brigadier Mazumdar, one of the best known Bengali officers, are unknown and his family was told that any inquiry would only invite trouble.[82]

Many doctors and surgeons were picked up from hospitals and their whereabouts are not known. At Sylhet all the doctors except Surgeon-General Dr. Shamsuddin fled across the border when the army entered the town. 'A major found Dr. Shamsuddin in the hospital operation theatre and shot him point blank.'[83] Even sick patients were reported to have been dragged out of hospital and killed.[84]

The PIA had dismissed about 2,000 Bengalis. Some university teachers reported for duty on 1 June; several of them fell into the hands of the Razakars. Bengalis were forbidden to approach major railway stations, port and dock installations. When 5,000 labourers returned to work at Chittagong docks on 1 May, they were driven away. The installations were reported to be operating by military, naval and non-Bengali personnel. Senior railway officials in Chittagong were shot and the workers' colony burned down. Even 250 porters were flown in from West Pakistan to replace the Bengalis at Dacca and Chittagong airports. The Bengali militiamen who responded to an amnesty call and surrendered in Dacca on 15 May 'were then seen being driven away in open trucks blind-folded with their hands tied behind their backs. A few days later hundreds of naked corpses were found in the Rivers Buriganga and Sitalakhya eyes covered and hands tied.'[85]

[82] *Sunday Times*, 20 June 1971.

[83] *Ibid.*

[84] *The Statesman*, Calcutta, 14 April 1971: 'Athens, April 13. West Pakistani troops dragged patients out of a hospital in Chittagong and executed them in the street, a Greek Merchant Navy officer just back from East Pakistan said in a newspaper interview published here today, reports AFP.'

[85] *Sunday Times*, 20 June, 1971. Also see the report of the New Delhi correspondent of the *New York Times* who was expelled from East Pakistan on 30 June: 'Army trucks roll through the half-deserted streets of the capital of East Pakistan these days, carrying "anti-state" prisoners to work-sites for hard labor. Their heads are shaved and they wear no shoes and no clothes except for shorts—all making escape difficult... Street designations are being changed to remove all Hindu names as well as those of Bengali Moslem nationalists as part of a campaign to stamp out Bengali culture... Those are but a few of the countless evidences, seen by this correspondent during a recent visit to the

It has been reported that 'on an average about 300 people (including women) were being transported daily to the Dacca cantonment.'[86] The *Daily Telegraph* of London revealed the existence in the military cantonments of Dacca, Chittagong, Jessore and Comilla, of detention camps behind high walls in which thousands of Bengalis were held in terrible conditions. The prisoners lived in terror of their lives.[87] Suspected sympathizers of the Awami League, wives and children of the members of the Mukti Bahini (liberation forces), journalists and students and many others were being kept in these detention camps. They were provided with a handful of rice with a little salt and two glasses of drinking water with no washing or sanitary facilities. The prisoners lived in 'sub-human conditions' in the concentration camps. A young man was shot dead for allegedly trying to escape from prison and his blood-stained body was hung up at the camp gate for display. An old man was mercilessly beaten for making a complaint to a brigadier who had earlier inspected the camp.[88]

There was systematic pillage of movable property belonging to the Bengalis and expropriation of their immovable property. Only a few instances will be mentioned. 'Another victim was Jogesh Chandra Ghosh, 86, the invalid millionaire chemist. Ghosh, who did not believe in banks, was dragged from his bed and shot to death by soldiers who looted more than $ 1 million in rupees from his home. Looting was also the motivating force behind the slaying of Ranada Prasad Saha, 80, one of East Pakistan's leading jute exporters and one of its few philanthropists; he had built a modern hospital offering free

---

eastern province, that Pakistan's military regime is determined to make its occupation stick and to subjugate the region of 75 million people... In addition to the daily troops arrivals, the Government is bringing in wave upon wave of West Pakistanis to replace East Pakistanis in Government jobs. No Bengali is trusted with a responsible or sensitive post; even the man who cuts the grass at the Dacca airport is a non-Bengali. Few Bengali taxi drivers remain. Their jobs have been given to non-Bengali Moslem migrants from India such as the Biharis, who have identified and sided with the West Pakistani-dominated Government and who are serving as the army's civilian arm, informing and enforcing. The West Pakistanis are discouraging the use of the Bengali language and trying to replace it with their own, Urdu. Soldiers tell the Bengalis disdainfully that theirs is not really a civilized tongue and they should start teaching their children Urdu if they want to get along. Merchants, out of fear, have replaced their signs with signs in English because they don't know Urdu...' Sydney H. Schanberg, *New York Times*, 14 July 1971.

[86] Eye-witness account of a senior journalist from Dacca: *The Statesman*, Calcutta, 12 June, 1971.

[87] UNI Report quoting *Daily Telegraph*: *Amrita Bazar Patrika*, 4 July 1971.

[88] The ordeals of prisoners narrated by a former News Editor of an East Bengal daily: *The Statesman*, Calcutta, 23 May 1971.

medical care at Mirzapur, 40 miles north of Dacca.'[89]   In Chittagong, locked shops and houses in Laldighi and Riazuddin Bazaar were broken open by the army and handed over to non-Bengalis. Nearly all sequestrated property had to have signboards and nameplates in Urdu.   In the villages, houses were distributed among members of political parties which were humiliated in the last elections by the Awami League.   All Hindu bank accounts were frozen together with those of suspected Awami League supporters.[90]   Murray Sayle of the *Sunday Times* has disclosed that the homes, farms, crops, and small businesses and other assets of the Bengalis were being transferred under paper-thin legal devices to their political and religious enemies.[91]   There have been eye-witness accounts that valuable machinery of different industrial establishments, such as jute mills and paper mills in Chittagong, were dismantled and shipped to West Pakistan.[92]

There are several accounts of ransom demands by Pakistani troops and the Razakars. 'Many girls have reportedly been taken from fleeing families to be sold as prostitutes to the soldiers, particularly if their fathers could not pay a ransom for them.   According to an official who has toured the border, Pakistani troops and their anti-Hindu supporters are demanding $ 140 a person before letting family members leave East Pakistan.'[93] A journalist from Dacca had said:[94] 'There is no court of law functioning in Dacca—not even the martial law court.   The only arbiter is a firing squad.   Individual officers decide whether the latest captives should live or die—in most cases they die unless they can buy their lives from the officers by paying a handsome ransom. But even then payment to an officer cannot be a guarantee against death, because the victim might be arrested by a different officer.' Relatives of missing persons were reported to have received ransom demands from Razakars and junior army officers.[95]

Fresh Evidence After 16 December 1971

After the liberation of Dacca on 16 December 1971, fresh evidence began to accumulate corroborating the earlier version of war crimes and crimes against humanity and also disclosing the commission of genocidal acts and other crimes by the Pakistani troops or their

---

[89] *Time*, 3 May, 1971, page 22.
[90] *Sunday Times*, 20 June, 1971.
[91] *Sunday Times*, 11 July, 1971.
[92] The report of a professor from Chittagong: *Amrita Bazar Patrika*, 5 June, 1971.
[93] *Time*, 21 June, 1971, p. 13.
[94] *The Statesman*, Calcutta, 12 June, 1971.
[95] *Sunday Times*, 20 June, 1971.

collaborators some time before their surrender. *Newsweek* of 3 January 1972 states:

ATROCITIES: It may take years, in fact, for Bangladesh to recover from the ravages of the past few months. In their campaign to bring the Bengalis to heel, the Pakistanis focused their fury on the elite of Bengali society, ruthlessly murdering anyone who could be expected to make trouble. When the victorious Indians arrived in Dacca, they discovered open graves that contained the bodies of more than 125 of Bangladesh's most influential physicians, professors, journalists and lawyers, all of whom had been tied up and then bayoneted, garrotted or shot. And the presumption was widespread that efficient Pakistani assassination teams had committed similar atrocities elsewhere throughout the nation. 'The whole nation is a mass grave', said one Bangladesh official. 'Who knows how many millions they have killed?'

A Press Note issued by the Dacca University on 23 December 1971 gave the names of a number of distinguished teachers who were picked up by the collaborators of the Pakistani army a few days before the surrender and were believed to have been killed; it also confirmed the killing of several distinguished teachers of the University by the Pakistani troops in March 1971. A meeting of the Dacca University demanded the trial of all men of the Pakistani military and para-military forces and other collaborators responsible for the massacre of the University teachers and students—a massacre which was 'one of the worst in the history of mankind.' The meeting called for steps to ensure that those connected with the murders were treated as war criminals and deprived of the status of prisoners of war, and it appealed to the United Nations to take punitive action against the Government of Pakistan for the planned genocide in Bangladesh.[96]

Among the several intellectuals and professional men killed during the gruesome massacre of early December, the bodies of 14 Dacca University teachers (including Professor Muniar Chowdhury, Head of the Department of Bengali), a number of journalists and 27 medical practitioners were stated to have been identified. Many of the dead bodies were found scattered in shallow ponds and depressions in a deserted brickyard near Mohmmedpur on the outskirts of Dacca city, with hands tied behind their backs. Several bore bullet wounds and at least a dozen had been brutally butchered. Evidence has come to light to indicate that a plan to exterminate intellectuals and professional men

[96] *Hindusthan Standard*, 24 December 1971.

was finalized on 9 August 1971 and it was being systematically executed by collaborators and merceneries belonging to organizations like al-Badar and al-Shams who used to receive regular salaries from the Pakistani army, and that liaison was maintained between the military administration and those organizations. Documentary evidence indicated that, among others, Brigadier Raza, Brigadier Aslam, Brigadier Sharif, Brigadier Bashier and Brigadier Saffi of the Pakistani army were directing the operations. It has also been alleged in Bangladesh Government circles that Major-General Rao Farman Ali, Military Adviser to the civilian Governor, was responsible for drawing up the blue print of 'Operation Gestapo' that accounted for a vital number of deaths in Bangladesh since March 1971; Brigadier Bashir, Martial Law Administrator of Dacca, Lt.-Col. Hizazi, Sector Commander, Dacca, and the Deputy Superintendent of Police Mr. Faridi, were involved in the planned execution of the Bengalis.[97]

A volume of evidence has come to light disclosing the planned execution of Bengalis, particularly Hindus, since 25 March 1971 by the Pakistani troops and their collaborators at Chandpur, Feni, Chittagong, Gopalganj, Madaripur, Faridpur and other areas in Bangladesh. The pattern was uniform. The operations took place during the early phase of the military action and were periodically repeated until the surrender. The Pakistani troops and their supporters would arrive at a town and shout. 'Where are the Malauns (Hindus), where are the Awami Leaguers? Kill them, loot and burn their houses.' After the killings, the houses and shops of the Bengalis, particularly the Hindus, would be plundered and then set on fire. Doors, windows and even wooden beams would be removed. Hindu temples would be desecrated, images broken and thrown out and valuables removed. Even the modest house of Sheikh Mujib in Tungipara in Faridpur district was destroyed. Women were violated on a large scale.[98] It has been reported that 700 women stripped of their clothes were found and recovered from Moinamati cantonment.[99] The journalists have found human skulls and bones lying scattered in many places, dumped into trenches or thrown into rivers. 20 per cent of the population of Faridpur was believed to have been slaughtered.[100]

The existence of an extermination camp at Hariharpara, a village near Dacca, was revealed by Mr. Lewis M. Simons in his despatch

[97] *The Statesman*, Calcutta, 19, 21, 27 and 29 December 1971, *Hindusthan Standard*, 24 December 1971 and 8 January 1972.
[98] See Ranajit Roy's reports in the *Hindusthan Standard*, 27, 29 December 1971, 5 and 7 January 1972.
[99] *Ananda Bazar Patrika*, 8 January 1972.
[100] *The Statesman*, Calcutta, 28 December 1971, 1 January 1972 and Ranajit Roy's reports mentioned above.

16

to the *Washington Post* (carried by the *The Statesman* of 23 January 1972). Pakistani firing squads were reported to have eliminated 20,000 Bengalis in that village. Quoting eyewitnesses the correspondent had said that beginning from sunset each evening the soldiers dragged the Bengalis, men and women, bound together in batches of six and eight, to the Buriganga front to be killed. 'While their executioners loomed above them on a wooden pier they were made to wade out into knee-deep water. Then the rifles opened up. The firing and the screaming shattered the hot night air until dawn. Each morning village boatmen were forced to bring their high-powered craft into the bloody water and haul the bodies out to mid-stream where they were cut loose to drift downwards.' The correspondent also said that victims were brought to Hariharpara by trucks from other villages and from the nearby town of Narayanganj and Dacca. 'Their hands tied behind the backs, they were kept prisoners in a large riverside warehouse of the Pakistani National Oil Company until their time came to die.'

Application of Legal Norms to Facts Alleged: Trial of the Criminals

The allegations are of a very serious nature. Foremost among all charges against the Yahya regime is the charge of genocide. Dealing with a few instances representing a small fraction of the authenticated accounts of widespread killing specially of youth and educated people, the *Saturday Review* was of the opinion that what had happened in East Bengal 'appears to be a *provable case of genocide.*'[101] (italics added). The *Washington Daily News* did not have any doubt that genocide had been committed in East Bengal: 'What, we ask, is so bad about sanctions against *mass murder and genocide* ? For that is exactly what the West Pakistani-dominated army committed against helpless Bengalis of East Pakistan... The Bengalis in the east voted overwhelmingly for home rule in the only free election in Pakistan's history. Instead they got the *genocidal assault* by the western army, which is still *shamefully going on.*'[102] (italics added). Again, the *Palaver Weekly* of Ghana comments:[103]

On March 25, 1971 under cover of darkness, one of the most gruesome crimes in the history of mankind was perpetrated by a blood-thirsty military junta against a whole population of seventy-five million, constituting the majority of the people of Pakistan. Many newspapers, reputed for their objectivity, have come out with documentary evidence in the form of photographs

[101] The *Saturday Review* (USA). 22 May 1971.
[102] *Washington Daily News.* 30 June 1971.
[103] *Palaver Weekly.* Ghana, 8 July 1971.

and eye-witness reports of one of the *greatest genocide exercises* in the *annals of man*. Eminent British M.P.s and statesmen, including Presidents and Prime Ministers and the U.N. Secretary-General have directly or indirectly voiced the strongest expressions against the crime. According to *all available* evidence and report the *awful genocide* which was deliberately planned and executed ruthlessly by the West Pakistan Army and has been marked, among other unspeakable atrocities, by the systematic decimation of East Pakistan's intellectuals and professionals, including eminent professors, lawyers, journalists, doctors, students, etc., is still continuing. (italics added)

Apart from the breach of the Genocide Convention of 1948, there is an appalling list of the transgressions of human rights, war crimes and crimes against humanity including infringements of the humanitarian principles of the Hague Convention IV, Geneva Protocol of 17 June 1925 read with the General Assembly resolution 2603A (XXIV) of 16 December 1969, the Geneva Conventions of 1949, the Law of the Nuremberg Charter, the Law of the Nuremberg Judgment, the humanitarian principles of the Convention on the Non-Applicability of Statutory Limitations to War Crimes and Crimes against Humanity adopted by the General Assembly on 26 November 1968, and the basic principles for the protection of civilian population in armed conflicts laid down by the General Assembly in resolutions 2675 (XXV), 2676 (XXV) and 2677 (XXV) of 9 December 1970.

I have set out in an Annexure to this chapter in tabular form the nature of the charges or allegations and the corresponding international legal norms alleged to have been infringed. The list is illustrative, not exhaustive, and prepared on the basis of the allegations publicly made so far. Many of the allegations were not even denied by the Pakistani authorities.

As will have been observed, much of the data in this chapter comes from disinterested international observers and journalists. By and large, the data collected from the evacuee sources is corroborated by intrinsic evidence and by circumstantial evidence, and accepted as dependable by impartial observers. Since during the months under discussion, foreign journalists were either expelled from East Bengal by the Pakistani authorities or their freedom severely restricted in addition to complete censorship of the Press in Pakistan, the normal channels of communication were not available. In the circumstances, there were no other dependable sources for collecting information than those from which the data in this Chapter has been compiled.

In its resolution 2712 (XXV) of 15 December 1970, the General Assembly urged the importance of a thorough investigation of war crimes and crimes against humanity, for the punishment of the guilty, and for compensation to the victims. These were declared to be necessary for the prevention of similar crimes now and in the future as well as for the protection of human rights and fundamental freedoms without which international peace and security could not be safeguarded. International responsibility was therefore attracted.

Inadequacy of the Nuremberg Precedent

The object of this chapter is to emphasize the need for a thorough investigation into the serious allegations of heinous crimes and for a fair trial so that those who are guilty do not escape punishment and yet those who are innocent are not victimized, and for compensation to the victims of those crimes. Sheikh Mujibur Rahman, in a television interview conducted by Mr. David Frost, said: 'Three million people have been killed, including children, women, intellectuals, peasants, workers and students. At least 25,000 to 30,000 homes were burnt and looted. We are still calculating and the final figure could be even more than three million. Daughters were raped in front of their fathers and mothers raped in front of their sons. I cannot stop my tears when I think of it.'[104]

In the proposed trial emphasis should be given to the crime of genocide and other crimes against humanity as distinct from war crimes *simpliciter* although in many cases they would cover common areas. The importance of this aspect should not be lost sight of in formulating the terms of reference of the proposed tribunal or tribunals to be entrusted with the trial of the criminals in Bangladesh. The mistake of the Nuremberg trials should not be repeated. The Nuremberg Tribunal was in substance a tribunal for trial of 'crimes against the peace' and 'war crimes' only; its jurisdiction in respect of 'crimes against humanity' was severely restricted, as will have been observed, by the requirement of their connection with 'crimes against the peace' or 'war crimes.' A perusal of the Nuremberg judgment will show how seriously handicapped the tribunal was, by reason of such limitation, in the punishment of persons accused of crimes against humanity committed before the commencement of the

[104] A Reuter and AP report from London: *The Statesman*, Calcutta, 18 January 1972. Also see *Time*, 24 January 1972: 'Mujib added that he found his country worse off than he had expected. "Very few times have I wept", he said. "This time I wept. We have almost 3,000,000 dead. I am sure of that figure because my organization is in every village; they know who has been killed." Then, with visible emotion, he asked: "Why did the United States Government remain silent?'

war. At Nuremberg '... only two of the accused were found guilty of crimes against humanity alone.'[105] Professor Lauterpacht had observed:

> The same, in a different sphere, applies to the charge of crimes against humanity—a provision of significance inasmuch as it affirmed the existence of fundamental human rights superior to the law of the State and protected by international criminal sanction even if violated in pursuance of the law of the State. However, the provisions of the Charter (Nuremberg Charter) in this matter were somewhat ambiguous. In their original formulation they seemed to give to the Tribunal jurisdiction with regard to crimes against humanity irrespective of their connection with crimes against the peace or war crimes. As the result of a Protocol subsequently signed on October 6, 1945, the semi-colon, in the English and French texts, after the words 'during the war' in Article 6(c) was replaced by a comma, to correspond with the Russian text. In consequence, though for no apparent imperative reason, the Tribunal held that it had jurisdiction only in respect of such acts enumerated in Article 6(c) as had taken place after the commencement of the war. In so far as crimes against humanity were, prior to the war, committed in pursuance of a policy of initiation and preparation of a war of aggression, they ought to have been considered to fall within the jurisdiction of the Tribunal. It is possible that an international military tribunal concerned primarily with war crimes proper may not have been the proper agency for exacting punishment for crimes against humanity. For the *cumulation of jurisdiction* in respect of war crimes and crimes against humanity tended both to draw uninformed criticism upon the charge of war crimes and, in the end, to *reduce the effectiveness of the charge of crimes against humanity*.[106] (emphasis added)

The judgment of the Nuremberg Tribunal was delivered on 30 September 1946. The Genocide Convention was approved by the General Assembly on 3 December 1948. Although the Nuremberg Tribunal had dealt with the planned extermination of Jews by Nazi Germany, it had no occasion to deal with the crime of genocide as defined in the Genocide Convention. Genocide, whether committed in peace time or in war, is a crime under international law. The inadequate precedent of the Nuremberg Tribunal should not therefore deter the proposed tribunal from punishing the guilty in accordance with the subsequent developments of legal norms in this field.

[105] *Oppenheim's International Law*, Vol. II, op. cit., p. 579.
[106] *Ibid.*, pp. 579-80, f.n. 5.

Reasons why Trial should be held in Bangladesh

Broadly speaking, the allegations of war crimes, genocide and other crimes against humanity committed in Bangladesh involve three categories of persons: (a) civilian collaborators of the Pakistani troops, both armed and unarmed; (b) Pakistani troops who had surrendered to the Indian Commander in Bangladesh who also happened to be the Commander of the Joint Command of Bangladesh and Indian forces; (c) persons like Yahya Khan, Tikka Khan, and other leaders of the Pakistani armed forces against whom serious accusation of genocide and other crimes have been made and who are physically beyond the territorial jurisdiction of India and Bangladesh.

With regard to the first category, a number of civilian collaborators of the Pakistani troops suspected of criminal acts have already been apprehended. They include unarmed civilians and high public officials like Dr. A. M. Malik and some of his colleagues as well as armed civilians such as Razakars, members of the so-called peace committees and of such organizations as al-Badar and al-Shams to name a few. The Bangladesh Government had announced its plan to appoint a commission to collect evidence of genocide and for a judicial tribunal for the trial of the accused. The government had promised that there would be no witch-hunting and the alleged offenders would receive a fair trial. Since the suspected criminals are in the custody or within the territorial jurisdiction of the Bangladesh Government, and they are beyond the ambit of Article 4 of the Geneva Convention Relative to the Treatment of Prisoners of War of 12 August 1949, enumerating the categories of persons entitled to be treated as prisoners of war, the authority of the Bangladesh Government to try those persons for criminal acts including genocide according to the law of the land and international law is beyond question. Most of the crimes alleged to have been committed are common crimes in every civilized society.

Regarding the second category, there are serious allegations against many members of the Pakistani armed forces. The instrument of surrender[107] contemplated that the Pakistani officers would 'be treated with dignity and respect that soldiers are entitled to in accordance with the provisions of the Geneva Convention'. However, the Government of Bangladesh was reported to have formally requested the Government of India for the custody of the prisoners of war responsible for genocide for a fair trial by a tribunal in Bangladesh. The Bangladesh Government contended that the Pakistani troops and their collaborators suspected of genocidal acts were not entitled to

[107] *The Statesman*, Calcutta, 18 December, 1971.

the protection of the Geneva Convention.[108]   In a letter dated 14 January 1972, addressed to the Secretary-General of the United Nations, India's permanent representative at the UN, Mr. Samar Sen, pointed out that under the Geneva Conventions, whether relative to prisoners of war or civilians, no immunity was guaranteed to the prisoners of war or to protected persons from trial by competent courts for the offences committed by them prior to capture or protection; and the Joint Command of Bangladesh and Indian forces has the right to demand, on behalf of the Government of Bangladesh, that persons who had committed grave offences such as genocide, war crimes and crimes against humanity should be taken into custody pending appropriate legal action under the law of the land and under international law.   It would be within the sovereign right of the People's Republic of Bangladesh to bring the guilty persons to account by trials in competent courts following fair procedures and assuring the accused full opportunity for defending themselves.   'Pakistan, being a party to the Geneva Conventions as well as the Convention on Genocide, 1948, should be aware of its responsibility as well as of the responsibility of its armed forces, public officials or private individuals for these offences whether they are committed in time of peace or in time of war.'[109]

One can think of several cogent reasons in support of the contention that the trial of persons accused of heinous crimes should take place in Bangladesh.

First, the geographical location of the crime is in Bangladesh. The victims are the citizens of the independent State of Bangladesh. Vital evidence is to be found in Bangladesh.   It provides the most convenient forum for such trials.   It will be recalled that the original Allied Declaration on war crimes signed in Moscow on 30 October 1943, and made public in Moscow by Churchill, Roosevelt and Stalin on 1 November 1943, stated *inter alia:*   (a) that members of the German armed forces and of the ruling party responsible for atrocities, massacres, executions and killings of hostages in occupied territory would *'be brought back to the scene of their crimes and judged on the spot by the peoples they have outraged'*; and (b) that the major war criminals 'whose offences had no particular geographical location' would be punished by a joint decision of the Allied Governments.[110] (emphasis added)

---

[108] See the speech of the then Bangladesh Home Minister, Mr. A. H. M. Kamaruzzaman at Dacca on 7 January 1972: *The Hindusthan Standard,* 8 January 1972.

[109] *The Statesman,* Calcutta, 18 January 1972.

[110] For text of the Declaration, see *History of the United Nations War Crimes Commission* (1948), p. 107.

While the Nuremberg Tribunal was set up pursuant to the agreement of 8 August 1945 between the victorious Allied Governments for the trial of 22 major war criminals whose offences had no particular geographical location, several tribunals established by the national authorities of various allied States exercised jurisdiction against members of the German armed forces and civilians in respect of charges of war crimes. The principle that persons accused of such crimes were to be judged in the vicinity of their alleged crimes, and by a tribunal of the people victimized, became firmly established after the Second World War.[111]

A few instances may be cited: (a) In the case of the *Peleus* (a Greek vessel chartered by the British), some German naval officers and members of the crew of a German U-Boat, after torpedoing the *Peleus* near mid-Atlantic, machine-gunned and threw hand-grenades at members of its crew while they were on rafts or pieces of wreckage; all except three of the *Peleus*' crew were killed or later succumbed to their wounds. The crew of the *Peleus* consisted of several nationalities including Greek and British. The accused persons were tried at Hamburg by a British military court in which Greek military officers also served. Three of the accused were sentenced to death and were executed at Hamburg on 30 November 1945. (b) Some captured Americans were shot in Italy without trial under an express order of General Anton Dostler, a German commander. Dostler was tried in Rome by a U.S. military commission, found guilty and sentenced to death. (c) Gerald Hood, a British pilot, was shot by Schweinberger at the base of the skull under the order of Sandrock in Holland. A Dutch national, Bote, was also killed in similar circumstances. Sandrock and Schweinberger were tried by a British military court (in which Dutch military officers also served) which sat in Almelo, Holland, and there was an agreement with the Dutch Government in this respect. Sandrock and Schweinberger were sentenced to be hanged and the sentences were executed on 13 December 1945. (d) Three American airmen were forced to land near the Jaluit Atoll in the Marshall Islands and were taken to a Japanese naval headquarters at Emidj Island and were shot without trial under orders of Rear-Admiral Masuda. Late in 1945, after the United States had captured the area, a U.S. military commission was set up and five Japanese officers who carried out Masuda's order were tried and three of them were sentenced to be hanged. Masuda, who had earlier confessed that he had ordered the killing, committed suicide before

---

[111] The efforts made by the United Nations War Crimes Commission, an important inter-allied body set up by a diplomatic conference in October 1943, resulted in a considerable body of case law which clarified numerous aspects of the law of war and revealed the considerable potentialities of its judicial enforce-

the trial. The indictment against the five Japanese officers charged with murder stated that the criminal acts were committed 'in violation of the dignity of the United States of America, the international rules of warfare and the moral standards of civilized society.' An objection to the phrase 'moral standard of civilized society' on the ground that it was non-legal and improper was overruled. (e) Some German civilian officials of a firm of suppliers of poison gas with knowledge that it was to be used to kill inmates of concentration camps, were tried by a British military court in Hamburg in March 1946. The owner and the principal executive of the firm were sentenced to death by hanging.[112]

Second, the theory of the universality of jurisdiction over war crimes will fully support the contention that the criminals in question should be tried by an appropriate tribunal in Bangladesh. The theory, as propounded by Professor Willard B. Cowles, states that in international law, every independent State has jurisdiction to punish war criminals in its custody regardless of the nationality of the victim, the time it entered the war or the place where the offence was committed.[113]

The principle was accepted by the United States Military Commission in Insane Asylum Murders Case. There were on trial some Germans in charge of a sanatorium at Hadamar, Germany, in which, among others, the victims were a large number of Polish and Russian nationals who were put into the sanatorium allegedly for treatment of tuberculosis. It was established that the Poles and the Russians were neither examined nor treated for tuberculosis and they died as a result of overdoses of narcotics within a few days of arrival. There were burials in mass graves in the cemetery of the sanatorium. The trial took place at Wiesbaden, Germany, by a US military com-

---

ment. The main source of these decision is the *Law Reports of Trials of War Criminals*, 15 vols. (selected and prepared by the United Nations War Crimes Commission and published for it by His Majesty' Stationery Office (1946-1949). The last volume contains a detailed legal analysis of the decisions. Also see *Oppenheim's International Law*, Vol. II, pp. 582-6. The literature on the subject of the Nuremberg Tribunal is vast and a selective bibliography can be found in Oppenheim, vol. II, pp. 580-81. For the judgment of the International Military Tribunal of the Far East, delivered on 4 November 1948, see *Annual Digest and Reports of Public International Law Cases*, 1948. *Also see International Military Tribunal for the Far East, Dissentient Judgment of Justice R. B. Pal* (Sanyal & Co., Calcutta, 1953).

[112] The cases were reported in *Law Reports of Trials of War Criminals*, *ibid.* Vol. I. Also see the *Trials of War Criminals* (Non-Nuremberg) by Professor Willard B. Cowles (1948), 42 AJIL, pp. 299-319, for an excellent discussion of the issues involved in the trials.

[113] *Universality of Jurisdiction Over War Crimes*; 33 California Law Review, pp. 177-218 (1945). Also see (1948) 42 AJIL, pp. 312-3, f.n. 13.

17

mission. The question of jurisdiction of the tribunal was raised. No American national was among those killed at Hadamar and when the crimes took place the territory was not under American control. The Commission held that it had jurisdiction. The Notes of the case published in the Law Reports of Trials of War Criminals, states, *inter alia*:

> The following reasons sustaining the Commission's jurisdiction can be adduced: (a) the general doctrine recently expounded and called 'universality of jurisdiction over war crimes' which has the support of the United Nations War Crimes Commission and according to which every independent State, has, under International Law, jurisdiction to punish not only pirates but also war criminals in its custody, regardless of the nationality of the victim, or of the place where the offence was committed, particularly where, for some reason, the criminal would otherwise go unpunished...[114]

Bangladesh is therefore fully competent not only to try the criminals in its custody but also other criminals whose custody the Government of Bangladesh can lawfully demand for the purpose of such trials.

Third, since the predominant charge is a charge of genocide, the appropriate forum for the trial of the criminals is a competent tribunal in Bangladesh. Article VI of the Genocide Convention contemplates two possible forums for trial of persons charged with genocide or other punishable acts enumerated in Article III. These forums are: (a) *a competent tribunal of the State in the territory of which the act was committed* or (b) by such international penal tribunal as may have jurisdiction with respect to those contracting parties which shall have accepted its jurisdiction. Since at present the second forum does not exist, the first forum is the only available one under the Genocide Convention in respect of the crime of genocide in Bangladesh. Bangladesh is a State recognised by several countries. The distinction made between a 'State' and a 'contracting party' in respect of the two forums envisaged in Article VI makes it clear that the competency of a Bangladesh tribunal to try persons for the crime of genocide committed in time of peace or in time of war is beyond doubt and is not dependent upon Bangladesh becoming a party to the Genocide Convention.

Fourth, in terms of Article VII of the Genocide Convention, India as a contracting party is under a pledge to grant extradition in accordance with its laws and treaties in force. The pledge can be fulfilled

[114] Also quoted by Professor Cowles (1948), 42 AJIL, pp. 312-3, *ibid.*

under appropriate municipal legislation in India and by appropriate treaties between India and Bangladesh. If it be contended that a treaty between India and Bangladesh for extradition cannot at the moment be considered to be a treaty between two contracting parties within the meaning of Article VII, the answer is that for granting extradition an appropriate executive fiat is enough and a treaty is not indispensable. 'In some countries, like Switzerland, Sweden, Turkey, Argentina and France, the power of the executive to extradite offenders is not dependent upon the existence of a treaty of extradition'.[115]

Fifth, the Genocide Convention having the character of *jus cogens* (i.e. norms with which treaties must not conflict), its provisions must prevail over all other treaties including the Geneva Conventions. If, therefore, there are any provisions in the Geneva Convention relating to prisoners of war which conflict with India's obligation to send Pakistani troops to Bangladesh for trial in response to the request of the Bangladesh Government, the obligations under the Genocide Convention must prevail.

Sixth, at the time of their unconditional surrender on 16 December 1971, the Pakistani troops were fully aware that they were surrendering to the joint command of the Bangladesh and Indian forces which came into existence by an agreement between the two countries on 10 December 1971. Accordingly, it would be futile for the Pakistani troops, whose extradition has been sought by the Bangladesh Government, to deny the status of the Bangladesh Government or its right to try such persons for criminal acts under the cloak of the Geneva Convention relating to prisoners of war.

Seventh, there is in fact no conflict between the Genocide Convention and the Geneva Convention on the question of the trial of the Pakistani prisoners by an appropriate tribunal in Bangladesh. The Geneva Convention does not provide a charter of immunity from trials for war crimes, genocide and other crimes against humanity. This becomes clear if one analyses the following disciplinary and penal provisions of the Geneva Convention relating to prisoners of war.[116] The relevant provisions are divided into three parts:

(I) *General Provisions (Article 82-88)*

Except Article 85 the other provisions relate to offences committed by prisoners of war and not to offences committed prior to capture. In respect of trials for such offences, disciplinary rather than judicial measures and punishment are recommended and certain judicial safe-

---

[115] *Oppenheism's International Law*, Vol. II, op cit., page 588, f.n. 4.

[116] For text of the Geneva Convention relating to Prisoners of War, see (1950) Vol. 75, *United Nations Treaty Series*, I Nos. 907-973, pp. 135-285.

guards are provided. Accordingly, these provisions have no relevance with regard to the criminal acts in Bangladesh under consideration.

Article 85 provides: 'Prisoners of war prosecuted under the laws of the Detaining Power for acts committed prior to capture shall retain, even if convicted, the benefits of the present Convention.' Safeguards, therefore apply, not before, but after, conviction. The safeguards guaranteed consists mainly in the promise of humane treatment during imprisonment, certain delays concerning the carrying out of the death penalty and access to a protecting power. Professor Lauterpacht felt that while the safeguards in the long run might not defeat the ends of justice, there was some justification in the view that the deterrent element inherent in capital punishment for war crimes was bound to be weakened by the requirement of the lapse of a period of six months from the notification to the protecting power till the execution.[117]

In any event the aforesaid safeguards would not be available when the prosecution is for offences under international law such as war crimes, genocide and other crimes against humanity. The reservation of Soviet Russia and some other East European countries to Article 85 brings out this point. In its reservation to Article 85, the USSR stated: "The Union of Soviet Socialist Republics does not consider itself bound by the obligation, which follows from Article 85, to extend the application of the Convention to prisoners of war who have been convicted under the law of the Detaining Power, in accordance with the principles of the Nuremberg trial, for war crimes and crimes against humanity, it being understood that persons convicted of such crimes must be subject to the conditions obtaining in the country in question for those who undergo their punishment."[118]

(II) *Disciplinary Sanctions* (*Article 89-98*)

These provisions relate to the consequences of escape or attempt to escape by prisoners of war, the kind of punishment and their duration, humane treatment of prisoners of war accused of offences against discipline, procedure to be followed before a disciplinary award is pronounced etc. The provisions have nothing whatsoever to do with the crimes in Bangladesh under consideration.

(III) *Judicial Proceedings* (*Articles 99-108*)

Article 99 provides:

No prisoners of war may be tried or sentenced for an act which

---

[117] Oppenheim, op. cit., Vol. II, page 387, f.n. 3.
[118] (1950) 75 UN Treaty Series, op. cit., p. 460.

is not forbidden by the law of the Detaining Power or by international law, in force at the time the said act was committed. No moral or physical coercion may be exerted on a prisoner of war in order to induce him to admit himself guilty of the act of which he is an accused.

No prisoner of war may be convicted without having had an opportunity to present his defence and the assistance of a qualified advocate or counsel.

The reference to an act forbidden by international law in Article 99, which did not appear in the Convention of 1929, was intended to remove any doubt as to the right of the detaining power (for instance, India in the instant case) to try prisoners of war for war crimes.[119] This is an enabling provision and should India exercise its jurisdiction to try prisoners of war for war crimes certain judicial safeguards must be provided. For instance, the prisoner has a right to assistance by one of his fellow prisoners, to defence by a qualified counsel of his own choice and, if necessary, to the services of a competent interpreter (Article 105). The Convention contains detailed provisions designed to ensure a fair trial to prisoners of war.

Article 102 provides that a prisoner of war can be validly sentenced only if the sentence has been pronounced by the same courts and according to the same procedure as in the case of members of the armed forces of the detaining power. Article 104 provides that three weeks' notice must be given to the protecting power of the intention to initiate proceedings specifying the charges, the law applicable, the court and the date and place of the opening of the trial.

It can be argued with considerable force that Article 102 does not apply to the Pakistani prisoners of war in respect of trial for crimes committed before their surrender and further that non-compliance with Article 104 is not fatal to the jurisdiction of the tribunal. A precedent may be cited. A plea to the jurisdiction of the United States Military Commission, similar to the plea raised in the Dostler case mentioned before, was decided by the United States Supreme Court in *Ex parte Yamashita*.[120] Article 63 of the Geneva Convention of 1929 (corresponding to Article 102 of the 1949 Convention) provided that 'sentence may be pronounced against a prisoner of war only by the same courts and according to the same procedure as in the case of persons belonging to the armed forces of the detaining power.' In the Dostler case, it was argued by the defence that the only proper method to try Dostler would be by a

[119] This is Professor Lauterpacht's view: see *Oppenheim's Internationl Law*, Vol. II, p. 390.

[120] *Ex parte Yamashita* (1946), 327 US p. 1: 90 Lawyers ed., p. 499.

United States court martial. The prosecution contended that the relevant provisions of the Geneva Convention pertained only to offences committed by a prisoner of war after capture, not to offences committed against the law of nations prior to becoming a prisoner of war. To this, Professor Cowles adds a further argument: 'The Prosecution might have added that under Article 1 of the Geneva Convention only individuals who have conducted their operations in accordance with the laws and customs of war have the rights of prisoners of war under that treaty. War criminals have not so conducted themselves.'[121]

Analysing the relevant provisions of the Geneva Convention of 1929, the Supreme Court of the United States dealt with a similar jurisdictional plea and observed in *Ex parte Yamashita*:

"But we think examination of Article 63 in its setting in the Convention plainly shows that it refers to sentence 'pronounced against a prisoner of war' for an offence committed while a prisoner of war, and not for a violation of the law of war committed while a combatant... Punishment is of two kinds—'disciplinary' and 'judicial', the latter being the more severe. Article 52 requires that leniency be exercised in deciding whether an offence requires disciplinary or judicial punishment. Part 2 of Chapter 3 is entitled 'Disciplinary Punishment', and further defines the extent of such punishment, and the mode in which it may be imposed. Part 3, entitled 'Judicial Suits', in which Article 63 is found, describes the procedure by which 'judicial' punishment may be imposed. The three parts of Chapter 3, taken together, are thus a comprehensive description of the substantive offences which prisoners of war may commit during their imprisonment, of the penalties which may be imposed on account of such offences, and of the procedure by which guilt may be adjudged and sentence pronounced. We think it clear, from the context of these recited provisions, that *part 3*, and *Article 63* which it contains, *apply only to judicial proceedings* directed against a prisoner of war for *offences committed while a prisoner of war*." (emphasis added).

With regard to the fact of failure to give notice of the trial to the protecting power under Article 60 (corresponding to Article 104 of 1949 Convention), the Supreme Court held: "Article 60 of the Geneva Convention of July 27, 1929, 47 Stat 2051, to which the United States and Japan were signatories, provides that 'At the opening of a judicial proceeding directed against a prisoner of war, the detaining Power shall advise the representative of the protecting Power thereof as soon as possible, and always before the date set for the opening of the trial.' Petitioner relies on the failure to give the prescribed notice to the protecting power to establish want

[121] (1948) 42 AJIL, p. 305.

of authority in the commission to proceed with the trial. For reasons already stated, we conclude that Article 60 of the Geneva Convention, which appears in Part 3, Chapter 3, Section V, Title III of the Geneva Convention, applies only to persons who are subjected to judicial proceedings for offences committed while prisoners of war."[122]

An examination of the relevant provisions in their setting in the Convention of 1949 will support the argument that the benefits of Articles 102 and 104 are not available to the Pakistani prisoners of war for offences under international law committed prior to their surrender. The said provisions appear in Part III (Captivity), Section VI (Relations between Prisoners of War and the Authorities), Chapter III (Penal and Disciplinary Sanctions).

The question of release and repatriation of the Pakistani prisoners of war who might be charged with indictable offences cannot arise until the completion of the proceedings against them and, if necessary, until the completion of punishment (Article 119).

Serious allegations of war crimes, genocidal acts and other crimes against humanity have been made against high officials of the Pakistani military junta, including Yahya Khan and Tikka Khan. If on a proper investigation charges are framed against persons within the jurisdiction of a party to the Geneva Convention, be it Pakistan or any other country, it will be the duty of such country to search for the criminals, regardless of their nationality, and to prosecute them before its own courts or to hand them over to another party for trial provided a *prima facie* case was made out against them (Article 129). Such responsibility extends to 'grave breaches' enumerated in Article 130: wilful killing, torture or inhumane treatment, including biological experiments, wilfully causing great suffering or serious injury to body or health etc. Although the terms 'war crimes' and 'crimes against humanity' were not used in the Geneva Convention, the same will obviously be covered by the definition of 'grave breaches', as will have been observed from the recent trends in the punishment of criminals discussed earlier.

Although the appropriate time for the United Nations intervention was when the impugned acts were committed, 'for the prevention and suppression of acts of genocide' under Article VIII of the Genocide Convention, and nothing was done, yet a report from Dacca on 11 January 1972 indicated that the Bangladesh Government had decided to move the United Nations formally for the appointment of an international commission for genocide alleged to have been committed by the Pakistani occupation forces.[123] This established the

---

[122] (1946) 327 US, pp. 21-24:90 Lawyers ed., pp. 512-14.
[123] Addressing a public meeting at Tangail in Bangladesh on 24 January 1972,

bona fide desire of the Bangladesh Government for a fair trial. An international tribunal can be set up for such a trial either by the United Nations with the consent of Bangladesh, or by an agreement between India and Bangladesh as victorious allies in the December war following the precedent of the Nuremberg tribunal, or by the Bangladesh Government itself. Should such an international tribunal consisting of persons whose integrity cannot be questioned be set up, it will be the duty of every country having the custody of any persons alleged to have committed the crimes to hand them over for trial in Bangladesh.

Some Guidelines for the Proposed Tribunal

The proposed tribunal or tribunals for trials in respect of criminal acts in Bangladesh will doubtless be guided by the relevant principles of municipal and international law, numerous precedents, international conventions and agreements, and the resolutions of the United Nations between 1946 and 1970. Among the principles which the tribunal may find useful in the context of the crimes in Bangladesh, the following four may serve as important guidelines:

First, *the Principle of Individual Responsibility*. As the Nuremberg Tribunal pointed out: "The principle of international law, which, under certain circumstances, protects the representatives of a state, cannot be applied to acts which are condemned as criminal by international law. The authors of these acts cannot shelter themselves behind their official positions in order to be freed from punishment in appropriate proceedings. Article 7 of the Charter expressly declares: 'The official position of Defendants, whether as heads of State, or responsible officials in Government departments, shall not be considered as freeing them from responsibility, or mitigating punishment'. On the other hand, the very essence of the Charter is that individuals have international duties which transcend the national obligations of obedience imposed by the individual state. He who violates the laws of war cannot obtain immunity while acting in pursuance of the authority of the state if the state in authorizing action moves outside its competence under international law."[124]

The principle was reiterated in Article IV of the Genocide Convention, viz. 'Persons committing genocide or any other acts enumerated in Article III shall be punished, whether they are constitu-

---

Prime Minister Sheikh Mujibur Rahman reiterated his demand for a trial by some world body of Pakistan Army personnel responsible for 'history's worst killing and genocide' which had overshadowed the barbarism of Hitler. (*The Statesman*, Calcutta, 25 January 1972).

[124] (1947) 41 AJIL, p. 221.

tionally responsible rulers, public officials or private individuals.' And again the principle was reaffirmed and elaborated in Article II of the 1968 Convention on Non-Applicability of Statutory Limitations to War Crimes and Crimes Against Humanity adopted by the UN General Assembly on 26 November 1968.

Second, *Plea of Superior Orders Inadmissible.* A plea of superior orders is inadmissible as an absolute defence although it might be taken into consideration in mitigation of punishment. As the Nuremberg Tribunal had observed:[125]

> It was also submitted on behalf of most of these defendants that in committing what they did they were acting under the orders of Hitler, and therefore cannot be held responsible for the acts committed by them in carrying out these orders. The Charter specifically provides in Article 8: 'The fact that the Defendant acted pursuant to the order of his Government or of a superior shall not free him from responsibility, but may be considered in mitigation of punishment.' The provisions of this Article are in conformity with the law of all nations. That a soldier was ordered to kill or torture in violation of the international law of war has never been recognized as a defence to such acts of brutality, though, as the Charter here provides, the order may be urged in mitigation of the punishment. The true test, which is found in varying degrees in the criminal law of most nations, is not the existence of the order, but whether moral choice was in fact possible.

Professor Lauterpacht had observed:

> However, subject to these qualifications, the question is governed by the major principle that members of the armed forces are bound to obey lawful orders only and that they cannot therefore escape liability if, in obedience to a command, they commit acts which both violate unchallenged rules of warfare and outrage the general sentiment of humanity... No principles of justice and, in most civilized communities, no principle of law permits the individual person to avoid suffering or even to save his life at the expense of the life—or, as revealed in many war crimes trials, of a vast multitude of lives—or of sufferings, on a vast scale, of others. Moreover, there is as a rule no question of danger to life, following upon disobedience, in the case of officers or other persons in positions of authority. It is, as a rule, probable that disobedience on the part of such persons, far from exposing

[125] *Ibid.*

18

them to immediate danger, may result in the modification or withdrawal of the unlawful order.[126]

Third, *Vicarious Liability of Commanders.* The inverse case of the responsibility of commanders for war crimes committed by subordinate members of the armed forces is equally well setttled. As Professor Lauterpacht had observed:

When troops under a general in command of a locality or province in occupied territory commit massacres and atrocities against the civilian population or prisoners of war, there may arise, in addition to the criminal responsibility of the actual perpetrators, the responsibility of the commander. Such responsibility arises, directly and undeniably, when the acts in question have been committed in pursuance of an order of the commander concerned, or if he has culpably failed to take the necessary measures to prevent or suppress them. The failure to do so raises the presumption—which for the sake of effectiveness of the law cannot be regarded as easily rebuttable—of authorisation, encouragement, connivance, acquiescence or subsequent ratification of the criminal acts. In numerous war crimes trials—of which the case of *General Yamashita,* sentenced in 1946 to death by a United States Military Commission in Manila, is the most significant example—held after the Second World War, various tribunals acted upon that principle. The latter has also been recognised in the legislation, relating to war crimes, of some countries. However, it is probable that the responsibility of the commander goes beyond the duty as formulated above. He is, it is believed, also responsible if he fails, negligently or deliberately, to inflict punishment or to insist by all means at his disposal—including, in extreme cases, relinquishment of his command—on the infliction of punishment upon the guilty... Any deviation from that principle is calculated to endow commanding officers with immunity for crimes which, as active or passive accomplices, they may have committed at the instance of a higher authority.[127]

Fourth, *Liability for Membership of Criminal Organizations.* Following the Nuremberg precedent, it may be necessary for the proposed tribunal in Bangladesh to declare the criminal character of certain groups and organizations like the Razakars, the so-called peace committees, al-Badar and al-Shams and to punish the members there-

[126] *Oppenheim's International Law,* Vol. II, pp. 569-72.
[127] *Ibid.,* pp. 572-4.

of for participation in heinous crimes. The tribunal will also have to consider whether the Leadership Corps of the military junta, General Staff of the Pakistani armed forces, the civilian government set up by the military junta, the security organizations of the Pakistani army in Bangladesh and similar other groups or organizations, should be declared as criminal groups or organizations. The terms of reference of the proposed tribunal or tribunals will have to make adequate provisions in this regard and to arrange to bring individuals to trial for membership of such groups or organizations.[128]

Illegal Trial of Sheikh Mujibur Rahman

There was a public announcement by General Yahya Khan about the trial of Sheikh Mujibur Rahman to be held *in camera* before a military court without the assistance of a freely chosen lawyer. There was very little reliable evidence as to the progress of the trial. Apart from Sheikh Mujib, some important Awami League leaders were reported to have been tried *in absentia* by military courts and their property was ordered to be sold by public auctions. On 18 December 1971, a spokesman of the Pakistan Government said at Islamabad: 'The trial (of Sheikh Mujib) has ended. All the witnesses have been examined. The verdict may be soon or it may be at the end of the month.'[129]

Although after the release of Sheikh Mujib on 8 January 1972, the trial has become infructuous, yet it will be useful to examine briefly the principles of international law involved in a similar situation, both with regard to the nature of the charges and the procedure to be followed.

What was the offence of Sheikh Mujib? In his broadcast on 26 March 1971, President Yahya Khan had said: "Sheikh Mujibur Rahman's action of starting his non-cooperation movement is an act of treason." Was that an offence? As already indicated, under no system of jurisprudence in a civilized country, nor under the municipal law of Pakistan as on 25 March, can a non-violent non-cooperation movement for transfer of power to the elected representatives of the people be considered an act of treason.

[128] Article 9 of the Nuremberg Charter conferred the power on the Tribunal to declare a group or organization of which the individual concerned was a member as a criminal organization. Article 10 provided for the trial of individuals for membership of such criminal organizations. For the judgment of the Nuremberg Tribunal on this aspect, see (1947) 41 AJIL, pp. 249-72. The accused organizations considered by the Tribunal were the leadership corps of the Nazy Party, Gestapo and SD, SS, the SA, the Reich Cabinet, and General Staff and High Command.

[129] The Statesman, Calcutta, 19 December 1971.

Was Mujib then guilty of any offence under international law? Let us assume he had inspired the movement for independence of East Bengal and the subsequent dismemberment of Pakistan. A movement for dismemberment of a country is only forbidden by international law when a section of the people, in a constitutional regime with adequate guarantees of fundamental human rights, makes an attempt by unconstitutional means to destroy the territorial integrity of the state concerned. The Declaration on Principles of International Law, adopted by the General Assembly by Resolution 2625 (XXV), makes it clear that only a state possessed of a popular Government in a constitutional regime can raise the defence that self-determination does not permit the dismemberment of a country. Where, however, the majority is denied its democratic right to bring about a constitutional regime, the revolutionary right of the majority to the dismemberment or division of a state to achieve self-determination has never been in doubt in international law. It is one of the legitimate and permissible modes for implementing self-determination in contemporary law.

It will have been observed that Article 3 of the Geneva Convention of 1949 imposed certain minimum obligations of a humanitarian character upon the Government of Pakistan with regard to the procedure for trial of political prisoners. It is in respect of such trials that Professor Lauterpacht had observed: 'Utmost restraint—dictated, in addition, by the apprehension of provoking reprisals—must be exercised in the matter of trials arising from what is in essence a political crime of treason and rebellion.'[130]

The persons protected by Article 3 are entitled to claim, in respect of their trials, the minimum judicial safeguards recognized as indispensable by civilized people. Some of these norms can be found in Articles 10, 11 and 12 of the Universal Declaration of Human Rights of 6 December 1948. The minimum norms of judicial safeguards require:

First, the accused can only be tried by a regular, impartial and independent municipal court and not by a military court. Even under Articles 64, 65 and 66 of the Geneva Convention, civilians should normally be tried by a regular municipal court, and only in certain exceptional cases can a properly constituted, non-political military court claim jurisdiction. President Yahya could not have invoked these exceptional provisions because he did not recognize the armed conflict with the Bengali people as an international war. Second, the accused must be presumed to be innocent until proved guilty according to law at a fair trial in a regular court. Third, he cannot be tried for commission or omission in respect of any act which was not

---

[130] *Oppenheim's International Law*, Vol. II, p. 211.

an offence under the national law of Pakistan as on 25 March. There can be no *ex post facto* criminal law in a civilized society. Even a military court is bound by this rule by reason of Article 65 of the Geneva Convention which provides that the penal laws promulgated by the occupying power shall not be retroactive. Fourth, the accused must be given full particulars of the offences alleged against him. Fifth, he is entitled to be assisted by a qualified lawyer of his own choice who should be able to visit him freely and enjoy the necessary facilities for preparing the defence. Sixth, he should have a right of appeal in accordance with the regular municipal law of Pakistan.

Any trial held or sentences passed in breach of these minimum norms of a fair trial would have amounted to a serious transgression against human rights guaranteed by the Universal Declaration of 1948. The secret trial of Sheikh Mujib or any other Awami League leader in a similar situation by a military court was therefore held in complete breach of the human rights provisions in contemporary law.[131]

It was the duty of the international community to prevent from the beginning the commission of such atrocious breaches of human rights. Although there is at present no international penal tribunal or criminal court for punishing the persons guilty of breaches of human rights or for protecting the victims thereof, the ex-Secretary-General, U Thant, had observed that 'if there are breaches of human rights which contravene the provisions of the Declaration of Human Rights, then all such breaches should be brought to the attention of the United Nations, by *some means or another.*'[132] (emphasis added). International responsibility was therefore attracted in this field of war crimes and crimes against humanity in East Bengal since March 1971.

---

[131] 'Who Should be in Dock?', for text of the talk by Subrata Roy Chowdhury, All India Radio, Calcutta Station on 29 July, 1971, see The Hindusthan Standard (Calcutta), 30 July 1971.

[132] U.N. Press Release SG/SM 1200, at 7 (1969); (1970) 64 AJIL, July, p. 613.

ANNEXURE
WAR CRIMES, GENOCIDE & OTHER CRIMES AGAINST HUMANITY: APPLICATION OF LEGAL NORMS TO FACTS ALLEGED

Nature of the Charges or Allegations

Infringements of International Legal Norms

1. There was a common plan or conspiracy to eliminate a substantial part of the Bengali population in East Bengal consisting of the leaders and followers of the Awami League in general and the Hindu community in particular. The *mens rea* or the intention to eliminate a substantial part and to stifle all political opposition to the military regime by a reign of terror is evidenced inter alia by a contingency battle plan carefully prepared, the military government's policy as disclosed by Major-General Shaukat Raza and other military officers at the Eastern Command Headquarters at Dacca. This is further corroborated by evidence discovered since 16 December 1971, to wit, a meticulous plan to exterminate intellectuals of Dacca, partially executed early in December; planned killings in extermination camp in Hariharpara.

By itself the conspiracy to commit genocide amounts to a crime under Article III(B) of the Genocide Convention and also under Article 6 of the Nuremberg Charter. Leaders, organizers, instigators and accomplices participating in the common plan or conspiracy are punishable under Article III(B) and (E) of the Genocide Convention and Article 6 of the Nuremberg Charter.

2. The overt act of killing over a million Bengalis in execution of the conspiracy aforesaid or independently thereof. The victims were the political leaders, followers and sympathizers of the Awami League, the intelligentsia, teachers, students, civil servants, doctors, journalists, members of the police force, militiamen who responded to the call of amnesty, peasants and villagers, workers, ordinary men, women and children. In particular the target was the Hindu commu-

These acts would amount to a crime of genocide under Article II(A) and as such punishable under Article III(A) of the Genocide Convention; and a crime against humanity under Article 6(c) of the Nuremberg Charter read with the Nuremberg Judgment; and also a crime under the humanitarian principle of Article I(b) of the Convention of 1968. The Pakistani troops and others who committed the genocide as also those who directly and publicly incited them to commit genocide are punishable. And the commanders are

Nature of the Charges or Allegations	Infringements of International Legal Norms
nity. People were killed *en masse*, in groups and individually.	vicariously liable. Hired assassins and civilian collaborators of the Pakistani army including Razakars, members of al-Badar, al-Shams and Peace Committees are also punishable and their organizations liable to be declared criminal following the precedent of the Nuremberg Charter. This is also a crime under Article 6(b) of the Nuremberg Charter read with Article 46 of the Hague Convention (IV) as also under Article 3(1)(a) of the Geneva Convention of 1949. These provisions are to be read along with resolution 2677(XXV) of the General Assembly calling upon all parties to any armed conflict to observe the rules laid down inter alia in the Hague Convention of 1907 and the Geneva Conventions of 1949.
3. There have been indiscriminate air attacks and random bombing of undefended cities, towns and villages. The ordinary civilian population who did not actively take part in the operations of the liberation forces of East Bengal were the victims.	This would amount to a crime under the customary law of the immunity of civilian population as also under Article 25 of the Hague Convention (IV). This is also a violation of the principles for the protection of civilian populations in armed conflicts of all types as laid down by the General Assembly in resolution 2675 (XXV) of 9 December 1970. These provisions are to be read along with resolution 2677 (XXV).
4. As a result of indiscriminate air attacks, heavy shellings from warships and gunboats and the operations of the Pakistani troops in the field (e.g. 'kill and burn mission'), extensive devastations of private and public properties were caused in East Bengal. The devastation was on a scale reminiscent of World War II. University buildings, charitable and educational institutions, temples and mosques, hospitals, public buildings and the properties and dwellings of private persons were destroyed or wilfully damaged.	This amounts to a crime under Article 6(b) of the Nuremberg Charter read with Articles 25, 46 and 56 of the Hague Convention (IV) and Article 53 of the Geneva Convention of 1949 relating to civilians. The provisions are to be read along with resolution 2677 (XXV).

Nature of the Charges or Allegations	*Infringements of International Legal Norms*
5. Various patterns of killing, cruelty and torture were devised by the Pakistani troops and mercilessly carried out; to wit, roasting people alive, shooting school children and pregnant women, shooting a baby in mother's arm, the lobe of a boy's ear shot away at close range, the burial alive of a husband in front of the wife, children murdered and daughters violated in front of their parents, babies thrown up to be caught on bayonets, children sliced up like meat and draining blood out till the victim dies.	The atrocities amount to crimes against humanity within the definition of Article 6(c) of the Nuremberg Charter, the Nuremberg Judgment, Article 3(1)(a) of the Geneva Convention of 1949 and the humanitarian principles in Article 1(b) of the 1968 Convention; Article II(B) of the Genocide Convention.
6. There were numerous incidents of outrages on women; to wit, continuous raping, raping to death, killing the girls raped, enforced prostitution, detention of women for ransom, sterilization of women, turning out pregnant women as destitutes, deportation of women to West Pakistan and forced marriages.	These amount to crimes under Article 6(b) of Nuremberg Charter read with Article 46 of the Hague Convention (IV); Article 6(c) of Nuremberg Charter prohibiting murder, enslavement, deportation and other inhumane acts, read with Nuremberg Judgment; Article 3(1)(a) of the Geneva Convention of 1949 prohibiting violence to life and person, cruel treatment and torture; Article 3(1)(c) of Geneva Convention prohibiting outrages upon personal dignity, in particular humiliating and degrading treatment; Article 27 of the Geneva Convention providing that women shall be especially protected against any attack on their honour, in particular against rape, enforced prostitution and any form of indecent assault; Article 32 of the Geneva Convention prohibiting not only murder and torture but any other measures of brutality whether applied by civilian or military agents. These would also amount to genocidal acts under the Genocide Convention of 1948, to wit, causing serious bodily or mental harm, Article II(B); deliberately inflicting conditions of life calculated to bring about their physical destruction, Article II(C); imposing measures intended to prevent births within the group, Article II(D).

Nature of the Charges or Allegations	Infringements of International Legal Norms
7. Extermination and/or persecution of minorities, particularly the Hindu community; to wit, killing Hindus indiscriminately in execution of a plan or conspiracy to kill, terrorizing Hindus and compelling them to leave East Bengal; torture and cruelties; looting and destruction of their properties.	The impugned acts amount to crimes under Article 6(b) of the Nuremberg Charter read with Article 46 of Hague Convention (IV); Article 6(c) of the Nuremberg Charter prohibiting murder, extermination and other inhumane acts and also persecution on political or religious grounds; the law of the Nuremberg Judgment; genocidal acts under Article II(A), (B), (C), and (D) of the Genocide Convention; and the humanitarian principle in Article 1(b) of the Convention of 1968.
8. Use of chemicals and napalm resulting in loss of civilian lives and destruction of paddy and jute plantations.	These amount to violations of Geneva Protocol of 17 June 1925 read with draft resolution L. 489 (of which Pakistan was one of the sponsors) adopted by the General Assembly in resolution 2603A (XXIV) of 16 December 1969.
9. There was a systematic pillage of movable properties of civilians from private residences and shops, particularly belonging to the members of the Hindu community.	This amounts to a crime under Article 47 of the Hague Convention (IV). This has to be read along with resolution 2677 (XXV).
10. Large-scale confiscation, expropriation and sequestration of properties such as houses, farms, crops, small businesses and other assets of Bengalis and the transfer thereof to 'their political and religious enemies'.	This amounts to a crime under Article 6(b) of the Nuremberg Charter read with Article 46 of the Hague Convention (IV).
11. Instead of collecting the wounded and sick and taking proper care of them, in many cases they were killed or thrown into flames. Even sick patients were dragged out of hospital and shot.	This amounts to a breach of Article 3(2) of the Geneva Convention of 1949.
12. Bodies of dead and living persons were piled together and then the soldiers poured petrol and set them alight. There are several cases when Bengalis were buried alive. Instead of adequate funeral arrangements, dead bodies were dumped into mass graves or thrown into rivers, wells and ponds. Even road	These acts amount to violations of the customary rule of international law that dead bodies shall not be mutilated but shall be collected and buried or cremated; Articles 15 and 17 of the relevant Geneva Convention of 1949, read along with resolution 2677 (XXV).

19

Nature of the Charges or Allegations	*Infringements of International Legal Norms*
barricades were erected with dead bodies.	
13. Religious convictions and practices of Moslems, Hindus, Christians and Buddhists were not respected. Moslem priests and devout Moslems were shot. Soldiers refused to allow removal of the decomposing bodies despite the Moslem belief in prompt burial. Funeral requirements according to religious rites were denied. Cremation according to Hindu religious rites were denied. Mosques and Hindu temples were bombed and Buddhist monasteries and Christian churches were attacked and valuable possessions of the monasteries looted.	These acts amount to crimes under Article 6(b) of the Nuremberg Charter read with Articles 25, 46 and 56 of Hague Convention (IV).
14. Detention camps were set up inside military cantonments of Dacca, Chittagong, Jessore and Comilla where thousands of Bengalis, suspected sympathisers of Awami League, journalists and students, wives and children of the members of the liberation forces— were being held in terrible conditions. These were civilian prisoners living in terror of their lives and in 'sub-human' conditions with inadequate food and drinking water and no washing or sanitary facilities.	These amount to crimes under Article 6 of the Nuremberg Charter read with the Nuremberg Judgment relating to the treatment of prisoners in the concentration camps in Germany before extermination. This also amounts to a violation of the humanitarian principles in the Geneva Convention of 1949 relating to prisoners of war, read along with resolutions 2676 (XXV) and 2677 (XXV) of 9 December 1970, applicable *mutatis mutandis* to non-combatant or civilian prisoners in an armed conflict.
15. Many orphaned Bengali children were taken away to West Pakistan or committed to the custody of the supporters of the military regime to make them immune from the influence of Bengali culture.	If such transfers took place on any significant scale, this may amount to genocide within Article II(E) of the Genocide Convention, viz. forcible transfer of children of one group to another, as it was in pursuance of an intent to destroy in part the Bengali people.
16. The extent of devastation is an indication of the punitive measures involved in the military operations. Punitive measures were also taken after the withdrawal of the resistance forces. Whether directed against the general populace or particular elements, the object was	This offends Article 3 of the Geneva Convention of 1949 which protects persons taking no active part in the hostilities, from violence and inhumane treatment; Article 33 which prohibits collective penalties and likewise all measures of intimidation or terrorism. This is contrary to principle (7) of the

Nature of the Charges or Allegations	Infringements of International Legal Norms
to foster fear among the population at large. Evidence on this point can be found, among others, in the report of the World Bank special mission and the eyewitness account of its economic member Mr. Henrik van der Heijden.	General Assembly resolution 2675 (XXV) which provides that civilian populations or individual members thereof should not be the object of reprisals. This also offends Article 50 of the Hague Convention (IV).
17. As a result of the devastating Army operations and large-scale destruction of civilian dwellings, thousands of Bengalis have become homeless, destitute and vagrants, facing starvation and death, and undergoing humiliating and degrading treatment.	In so far as the military operations were undertaken in pursuance of a common plan or conspiracy to destory a substantial part of the Bengali people, the impugned acts would amount to 'genocide' within Article II(C) of the Genocide Convention. They also offend Article 3(1) (c) of the Geneva Convention of 1949.
18. As a result of the Army operations, and a deliberate policy of terror and persecution, ten million Bengalis had to flee East Bengal and take shelter in India as evacuees and destitutes.	In so far as this was directly a consequence of a common plan or conspiracy to destroy a substantial part of the Bengali people and the policies executed in pursuance thereof, the impugned acts amount to genocide within Article II(B) and (C). They also offend the humanitarian principles embodied in Article I(b) of the Convention of 1968, viz. eviction by armed attack or occupation and inhuman acts resulting from racial policies, and the crime of genocide, are crimes against humanity.
19. The follow-up military actions viz. 'cleansing process' and 'rehabilitation effort' include, among others, listing of suspects of all supporters and sympathizers of Awami League, Gestapolike pick-up of suspects, elimination of suspects in the black list, and imprisonment or dismissal from employment of the suspects in the grey list, transfer of civil servants in the grey list to West Pakistan, large-scale dismissal of Bengali employees and workers and in many cases replacement thereof by people from West Pakistan.	The impugned acts amount to crimes against humanity within Article 6(c) of the Nuremberg Charter, viz. murder, extermination, enslavement, deportation and persecution on political grounds, of the Bengali people. They are also crimes under the Genocide Convention.
20. The overall picture from the evidence discloses the fundamental	Contemporary norms of self-determination as laid down in the Declaration on

Nature of the Charges or Allegations	*Infringements of International Legal Norms*
objective of the military operations: the suppression of the right to self-determination of the Bengali people by ruthless military operations, and by a reign of terror and persecution. All political opposition was intended to be stifled to ensure a status of subordination or colonial status for East Bengal in relation to West Pakistan.	Principles of International Law adopted by the General Assembly in resolution 2625 (XXV) make it the duty of a non-representative government to refrain from forcible suppression of the movement for self-determination, and recognize the right of the people to resist such forcible action. Further, fundamental human rights (including the right to self-determination) are applicable to all situations of armed conflict under principle (1) of resolution 2675 (XXV). Therefore, recourse to military action by the non-representative government in Pakistan was illegal in international law. The impugned acts also amount to crimes against humanity within Article 6(c) of the Nuremberg Charter as interpreted by the Nuremberg Judgment. The murder of political opponents, a policy of terror with a view to stifling all resistance, 'a systematic rule of violence, brutality and terror', 'consistent and systematic inhumanity' will be considered as crimes against humanity in terms of the principles laid down in the Nuremberg Judgment, and genocidal acts within Article II of the Genocide Convention.

CHAPTER FOUR

THE EMERGENCE OF BANGLADESH

Introduction

From 26 March 1971 when the People's Republic of Bangladesh is deemed to have come into being till 16 December 1971 when liberated Dacca became the 'free capital of a free country', any analysis of events will show that the predominant common legal test of recognition of statehood or recognition of a government was fully satisfied in the instant case. The common test is effectiveness of governmental authority evidenced by popular support freely expressed. It is an acknowledged fact that the men who proclaimed the birth of the new State, formed the new government, led and won the nine-month war of liberation were, and still are, accredited leaders of the people of Bangladesh. By and large, the entire nation responded to the call of their leaders and participated in the national struggle that culminated in a complete victory. Popular leadership and popular support therefore provided the infrastructure of the new State and its government from the very inception.

A brief analysis of the events between 25 March and 16 December 1971 will be relevant for three purposes: first, for a brief historical picture of the birth and progress of the new State and its government; second, for appreciation of the first successful war of liberation by a non-aligned people during the regime of the United Nations Charter and third, for an objective assessment of the period from which the government of the new State can be said to have become entitled to international recognition by compliance with the traditional test of territorial control.

Proclamation of Independence

The Proclamation of Independence Order of 10 April 1971,[1] issued from Mujibnagar, Bangladesh, and operative retrospectively from 26 March 1971, provides as follows:

> Whereas free elections were held in Bangladesh from 7th December, 1970 to 17th January, 1971, to elect representatives for the purpose of framing a Constitution, and whereas at these

[1] For text see *Bangla Desh Documents* (External Affairs Ministry, New Delhi), September 1971, pp. 281-2; *The Sunday Standard*, 18 April, 1971.

elections the people of Bangladesh elected 167 out of 169 representatives belonging to the Awami League, and whereas Gen. Yahya Khan summoned the elected representatives of the people to meet on 3 March 1971 for the purpose of framing a Constitution, and whereas the Assembly so summoned was arbitrarily and illegally postponed for an indefinite period, and whereas instead of fulfilling their promise and while still conferring with the representatives of the people of Bangladesh, Pakistan authorities declared an unjust and treacherous war, and

Whereas in the facts and circumstances of such treacherous conduct *Bangabandhu Sheik Mujibur Rahman,* the undisputed leader of 75 million people of Bangladesh, in due fulfilment of the legitimate right of self-determination of the people of Bangladesh, *duly made declaration of independence at Dacca on March 26, 1971,* and integrity of Bangladesh, and whereas in the conduct of a ruthless and savage war the Pakistani authorities committed and are still committing numerous acts of genocide and unprecedented tortures, amongst others on the civilian and unarmed people of Bangladesh, and whereas the Pakistan Government by levying an unjust war and committing genocide and by other repressive measures made it impossible for the elected representatives of the people of Bangladesh to meet and frame a Constitution, and give to themselves a government and whereas the people of Bangladesh by their heroism, bravery and revolutionary fervour have *established effective control over the territories of Bangladesh,* we the elected representatives of the people of Bangladesh, as honour bound by the mandate given to us by the people of Bangladesh whose will is supreme duly constituted ourselves into a Constituent Assembly, and having held mutual consultations, and in order to ensure for the people of Bangladesh equality, human dignity and social justice, *declare and constitute Bangladesh* to be sovereign People's Republic and thereby *confirm the declaration of independence* already made by *Bangabandhu Sheikh Mujibur Rahman,* and

Do hereby confirm and resolve that till such time as a Constitution is framed, *Bangabandhu* Sheikh Mujibur Rahman shall be the *President* of the Republic and that Syed Nazrul Islam shall be the Vice-President of the Republic and that the President shall be the Supreme Commander of all the armed forces of the Republic, shall exercise all the executive and legislative powers of the Republic including the power to grant pardon, shall have the power to appoint a Prime Minister and such other Ministers as he considers necessary, shall have the power to levy taxes and expend monies, shall have the power to summon and adjourn the Constituent Assembly, and do all other things that may be necessary to give to the people of Bangladesh an orderly and just government.

We the elected representatives of the people of Bangladesh do further resolve that in the event of there being no President or the President being unable to enter upon his office or being unable to exercise his powers and duties due to any other reason whatsoever, the *Vice-President* shall have and *exercise all the powers*, duties and responsibilities herein conferred on the President. We further resolve that we *undertake to observe* and give effect to all duties and obligations devolved upon us as a member of the family of nations and by the *Charter of the United Nations*. We further resolve that this proclamation of independence shall be deemed to have come into effect since 26th day of March, 1971.

We further resolve that to give effect to this our resolution, we authorise and appoint Prof. M. Yusuf Ali, our duly constituted potentiary to give to the President and Vice-President oaths of office. (emphasis added)

The Government of Bangladesh:
26 March to 15 December 1971

Mr Tajuddin Ahmed, who was duly appointed Prime Minister by the Acting President, Syed Nazrul Islam, made a broadcast to the nation from *Swadhin Bangladesh Betar Kendra* on 11 April 1971 in which he announced his government's plan for conducting the war of liberation and invited the World Press, diplomatic and political observers 'to tour the liberated areas and witness the reality of a free Bangladesh', the world's eighth largest country. He referred to the 'epic resistance' of his people 'against the colonial army of occupation from West Pakistan', called upon his people to 'join the liberation struggle' and to put their services at the disposal of the Government of Bangladesh. 'There should be no collaboration with the army of occupation'. The Prime Minister said: 'There can be *no doubt* about the *outcome of the final struggle*. Victory is ours, armed by our own courage and sacrifice. This is now to be gradually realized by the enemy. They thought that it would be an easy victory and that Bengalis would be quickly intimidated by the sight of modern weapons. That we should withstand their murderous attack and now fight back has upset their well-laid plans.'[2] (emphasis added)

A Press report on 14 April 1971 announced the names of three other Ministers of Mr Tajuddin Ahmed's Cabinet: Mr Khondakar

---

[2] For text of the speech, see *Bangladesh Documents* (External Affairs Ministry, New Delhi), September 1971, pp. 282-6.

Moshtaque Ahmed, Mr A. H. M. Kamaruzzaman and Mr Mansur Ali.[3] The Bangladesh Government also appealed to India and 'other democratic countries of the world to take note of the formation of the government and recognize it and establish diplomatic relations'.

At a largely attended public meeting held at Mujibnagar on 17 April 1971 at which were present about fifty foreign journalists, the birth of the new State and the inauguration of its government were publicly proclaimed, and the Prime Minister declared that *his government's writ ran through 90 per cent of the territory, except for the cantonments and a few administrative headquarters which were being held by the Pakistan Army*. The Acting President pointed out that their struggle was for the political, cultural and economic emancipation of the people of Bangladesh as well as for their very existence and 'win we must today, tomorrow or the day after'. The Prime Minister regretted that the arms secured by the Pakistan Government from foreign countries were being used against the unarmed people of Bangladesh; he appealed for recognition of his government and arms assistance from foreign countries.[4] In a statement issued on 17 April 1971 after the inauguration of the new government, the Prime Minister said:

> Bangladesh is at war.   It has been given no choice but to secure its *right of self-determination through a national liberation struggle* against the *colonial* oppression of West Pakistan... *Pakistan is now dead and buried under a mountain of corpses.* The hundreds and thousands of people murdered by the army in Bangladesh will set an impenetrable barrier between West Pakistan and the people of Bangladesh. By resorting to *preplanned genocide*, Yahya must have known that he was digging Pakistan's grave. The subsequent massacres perpetrated on his orders by his licensed killers on the people were not designed to preserve the unity of a nation. They were acts of social slaughter and sadism devoid of even the elements of humanity. Professional soldiers, on orders, violated their code of military honour and were seen as beasts of prey, indulged in an orgy of murder, rape, loot, and destruction unequalled in the annals of civilization. These acts indicated that the concept of two countries is already deeply rooted in the minds of Yahya and his associates who would not dare commit such atrocities on their own countrymen... They ('those great powers who chose to ignore this largest single act of genocide since the days of Belsen and Auschwitz') must realize that Pakistan is dead, murdered by

[3] *The Statesman*, Calcutta, 14 April, 1971.
[4] *The Sunday Statesman*, New Delhi, 18 April 1971.

Yahya—and the *independent Bangladesh is a reality* sustained by the indestructible will and courage of 75 million Bengalis who are daily nurturing the roots of this new nationhood with their blood. No power on earth can unmake this new nation and sooner or later both big and small powers will have to accept it into the world fraternity. It is, therefore, in the interest of politics as much as of humanity, for *the big powers to put* their full *pressure on Yahya* to cage his killers and bring them back to West Pakistan... We now *appeal* to the *nations of the world for recognition and assistance*, both material and moral, in our struggle for nationhood. *Every day this is delayed a thousand lives are lost and most of Bangladesh's vital assets are destroyed.* In the name of humanity act now and earn our undying friendship. This we now present to the world as a Case of the people of Bangladesh. No nation has a greater right to recognition, no people have fought harder for this right.[5] (emphasis added)

From its embryonic stage, and despite severe handicaps, the Government of Bangladesh began to acquire several attributes of a regular governmental organization—both civil and military. The organization of the Mukti Bahini (liberation forces) became its principal task.

Mukti Bahini and the War of Liberation
Organizational set-up

The Mukti Bahini was composed of thousands of young men from every walk of life in Bangladesh—experienced soldiers and para-military forces, students and teachers, workers and peasants—completely dedicated to the cause of liberation of their country and fully convinced that there was no alternative but to win the war of survival. They had seen and endured so much suffering that to them life without freedom was meaningless. From the beginning they seemed to have responded to the spirit of resistance outlined for them by Andre Malraux, the eminent French writer and formerly General de Gaulle's Minister of Culture: 'East Bengal is not defending a political system, it is defending its life. It must answer like Vietnam: If we must die, we will die, but this will cost you so much that you will end up by going away.'[6]

In due course history will doubtless record the story of the epic

[5] Statement of the Prime Minister, Mr Tajuddin Ahmed, circulated by the Government of Bagladesh and also reproduced in *Bangladesh Documents,* op. cit., pp. 291-8.
[6] Malraux's letter to J. P. Narayan, *The Statesman,* Calcutta, 11 September 1971.

struggle and indomitable courage of the liberation forces of Bangladesh. I have neither the qualifications nor the pretension even to try to attempt the task of a military historian in respect of a nine-month war only recently terminated. Nevertheless since some appreciation of the progress and achievements of the liberation forces is relevant to the issues discussed in the book, I have made a modest attempt to relate briefly the story of the Mukti Bahini. Much of the data comes from contemporary reports in newspapers and journals, war bulletins of the Bangladesh Government, as also from my personal notes compiled from my periodic visits to the training camps and frequent contacts with several Mukti Bahini youths and Awami League leaders.

India's Prime Minister, Mrs Indira Gandhi, told the Lok Sabha on 6 December 1971: 'The valiant struggle of the people of Bangladesh in the face of tremendous odds has opened a new chapter of heroism in the history of freedom movements... The East Pakistan Rifles and the East Bengal Regiment became the Mukti Bahini which was joined by thousands of young East Bengalis determined to sacrifice their lives for freedom and the right to fashion their future. The unity, determination and courage with which the entire population of Bangladesh is fighting has been recorded by the entire world Press.'[7]

The Mukti Bahini, originally known as Mukti Fauj, came into existence spontaneously on the night of 25-26 March 1971 when it became clear that the Pakistani Army was launching a war of genocide to suppress the self-determination of the Bengali people, sparing not even the police and servicemen. Colonel Osmani told Mr Khushwant Singh: 'If the Pakistanis had only limited their action against selected politicians, Bengalis in the army and the police might have stayed neutral. It was only when information got around that the Pakistani Army was out to kill Bengali intellectuals and servicemen as well that we revolted to a man. The Mukti Bahini was manufactured overnight by the Pakistani Army.' Since senior Bengali officers were either transferred to West Pakistan or assigned non-operational jobs some weeks prior to the army crackdown, it was the junior officers like Major Usman, Major Khaled Musharraff and Major Zia who led the revolt. Bengali soldiers and policemen rallied round the young officers and within a few days they had an army of about 10,000 trained men. Colonel Osmani, elected to the National Assembly on a ticket of the Awami League, became their Commander-in-Chief.[8]

[7] *The Statesman*, Calcutta, 7 December 1971.

[8] Khushwant Singh, 'The Freedom Fighters of Bangla Desh': *Illustrated Weekly of India*, 19 December 1971, pp. 21-2.

Composed of both men and women, Muslims and Hindus, the Mukti Bahini consisted of four main groups:

(i) Regular troops comprising officers and men from the former East Bengal Regiment.

(ii) Members of the East Pakistan Rifles, a para-military force, trained as frontier guards; the Police; Ansars and Mujahids, trained as home guards to maintain peace in the cities. About 10,000 of these men belonging to the first two categories survived the Pakistani Army action of 25 March and they formed the hard core of fighters of the Mukti Bahini.

(iii) Volunteers recruited by the Mukti Bahini comprising students and young men from every walk of life. A majority of this group consisted of boys between 15 and 20 years of age from high schools or universities. Besides, factory workers, office clerks, peasants and villagers volunteered in thousands and it became virtually impossible to accommodate all of them due to lack of resources and amenities. In this group one could find people with different political ideologies but united in their determination to win the war of liberation.

(iv) The fourth group, known as the Mujib Bahini, consisted of eminent student leaders and their followers. They were intensely patriotic young men wholly dedicated to upholding and implementing the idealism of Sheikh Mujib. To them Sheikh Mujib was not only a person, but a spiritual symbol, the manifestation of an idealism, a political philosophy that in due course was destined to travel beyond the borders of Bangladesh. This idealism came to be known as Mujib-bad.

The Mujib Bahini, the militant section of the student community, was the political armed cadre of the Chhatra League or the Students' League, which again was the students' wing of the Awami League. It was the student community in Bangladesh which first raised the slogan for independence and burnt the Pakistani flag. The Mujib Bahini was successor to the Bengal Liberation Front which was formed in March 1971 to wage an armed struggle against the Pakistani army of occupation. To them the independence of Bengal would remain somewhat incomplete till the Bangabandhu was released to lead the new nation. During the war of liberation, the Mujib Bahini forces went through an arduous and rigorous training course, accomplished themselves in the technique of using sophisticated weapons, and added considerably to the strength and success of the liberation forces.

This group was led by well-known student and youth leaders like Mr Nur-e-Alam Syddiquee (President, Students' League), Mr Shahjahan Siraj (General Secretary, Students' League), Mr A. S. M. Abdur Rob (Vice-President, Dacca University Students' Union),

Mr Abdul Kuddus (Makhan) (General Secretary, Dacca University Students' Union), Mr Fazlul Haq (Moni), Mr Sirajul Alam Khan, Mr Abdur Razzaque (President, Awami League Volunteer Corps) and Mr Tofail Ahmed, a former President of the Students' League and an Awami League MNA elect. The first four were the top leaders of the powerful Bangladesh Central Students' Action Committee.

Although the training period varied with the exigencies of the situation and depended upon the tasks assigned, normally the limit was a period of six months. The location of the training centres was necessarily kept secret but there were many of them along the borders between Bangladesh and India. In these training centres, illiterate village youth from the peasantry clad in vests and tucked up *lungis* mingled happily with young men from urban areas in terylene shirts and bellbottomed jeans and jointly participated in parades and drills based on command words in English. The eldest son of the President of Bangladesh, Kamal (who on completion of his training became a Lieutenant of the Mukti Bahini) and the offspring of a poor peasant were all treated alike. Many of these village youths, trained by the Mukti Bahini, had courageously faced the Pakistanis in the front line during the closing phase of the liberation movement and it was these unsophisticated young men whom Captain Huda had led to the successful liberation of Kaligunj.[9]

By the end of November 1971, according to Major M. A. Zalil, Commander of Sector 9, the Mukti Bahini had already a strength of 150,000 men and the number was swelling by hundreds everyday: 'We are having a hard time in equipping and clothing them properly.'[10]

The change of nomenclature from the Urdu word 'Fauj' to the Bengali word 'Bahini' two months after its birth was indicative of the expansion of a purely land-based guerrilla army into one with armed boats operating in rivers, frogmen who began to sink Pakistani ships with limpet mines, and eventually a proper Air Force. Group Captain Khondarkar was appointed Air Marshal of the Bangladesh Air Force which had a number of trained pilots, although at the material time there were no aircraft or an air base.[11] The naval wing of the Mukti Bahini, however, achieved great distinction.

The *Newsweek* of 27 December 1971 said that 'considering the recent performance of the Mukti Bahini guerrillas', 'the reputation' that the Bengalis were 'more adept at talking... than at fighting' is 'perhaps undeserved'. Moazzam Ahmed Chaudhury of Sylhet

[9] *The Statesman*, Calcutta, 3 December 1971.

[10] *Ibid.*

[11] Khushwant Singh, op. cit., p. 23.

explained to Mr Khushwant Singh how the youth of Bangladesh 'acquired the iron in their souls'. 'You know we are a peace-loving people. It is the savagery of these Pathans, Bilochis (from Baluchistan) and Punjabis that turned us into fighting men. They did not even spare our women and children. Even a timid animal will turn round to protect its mate and its young.' Again, Colonel Osmani told Mr Singh: 'Tell those American friends of yours that what the Pakistani Army did to our people on the night of the 25th and 26th March were worse than a hundred My Lais. We will not rest till we have totally exterminated them. Their corpses will rot in Bangladesh; we'll send their ghosts to West Pakistan.'[12]

The emotional involvement of the liberation forces was perfected by an intensive and arduous training that accounted for its successful operational skill. Under the guidance of Colonel Osmani, the commanders of the Mukti Bahini displayed remarkable leadership in organizing and training the liberation forces, in planning and coordinating the military strategy and in conducting commando operations, guerrilla and positional warfare.

The moral and political leadership of the Mukti Bahini was primarily provided by the leaders and intellectuals of the Awami League, and by hundreds of teachers from universities and colleges in Bangladesh. One instance will suffice. Two distinguished teachers of Bangladesh, Professor Mazharul Islam, M.A. (Dacca), Ph. D. (Rajshahi), Ph.D. (Indiana), F.R.A.S. (London), and Mr Abu Sayeed, formerly of Rajshahi University and an MNA elect, in discharge of the duties assigned by the Bangladesh Government, visited the liberated areas adjoining Jalangi and Shikarpur between 1 and 10 August 1971. Every day they talked to the freedom fighters, explained the political philosophy and the implications of the war of liberation, prepared them psychologically for the tasks ahead, instructed them about guerrilla tactics and sent off groups of freedom fighters, each group consisting of 30 to 50 young men, to the operational fronts inside Bangladesh. The freedom fighters were given hand-grenades, dynamites, LMG, ·303 rifles and sufficient ammunition. They were sent to operate in the interior villages of Rajshahi, Pabna and Kushtia districts. After a solemn promise of supreme sacrifice for the liberation of their motherland, the freedom fighters in disguise of farmers, small traders or village labourers left for their operational centres in country boats.[13]

---

[12] *Ibid.*, p. 23.

[13] This incident was narrated to the writer by Professor Islam. Professor Islam had earlier taken active part along with many of his pupils in the operations of the Mukti Bahini.

Operations of the Mukti Bahini: Five Phases:

The operations of the liberation forces can be conveniently, though somewhat arbitrarily, divided into five stages:

1. 26 March to end of May 1971: spontaneous but uncoordinated resistance.
2. June/July 1971; phase of organization and use of guerrilla tactics.
3. August/September 1971: stepping up of operations.
4. October to 3 December 1971: taste of success.
5. 3 December to 16 December 1971: joint operations with the Indian forces: partisans in the same cause.

1. During the first phase from 26 March to the end of May 1971, the resistance of the people to the onslaughts of the Pakistani Army was spontaneous but inevitably disorganized and uncoordinated. In the regions of Sylhet/Comilla, Chittagong/Noakhali, Mymensing/Tangail, the south-west region and north Bengal, many areas were liberated and the Pakistani troops in many places were compelled to take shelter within the limits of the cantonment areas.[14] The lack of organization, coordination and planning and insufficiency of arms and ammunition, however, made it impossible for the liberation forces to maintain their control of the liberated areas. It was an unequal battle between a determined but insufficiently equipped Mukti Bahini in its infancy, and the vastly superior armed forces of West Pakistan supported by sophisticated foreign weapons and ammunition. As a result, Pakistani forces soon regained control of towns, the main road and rail communication links. The military operations of the Pakistani forces against purely civilian areas were completely disproportionate to the threat presented by a disorganized, popular and essentially civilian resistance, and disclosed a pattern of brutality which has since shocked the conscience of the world. The victory during the first round did not however ensure the ultimate victory of the Pakistani forces in an area ideally suited for guerrilla warfare and where the technique of resistance was soon to be transformed into guerrilla tactics after the initial error of direct confrontation with the armed forces of West Pakistan. As early as on 2 April 1971, Mervyn Jones wrote in the *New Statesman,* London: 'Certainly, though the army may have won the first round by sheer brutality, maintaining a detested suzerainty over 73 million people isn't like sending the police to Anguilla. Bengal has no forests or mountains

---

[14] See the English translation of an address by Mr Tajuddin Ahmed, Prime Minister, broadcast by *Swadhin Bangla Betar Kendra* on 11 April 1971, *Bangladesh Documents* (External Affairs Ministry, New Delhi), September 1971, pp. 282-6.

except on its eastern borders; but in its odd way it is a fine guerrilla country.'

The reason for the transformation from conventional to guerrilla warfare was explained by Colonel Osmani: 'In the earlier stages, I trained my men along conventional army lines and fought traditional style battles. We hoped foreign powers would intervene, stop the unequal fight and tell the Pakistanis to get the hell out of Bangla Desh. When that did not happen and the Pakistanis brought in four and a half divisions (80,000 men) equipped with tanks, heavy guns and bombers, I decided to change my tactics. Early last May, I reorganized my forces into decentralized guerrilla bands and changed the technique of fighting from pitched battles to commando type ambush. We had to concede some ground but we succeeded in forcing our enemy to scatter his forces on a vast, hostile countryside. We cut his lines of communication, we harass him all the time. We kill over a hundred a day; they take plane loads of coffins every day to West Pakistan.'[15]

2. During the second phase, in June/July, the freedom fighters not only reorganized themselves and worked out a well-coordinated plan, the Mukti Bahini became a force to be reckoned with which the Pakistani forces were finding increasingly difficult to subdue. The Mukti Bahini during this period emerged as an organized, cohesive force divided mainly into three categories: (i) regular troops consisting of officers and men from the former East Bengal Regiment; (ii) sector troops comprising mainly of para-military forces like the East Pakistan Rifles; and (iii) guerrilla bands consisting of students and young men from every walk of life and efficiently trained in the tactics of guerrilla warfare. The activities of all the three groups were coordinated under a central command. A workable communication system linking action areas with their respective sector commands was set up. Each command unit was now equipped with its political wing whose task was to maintain contact with the people and to make them understand the requirements of a war of liberation. During this period trained commando groups operated from border areas and inflicted increasingly heavy casualties on the enemy, while the guerrillas, operating from within the civilian population, caused increasing harassment to the occupation forces.

The operation of the liberation forces was being conducted through several sectors: the Rangpur-Dinajpur-Rajshahi sector; the Dacca-Comilla-Chittagong sector; the Mymensingh-Sylhet sector; and the Kushtia-Jessore-Khulna sector; each sector having several sub-sectors. By this time, the strength of the Mukti Bahini exceeded 50,000

[15] Khushwant Singh, 'The Freedom Fighters of Bangla Desh', *Illustrated Weekly of India*, 19 December 1971, p. 40.

men with still larger numbers under training in various camps in Bangladesh.[16] The Mukti Bahini fought the war mainly with arms and ammunition captured in ambushes on Pakistani troops or arms which the former officers of the EBR and EPR brought along with them. About the sources of weapons, Colonel Osmani had said:[17] 'Soldiers and policemen brought them when they came over to the liberation side; others we captured from the enemy. We also buy them from friendly sources by money sent over by Bengali communities settled in foreign lands.' Among numerous instances of the capture of arms and ammunition reported in the Press, one can refer to the recovery of a large number of Pakistani arms and ammunition at Kaligunj which included 4 rocket launchers, 30 rocket shells, 650 pieces of mortar bombs, 22,000 rounds of ·303 ammunition, 12 machine-guns, besides 6 guns and speed boats.[18] Indian assistance to the liberation forces mainly consisted of moral support but very little material assistance. In fact, the denial of material assistance by India was a serious general grievance of the liberation forces.

Notable successes resulting from the execution of guerrilla tactics were achieved: frequent raids at Pakistani Army positions and the killing of Pakistani troops, the blasting of bridges and culverts, the sinking of ships after the explosion of mines laid out by frogmen, the destruction of rivercraft and gunboats, the disruption of rail and road communications and tele-communication links, frequent ambushes of Pakistani troops, to name a few. The important factors which accounted for the success of guerrilla warfare in Vietnam were also present in East Bengal, namely, topography of the terrain and the support of the population. By the end of July, the diminishing control of Pakistan's military regime was confined to the main cities of Bangladesh while the writ of the Government of Bangladesh ran throughout the countryside. When asked how much of the territory of Bangladesh was under the control of the Government of Bangladesh, the then Foreign Minister, Mr Khondakar Moshtaque Ahmed observed: 'It is very difficult to be precise. Where the Pakistani Army is present physically they are in control. The rest is ours. At night all they control are the barracks they sleep in. Our boys avoid direct confrontation with them. They have tanks and airplanes. Our boys only rifles, hand-grenades, sten and machine-guns. As soon as we obtain heavy armour we shall take them on in the open field. It won't be very long.'[19]

---

[16] Various War bulletins of Bangladesh Forces HQ, Public Relations Department, June, July 1971. *The Statesman*, Calcutta, 22, 23 July 1971.

[17] Khushwant Singh, op. cit., p. 23.

[18] *The Statesman*, Calcutta, 3 December 1971.

[19] Khushwant Singh, op. cit., p. 41.

International observers have recorded the successful operations of the Mukti Bahini. Peter R. Cann wrote in the *Wall Street Journal,* New York, 23 July 1971: 'An Army rule is being challenged by Bengali guerrilla forces (Mukti Bahini or liberation army) that seem to have massive support among the Bengali population.' On 31 July 1971, the *Christian Science Monitor* commented in its editorial: 'Today, four months later, the Pakistani Army controls the main cities of Bengal but not the countryside. Resistance is increasing. The guerrillas have been able twice to knock out the power stations serving Dacca, the capital. They frequently cut the rail links from Dacca to the other cities. The occupying Punjabi (West Pakistan) Army faces precisely the same prospect in Bengal that the Thieu regime in South Vietnam faced back before massive American intervention—the prospect of a pacification programme stretching endlessly into the future.' *Newsweek* of 2 August 1971 pointed out: 'All over the country, the resistance is rapidly taking the earmarks of a classical guerrilla warfare. And East Pakistan is an ideal guerrilla terrain reminiscent of South Vietnam's Mekong Delta—a labyrinth of sunken paddies, jute fields and banana groves... Most important, however, is the fact that the rebels now seem to be winning what every guerrilla needs—the support of the populace.' *Time* Magazine of 2 August 1971 observed: 'Resistance fighters already control the countryside at night and much of it in the day time.' It also pointed out that young recruits of the Mukti Bahini, many of them students, were being trained to blend in with the peasants, who fed them, and served as lookouts, scouts and hit-and-run saboteurs.

3. The third phase (August/September, 1971) witnessed a rapid increase in the frequency and scale of the Mukti Bahini operations.[20] The Pakistani forces were considerably demoralized owing to the increasing number of casualties, widespread sabotage, the hostility of the entire population and terrorization of the Razakars and local collaborators by the Mukti Bahini, progressive disruption in communication links and a complete failure of counter-insurgency military action. The Pakistani forces trained in anti-guerrilla warfare found it impossible to succeed because of the absence of a political base to operate. The stratagem of terror was thoroughly inconsistent with counter-insurgency military measures designed to win over a hostile population.[21]

About the achievements of the Mukti Bahini, Colonel Osmani had

[20] The various war bulletins of Bangladesh Forces HQ, Public Relations Department, August, September 1971; also see, *The Statesman*, Calcutta, 18, 19, 21 September 1971.

[21] Hironmoy Karlekar, 'Mukti Bahini Offensive: Pak Strongholds Under Pressure.' *The Statesman*, Calcutta, 1 December 1971.

21

claimed: 'Up to the end of September, we had killed 25,000 Pakistani soldiers, sunk 21 ships, destroyed over 600 bridges and culverts and totally dislocated rail, road and river communication. You can check up for yourself. Few trains run in Bangla Desh and shipping in Chalna is non-existent. We will soon put Chittagong out of commission.'[22]

Vast areas were effectively liberated from the occupation forces. In one sector alone, the Mukti Bahini consolidated its position in an area of about 500 sq. miles, liberated earlier, comprising parts of Rangpur and Mymensingh districts. The Pakistani Army was pushed back from this area; and a Bangladesh cantonment was set up at Rahumari,[23] from where arms and ammunition were supplied for operations in Bogra, Sirajganj, Jamalpur , Jagannathganj, Mymensingh and Tangail. Another area of about 400 sq. miles was liberated with its headquarters at Tetulia.[24] These instances are only illustrative, not exhaustive.

While on the one hand there was progressive demoralization in the Pakistani camp, the unity and solidarity of the people of Bengal

[22] Khushwant Singh, 'The Freedom Fighters of Bangla Desh': *Illustrated Weekly of India*, 19 December 1971, p. 40. Although it is very difficult to verify the number of casualties on Pakistani side during this period, reports in the Western Press admitted that at least 2,500 Pakistani troops were killed and 10,000 were wounded. *Time*, 2 August 1971. The Indian Institute for Defence Studies and Analyses had put the figure of Pakistanis killed in Bangladesh at about 6,000. With regard to loss and damage inflicted, Khushwant Singh states: 'There are however two fairly reliable sources of information: Bengali crew (lascars) on ships coming from East Pakistan ports and correspondents of foreign radio, television and newspapers who have sporadically been allowed out of Dacca to see things for themselves. Lascars have confirmed stories of damaged ships. In the third week of September, the 16,000-ton British carrier *Teviot Bank* was seriously damaged at Chalna. Immediately thereafter another British vessel, the 10,000-ton *Chakdina* was hurt and forced to return for repairs to Calcutta. Lascars reported seeing two Pakistani steamers, a coastal tanker and many barges lying half submerged in Chalna. On Pakistan's Independence Day (August 14) the *Ohrmazo* was attacked in Chittagong.' Khushwant Sing, op. cit., p. 40. Also see, *The Statesman*, Calcutta, 4 January 1972, 'Mukti Bahini Played Vital Role in Bangladesh' which states, *inter alia*: 'A special group of guerrillas was trained up as naval commandos and in August blew up more than 50 large steamers and a number of ships at the same hour on the same day at Chittagong, Chandpur, Ashugunge, Narsinghdi and Narayangunge. In order to cripple the military rulers economically, the commandos burnt more than 200,000 bales of jute at different ports and destroyed a factory which manufactured fibre glass for gunboats. In order to terrorize collaborators, the gurrillas killed a former Governor, Abdul Monem Khan, a Vice-Chairman of the railway and about 600 'Peace Committee' members. They also killed Razakars and al-Badar and al-Shams men to stop their acting as enemy agents.'

[23] *The Statesman*, Calcutta, 18 September 1971.

[24] *The Statesman*, Calcutta, 20 October 1971.

behind the operations of the Mukti Bahini became still more pronounced. From the beginning of the struggle the political parties of Bangladesh had combined to support the Government of Bangladesh and the Mukti Bahini in the war of liberation. As early as on 20 April 1971, Professor Muzaffar Ahmed, President of the pro-Soviet National Awami Party, gave 'a clarion call to all the sons and daughters of Bangladesh to carry forward the armed struggle with renewed vigour and determination till its victory.'[25] On 22 April 1971, the revered elderly leader of Bangladesh, Maulana Abdul Hamid Khan Bhasani, leader of the pro-Chinese National Awami Party, appealed to his own people for complete unity and solidarity till victory was won. He said: 'I appeal to all the people of East Bengal, I appeal to the peasants, workers, blacksmiths, pottery workers, boatmen, weavers, persons engaged in cottage industries, students, traders, intelligentsia and service holders and others to forge a unity like steel... At the present moment, unity, mental strength and burning patriotism are most vital weapons. Our victory is certain. God hates oppressors and traitors. We will definitely get the blessings of Allah in our great struggle and we will establish a free sovereign happy and prosperous Bangla Desh in East Bengal.'[26] On 3 May 1971, the Central Committee of the Communist Party of East Pakistan (Bangladesh) in its communication to fraternal Communists and Workers' Parties said:[27] 'Judging from all the above facts, all democrats of the world should be fully convinced that the present struggle for the liberation of our motherland is a just struggle against native and foreign reactionaries who are enemies of humanity and peace. The defeat of these reactionaries in Bangla Desh will strengthen the forces of democracy and peace in the South-East Asia region.' Eventually, a significant step was taken on 9 September when a Consultative Committee of five major political parties—the Awami League, the National Awami Party (Bhasani), the National Awami Party (Muzaffar), the Communist Party of Bangladesh and the Bangladesh National Congress—was formed to ensure a sense of participation in the liberation struggle among all shades of people and opinion engaged in the freedom movement. This was an expression of total unity in leadership and rank and file in the struggle for national liberation.

4. During the fourth phase (October to 3 December 1971) one can find unmistakable indications of the eventual victory of the Mukti Bahini and the certainty of the ultimate defeat of the occupation

---

[25] *Bangladesh Documents* (External Affairs Ministry, New Delhi), September 1971, p. 298.
[26] *Ibid.*, pp. 303, 306.
[27] *Ibid.*, pp. 307, 317.

forces, *even without participation of the Indian armed forces.* During this period, instead of continuing to rely exclusively on guerrilla warfare and commando operations, the Mukti Bahini engaged the Pakistani units in important positional warfare. There was a judicious combination of commando operations, guerrilla and positional warfare. The strength of the Mukti Bahini increased enormously during this period; by the end of October about 100,000 Mukti Bahini forces were operating in Bangladesh and the Pakistani Army losses had risen to 189 per day.[28] In Dacca, a series of attacks on public buildings by more than 800 guerrillas were reported by a foreign correspondent.[29]

There were many other reports of increasing Mukti Bahini activities in the capital city of Dacca, the stronghold of the Pakistani Army, and their increasing impact on the morale of the Pakistani troops. On 9 October, a bomb exploded in the West Pakistan-controlled Habib Bank in central Dacca, killed five men and injured another thirteen. The next day, a few blocks away from the Habib Bank, a building housing the World Bank had one of its floors wrecked and a jute godown gutted.[30] A few of numerous other known incidents are: (a) the frequent disruption of power, water supply, etc.; (b) sinking of a steamer carrying Pakistani troops by the Mukti Bahini operators on the river Buriganga while it was proceeding from Sadaraghat in Dacca to the village of Jinjira during October. There were no Pakistani survivors; (c) Monem Khan, who was Governor of East Bengal for the longest period under the military regime of Ayub Khan, was killed by the Mukti Bahini operators early in October in his own home at Dacca not very far from the cantonment; (d) in October a bridge on the Asian Highway, 20 miles away from Dacca, was blown off by the Mukti Bahini operators and in the process a commander of the Mukti Bahini was killed. Again, bombs exploded in front of several banks, offices and markets and in the Motijheel area of Dacca in the month of October creating considerable panic and terror, and dislocation of normal trade and business; (e) in November, in the heart of Dacca, places like Green Road were being periodically controlled by the liberation forces and it became extremely difficult for the Pakistani troops to enter the areas. In front of New Market one evening a dozen Pakistani troops were killed by the guerrillas. Several Pakistani soldiers were killed early in November in their camps inside the Jehangirnagar University campus in Shavar, about 15 to 20 miles away from Dacca.

[28] Reported in the *Sunday Times,* London, from its correspondent in Bangladesh, carried by *The Statesman,* Calcutta, 2 November 1971.
[29] *Ibid.*
[30] Khushwant Singh, op. cit., p. 40.

On the subject of dislocation of trade, Khushwant Singh has said: "Bangladesh observers in India assess that in peacetime, transport of goods was 38% by rail, 34% by road and 28% by river. Today rail and road is below 10% of the normal and river transport is completely dislocated. Jute which was East Pakistan's chief foreign-exchange earner is transported by coolies. Industrial production is down by 35% of the normal. Tobacco down by 40%. Eleven tea plantations near the border have closed down; others are producing 25% of the normal. All this is ascribed to the Mukti Bahini which has been paid a back-handed compliment by the *Pakistan Observer* of Dacca as 'a pitiless perpetrator of death and destruction... creating a sense of unreality with their hit-and-run raids and creating an atmosphere of chaos and uncertainty.' "[31]

The Statesman, Calcutta, of 13 November 1971, carried a map of East Bengal indicating the areas liberated by the Mukti Bahini, the areas where it was fighting for control and the areas which were still being held by the Pakistani Army. This indicated that West Pakistan's control decreased steadily as the liberation forces stepped up their guerrilla offensives. By then the Mukti Bahini was in virtual control of the upper reaches of the Padma river and very active in the delta region as well. The struggle was increasingly focussed on the vital 150 km stretch between the Faridpur and Agartala border and Dacca stood at the turbulent centre of this area.

To illustrate the mounting offensives by the Mukti Bahini during early November 1971, one may refer to *The Statesman* of 10 November 1971 which reveals that in a battle against the Pakistani forces the Mukti Bahini was maintaining its encirclement of Radhanagar for over a week. It overtook for a while Gowanighat in a frontal attack and captured Gourinagar in a dawn attack. Pakistani forces were driven out of Barni, Dakterbar and Duliargaon. In physical control of over 800 sq. km. in Kushtia district, the Mukti Bahini launched a fierce assault on the sub-divisional town of Meherpur, a well-fortified Pakistani bastion, gained control of 17 out of 22 border outposts in the district and liberated fresh areas around Jibannagar police station. In Jessore sector, the freedom fighters were active in Harinagar and Ghaziakhali areas, interfering with the movement of naval craft and gunboats. After a fresh offensive on 8 November on the west bank of river Mathabhanga, the Mukti Bahini gained control of extensive areas in Bamundihi and Gagni. In yet another sweep along the western side of river Bhairab, the liberation forces claimed Natuda, Ratanpur and Maniknagar.

Between the third week of November and 3 December, the opera-

---

[31] *Ibid.*, p. 41.

tions of the liberation forces were becoming so extensive and effective that their eventual success was almost assured though a decisive early victory still could not be predicted. By the end of November, extensive areas in Dinajpur, Kushtia, Khulna and Jessore were liberated by the Mukti Bahini; the encirclement of Sylhet was almost complete; a 4,000 sq. km. area in the Rangpur-Durgapur sector was fully liberated after grim encounters; strategic bridges were blown up in Dacca; increasingly successful operations were reported from Jessore, Dinajpur, Mymensingh, Noakhali, Kushtia and other areas. Pakistani authorities admitted the fall of Radhanagar and a three-pronged attack on Sylhet area, the withdrawal of Pakistani forces to Panchnagar in Dinajpur sector and shelling in the heart of Jessore town.[32] In the Mymensingh sector, the liberation forces were closing in on the Pakistani Army outpost at Kamalpur and its imminent fall was predicted; having consolidated their position around Feni, the freedom fighters launched an all-out attack on the strategic town of Noakhali and a fierce battle was in progress. Having gained control of Jibannagar police station in Kushtia district, the Mukti Bahini was moving fast towards the strategic town of Chuadanga; Pakistani Army positions at Natuda, Kapasdanga and Darsana were besieged from all sides.[33]

During the first three days of December, successful Mukti Bahini offensives were reported from all fronts of Bangladesh—the Sylhet, Noakhali, Mymensingh, Jessore, Dinajpur, Khulna, Kushtia and Chittagong sectors. The Bahini forces liberated vast areas in those sectors, intensified their attacks on Kamalpur, Feni and the strategic airbase at Shamsernagar, encircled the Pakistani positions in Akhaura, Ganganagar and Rajarkot in the Comilla district, launched a three-pronged frontal offensive on Pakistani strongholds from Brahmanbaria in the north to Akhaura in the south along the Dacca-Comilla-Mymensingh-Sylhet rail route and completed the encirclement of the Pakistani troops. Again, there was no alternative for the Pakistani troops but to get involved in a war of attrition in the Jessore sector. While the regular forces of the Mukti Bahini were confronting the Pakistanis at their positions outside the cantonment, others were getting at the rear of the forward positions of the Pakistanis trying to cut off their lines of communication.[34] By this time, it was reliably predicted that the crucial battle of Jessore was being decided in favour of the liberation forces. *Newsweek* of 6 December 1971 carried a report from its correspondent, Tony Clifton, which states: 'Indeed, many foreign military attaches in New Delhi predicted that

[32] See *The Statesman*, Calcutta, 27, 28, 29, 30 November and 1 December 1971.
[33] *The Statesman*, Calcutta, 1 December 1971.
[34] *The Statesman*, Calcutta, 2, 3 and 4 December 1971.

Jessore would fall to the Mukti Bahini by the end of this week—thus setting the scene for the proclamation of an independent Bangla Desh and, perhaps, a retaliatory declaration of war by Pakistan against India.'

Indeed, by the middle of November 1971, the comparatively favourable position of the Mukti Bahini was internationally acknowledged. *Newsweek* of 22 November 1971 records: 'From the moment last March that Pakistan's President Mohammed Yahya Khan unleashed a reign of terror against the Bengalis of East Pakistan, his army has been embroiled in a bloody—and losing—guerrilla war there. By now, the Bengali insurgents—known as the Mukti Bahini—claim a force of 100,000 soldiers and control roughly one-fourth countryside of East Pakistan. Last week, *Newsweek* Senior Editor Arnaud de Borchgrave travelled deep into guerrilla territory and filed this report: "... Already, Pakistan's superiority over the rebels in arms and equipment is dwindling... the guerrillas have continued week by week to expand their control over the countryside.' Government officials, civil servants and village leaders by the scores now work covertly with the rebels and, except at occasional river-crossing points, government troops are rarely seen outside the cities and towns. Most of the country is rebel territory by night and an ever larger area is rebel territory by day as well. And the government, with its order last week to impose collective fines on villages where guerrilla activity occurs, tacitly conceded its military control of East Pakistan is slipping. Yet, at the same time, the Army still tries to maintain the fiction that rebel activity is almost nil." '

The assistance of the Indian Armed Forces after this period undoubtedly contributed to the early termination of the war of liberation and a decisive victory which, in any event, would have been ultimately achieved by the Mukti Bahini had it fought the war alone. By the end of November, the strength of the Mukti Bahini not only equalled that of the Pakistani Army, but was progressively increasing. Well-fortified strongholds of the Pakistani Army in their cantonments at Moinamoti, Comilla, Dacca, Chittagong and Jessore were under increasing pressure. As a result of large-scale disruption of surface communications and guerrilla activities at ports against incoming vessels, the mobility of the Pakistani forces was being increasingly hampered and their plans seriously threatened. The Pakistani Army was bound to suffer defeat ultimately[35] but perhaps not before a further period of bitter and bloody fighting involving heavy casualties. To the Mukti Bahini, India's participation in the war came as

[35] Hironmoy Karlekar, 'Mukti Bahini Offensive—Pak Strongholds Under Pressure' *The Statesman*, Calcutta, 1 December 1971.

a 'windfall',[36] a sudden unexpected advantage, that hastened the liberation which otherwise would have been somewhat delayed.

5. During the last phase (3 December to 16 December 1971) a full-scale war broke out in the subcontinent after Pakistani aerial attacks at 5·30 p.m. on 3 December 1971. In a midnight broadcast to the nation, Mrs. Gandhi declared: 'Today, the war in Bangladesh has become a war on India.'[37] After that Indian troops moved in massive strength in all sectors in Bangladesh and in concert with the Mukti Bahini began to operate against the West Pakistani occupation forces. The IAF went into action and pounded Dacca and Jessore airfields in Bangladesh. The Indian Navy also organized a total blockade of the entire Bangladesh coast. The operations of the allied forces of Bangladesh and India were swift and decisive. Akhaura was captured on 5 December. While announcing recognition of the People's Republic of Bangladesh and the Government of Bangladesh on 6 December 1971, Mrs. Gandhi said: 'The people of Bangladesh battling for their very existence and the people of India fighting to defeat aggression now find themselves partisans in the same cause.'[38] On 7 December 1971, Jessore and Sylhet were completely liberated. On 8 December Comilla was liberated and the move to encircle Dacca commenced. One column of Indian troops, moving westward from Laksham, reached the outer defences of Chandpur and Daudkandi. With the liberation of Chandpur and Bhairab Bazar on 9 December, the allied forces held a commanding position on the Meghna river.

On 10 December, a formal agreement between India and Bangladesh was executed which provided that the armed forces of the two countries would act 'in full concert and co-operation' under a unified command and the commanders of the two forces would report periodically to their respective Prime Ministers.[39] On 10 December the allied forces crossed over to the western bank of the Meghna. On 11 December Mymensingh and Kushtia were liberated. It was reported that Major-General Farman Ali, military adviser to the civilian Government set up by the junta, bypassed the local commander and Islamabad and directly appealed to the U.N. Secretary-General to help pull out the Pakistani troops from Bangladesh. On 12 December, the allied forces were within 30 miles of Dacca. On 13 December Tangail was liberated, all escape routes from Dacca were sealed and the allied forces, moving with speed and precision from the north and east, were closing their ring around Dacca defences. On 14 December Indian troops were 10 to 15 km from Dacca. A part of the Pakistani

[36] *Newsweek*, 22 November 1971.
[37] *The Statesman*, Calcutta, 4 December 1971.
[38] *The Statesman*, Calcutta, 7 December 1971.
[39] *The Statesman*, Calcutta, 11 December 1971.

garrison led by a Brigadier surrendered at Joydevpur. Chittagong harbour was set ablaze by repeated pounding from aircraft and ships of the Indian Navy. On 15 December, in response to the final message from General Manekshaw, the Chief of the Indian Army, Lieut-General Niazi, Commander-in-Chief of the West Pakistan Forces in Bangladesh, requested a cease-fire and was given time till 9 a.m. on 16 December to surrender. On 16 December, the Pakistani Army surrendered unconditionally in Bangladesh.[40] The war of liberation was thus finally won.

During the last phase the allied forces of Bangladesh and India fought together 'as partisans in the same cause' and won it at record speed. Historians in future will no doubt collect and analyse the relevant evidence and assess the contribution made by the Mukti Bahini to the final victory in Bangladesh. In the meantime, available evidence has established that without the Mukti Bahini it would not have been possible to overrun the Pakistani troops so quickly. General Niazi of the Pakistan Army conceded the effectiveness of the Mukti Bahini when he said that Indian Army had an advantage over the Pakistani forces in 'the considerable help' provided by the Mukti Bahini. The Indian Army commanders in the Eastern sector including General Aurora paid warm tributes to the important role played by the Mukti Bahini during the last phase of the war of liberation in Bangladesh.[41]

Civil Administration: 25 March—15 December 1971

Apart from military operations, the Government of Bangladesh from its very inception made diligent efforts to implement the discipline of a civil administration, particularly in the liberated areas. Regular directives provided administrative guidelines to civil servants. The administrative apparatus at the headquarters functioned

[40] For a brief report on the progress of the war, see 'A Chronicle of Victory', *Hindusthan Standard*, 17 December 1971; The *Illustrated Weekly of India*, 16 January 1972, pp. 6-17.

[41] *The Statesman*, Calcutta, editorial 'The Struggle Before the War', 19 December 1971. Also see *The Statesman*, 30 December 1971: Major General G. Nagra of the Indian Army admitted that without the Mukti Bahini it would not have been possible to overrun the enemy so quickly. See *The Statesman* report 'Mukti Bahini Played a Vital Role in Bangladesh', 4 January 1972: 'The spade work done by the Mukti Bahini for months, particularly in the Dacca-Comilla-Mymensingh sector, was one of the major factors that had helped the allied forces to advance towards Dacca at a record speed. About 20,000 Mukti Bahini guerrillas were engaged in work of "softening-up" enemy bases deep inside Dacca, Noakhali, Comilla, Chittagong, South Mymensingh, South Sylhet, Madaripur sub-division of Faridpur. Again the heli-landing by Indian troops at Raipura and Narsinghdi—an operation which brought the Indian Army at Dacca's doorsteps—was largely made possible by the guerrillas as the landing areas were under their direct control.'

22

through various departments: Defence, General Administration, Relief and Rehabilitation, Home affairs including Food, Foreign Affairs, Law and Parliamentary Affairs, Cabinet Affairs, Finance, Health and Social Welfare, Information and Broadcasting, Planning Commission, etc.

Even during the early stages, the civil administration of the Bangladesh Government was duly established in the liberated areas. For instance, at Rahumari, a civil and police administration had been functioning without interruption since the middle of July 1971. A zonal administrator, police officers and circle officers maintained law and order and normal relations as were possible during a national struggle for liberation. Levies on jute, eggs and milk and local rates from weekly markets were collected by the civil officers of the local committees for meeting the expenses of civil administration and for feeding the freedom fighters. Primary schools and shops were opened and Bangladesh flags could be seen everywhere. There was no interference by the Mukti Bahini in the normal and regular administration by civilian officers.[42] In another liberated area of 400 sq. miles with headquarters at Tetulia, the town of Tetulia was policed by 26 men and the telephone network functioned normally and the administration was conducted under the overall supervision of a civil administrator.[43]

In almost all other liberated areas, civil administration was set up, e.g. Dahagram in north Rangpur, Panchagar in Dinajpur, Ramgarh in Chittagong, Rohonpur in Rajshahi and Pragpur in Kushtia. The pattern of administration was the same. Administrators, circle officers and police officers were regularly appointed by the Bangladesh Government and they functioned with complete cooperation from the local population. Hundreds of teachers at secondary and primary levels were appointed by the Bangladesh Government for the liberated areas. Schools, shops and weekly markets were functioning. A very significant achievement of the Bangladesh Government was the tremendous improvement in the law and order situation in the liberated areas under its control. There were hardly any thefts or other crimes. Normalcy was maintained not only in the liberated areas adjoining the Indian borders but also in areas deep inside Bangladesh such as Tangail district, Potuakhali district, and Banowarinagar-Faridpur, a police station in the Pabna district.

In foreign affairs, the activities of the Bangladesh Government, long before the liberation of Dacca, attracted much public attention. Bangladesh Missions were set up in Washington,

---

[42] For an account of the civil administration at Rahumari, see *The Statesman*, Calcutta, 18 September 1971.

[43] *The Statesman*, Calcutta, 2 October 1971.

New York, London, Sweden, Hongkong, Delhi and Calcutta. Many Bengali members of the diplomatic and consular services shifted their allegiance to the Government of Bangladesh. These included Pakistan's Ambassadors to Iraq and Philippines and the Deputy High Commissioner in Calcutta. The *Time* Magazine of 6 December 1971 estimated that some 130 Bengali diplomats defected from the Pakistani Missions around the world. Mr. Justice Abu Sayeed Chowdhury led a 16-member Bangladesh delegation to the twenty-sixth session of the United Nations General Assembly with a view to explaining unofficially to the representatives of the world community the case for independence of Bangladesh and for the recognition of its status. Strenuous efforts were made to arouse the conscience of the world for cessation of supplies of arms and ammunition to the Government of Pakistan and for recognition of the Government of Bangladesh.

Performance of the Bangladesh Government:
16-31 December 1971

Between the liberation of Dacca on 16 December and the end of the year, the Government of Bangladesh was firmly established all over the territory of Bangladesh and the authority of the rival claimant, Pakistan,[44] was completely destroyed. The Acting President, Syed Nazrul Islam, told a Press conference in Dacca on 29 December: 'Just within 10 days after the Pak soldiers' surrender, the law and order has been fully established, the rule of law is functioning and complete peace prevails throughout Bangladesh.'[45]

By the end of the year, a 9-member Cabinet[46] headed by the Prime Minister, Tajuddin Ahmed, was in complete control of the administration of the country. The restoration of law and order, the rehabilitation of the refugees and the programme of economic reconstruction, presented difficult but manageable problems, and the new government displayed its ability to face them with fortitude and courage.

Despite President Z. A. Bhutto's allegation to the members of the Security Council that there were 'revenge killings in Bangladesh,'[47] the fact remains that firm steps were taken by the Government of Bangladesh for the protection of the life and property of all residents irrespective of nationality. At the request of the Bangladesh authorities, the Indian troops during the first few days played an important role in the restoration of law and order. According to the Planning

[44] *Time* Magazine, 27 December 1971: 'At week's end, Bangladesh's Acting President, Syed Nazrul Islam, and his government were already settled in Dacca and Washington was stated to be considering recognition of the new nation.'
[45] *Hindusthan Standard*, 30 December 1971.
[46] *The Statesman*, Calcutta, 30 December 1971.
[47] *The Statesman*, Calcutta, 25 December 1971.

Cell of Bangladesh, normalcy in the country could be immediately restored by organizing defence parties at all levels from villages to districts and in the different wards in towns and municipal areas. The Cell had suggested that each village defence party should consist of 10 volunteers and these would be the basic units to be supervised by the district police.[48]

There were two formidable difficulties: first, the 40,000-strong police force of Bangladesh was severely reduced in strength on account of deliberate killings of Bengali policemen by the West Pakistani army during the preceding nine months. The administrative problem of transforming the disciplined members of the liberation forces into an organized civilian force could not be solved overnight. The Mukti Bahini, nevertheless, played an effective policing role in the initial stages and at the request of the Government of Bangladesh, the Indian Army also played its part in the preservation of law and order. Second, the atmosphere was charged with the accumulated grievances of the previous nine months and it was surcharged with the disclosure of the news of the planned massacre of the Bengali intelligentsia including teachers, writers, journalists, doctors and lawyers by the occupation forces or their henchmen on the eve of surrender. It was not an easy task to persuade the liberated victims of repression to exercise restraint. Nevertheless, the new government spared no efforts and succeeded in restraining people from taking the law into their own hands. Except for some stray incidents, there were no general reprisals against collaborators of the army of occupation including many non-Bengalis in Bangladesh. The new government repeatedly declared that the collaborators of the occupation forces who were responsible for war crimes and crimes against humanity would be rounded up and tried according to the law and the people themselves should not take the law into their own hands.[49]

[48] *The Statesman*, Calcutta, 24 December 1971.

[49] The Acting President said on 23 December that the Razakars and members of the al-Badar party who had killed many Bengali intellectuals would be tried and would be spared if found not guilty; there would be no witch-hunting in the process. The Prime Minister, Tajuddin Ahmed, said that those who had collaborated with the occupation army would be tried for the crimes by a tribunal: 'But do not take the law into your own hands'. A large number of persons including Razakars and members of the al-Badar and al-Shams suspected of criminal activities were rounded up by the police. The situation became more complicated because a large number of Bihari Muslims and other supporters of the army of occupation were fully armed by the military authorities before surrender. As a result, in some residential areas the restoration of law and order became difficult. At the same time, reports were pouring in that the safety and security of 400,000 Bengalis in West Pakistan were in danger. The Bangladesh Government requested the Red Cross organization to look after the interests of the Bengalis in West Pakistan and also promised to help the Red Cross to do relief work among the

It was in response to the improved situation that Mrs. Gandhi told a press conference in New Delhi on 31 December that since the Bangladesh Government was already in full control of the situation, the earlier fear that Indian troops might have to stay on in the interest of the safety of the non-Bengalis proved unfounded and accordingly, a large number of Indian troops had already been pulled out. Although a few reprisals against 'Bihari Muslims' had indeed taken place in the first few days after the liberation, it was strange, said Mrs. Gandhi, that the Western Press tended to blow some of those incidents out of proportion. There appeared to be a lack of a sense of proportion in judgment of acts of reprisal, and the situation was not viewed in perspective. Some sections of the Western Press were 'printing horrible pictures' of incidents relating to some twenty deaths while the annihilation of a million people earlier and the butchery of 280 intellectuals on the eve of the surrender seemed to have made no impact. On the whole, Mrs. Gandhi said, the people of Bangladesh had behaved with remarkable restraint after liberation considering what they had gone through.[50]

As a result of the progressive improvement of the law and order situation, the refugees started the return journey from India to Bangladesh immediately after the liberation of Dacca. The weekly international commentary in *Pravda*, Moscow, on 26 December 1971 said that the anxieties of the past weeks were gradually calming down in the last few days with the normalization of the situation in East Bengal and the beginning of the return of the East Bengal refugees who had fled to India because of the terror of the military regime of Pakistan. On 20 December 1971, *Time* magazine wrote: 'And so at week's end the streams of refugees who walked so long and so far to get to India began making the long journey back home to pick up the threads of their lives. For some there were happy reunions with their relatives and friends, for others tears and the bitter sense of loss for those who will never return. But there were new homes to be raised, new shrines to be built and a new nation to be formed. The land was there too, lush and green. "Man's history is waiting in patience for the triumph of the insulted man", Rabindranath Tagore, the Nobel-prize-winning Bengali poet, once wrote. Triumph he had but at a terrible price.'

non-Bengalis in the areas around Dacca. *Hindusthan Standard*, 25, 26 and 27 December 1971. *The Statesman*, Calcutta, 28 December 1971.

[50] *The Statesman*, Calcutta, 1 January 1972. One can perhaps refer in this context to the article captioned 'Vengeance After Victory' and the pictures printed in *Time* magazine of 3 January 1972, and the article captioned 'Birth Pangs of Bangladesh' with pictures printed in *Newsweek* of 3 January 1972. The incident involved alleged atrocities against four suspected Pakistani quislings witnessed by Western newsmen.

The Acting President of Bangladesh announced that his government had worked out a comprehensive plan for bringing back the refugees and for resettling them—a programme to which the Bangladesh Government was fully committed.[51] By the end of the year, according to official figures, since the surrender of the Pakistani Army in Bangladesh nearly 340,000 refugees had left West Bengal, Assam, Meghalaya and Tripura and crossed the border into Bangladesh. Of those, about 118,000 were from West Bengal. The refugee movement on a much wider scale under the Dispersals Scheme was to begin on 1 January 1972. On 30 December Mr. A. H. M. Kamaruzzaman, the Bangladesh Home and Rehabilitation Minister, visited the refugee camps near Calcutta and urged the inmates to go back to Bangladesh and assured them that the miscreants and collaborators who were responsible for their miseries were being rounded up and would be brought to trial. He said: 'You have stayed here for nine months taxing the resources of this great friendly nation. We have upset her economy badly. You should not stay here as evacuees but go back and take part in the national reconstruction.'[52] He assured the refugees that they would get back their property. He further said that the dispersal of refugees would be completed by 25 March 1972. On the last day of the year, Mrs. Gandhi expressed the hope that most of the refugees would return home by the end of February 1972. Although at an earlier stage, a great majority of them did not wish to go back partly because of the fear of being killed and partly because they could not foresee the liberation, there was no reason for them to stay on now as their country had been liberated.[53]

It was announced that the members of the National Assembly and Provincial Assembly of Bangladesh elected during the December 1970 elections would form a Constituent Assembly and would frame the constitution for the People's Republic of Bangladesh. In the December elections 169 M.N.A.s and 288 M.P.A.s were elected in Bangladesh, a number of whom were killed by the Pakistani Army during the period of occupation. Re-elections would be necessary in constituencies where seats had become vacant. The task of framing a constitution would not be a difficult matter and could be completed in about a month's time.[54] The Constituent Assembly was expected to

---

[51] *Hindusthan Standard*, 29 December 1971.

[52] *The Statesman*, Calcutta, 31 December 1971; *Hindusthan Standard*, 31 December 1971.

[53] *The Statesman*, Calcutta, 1 January 1972.

[54] The statement of Abdus Samad Azad, the then Political Adviser to the Government of Bangladesh who since became the Foreign Minister; *The Statesman*, Calcutta, 28 December 1971.

finalize the constitution emphasizing the three fundamental concepts of democracy, socialism and secularism and pending the enforcement thereof, the Government would function according to the Declaration of Independence of April 1971.[55] The Acting President assured his people of full protection of fundamental human rights.[56] One of the first acts of the new government was to declare Bengali as the only official language[57] and thus the dream deferred for the last 24 years was eventually realized.

As a result of the Indian Army tactics of bypassing civilian areas and its rapid advance, the damage to Bangladesh economy, Mrs. Gandhi felt, was not as great as was originally feared.[58] The Planning Cell of the Bangladesh Government produced a scheme for the reconstruction of the country and for the rehabilitation of the refugees, the implementation whereof was expected to cost Rs. 700 crores. Of this amount Rs. 280 crores could be raised locally and the rest was to be arranged by way of loan assistance from India.[59] One of the earlier estimates attributed to the Indian Planning Commission puts the cost of reconstruction at Rs. 656 crores.[60]

By a Presidential order of 26 December 1971, the Bank of Bangladesh was formally set up with its headquarters at Dacca and, as successor to the State Bank of Pakistan, it was to take over all assets

[55] The statement of the Acting President of Bangladesh on 25 December 1971; *Hindusthan Standard*, 27 December 1971. In her Lok Sabha speech of 6 December 1971, Mrs. Gandhi said: 'Honourable members will be glad to know that the Government of Bangladesh have proclaimed their basic principles of /State policy to be democracy, socialism, secularism and establishment of an egalitarian society in which there would be no discrimination on the basis of race, religion, sex or creed.' *The Statesman*, Calcutta, 7 December 1971.

[56] *Hindusthan Standard*, Calcutta, 30 December 1971.

[57] *The Statesman*, Calcutta, 25 December 1971.

[58] *The Statesman*, Calcutta, 1 January 1972.

[59] *The Statesman*, Calcutta, 24 December 1971. According to the Rehabilitation Minister of Bangladesh, of the total sum of Rs. 2000 crores needed for the rehabilitation of the refugees, the immediate requirement was for Rs. 700 crores; in view of the limited resources of Bangladesh, some friendly countries who had supported the cause of liberation would be requested to provide financial and material assistance. *The Statesman*, Calcutta, 1 January 1972.

[60] *The Statesman*, Calcutta, 20 December 1971. *Time*, 27 December 1971: 'Meanwhile, the huge task of reconstruction in Bangladesh begins. India has already set a target date of January 31 as the goal for the return of all 10 million refugees. Free bus service is being provided and vehicles loaded down with belongings and passengers have begun rolling back across the borders of Bangladesh. The Indian Planning Commission, who charts India's overall development program, estimates that it will take nearly $ 900 million for essential reconstruction work in Bangladesh and for the refugees' rehabilitation. Bridges, buildings, roads and almost the entire communications network must be restored.'

and branches of its predecessor.[61] By another Presidential order, the new government took over the management and control of banks in Bangladesh whose headquarters were situated in Pakistan. It was also announced that the new government would soon nationalize all banks and insurance companies in implementation of its socialistic policy.[62] Earlier, the Bangladesh Government was reported to have planned a new currency system of its own, and pending the implementation of such a plan, the Pakistani currency with its fluctuating exchange rate would be accepted as legal tender. With a view to building a gold reserve for the currency, the Bangladesh Government intended to appeal to the people for deposits of gold holdings to the Bank of Bangladesh which would issue gold bonds to the depositors; as the country's economy improved the private depositors would get back their gold. According to an estimate based on the Pakistani report, the total monetary assets in Bangladesh early in 1971 had been Rs. 536 crores—Rs. 231·6 crores of currency in circulation, Rs. 286·8 crores as deposits in scheduled banks and Rs. 17·6 crores in postal deposits. A large amount of paper currency was however destroyed by the Pakistani troops a few days before the surrender. The Bangladesh Government had not yet been able to ascertain how much of the monetary assets was still available by the end of the year.[63] An important question likely to arise soon would relate to the assets which are the legitimate share of the Bangladesh Government as larger half of the former State of Pakistan. These assets would include a share of defence equipment, Pakistan International Airlines, foreign exchange assets and assets held overseas in terms of property.[64]

Apart from the preservation of law and order and the rehabilitation of the refugees, some of the immediate primary tasks for the reconstruction of the country appeared to be as follows: (a) the organization of an effective administrative infrastructure; (b) the maintenance of the cycle of agricultural production; (c) the rehabilitation of the industries and foreign trade; (d) the restoration and improvement of communications.[65]

On 18 December the Bangladesh Government called upon all its employees—those who had left their posts during enemy occupation but remained inside Bangladesh and those who had left posts and crossed over to a neighbouring country—to return to their posts.[66]

[61] *The Statesman*, Calcutta, 31 December 1971.

[62] *The Statesman*, Calcutta, 31 December 1971.

[63] *The Statesman*, Calcutta, 24 December 1971.

[64] *The Statesman*, Calcutta, 20 December 1971.

[65] *The Statesman*, Calcutta, editorial, 'And Now to Reconstruction'; 20 December 1971.

[66] *The Statesman*, Calcutta, 19 December 1971.

Steps were taken by the new government for providing the administrative infrastructure not only at the capital city of Dacca but in district towns and villages as well. For instance, the Rehabilitation Department with only 13 clerks and a section officer at the time of surrender of the Pakistani army had already been provided with a Rehabilitation and Relief Secretary assisted by two joint secretaries, four deputy secretaries, an additional deputy secretary for each of the 19 districts with subdivisional relief officers under him; at the village level, *gram panchayats* had been included in the relief and rehabilitation work.[67] The administrative personnel had responded overwhelmingly to the call of the Prime Minister to meet the difficult challenge, and accepted ungrudgingly a reduction in pay scales with a salary ceiling of Rs. 1,000 as a 'temporary austerity measure' announced on 29 December.[68]

The Planning Cell made a detailed study of the report of the Administrative Reforms Commission of India and the Fulton Committee's report of the United Kingdom and had already prepared the outlines of a scheme suggesting measures for setting up of an administrative infrastructure consistent with the tasks to be accomplished.[69]

The agricultural economy of Bangladesh has been traditionally based on two crops, rice and jute. It was felt to be of utmost importance that the cycle of agricultural production should not be disrupted and that the normal channel of essential agricultural inputs like credit and fertilizers should be maintained.

Bangladesh had about 3,000 industrial units of which 30% were owned by the West Pakistanis. The Planning Cell of Bangladesh suggested that the management of all Pakistani-owned industrial units should be immediately taken over by the government and each unit should have an administrator appointed by the government. The takeover of the management of the industrial units in the public sector which were previously owned by the East Pakistan Industrial Development Corporation was not expected to present any problem.[70] The Bangladesh Government had announced its decision to take over 27 jute mills, 13 jute exporting firms and 7 jute baling presses with immediate effect to be operated by the Jute Board in the public sec-

---

[67] The statement of the Rehabilitation Minister of Bangladesh, *The Statesman*, Calcutta, 1 January 1972.

[68] *The Statesman*, Calcutta, 30 December 1971.

[69] *The Statesman*, Calcutta, 24 December 1971. In recognition of the calibre, dedication, training and intelligence of Bangladesh officials, Mrs. Gandhi felt that too much of administrative guidance from India was unnecessary. *The Statesman*, Calcutta, 1 January 1972.

[70] *The Statesman*, Calcutta, 24 December 1971.

tor,[71] and also a large number of cotton mills.[72] Already the management of 22 tea estates, 4 tea blending, packaging, distributing and warehousing companies had been taken over by the new government to be operated by the Tea Board in the public sector.[73]

The extent of damage suffered by the key jute and paper industries was still not very clear by the end of the year. Apart from the replacement of machinery and buildings, critical personnel requirements were anticipated in respect of industrial units owned or managed by the West Pakistanis. The reconstruction of the Chittagong refinery reported to have been severely damaged would naturally become an urgent but expensive project. The power system, however, appeared to have remained intact except for minor damage.[74]

The immediate requirements of food imports had been worked out by the Planning Cell. India and the Soviet Union were expected to provide considerable assistance in respect of food shipments.[75]

In the field of foreign trade, while long-term patterns would inevitably be linked up with the proposed economic planning of the new nation, available indications by the end of the year presented a picture far from gloomy. It might not be too difficult to secure the immediately essential imports like foodgrains, coal, petroleum, oils and other essential consumer goods. The capacity to pay for these imports immediately was necessarily limited. Nevertheless, Bangladesh was expected to resume shortly its export of raw jute, fish and newsprint to India, and the gap between the costs of imports and earnings from exports, likely to be considerable, would still not present any insurmountable problem. Help and assistance from friendly countries had been assured; close collaboration between Bangladesh and India[76] was almost guaranteed, and the two countries in their mutual interests were already working out mutually beneficial trading patterns. *Newsweek* of 27 December 1971 said: 'On the bright side, independence should bring some substantial benefits for under the discretionary rule of West Pakistan, East Bengal produced more than 50% of Pakistan's export earnings, but received only a grudging 30% of the government's national budget. And now Bangladesh should be able to reopen traditionally profitable trading pattern in jute and tea (the nation's primary exports) with India.'

Apart from India, many other countries, including France and

[71] *The Statesman*, Calcutta, 31 December 1971.
[72] *The Statesman*, Calcutta, 1 January 1972.
[73] *The Statesman*, Calcutta, 1 January 1972.
[74] *The Statesman*, Calcutta, 20 December 1971.
[75] *Newsweek*, 27 December 1971.
[76] *The Statesman*, Calcutta, 20 December 1971, 1 January 1972.

Britain, Soviet Union, and East European and Middle Eastern countries, had already expressed their desire to establish trade, economic and friendly relations with Bangladesh. Some of these countries were interested in importing from Bangladesh jute, jute goods, hides, skins and tobacco while exporting river vessels, tankers, ships, medicine, tractors, chemicals and chemical goods to Bangladesh.[77]

In the field of communications, substantial damage to the Chittagong and Chalna ports and to the key bridges as well as to the railway system presented a difficult problem but the work of repair or reconstruction had already made good progress. In fact, Indian Army engineers, Indian Post and Telegraphs technicians and Indian railway officials helped the Bangladesh government in this field. Telegraph and telephone links between Dacca and almost all other parts of the country were established, and telecommunication links with the outside world were restored. Indian Army technicians had built numerous pontoon bridges over rivers and canals. Railway services were resumed in many areas. The Indian Airlines came forward to help restore the communication links by running services between Calcutta and Dacca and between the different cities in Bangladesh. Bangladesh enjoys a natural system of waterways ideally suited for transport operations. No outside technical help was needed for restoration of the inland water transport. Steamer and launch services to different inland terminal points had started. However, a number of inland water transports had to be replenished because hundreds of steamers, launches and barges were sunk by the Mukti Bahini naval commandos during the liberation struggle.[78]

Between Bangladesh and India, one could reasonably predict that collaboration in war was about to mature into a more enduring collaboration in peace. The need arose, not merely from shared sentiments in human values during a crisis, but equally from an identity of views in matters of declared State policy, both internal and external. Above all, the need arose from the physical reality of natural interdependence between Bangladesh and the north-eastern and eastern regions of India. It was in response to such an imperative need for collaboration that comprehensive plans for joint participation in the reconstruction of Bangladesh were in the offing by the end of the year.

Although at the end of the year no other country except India and Bhutan had granted *de jure* recognition to the Government of Bangladesh, there were clear indications that a number of countries had expressed their desire to establish trade and friendly relations with Bangladesh. Mutual contacts between the representatives of

[77] *The Statesman*, Calcutta, 28, 31 December 1971
[78] *The Statesman*, Calcutta, 31 December 1971.

the United Nations, many foreign countries including the Soviet Union, France, Britain and East European countries, and Bangladesh, were established.[79]

The new government time and again had reiterated that the foreign policy of Bangladesh would be one of non-alignment, co-existence and non-interference in other countries' internal affairs. The government appealed for friendly relations with all countries including the USA and China despite their adverse role during the liberation struggle. Britain and France were praised for their neutral attitude during the liberation war, and Bangladesh expected a gesture of friendship from them.[80] Earlier, Mrs. Gandhi had informed the Indian Parliament in her recognition speech of 6 December 1971 that with regard to foreign relations, 'the Bangladesh Government has expressed their determination to follow a policy of non-alignment, peaceful co-existence and opposition to colonialism, racialism and imperialism in all its manifestation.'[81]

The performance of the new government during the first two weeks after the liberation of Dacca removed all doubts about the viability of Bangladesh. Having recovered from its terrible birth pangs, Bangladesh was well on the way of:

(a) Bringing back the 10 million Bengalis who sought asylum in India;

(b) Overcoming the seemingly insuperable difficulties of the restoration of public order throughout the territory of Bangladesh;

(c) Undertaking with ability, confidence and courage the task of reconstruction of the country with an economy battered by 25 years of colonial exploitation and nine months of struggle for liberation.

The reality of the emergence of Bangladesh, the eighth nation of the world in terms of population, could no longer be ignored by the international community.

The important task which still remained unaccomplished by the end of the year was to secure the release of Bangabandhu Sheikh Mujibur Rahman, President of Bangladesh. For the people of Bangladesh, the war of liberation would not come to an end until their beloved leader was freed from his detention in West Pakistan and had returned to Bangladesh to lead his people. However, while the

---

[79] On 31 December 1971 Mrs. Gandhi said that the world should recognize the realities of the situation, and one such reality was the emergence of Bangladesh. Even without formal recognition of government, the international community could help in the reconstruction of Bangladesh. *The Statesman*, Calcutta, 1 January 1972.

[80] UNI report of the views of the Acting President of Bangladesh: *Hindusthan Standard*, 29 December 1971.

[81] *The Statesman*, Calcutta, 7 December 1971.

people of Bangladesh were about to launch the final phase of their liberation struggle by a still stronger mobilization of international public opinion, President Bhutto of Pakistan, on 3 January 1972, announced his decision to release Sheikh Mujib unconditionally.[82]

He kept his promise, and Dacca celebrated the home-coming of her hero in an unprecedented welcome to the founder of Bangladesh on 10 January 1972. Within two days of Mujib's return Bangladesh introduced a parliamentary system of government after 13 years of military dictatorship. Sheikh Mujibur Rahman resigned from his office as President and Mr. Justice Abu Syed Chowdhury was sworn in as President of Bangladesh. Sheikh Mujibur Rahman became the Prime Minister of the Government of Bangladesh on 12 January 1972. His cabinet included all the members of the earlier government headed by Mr. Tajuddin Ahmed. The cabinet as reconstituted on 13 January consisted of: Sheikh Mujibur Rahman, Prime Minister, with additional portfolios of Cabinet Affairs, Establishment Division, Defence, Home Affairs, and Information and Broadcasting; Syed Nazrul Islam, Industry, Trade and Commerce; Tajuddin Ahmed, Finance, Revenue and Planning; Mansur Ali, Communications; Khondakar Moshtaque Ahmed, Power, Irrigation and Flood Control; Abdus Samad Azad, Foreign Affairs; A. H. M. Kamaruzzaman, Relief and Rehabilitation; Sheikh Abdul Aziz, Agriculture, Local Government, Rural Development and Co-operative; Professor Yusuf Ali, Education and Cultural Affairs; Zahur Ahmed Chowdhury, Health, Labour, Social Welfare and Family Planning; Phanibhusan Mazumdar, Food and Civil Supplies; and Kamal Hussain, Law, Parliamentary Affairs, Constitution-making and Works and Housing. Further additions to the cabinet were likely to be made. The National Anthem chosen by the new cabinet was the one which inspired the 150,000 freedom fighters of Bangladesh, Rabindranath Tagore's *Amar Sonar Bangla, ami tomay bhalobasi* (My golden Bengal, I love you.)

Mujib's return to Bangladesh was not only the fulfilment of the cherished dream of 75 million Bengalis since his arrest on 26 March 1971, it was also the catalytic agent which immediately brought about a transformation in the political atmosphere in Bangladesh. All doubts about the leadership were resolved, all fears settled; firm plans were outlined for social and economic justice, and for the political, cultural and moral rehabilitation of the people, who had suffered the fate of serfs for a period of 24 years. Any lingering doubts in the minds of political observers who had been watching the Mujib-Bhutto talks since Yahya's fall on 19 December were firmly set at rest with Mujib's announcement in Dacca that links with Pakistan

[82] *The Statesman*, Calcutta, 4 January 1972.

had been completely snapped and the word Pakistan had been 'erased in Bangladesh' (Press Conference, Dacca, 14 January 1972).

The Military Junta's Political Experiments
26 March-20 December 1971

Early in December President Nixon was reported to have said in Washington: 'We have followed with sympathetic interest the efforts of the Government and people of Pakistan to achieve an amicable settlement in East Pakistan. We have also welcomed the efforts of President Yahya to reduce tensions in the subcontinent.'[83]

Prime Minister, Indira Gandhi, in her letter of 15 December 1971, told President Nixon: 'War could have been avoided if the power, influence and authority of all States and, above all, of the USA, had got Sheikh Mujibur Rahman released. Instead we were told that a civilian administration was being installed. Everyone knows that the civilian administration was a farce: today, the farce has turned into a tragedy. Lip service was paid to the need for a political solution, but not a single worthwhile step was taken to bring this about. Instead, the rulers of West Pakistan went about holding farcical elections to seats which had been arbitrarily declared vacant.'[84]

It, therefore, becomes relevant to consider the efforts made by the military regime for an amicable settlement with which President Nixon was in sympathy but Mrs. Gandhi found farcical and tragic.

It will have been observed that after the Constitution of 1956 was abrogated and martial law proclaimed, the military junta led by General Ayub Khan came to power by a bloodless *coup* on 27 October 1958.

On 25 March 1969 General Yahya Khan replaced General Ayub Khan and on 31 March appointed himself President of Pakistan, admitting frankly that the people did not bring him to power, he came himself. The first national elections in the history of Pakistan held in December 1970 gave an overwhelming mandate to Sheikh Mujib's Awami League for a constitution based on the six-point programme. The Awami League had an absolute majority in the still-born National Assembly. In breach of his declared promise to transfer power to the elected representatives of the people, General Yahya banned the Awami League, imprisoned Sheikh Mujib and other Awami League leaders, and launched a war of genocide and a reign of terror and persecution in East Bengal on and from 25 March 1971.

After the death of a million Bengalis in the military operations, and the forcible eviction of about ten million people, President Yahya indicated his policies for a civilian government in East Bengal and

[83] *The Statesman,* Calcutta, 8 December 1971.
[84] *The Statesman,* Calcutta, 17 December 1971.

for a constitutional regime in Pakistan. On 31 August 1971 President Yahya appointed Dr. A. M. Malik as civilian Governor of East Pakistan 'in keeping with his pledge to restore civilian rule'. The official communique stated that the responsibility for running East Pakistan's civil administration would be entirely in the hands of the new Governor and his ministers to be approved by the President, and the role of the armed forces would be limited to ensuring the country's defence and providing assistance to the civilian government, if called upon to do so. Lieutenant-General Amir Abdullah Khan replaced Lieutenant-General Tikka Khan as Martial Law Administrator of East Pakistan.[85]

Apart from the non-representative character of the Governor, the functioning of the civil administration within the scheme of martial law administration was rather a strange way of restoring civilian rule. Even Mr. Z. A. Bhutto challenged the representative status of the new Governor and pointed out that candidates defeated in the last general elections were associated with the new administration. The *New York Post* had perhaps correctly assessed the situation and described it as 'a vain attempt to evade further condemnation of their own martial lawlessness... Malik is not a duly elected leader of the East Bengalis, nor has he any claim on that office. The only man who qualifies on both the counts is Sheikh Mujibur Rahman, head of the Awami League, whose party was the overwhelming victor in East Bengal's first election late last year.'[86]

The next step was the release of a number of persons from detention camps and jails in Dacca, Comilla, Jessore, Chittagong, Natore and Rangpur following a 'general amnesty' granted by President Yahya to all persons accused of 'anti-state crimes' in East Bengal except those already charged. The general amnesty did not however apply to members of the National Assembly and the Provincial Assembly and to certain 'limited number of individuals against whom criminal proceedings have been instituted.' The official spokesman pointed out that Sheikh Mujibur Rahman, facing trial before a military tribunal on a charge of waging war on the state, was not included in the amnesty order. The official communique described the amnesty as 'another step forward in the President's resolve to restore normal conditions in the country.'[87]

[85] *The Statesman*, Calcutta, 1 September 1971.

[86] *New York Post* editorial quoted in the *Statesman*, 4 September 1971.

[87] *The Statesman*, Calcutta, 6 September 1971. Also see the *Statesman*, 2 October 1971, for a UNI report: A former Bengali officer of the PAF, who recently escaped from captivity in Dacca Cantonment, described Yahya's amnesty offer as a 'hoax', designed to deceive world opinion. He disclosed that some officers who surrendered on the declaration of amnesty on an earlier occasion were

To eliminate all possible opposition to the military junta, and preceding the imposition of a constitution by President Yahya, certain unusual steps were taken. 97 National Assembly seats,[88] and 105 Provincial Assembly seats, won by the Awami League during the December elections, were arbitrarily declared vacant by the military government. In respect of the seat held by Sheikh Mujibur Rahman, a decision was to be taken after the verdict of the military court. The by-elections were to be held in respect of the seats declared vacant by the second week of December 1971.[89]

President Yahya appointed a committee for drafting a provisional constitution for 90 days. The constitution was to be presented to the National Assembly when convened after the by-elections to fill the seats of the disqualified Awami League members were held. The Assembly could have suggested amendments by a simple majority within three months provided there was a 'consensus of the federal units'. Any amendments which the President found unacceptable were to be returned to the Assembly for reconsideration. The Assembly could have again sent them to the President with modifications or in the original form; if they were still unacceptable to the President, the amendments 'will have fallen'. Any amendments which in the opinion of the President militated against the territorial integrity of Pakistan or the ideology of Pakistan were not to be accepted.[90]

India's reactions to the measures taken by the Pakistani rulers till September were expressed by Mr. Swaran Singh, Minister of External Affairs, addressing the General Assembly of the United Nations on 27 September. He said: 'Apart from accusing others for their own unwise and deadly activities, the rulers of Pakistan have taken a number of measures which are no more than an eye wash. How unrealistic these measures are can be judged from the impact that these had on the flow of refugees. The President of Pakistan has from time to time called upon the refugees to go back; yet the flow continues in ever increasing numbers into India. A so-called civilian government in East Pakistan which consists of men who have no representative character whatsoever and who are mere figureheads are obliged to take orders from the military commanders. An amnesty is proclaimed but Sheikh Mujibur Rahman and other elected representatives are at the same time treated and tried as traitors. We wit-

---

arrested and put into 'concentration camps'. A large number of Bengali civilian, army and air force officers were still being 'tortured in concentration camps.'

[88] *Weekly Joi Bangla*, 24 September 1971.

[89] *The Statesman*, Calcutta, 28 September 1971.

[90] *The Statesman*, Calcutta, 19 September 1971.

ness the strange spectacle that the party which would have by right formed the Government of Pakistan has been banned and disqualified from political activities. Half the elected representatives have been disqualified from sitting in the National Assembly. In our view the flow of refugees will not stop nor will the refugees already in India go back until a political solution acceptable to the elected representatives of the people has been found.'[91]

By the middle of November, it became clear that the military junta in Pakistan was trying to outmanoeuvre the people of Bangladesh and India by pushing through its normalization process including the convening of the National Assembly and the imposition of a constitution, without the authority or sanction of the duly elected majority party, the Awami League. President Yahya was not impressed by the efforts of those who appealed to him for a meaningful political solution acceptable to the people of Bangladesh. By 19 November 1971 when the USA sent words to India that the President of Pakistan was unwilling to release Sheikh Mujibur Rahman but was prepared to talk to any other Bangladesh emissary approved by him, it became clear that all hopes of a political solution acceptable to the people of Bangladesh had disappeared.[92]

Things began to move rather rapidly. With the background of progressively mounting Mukti Bahini offensives and series of reverses suffered by the Pakistani forces in Bangladesh, Yahya on the one hand tried to push through his scheme for a civilian government under military patronage and, on the other, openly threatened India with war. In aid of his first objective, uncontested candidates were declared elected to the National Assembly from the arbitrarily deprived seats of the duly elected members of the Awami League. Yahya announced the appointment of the 77-year-old Bengali politician, Mr Nurul Amin, as the Prime Minister-designate for a future civilian government, and Mr Zulfikar Ali Bhutto as his deputy, to which he promised to transfer some of his military regime's power.[93] It will be recalled that in the December elections, Sheikh Mujib's Awami League won 167 of the 169 Assembly seats and Nurul Amin won one of the two remaining seats. On 3 December 1971, Pakistan attacked several Indian airfields and thereafter declared war against India. Mrs. Gandhi announced the recognition of the People's Republic of Bangladesh on 6 December 1971 and within five hours, on the third day of the Indo-Pakistani war, Pakistan snapped diplomatic ties with India. On 14 December, Mr A. M. Malik, the Governor,

[91] *The Statesman*, Calcutta, 28 September 1971.

[92] S. Viswam, Political Commentary, *The Statesman*, Calcutta, 10 December 1971.

[93] *Time*, 20 December 1971.

and other members of his government tendered their resignation. The so-called civilian East Pakistan Government, deriving its title from the military junta, thus wholly ceased to exist. On 16 December, the Pakistani Army surrendered unconditionally to the Indian troops at Dacca and Bangladesh became completely liberated.

President Yahya had proposed to call the National Assembly on 27 December[94] to consider his draft constitution. His proposed broadcast over Radio Pakistan for announcing the salient features of his constitution never took place. After the liberation of Bangladesh, India declared unilateral cease-fire on 16 December and Pakistan responded on 17 December. The war in the western front came to an end at 8 p.m. on 17 December. On 20 December, President Yahya resigned from office and Mr Z. A. Bhutto became Pakistan's President again deriving his title from the martial law of the military junta.

The most powerful condemnation of the efforts of President Yahya for a political settlement came from President Bhutto himself, although he was silent about his own contribution to the dismemberment of Pakistan. In his broadcast on 20 December, he announced the 'liquidation' of the results of the by-elections held by the Yahya regime to fill the seats rendered vacant by the removal of the Awami League members of the National Assembly, describing the by-elections as 'an insult to the people'. The new President blamed 'the capricious and whimsical rule of the military dictators' for the plight of his country.[95] Again, on 3 January 1972, President Bhutto said: 'General Yahya had hidden a lot of things from the people... His politics were a fraud. They were treacherous.'[96] Still clinging to his illusion that 'East Pakistan is an inseparable and indissoluble part of Pakistan', and ignoring the reality of the existence of Bangladesh as a sovereign State, President Bhutto appealed to the people of 'East Pakistan not to forget us, and forgive us if they are angry with us.'[97]

The political experiments of the military dictator thus ended with devastating consequences. The attempts President Yahya made to impose a constitution upon the people of Bangladesh and the people of Pakistan, which apparently satisfied President Nixon, would have been described by President Wilson as futile efforts of an 'usurper', and his government 'a pretended government', a 'military despotism'. The efforts of General Yahya Khan designed towards the perpetuation of the hegemony of the military junta with a facade of civilian regime functioning under an imposed constitution was doomed to

[94] *The Statesman*, Calcutta, 21 December 1971.
[95] *Ibid.*
[96] *The Statesman*, Calcutta, 4 January 1972.
[97] *The Statesman*, 21 December 1971.

failure from the beginning as was predicted by enlightened public opinion throughout the world. A military regime *simpliciter* as in Greece, or a civilian government with a constitution imposed by the military regime as in Turkey or the attempted imposition of a civilian regime under military patronage as in Pakistan, are all equally destructive of the principle of self-determination, the sanction behind them being armed forces of the military junta, and not the will of the people voluntarily expressed. Even if General Yahya had succeeded in imposing a constitution of this nature and extracting the tacit acquiescence of the people of West Pakistan and Bangladesh, the resultant governmental authority would still not have acquired the legitimacy in international law, as will be discussed subsequently.

CHAPTER FIVE

INTERNATIONAL LEGAL NORMS
AND
DEFAULT IN BANGLADESH

Magnitude of Default

In every State, in the field of equal rights and self-determination, and human rights and fundamental freedoms, the international community has a definite responsibility in contemporary law. In these fields, the magnitude of the gulf between the rhetoric of law and the reality of response has nowhere been more startling than in the case of East Bengal, now known as Bangladesh.

The tragic story of self-determination for East Bengal is the story of the metamorphosis of an independent people in an independent country to a dependent people in a technically independent country. The status of the people of East Bengal, during the last 24 years, was admirably expressed by Sheikh Mujibur Rahman in one of his familiar Bengali phrases, *swadhin deshe paradhin nagarik,* which means, 'dependent citizens of an independent country'. The acquiescence of the international community to the persistent denial of the principle of equal rights and self-determination to the majority people of Pakistan during the last 24 years has been the first breach of international responsibility. Such acquiescence was prompted perhaps by the technical consideration that the problem was a matter of internal public order of an independent country and not the problem of a non-self-governing or trust territory within the meaning of Chapters XI and XII of the United Nations Charter. It will be my endeavour to show that this was a thoroughly erroneous assumption. First, because the matter of equal rights and self-determination has always been in contemporary international law a matter of international concern. And, secondly, even the technical ground does not hold good since East Bengal, where the majority of the Pakistani people resided, did in fact become a colony of West Pakistan. East Bengal satisfied all the tests of a colony known in contemporary law.

If the United Nations could severely condemn Ian Smith for the denial of majority rule and for his policy of racial discrimination, is it not surprising that similar policies of the Islamabad Government, ruthlessly executed through genocide and other horrid crimes against humanity, did not evoke even a mild protest from the world body? Ian Smith was at least honest. He frankly stated in December 1966: 'I cannot in all honesty claim that I am an advocate of majority rule... We will never negotiate with Britain while Mr Wilson is in his present position because he is waiting for us to reach the position of one man, one vote and this will not happen in my lifetime or Mr Wilson's lifetime.'[1]

In contemporary international law, a minimum standard of civilized behaviour is expected to be observed by every State. The newly developing concept of international public policy imposes this obligation on every civilized nation even without any conventional obligation. This is how the International Court of Justice treated the obligations of the Genocide Convention of 1948. The elementary provisions of human rights and fundamental freedoms can claim their source of authority both to the law of the United Nations regime and the modern concept of international public policy.

Although there is at present no viable international system which effectively deals with deliberate governmental violations of human rights, yet the provisions of the Charter and other important international instruments in this field can be reasonably considered as self-executing, depending, however, upon the degree of the United Nations response and the nature of its sanction. If such response is prompt and sincere, although the sanction is inadequate and the relief to the victim nominal, the international community will at least express a workable optimism, albeit a qualified one, in the efficacy of the world body; where, however, far from a formal condemnation or providing a sanction, the response of the United Nations is nil, the international community expresses great skepticism about its efficacy, because it really amounts to world body's acquiescence in the breaches committed by the violating State. Two instances of the former can be found in the attitude of the United Nations towards Southern Rhodesia and in the case of Arab refugees from Israel; two instances of the latter can be found in the case of Biafra and of East Bengal.

The tragic experience of the international community has been that the machinery of the United Nations, intended to be self-propelled, hardly moves of its own volition; in practice, its inertia or its energy originates from the will-force of the great powers. If the great powers are unanimous, the performance of the international machinery can be superb; if, however, there is a conflict of interest among the great powers, the movement of the world body becomes

---

[1] Quoted by Congressman Rosenthal of New York, Cong. Rec., Feb. 9, 1967 H 1246 and reproduced in (1968) 62 *American Journal of International Law* (AJIL), p. 2 f.n. 9.

stagnant. The world public opinion is bewildered in a case where the issue involved is one of human rights and fundamental freedoms, and there could be no reasonable apprehension of any conflict between the declared or enlightened interests of the great powers, yet the machinery of the United Nations is virtually stagnant.

For a period of 24 years, the right to self-determination was denied to the people of East Bengal. There can be no serious dispute that premeditated crimes against humanity were committed by Yahya's army of occupation. In magnitude and variety, the transgressions of human rights by Yahya Khan defied the imagination of civilized nations. A calculated genocide of the Bengali people was committed with merciless efficiency. There were inhuman acts of killings of civilians of all ages—*en masse,* in groups, and individually. Undefended towns, villages and dwellings were bombed indiscriminately. Civilians had been shelled and burned alive. Women were defiled. Private property was plundered. There was a forcible eviction of over ten million people to India and millions of others rendered homeless. The intelligentsia, political opponents and the minority communities were the particular targets of genocide. Even on a conservative estimate, the indictment of war crimes and crimes against humanity against the Yahya regime will be an appalling list.

The way in which the world body and the great powers were persuaded to acquiesce in such massive violations of human rights in East Bengal by the Islamabad Government is amazing. While discontinuing, since 28 October 1969, the long-standing practice of the UN Information Centres in receiving and forwarding individual complaints to the United Nations on human rights matters, U Thant observed: 'If there are breaches of human rights which contravene the provisions of the Declaration on Human Rights, then all such breaches should be brought to the notice of the United Nations by *some means or another.'*[2] Why did not U Thant himself follow his own principle in the case of East Bengal?

When there was a duty to speak and act, the United Nations and the great powers remained silent spectators to a deliberate rupture of fundamental international norms. Even though the most elementary international community standards were being brutally suppressed, the world body, far from using its coercive power or from taking any effective action, did not even utter a whisper of protest, did not even employ its watchdog machinery, did not even use its persuasive power to prevent the tragedy. It was only after the breach was perfected, and not while it was being committed, that a subsidiary organ of the United Nations first took notice of the events in East Bengal. And this minimal, inadequate and superficial response

[2] (1970) 64 AJIL 613.

was solely due to the fact that millions of people were successfully terrorized by the military oligarchy of Pakistan to flee to India. In their own right, the people of East Bengal did not receive any attention from the United Nations. No civilized nation could shut its frontiers to the helpless victims of a reign of terror and persecution. The forced exodus of ten million human beings in execution of a policy of genocide by itself amounted to an act of aggression against India by the Yahya regime. Even then the United Nations did not take any effective action against the guilty. Neither the Security Council nor the General Assembly followed its own precedent in the case of Arab refugees from Israel at least to affirm the inalienable rights of the evacuees from East Bengal to return, resume normal life, recover their property and homes and rejoin their families according to the provisions of the Universal Declaration. The world body did not ask the Islamabad Government to create conditions suitable for the return of the evacuees to their own country. At the twenty-sixth session of the United Nations, 47 speakers in the general debate in the General Assembly called for a political reconciliation in Pakistan, but none took the step of introducing the issue in the agenda of the General Assembly or the Security Council that might have led to action. No wonder the United Nations suffers from a severe decline in credibility.

The performance of the United Nations at the 26th session explains the reason why it has suffered from a severe decline in credibility. No steps were taken for a political reconciliation in Pakistan. The earlier attempts of India's Prime Minister during her tour of Western Europe and the USA did not succeed in enlisting any worthwhile international support to persuade General Yahya Khan to reach a political reconciliation with the Awami League leaders so that not only was the principle of self-determination vindicated but the 10 million refugees could also go back to their country, thereby removing the root cause of the tension in the subcontinent. Even then, the tragic war, which broke out in the subcontinent on 3 December 1971, 'could have been prevented had the rulers of Pakistan not launched massive attacks on India's airfields in broad daylight on 3 December.'[3] But when the war did break out, instead of attempting a genuine political solution, international effort was made, for the first time in the Charter regime, to utilize the machinery of the United Nations to stifle the war of liberation in Bangladesh when it was about to be successful. The international community led by the United States and China became a partisan to a descredited military rule against the struggle for liberation of 75 million Bengalis.

[3] See Prime Minister Indira Gandhi's letter of 15 December 1971 to President Nixon. *The Statesman*, Calcutta, 17 December 1971.

With these preliminary observations, we propose to enquire into some of the important areas of international responsibility, and to explore and find out the relevant international norms, to assess the extent of international default in matters of equal rights and self-determination, human rights and fundamental freedoms, in East Bengal.

Contemporary Law of Self-determination

While the philosophical edifice of the principle of equal rights and self-determination of peoples is founded on the dignity and worth of the human individual, emphasized so eloquently by Jefferson and Lincoln, its legal edifice in contemporary international law is founded on the Charter of the United Nations: Preamble, Articles 1(2), 13(1)(b), 55, 56, 59, 62(2), 68 and 76(c). Peaceful and friendly relations among nations are based on the respect for, and the fulfilment of, this principle. The realization of the principle will help create conditions of stability and well-being. It is with this end in view that the United Nations has undertaken the obligations, *inter alia,* to promote universal respect for, and observance of, human rights and fundamental freedoms for all without discrimination as to race, sex, language or religion. The basic constitutive Charter prescription is that the minimum conditions of a dignified human existence must be realized and maintained by member States by joint and separate action in co-operation with the UNO. Failure to realize this objective will necessarily result in a failure to create conditions of stability and well-being, thereby disturbing the very foundation of the Charter system.

Much progress was made between the third and twenty-fifth sessions of the General Assembly in promoting a common understanding of these rights and in formulating their contents. Apart from the Charter, the most important basic instrument is the Universal Declaration of Human Rights which 'is now widely acclaimed as a *Magna Carta* of mankind, to be complied with by all the participants in the world arena.'[4] While approving the Universal Declaration on 6 December 1948,[5] the General Assembly pointed out the importance of protecting these rights by a rule of law 'if man is not to be compelled to have recourse as a last resort to rebellion against tyranny and oppression.' Since then the international community concern for the realization of the principle by promoting the observance of human rights and fundamental freedoms has been expressed in a series of important resolutions of the General Assembly and in some conventions and covenants of outstanding significance.

---

[4] (1969) 63 AJIL, p. 262.
[5] For text, see *International Organisation*, 1949, Vol. III, pp. 202-6.

To mention only a few: (i) The Declaration on the Granting of Independence to Colonial Countries and Peoples, General Assembly Resolution 1514 (XV) of 14 December, 1960;[6] and Resolution 1541 (XV) of 15 December 1960;[7] (ii) The Declaration on the Elimination of all Forms of Racial Discrimination, General Assembly Resolution 1904 (XVIII) of 20 November, 1963[8] and the Convention on the Elimination of Racial Discrimination of 1966;[9] (iii) the General Assembly Resolution 2200 (XXI) of 16 December 1966 approving the International Covenant on Economic, Social and Cultural Rights and the International Covenant on Civil and Political Rights,[10] and (iv) the adoption of the Proclamation of Tehran, 1968, by a United Nations Conference on Human Rights.[11]

It will have been observed that in the context of the principle of equal rights and self-determination, emphasis has been shifted in contemporary international law from the traditional criteria of a homogeneous, ethnic and cultural group within a distinct geographical area to the modern criteria of individual human rights and fundamental freedoms. In its modern formulation one finds the fulfilment of the dream of Henry David Thoreau in his *Civil Disobedience* (1849) :[12]

> The progress from an absolute to a limited monarchy, from a limited monarchy to a democracy, is a progress toward a true respect for the individual. Even the Chinese philosopher was wise enough to regard the individual as the basis of the empire. Is a democracy such as we know it, the last improvement possible in government? Is it not possible to take a step further towards recognizing and organizing the rights of man? There will never be a really free and enlightened State until the State comes to recognize the individual as a higher and independent power, from which all its own power and authority are derived, and treats him accordingly.

While the importance of the principle has been repeated and reaffirmed time and again, the vagueness implicit in the expression was responsible for serious controversy in the past as to the precise legal contents of the right, legal criteria for its application, situations

---

[6] *U.N. Yearbook 1960*, p. 49.

[7] *Ibid.*, p. 509.

[8] (1964) 58 AJIL, p. 1081.

[9] (1966) 60 AJIL, p. 650.

[10] (1967) 61 AJIL, pp. 861-890.

[11] (1969) 63 AJIL, p. 674.

[12] *Living Ideas in America* (Harper), pp. 383-4.

in which the right becomes operative and the modes of its implementation. Between 1962 and 1970, at the request of the General Assembly, several Special Committees made great efforts for the codification of the modern principles of international law and for their elaboration. Finally, the work of the Special Committee which met in Geneva from 31 March 1970 to 1 May 1970 produced a report elaborating the declaration of seven principles of international law. The declaration was adopted by the General Assembly on 24 October 1970 by Resolution 2625 (XXV). This is known as the *Declaration on Principles of International Law Concerning Friendly Relations and Cooperation Among States In Accordance with the Charter of the United Nations.*[13] The Declaration will be referred to hereafter as 'the 1970 Declaration'. Of the seven principles, Principle (e) deals with equal rights and self-determination of peoples. All the seven principles are inter-related and each has to be construed in the context of the others. In view of this legal exposition of the highly emotive symbols of equal rights and self-determination, it is now possible to examine the question of the right to self-determination of the people of East Bengal in the light of five norms in contemporary law. These norms relate to:

A. Beneficiaries of the Right
and
The Manner of its Exercise.
B. Situations where Applicable.
C. Modes of Implementation.
D. Duties of the State:
(i) To promote self-determination.
(ii) To refrain from forcible suppression.
E. Rights of the People:
(i) To resist forcible action.
(ii) To receive international assistance.

Five Legal Norms : Colonial Status of East Bengal

A. BENEFICIARIES OF THE RIGHT AND THE MANNER OF ITS EXERCISE.

It is a trite observation that the right to self-determination is the right of the people—not of a king or military dictator or usurper of power or any other non-representative ruler—freely to *determine their political status* and to pursue their economic, social and cultural developments, without discrimination as to race, sex, language or religion. Correlative to the right of the peoples, there is the duty of the State to promote in good faith the realization and observance of

---

[13] *International Legal Materials,* Vol. IX, No. 6, Nov. 1970, pp. 1292-7.

this right. This will clearly appear from the elaboration of principles (e) and (g) of the 1970 Declaration.

The principle is one, though it embraces, like two sides of the same coin, two inseparably interlinked concepts: (i) equal rights of the people and (ii) self-determination of the people. One cannot exist without the other. Since men are created equals, there can be no freedom unless they are treated as equals. Since the source of governmental authority is the consent of the governed, there can be no freedom in tyranny or in a regime ruled by a dictator or a military junta or a non-representative government. The struggle is between right and wrong, between the legitimate right of the peoples to govern themselves and the pretended right of a king or non-representative ruler (whom Lincoln compares with a serpent) who exploits them. The modern formulation of this right can trace its foundation to Jefferson's famous declaration of 1776 and to the Lincoln concept of freedom and democracy, of liberty and equality, of peace and justice. As Abraham Lincoln had observed:[14] "That is the real issue. That is the issue that will continue in this country when these poor tongues of Judge Douglas and myself shall be silent. It is the eternal struggle between these two principles—right and wrong—throughout the world. They are the two principles that have stood face to face from the beginning of time; and will ever continue to struggle. The one is the common right of humanity, and the other the divine right of kings. It is the same principle in whatever shape it develops itself. It is the same serpent that says, 'You toil and work and earn bread, and I'll eat it.'"

So formulated, the right to self-determination amounts to a declaration of the forfeiture of the title of all non-representative rulers—colonial exploiters, an unpopular king or emperor, a military dictator or a military oligarchy, or a minority ruling over the majority by brute force.

This right can only be exercised by the implementation of the principle of majority rule with guarantees of minority rights. Every government derives its powers from the consent of the governed and such consent can only be expressed through free and genuine elections under a system of universal, equal and adult suffrage. It is again an expression of the Lincoln concept that, since unanimity is impossible and the rule of a minority as a permanent arrangement is wholly inadmissible, the rejection of the majority principle would mean anarchy or despotism in some form or other. The rule of a majority with adequate constitutional safeguards for the minority is

[14] *The Life and Writings of Abraham Lincoln,* edited by Philip Van Doren Stern (Modern Library, New York, 1940), p. 70; for brevity, hereafter referred to as *Writings of Lincoln.*

theretofore the only legitimate means of exercising the right to self-determination. The principle received an overwhelming endorsement from the United Nations in the Rhodesian case to which we shall revert later.

B. SITUATIONS WHERE APPLICABLE.

The situations in which the right to self-determination becomes applicable or operative is also indicated in contemporary law. It applies to every territory in which complete governmental powers have not been transferred to the people. The right unquestionably applies to a colony or a non-self-governing territory. But it will also apply to a technically independent territory where powers have not been transferred to the people. In this context the proposal of the United States before the 1966 U.N. Special Committee on Principles of International Law will be relevant. The proposal gave the principle *prima facie* applicability in the case of exercise of sovereignty by a State over a territory geographically distinct and ethnically or culturally diverse from the remainder of the State's territory, 'even though not as a colony or other non-self-governing territory.'[15]

It will be necessary to consider the significance of two important resolutions of the United Nations, viz. 1514 (XV) of 14 December 1960 read with 1541 (XV) of 15 December 1960. The celebrated resolution 1514 (XV), declaration on the granting of independence to colonial countries and peoples, criticizes 'colonialism in all its forms and manifestation' and recognizes 'the passionate yearning for freedom in all dependent peoples'. It then provides in paragraph 2 that 'all peoples have the right to self-determination' and specifies in paragraph 5 the territories and situations to which the right is attracted. Paragraph 5 states: 'Immediate steps shall be taken, in trust and non-self-governing territories or all other territories which have not yet attained independence, to transfer all powers to the peoples of those territories, without any conditions or reservations, in accordance with their freely expressed will and desire, without any distinction as to race, creed or colour, in order to enable them to enjoy complete independence and freedom.'

Resolution 1541 (XV), while laying down guidelines for determining whether or not an obligation exists to transmit information under Article 73(e) of the Charter, states in Principle IV: '*Prima facie* there is an obligation to transmit information in respect of a territory which is geographically separate and is distinct ethnically and/or culturally from the country administering it.' Principle V then provides: 'Once it has been established that such a *prima facie* case of geographical and ethnical or cultural distinctness of a terri-

[15] (1967) 61 AJIL, pp. 703, 724.

tory exists, other elements may then be brought into consideration. These additional elements may be, *inter alia,* of an administrative, political, juridical, economic or historical nature. If they affect the relationship between the metropolitan State and the territory concerned in a manner which arbitrarily places the latter in a position or status of subordination, they support the presumption that there is an obligation to transmit information under Article 73(e) of the Charter.'

In Principle (e) of the 1970 Declaration, there is again an affirmation that the right is of universal application although the separate and distinct status of a colony or other non-self-governing territory has been expressly recognized. It states: 'By virtue of the principle of equal rights and self-determination of peoples enshrined in the Charter, all peoples have the right freely to determine, without external interference, their political status and to pursue their economic, social and cultural development, and every State has the duty to respect this right in accordance with the provisions of the Charter.' The declaration further provides: 'The territory of a colony or other non-self-governing territory has, under the Charter of the United Nations, a status separate and distinct from the territory of the State administering it; and such separate and distinct status under the Charter shall exist until the people of the colony or non-self-governing territory have exercised their right of self-determination in accordance with the Charter, and particularly its purposes and principles.'

Therefore, in contemporary law the only relevant test is: Are the people of the territory concerned completely independent? And the only proof of an independent people is: Have all governmental powers been transferred to them unconditionally and without reservations in accordance with their freely expressed will and desire? Every territory—trust, colonial or non-self-governing, or any other territory including a technically independent territory—must satisfy the aforesaid test if it claims immunity from accountability to the international forum. The exemption from international accountability operates only in respect of a territory where the principle of self-determination has been implemented. Therefore, in every territory where the test is not satisfied, international responsibility is immediately attracted, irrespective of the status of the territory, for helping complete and unconditional transfer of power from the usurping authority to the people.

Any other interpretation will result in the startling paradox that only the dependent people in a dependent territory, but not the dependent people in a technically independent territory, are entitled to the benefit of equal rights and self-determination. No one will seriously suggest that the dependent people in Portuguese Angola or Rhodesia or the tribal peoples of Namibia have better rights in the field of self-determination than the people of Pakistan simply because of the fortuitous circumstance that Pakistan became technically independent in 1947. Since the right to self-determination or independence is the right of the people, not of the territory, and since the only test of independence is unconditional and effective transfer of all powers to the people, it will be illogical to contend that Pakistan was immune from international accountability for its failure to implement self-determination, even on the assumption that East Bengal was not a colony of the metropolitan West Pakistan. Pakistan's accountability to the international community would remain in full force until all the people of Pakistan had gained complete independence; till then the status of the Pakistani people could only be characterized as the status of a dependent people in a technically independent territory. The responsibility of the international community to help the people of Pakistan in their struggle against the usurper of power would remain fully operative till even the West Pakistani people became truly free and independent.

East Bengal was however a colony of West Pakistan according to the contemporary tests laid down in the Charter, Universal Declaration, Resolutions 1514 (XV) and 1541 (XV). The reasons are as follows: First, during the last 24 years, governmental powers were not wholly and unconditionally transferred to the people of Pakistan in the manner prescribed. Such powers remained in the hands of an administering authority without any popular base. At all material times the administering authority was manned by a different racial and cultural group, namely, a predominantly Punjabi-Pathan military oligarchy and civil bureaucracy; and it was located in a geographically distinct area, namely, West Pakistan, comparable to the metropolitan areas of the familiar colonial administrations. If contemporary norms of self-determination were followed in Pakistan, and the principle of majority rule with constitutional safeguards for the minority was implemented, it would have meant a government in which the people from East Bengal would have had a controlling voice. The persistent refusal of the West to implement self-determination reduced the majority people residing in East Bengal to a status of a dependent people in a nominally independent country. Secondly, the principle of self-determination having been denied, there was a *prima facie* presumption that East Bengal was a colony of West Pakistan because it was geographically alien and was distinct ethnically and/or culturally from the metropolitan West. The presumption becomes irrebuttable if one looks into the facts examined earlier and takes into consideration the historical, political, economic, cultural, linguistic, racial and administrative relations between the two wings. The inference seems natural that East Bengal was 'arbitrarily' placed by the West 'in a position or status of subordination' within the meaning of resolution 1541 (XV). International responsibility for East Bengal was therefore attracted on the additional ground that it was a colony of the West.

C.   MODES OF IMPLEMENTATION

The division of a State into two separate States has always been a permissible mode of implementing self-determination provided it is done in accordance with the will of the people concerned.   A recent example is the separation of Singapore from the Malaysian Federation.   As Quincy Wright had observed: 'There is no rule of international law forbidding revolutions within a state, and the United Nations Charter favours "self-determination of the people." Self-determination may take the form of the rebellion to oust an unpopular government, of colonial revolt, of an irredentist movement to transfer territory, or of a movement for the unification or federation of independent states. There is nothing in the Charter to prevent the latter, even if it destroys the independence of the participating states after their union.   Such a union occurred in the formation of the United States in the 18th century, the formation of Italy and Germany in the 19th century, and the formation of the United Arab Republic in the 20th century.   If divisions of a state or unions of states are formed primarily in accordance with the will of the peoples concerned, even if accompanied by some violence, neither international law nor the United Nations offers opposition. If, on the other hand, such changes are effected primarily by conquest, the case would be one of aggression, forbidden both by Charter and the contemporary international law.'[16]

The elaboration of Principle (e) of the 1970 Declaration has specified the modes of implementation: 'The establishment of a sovereign and independent State, the free association or integration with an independent State or the emergence into any other political status freely determined by a people constitute modes of implementing the right of self-determination by that people.'

This is really an improvement on Principle VI of resolution 1541 (XV) and has been formulated in a manner that it becomes applicable to all cases of self-determination and is not confined to a non-self-governing territory.

From Jefferson's famous declaration of 4 July 1776 till the declaration of the principles of international law by the United Nations in October 1970, there has been no dispute that, the principle that the

[16] Q. Wright, 'Intervention on Invitation' (1959), 53 AJIL, pp. 119, 121.

right of self-determination does not permit dismemberment of a country, is available only to a government which derives its authority from the will of the people expressed through periodic and genuine elections. Any other interpretation will only mean perpetuation of despotism or exploitative tyranny. Article 21(3) of the Universal Declaration points out that the legitimacy of a governmental authority is to be judged only on the basis of the will of the people: 'The will of the people shall be the basis of the authority of the Government; this will shall be expressed in periodic and genuine elections which shall be by universal and equal suffrage and shall be held by secret vote or by equivalent free voting procedures.'

The elaboration of Principle (e) of the 1970 Declaration, *inter alia*, provides: 'Nothing in the foregoing paragraphs shall be construed as authorizing or encouraging any action which would dismember or impair, totally or in part, the territorial integrity or political unity of sovereign and independent States *conducting themselves* in compliance with the principle of equal rights and self-determination of peoples as described above and *thus possessed of a government representing the whole people* belonging to the territory without distinction as to race, creed or colour.' (emphasis added)

It is therefore clear that the *military oligarchy of Islamabad* without any popular base was *not lawfully entitled to resist the movement for self-determination* launched by the Awami League on the *plea* that it would have amounted to *dismemberment of Pakistan.* If the State of Pakistan was possessed of a government representing the whole people including the majority residing in East Bengal and there was a constitutional regime ensuring rule by a majority with adequate guarantees to minorities, such a government alone could have resisted a movement by the minority, e.g. by the Punjabis or the Sindhis, for the dismemberment of the country on the plea of self-determination.

The principle so enunciated in contemporary international law is a corroboration of Jefferson's Declaration of Independence of 4 July 1776.[17] The movement for independence of Bangladesh can find no better source of inspiration than this most famous document of American history. It proclaimed the birth of a new nation and with matchless eloquence championed the cause of freedom of the oppressed people. One has yet to come across a more persuasive reasoning for separation of a country from the parent state and for dissolution of all political bonds between two peoples historically tied together. When separation becomes an impelling necessity, the birth of a new nation is inevitable: 'When in the Course of human events, it becomes necessary for one people to dissolve the political bonds which have connected them with another, and to assume among the Powers of

[17] Living Ideas in America, op. cit., p. 125.

the earth, the separate and equal station to which the Laws of Nature and of Nature's God entitle them, a decent respect to the opinions of mankind requires that they should declare the causes which impel them to the separation.'

In deference to the opinion of mankind Jefferson had explained the causes of separation: in the same way the world was informed by the people of East Bengal the reasons for their struggle for separation from Pakistan. The reasons for separation in America were: All men are created equal and they enjoy the 'unalienable Rights' of life, liberty and the pursuit of happiness. Governments are instituted among men 'deriving their just powers from the consent of the governed' for the purpose of securing these rights. Jefferson submitted facts to a candid world to show that: 'The history of the present King of Great Britain is a history of repeated injuries and usurpations, all having in direct object the establishment of an absolute Tyranny over these States... In every stage of these Oppressions We have Petitioned for Redress in the most humble terms: Our repeated Petitions have been answered only by repeated injury. A Prince, whose character is thus marked by every act which may define a Tyrant, is unfit to be the ruler of a free People.'

With the forfeiture of the title of an oppressive ruler, there arises the duty of the people to form a new government and to provide new guards for the purpose of securing the inalienable rights of the people: 'That whenever any Form of Government becomes destructive of these ends, it is the Right of the People to alter or to abolish it, and to institute new Government, laying its foundation on such principles and organizing its power in such form, as to them shall seem most likely to effect their Safety and Happiness. Prudence, indeed, will dictate that Governments long established should not be changed for light and transient causes; and accordingly all experience hath shown, that mankind are more disposed to suffer, while evils are sufferable, than to right themselves by abolishing the forms to which they are accustomed. But when a long train of abuses and usurpations, pursuing invariably the same Object evinces a design to reduce them under absolute Despotism, it is their right, it is their duty, to throw off such Government, and to provide new Guards for their security.'

If one applies these precepts of democracy and liberty to the history of Pakistan during the last 24 years, the case for independence of East Bengal by separation from Pakistan becomes incontestable. The Americans could only endure the oppressive rule of George III for a period of 16 years; the people of East Bengal suffered the exploitative tyranny of West Pakistan for a period of 24 years, including 13 years of repression and terror under a military oligarchy,

26

culminating in a war of genocide against the Bengali people.   It was
only when it became clear that there was not the slightest chance of
securing their inalienable human rights, and the military dictator
was determined to continue his reign of terror and oppression, that
the people of East Bengal decided to separate and to provide new
guards and a new government for their security.   Compared to the
repression and atrocities of Ayub Khan and Yahya Khan, the 'abuses'
and 'usurpations' of George III paled into insignificance.   Both in
America and Pakistan, the rupture came when 'evils' were no longer
'sufferable'.

The mode of implementing self-determination by separation also
finds support from the political philosophy of Abraham Lincoln.   A
constitutional regime means rule by a majority with proper checks
and balances and guaranteed rights for all.   The only alternative to
the majority principle is despotism or anarchy.   If a majority is
denied the democratic right to inaugurate a constitutional regime,
its revolutionary right to implement self-determination by dismemberment of the country is fully in consonance with the Lincoln concept.
We shall revert to the Lincoln concept while comparing the civil war
in the United States with the movement for self-determination in
East Bengal.

D.   DUTIES OF THE STATE:

(1) To promote self-determination.

(2) To refrain from forcible suppression.

We have already noticed that correlative to the peoples' right to
self-determination, there is the duty of every State to promote in
good faith the realisation of this right.   This is a positive duty. There
is also a negative duty to refrain from using force in suppressing any
popular movement for achieving self-determination.   Principle (e)
of the 1970 Declaration thus provides: 'Every State has a duty to
refrain from any forcible action which deprives peoples referred to
above in the elaboration of the present principle of their right to
self-determination and freedom and independence.'

Any threat or use of force with a view to depriving peoples of their
right to self-determination will amount to a threat or use of force in a
'manner inconsistent with the purposes of the United Nations' within
the meaning of Article 2(4) of the Charter. The correlation between
this prohibition and the right to self-determination has also been
brought out in the elaboration of Principle (a) which deals with the
threat or use of force in contravention of Article 2(4).   There again
the duty to refrain from any forcible action for suppressing self-
determination has been emphasized and it was also stated: 'The territory of a State shall not be the object of military occupation resulting

from the use of force in contravention of the provisions of the Charter.'

The obligations of the administering authority in Pakistan in relation to the movement for self-determination have to be considered in the context of the aforesaid norms.

E.   RIGHTS OF THE PEOPLE:

(1) To resist forcible action.

(2) To receive international assistance.

Corresponding to the duty of a State to refrain from forcible action for suppressing a movement for self-determination is the right of the people not only to resist such forcible action but also to seek and receive international assistance in support of their struggle.   Thus Principle (e) of the 1970 Declaration provides: 'In their actions against and resistance to such forcible action in pursuit of the exercise of their right to self-determination, such peoples are entitled to seek and to receive support in accordance with the purposes and principles of the Charter of the United Nations.'

The duty of the international community to render assistance to a peoples' movement for self-determination has been repeatedly emphasized in the Charter and in the 1970 Declaration.   For instance, in the context of Principle (e) it is stated: 'Every State has the duty to promote, through joint and separate action, the realization of the principle of equal rights and self-determination of peoples, in accordance with the provisions of the Charter, and to render assistance to the United Nations in carrying out the responsibility entrusted to it by the Charter regarding the implementation of the principle in order: (a) To promote friendly relations and co-operation among States; and (b) To bring a speedy end to colonialism having due regard to the freely expressed will of the peoples concerned; and bearing in mind that the subjection of peoples to alien subjugation, domination and exploitation constitutes a violation of the principle, as well as denial of fundamental human rights, and is contrary to the Charter of the United Nations.'

The duty of all states to cooperate with one another in matters of human rights and fundamental freedoms will also appear from the elaboration of Principle (d) which, *inter alia*, provides: 'States shall co-operate in the promotion of universal respect for and observance of human rights and fundamental freedoms for all, and in the elimination of all forms of racial discrimination and all forms of religious intolerence.'

International intervention—both pursuasive and coercive—is not only permissive but obligatory with a view to helping the establishment of a democratic regime freely determined by the will of the people in Pakistan. The failure to render such assistance to the movement for self-determination in Pakistan resulted in imperilling the peace and stability of the subcontinent.

Resume of Facts

The international norms discussed above have to be examined in the context of the facts set out in the earlier chapters. A resume of the relevant facts will perhaps be useful.

The constitutional history of Pakistan provides a classic example of persistent breaches of the contemporary tests for implementing self-determination. It also exposes the utter callousness of the international community in fulfilling its obligations for promoting self-determination in East Bengal. The first phase (14 August 1947 to 24 October 1954) witnessed a concerted effort by the West towards political and cultural subjugation of the East by employing force and various other repressive measures. The repressive laws were used against popular leaders who wanted autonomy and economic and political justice for East Bengal. When the United Front came into existence to implement its twenty-one-point programme for provincial autonomy, the ruling Muslim League tried to suppress the massive opposition by a reign of persecution. The movement, however, could not be suppressed by such repressive measures. In the 1954 elections held on the basis of adult franchise, the ruling Muslim League was completely routed and the opposition United Front won a stunning majority. There was therefore a clear mandate for the implementation of the twenty-one-point programme which envisaged provincial autonomy, economic prosperity, political freedom, repeal of repressive laws and release of political prisoners at the provincial level and the fulfilment of the democratic principle of majority rule at the Centre. The United Front Ministry was not permitted even to begin its effort for the implementation of its mandate and was summarily dismissed within two months of its coming into office. After such dismissal thousands were arrested and anyone in East Bengal who declared his faith in democracy was persecuted by some means or another. There was a complete press censorship. The instruments of oppression were military troops reinforced by a 40,000 strong police force.

At the central level, a Prime Minister enjoying the confidence of the legislature was unceremoniously dismissed and was replaced by a member of the Pakistani diplomatic corps then serving his term of office in the U.S.A. The constitution of 1954 was however allowed to be framed. In negation of the democratic principle of majority rule, the constitution deprived the people of East Bengal their due share in the legislative and executive branches of the central administration. East Bengal, in spite of its majority, was given only 50 per cent seats in the two Houses taken together.   Nevertheless, the constitution was approved as a compromise—a generous political accommodation by East Bengal.   The Constituent Assembly, however, introduced certain elementary measures to ensure parliamentary democracy, viz. that the Prime Minister and other ministers of the cabinet should be elected members of the parliament, the cabinet should be collectively responsible to parliament and the Governor-General as constitutional ruler should act on the advice of his ministers.   The introduction of these elementary provisions by the Constituent Assembly annoyed the Governor-General, Ghulam Mohammad, formerly a Punjabi civil servant without any popular sanction.   As a result, when parliamentary democracy was about to be inaugurated on the basis of the 1954 Constitution, the Governor-General reacted sharply and took the surgical step of dissolving the Constituent Assembly.

During the second period (25 October 1954 to 27 October 1958) the person at the helm of affairs was another civil servant, Iskander Mirza, who again had no popular sanction.   He was conspicuous for thriving on intrigues and conspiracies and for corrupting morals in public life.   No wonder there were frequent dismissals and installations of ministries at the Centre and at provincial levels.   Like his predecessor Ghulum Mohammad and his successor General Ayub Khan, Iskander Mirza had no faith in parliamentary democracy.   He told the people of Pakistan, trained in progressive realisation of self-government since 1861 and in parliamentary institutions for responsible government since 1909, that parliamentary democracy was not suited to their genius.   Accordingly, the bureaucratic head of state introduced his theory of controlled democracy which meant that the people must be controlled dictatorially until they had learned what Mirza thought was of the essence of democracy.

The second Constituent Assembly was however permitted to frame the Constitution of 23 March 1956 under the stewardship of Mirza. This Constitution was again conspicuous for its denial of provincial autonomy in East Bengal, denial of the principle of the majority representation at the Centre and the introduction of the impracticable parity system between the two wings of Pakistan.

The constitution-makers in Pakistan seem to have forgotten the lesson of Abraham Lincoln that rejection of the majority principle would only mean the introduction of anarchy or despotism in some form or other.

Nevertheless, when elections under the 1956 Constitution, promised for 1957 but postponed till 1958, were due, Iskander Mirza, on 7 October 1958, abrogated the Constitution, proclaimed martial law throughout Pakistan and dismissed the central and provincial governments and legislative bodies. Mirza appointed General Ayub Khan as the Martial Law Administrator. But within 20 days three Generals representing Ayub gave an ultimatum to Mirza and packed him off to England. On 27 October 1958 the military oligarchy came into power, and completed its 13th year on 27 October 1971.

The third period (27 October 1958 to 25 March 1969) is the regime of General Ayub Khan. He ruled the country for over a decade through a number of repressive laws introduced through Presidential Orders and Ordinances and Martial Law Regulations, mentioned earlier. Political parties were banned and political activities forbidden; political leaders were either disqualified or imprisoned or their movements were severely restricted.

General Ayub Khan used the familiar argument of a colonizer for denying parliamentary democracy to the people, viz. the inadequacy of political, economic, social and educational preparedness for a responsible government, an argument condemned by the United Nations in its famous Resolution 1514 (XV).

During his regime, Ayub Khan made two experiments with his political theories, broadly formulated by him on 'a warmish night' at a Hotel in London 1954. The first was the theory of basic democracy. Since the elected representatives of the people could not be trusted with national policies or political power Ayub conceded that a limited voice in local self-government might be granted to the people of Pakistan for the study and solution of local problems and for developing a sense of civic responsibility. This is what basic democracy meant. To a people used to local self-government since 1885 under the British Rule, such a system could create little enthusiasm. After eliminating all political opposition and banning all political parties and their activities, Ayub utilised a few thousand basic democrats for perpetuating his military regime and for denying popular government at the Centre and in the provinces.

Ayub also gave the country a constitution in 1962. In his constitution all powers were concentrated in his own hands; he was elected President indirectly by the basic democrats who, in their turn, were elected for the limited purpose of local self-government. In spite of popular demands, Ayub did not accept the principle of direct election on the basis of adult franchise. Ayub's constitution was not only expressly a denial of the parliamentary form of government to which the people were accustomed, it was a mockery of the presidential system of government known to constitutional lawyers. There was no separation of powers, no effective checks and balances. It was a denial of provincial autonomy to the people of East Bengal. It was a betrayal of the Lahore resolution of 1940 which was the foundation of the independent State of Pakistan. It was a denial of the majority principle of Abraham Lincoln. The pretended gift of fundamental rights in his constitution was totally nullified by the exclusion of all his repressive laws from the scope of those rights.

It was during Ayub's regime that Sheikh Mujibur Rahman's famous six-point programme was first announced. It was a programme for a constitutional regime in Pakistan on the basis of equality between its two wings. The support that Sheikh Mujibur Rahman received from his people was overwhelming. This unnerved the military dictator. In March 1966 Ayub threatened the people of East Bengal with a civil war if they were to take seriously the 'horrid dream' of autonomy envisaged by the six-point programme; Mujib, however, asked his people for a peaceful and democratic movement for the achievement of self-determination.

The reaction of the military dictator was one of anger and frustration. He used his repressive laws for terrorizing the political leaders of East Bengal. The worst victims of his repression were collectively the people of East Bengal, politically the Awami League and individually Sheikh Mujibur Rahman. During the period of little over a decade of the Ayub regime, Sheikh Mujib was the victim of the repressive laws of the military oligarchy for nearly nine years.

We have described the fourth period (25 March 1969 to 25 March 1971) as the period when the strategy of deception by the military dictator was practised and perfected in East Bengal. The popular leaders of East Bengal were deceived into talks for a political settlement by Yahya, while his generals were making final preparations for launching a war of genocide against the Bengali people. It was during this period that for the first time in 23 years national elections were held on the basis of adult franchise. General Yahya who appointed himself President of Pakistan frankly admitted: 'The people did not bring me to power. I came myself.'[18]

In Yahya's first address to the nation on 26 March 1969 he solemnly declared that his mission was the establishment of a constitutional government. He had repeatedly promised transfer of power to the people after the elections. His Legal Framework Order mentioned three important guidelines for the future constitution of Pakistan viz. (i) maximum autonomy for the provinces, (ii) adequate powers for the federal government and (iii) removal of economic and all other disparities between the two wings of Pakistan. Sheikh Mujib and his Awami League fought the elections on the basis of their six-point programme. The programme was not an innovation. It was basically similar to the twenty-one-point programme on the basis of which the United Front came into power in East Bengal in 1954. The six-point programme envisaged provincial autonomy for East Bengal

[18] *Time*, 2 August 1971.

and a federal structure for the centre. The programme was fully in compliance with the guidelines specified in Yahya's Legal Framework Order. Yahya must have thought so, otherwise it is inconceivable that a military dictator, in possession of total power, would permit the Awami League to contest the elections for implementing this programme. The elections were held on the basis of adult franchise in December 1970. According to all impartial observers the elections were free and fair and polling was heavy. Sheikh Mujib and his party received an overwhelming mandate from the people. The Awami League captured in its own right 160 seats out of 162 seats allotted to East Bengal in a National Assembly of 300 elected members. The remaining two elected members from East Bengal subsequently extended their full support to Mujib's six points. It was therefore an outstanding event in the history of modern democracy that all the elected members of the National Assembly from East Bengal were committed to the six-point programme put forward by the Awami League. Thus the Awami League and its supporters had an absolute majority in the National Assembly and were in a position to inaugurate for the first time a constitutional regime in Pakistan on the basis of the six-point programme. Had President Yahya followed the Lincoln precept that the alternative to the majority principle was despotism or anarchy, and had he permitted the normal democratic course for the return to a constitutional regime in Pakistan, the tragedy that has happened since 25 March 1971 could have been easily avoided. Yahya and his military generals were never serious about their promise of transfer of power to the people. What unnerved the military generals was the stunning victory of the Awami League. The junta never conceived that Sheikh Mujib would have an absolute majority in the National Assembly; a coalition with some West Pakistani parties was their expectation. No such civil government would be able to function without the blessings of the military oligarchy. This was more or less in tune with the thinking of the military generals in Turkey who had, at about the same time, in March 1971, given an ultimatum to Prime Minister Demirel to resign, who did resign. Demirel was in office and Mujib was yet to come to power. Both, however, suffered from the delusion that a parliamentary majority could alone either bring them to power or depose them.

On 1 March, President Yahya suddenly announced his decision to postpone the inaugural session of the National Assembly. This was apparently done in response to an unreasonable demand by a minority leader, Mr. Z. A. Bhutto (now President of Pakistan). This was done without the knowledge or consent of the majority leader, Sheikh Mujib. Mujib called for a general strike in protest. Several unarmed civilians were killed in Dacca by Yahya's troops. Sheikh Mujib then launched his non-violent non-cooperation movement. The spectacular success of the movement has no precedent in modern history. It not only proved the effectiveness of Mujib's authority in East Bengal, it demonstrated to the whole world the forfeiture of Yahya's authority. Yahya's writ did not run anywhere in East Bengal unless it was backed by bullets supplied by foreign countries. Not even one Judge of the High Court came forward to administer the oath of office to Tikka Khan, the newly appointed Governor.

In the meantime, the authority of Mr. Bhutto in West Pakistan was eroding swiftly. As we have seen, there were clear indications that at least 210 out of 300 elected members of the National Assembly, i.e., more than two-thirds, were pressing for immediate transfer of power to an interim government headed by Sheikh Mujib.

Between 16 and 25 March Yahya carried on talks in Dacca for a political settlement. Even as late as on 24 March it appeared to the Awami League leaders that there was nothing to prevent a settlement and the framing of an interim constitution for immediate transfer of power. On 25 March, while the Awami League leaders were given no indication of any breakdown of the talks, Yahya suddenly left Dacca and his army took Mujib into custody in the early hours of 26 March. By midnight the reign of terror had begun in full fury. The interval of 10 days had been fully utilised by Yahya's generals to implement the contingency plan by clandestine military preparations and troop movements.

In spite of an official news blackout, the event in Pakistan since 25 March 1971 became known to the whole world. A calculated genocide was committed against the Bengali people. *Newsweek* of 2 August 1971 characterized it as 'The Murder of a People.' International public opinion accepted the fact that crimes against humanity unequalled since Hitler's time were being committed by Yahya's army of occupation. The humanitarian principles of the Hague Convention IV, the Geneva Protocol of 1925, the Geneva Conventions of 1949, the laws of the Nuremberg Charter and Judgment, the Universal Declaration of 1948, the Genocide Convention of 1948 and the Basic Principles for the Protection of Civilians in Armed Conflicts laid down by the General Assembly on 9 December 1970 were violated with impunity.

The objects of the unspeakable cruelties and the heinous crimes against humanity were never in doubt. East Bengal with its majority population had to be reduced to a minority by a deliberate war of genocide. What the ballots had declared constitutionally had to be reversed by an indiscriminate use of bullets. East Bengal had to be kept as a colonial market for the products of West Pakistan. The

27

Bengali people were to accept a status of perpetual serfdom.   There was to be no return to the democratic principle of majority rule with safeguards for the minority.   This was how the shattered image of Pakistan as one nation was sought to be preserved.

American Civil War and the Independence Movement in East Bengal: Seven Points of Difference

Why should a majority secede if there is a democracy as envisaged by Abraham Lincoln? Yet there is a lingering suspicion in some quarters that the movement for the independence of East Bengal was a secessionist movement comparable to the attempt of some of the southern states in the USA during the 1861-1865 Civil War; accordingly, such a movement for the disintegration of Pakistan, it was felt, should have been condemned and suppressed as Abraham Lincoln had condemned and suppressed the insurrectionary movement in the United States.   *Time* magazine of 2 August 1971 stated: 'There is a case for Yahya's Lincolnesque attempt to hold the Pakistani house together; there is none for his methods.' The analogy is misleading; Abraham Lincoln's own writings will show that East Bengal's claim for independence was legally and morally incontestable, and Yahya had no case whatsoever. An argument of this sort is based on an inadequate appreciation of the vital differences between the two situations.   The situation in America was clearly explained by Abraham Lincoln in his first inaugural address of 4 March 1861, his message to the Congress on 4 July 1861, his second inaugural address of 4 March 1865 and in some of his contemporary writings.   There are seven main points of difference between the American Civil War and the independence movement in East Bengal.

1.   On 6 November 1860, Abraham Lincoln was elected the first Republican President of the United States. He was inaugurated as President on 4 March 1861.   Between these two dates seven States seceded from the Union: South Carolina, Mississippi, Florida, Alabama, Georgia, Louisiana and Texas.   On 4 February 1861, six of the seceded States met at Montgomery, Alabama, to form a Confederate Government.   There was an apprehension among some people in the South that their property and their peace and personal security would be endangered by the inauguration of the Republican Administration.   According to Lincoln, there never had been any reasonable cause for such apprehension.[19]   A powerful minority interest in the South had been preparing for secession for more than 30 years.   The South had an iron hand in the government of the whole country.   It elected Northern men as Presidents when they would favour its cause. It controlled the Senate absolutely and even the House when necessity

[19] *Writings of Lincoln*, op. cit., p. 647.

demanded. After the Dred Scott decision, it appeared that the South had apparently taken over the third and last branch of the government, i.e. the judiciary. Its victory was complete.[20]

The movement for secession started mainly because of the failure of the South to elect a President to their own liking. In a letter of 12 June 1863 Lincoln wrote: 'Prior to my installation here it had been inculcated that any State had a lawful *right to secede* from the National Union, and that it would be expedient to *exercise* the right whenever the devotees of the doctrine should *fail to elect a President to their own liking.* I was elected contrary to their liking; and, accordingly so far as was legally possible, they had taken seven States out of the Union, had seized many of the United States forts, and had fired upon the United States flag, all before I was inaugurated and, of course, before I had done any official act whatever. The rebellion thus begun soon ran into present civil war; and, in certain respects, it began on very unequal terms between the parties. The insurgents had been preparing for it more than 30 years, while the government had taken no steps to resist them.'[21] (emphasis added)

In his message to the Congress on 4 July 1861, Abraham Lincoln pointed out one of the vital issues involved in the secessionist movement in the USA. As Lincoln puts it: "Our popular government has often been called an experiment. Two points in it our people have already settled—the successful establishing and the successful administering of it. One still remains—its successful maintenance against a formidable internal attempt to overthrow it. It is now for them to demonstrate to the world that *those* who can fairly *carry an election* can *also suppress a rebellion*; that ballots are the ordinary and peaceful successors of bullets; and that *when ballots have fairly and constitutionally decided, there can be no successful appeal back to bullets*; that there can be no successful appeal, except to ballots themselves at succeeding elections. Such will be a great lesson of peace, teaching men that *what they cannot take by an election, neither can they take it by a war;* teaching all the folly of being the beginners of a war.'[22] (emphasis added)

The situation in Pakistan was just the reverse. For a period of nearly 24 years all attempts to establish a popular government and to inaugurate a constitutional regime were frustrated. In the first national elections held in December 1970 the people of Pakistan gave an overwhelming mandate to Sheikh Mujibur Rahman's Awami League to establish a constitutional regime on the basis of its six-point programme. There is evidence that more than two-thirds of

[20] *Ibid.*, pp. 60-61. Editor's comments.

[21] *Ibid.*, p. 757.

[22] *Ibid.*, p. 675.

the National Assembly were agreeable to an immediate transfer of power from the military oligarchy to a popular central government under the leadership of Sheikh Mujib. A military dictator, with the support of a minority leader, Mr Bhutto, then launched a war to upset the verdict of the people. The question therefore is: can a military dictator with the help of bullets suppress the mandate of the people given by ballots? When one applies Lincoln's concept to the situation in Pakistan, the answer must be emphatically negative. There was no question in Pakistan of any internal attempt by a minority, defeated in elections, to overthrow a popular government winning the elections.

2. The majority of the qualified voters in the USA including the southern states were against separation. As Lincoln pointed out in his message to the Congress on 4 July 1861: 'It may well be questioned whether there is today a majority of the legally qualified voters of any State, except perhaps South Carolina, in favour of disunion. There is much reason to believe that the Union men are the majority in many, if not in every other one, of the so-called seceded States. The contrary has not been demonstrated in any of them. It is ventured to affirm this even of Virginia and Tennessee; for the result of an election held in military camps, where bayonets are all on one side of the question voted upon, can scarcely be considered as demonstrating popular sentiment. At such an election, all that large class who are at once for the Union and against coercion would be coerced to vote against the Union.'[23]

Here again the situation in Pakistan was just the reverse. The attempt of the majority to establish a federal government on the basis of the six-point programme was frustrated by the military action of a dictator. The movement for independence of East Bengal was thrust upon a majority people. Such a movement cannot be compared with secessionist movement of the southern States which did not even receive the support of the majority of the people within those States. On the contrary, the American analogy which is relevant to the Pakistani context is the American movement for independence from a colonial rule. As we have already noticed, the strongest moral foundation of the movement in East Bengal is provided in Jefferson's famous document of 4 July 1776.

3. The alleged right of secession was sought to be exercised in the 1860s when the Federal Constitution of 1787, ordained and established by 'We the People of the United States', had been successfully functioning for a period of over 70 years. This is a popular constitution which assured minority rights and guaranteed a majority rule with checks and balances. Between 1774 and 1787, by a process of

trial and error, efforts were made for a more perfect Union. In the Articles of Confederation of 1778 all the then thirteen States agreed that the Union should be perpetual. Eventually, the preamble to the Federal Constitution provided that the object of the people of the United States was 'to form a more perfect Union'. Section 4 of Article IV of the Constitution provides that the United States 'shall guarantee to every State in this Union a republican form of government, and shall protect each of them against invasion; and on application of the Legislature, or of the Executive (when the Legislature cannot be convened) against domestic violence.' How can the Federal government fulfil this guarantee in a seceded State which later on rejects a republican form of government? None of the States had a State Constitution independent of the Union. For the fulfilment of this guarantee the necessary power to prevent secession has to be implied. As Lincoln had explained: 'The Constitution provides and all the States have accepted the provision, that 'the United States shall guarantee to every State in this Union a republican form of government.' But lf a State may lawfully go out of the Union, having done so, it may also discard the republican form of government; so that to prevent its going out is an indispensable means to the end of maintaining the guarantee mentioned; and when an end is lawful and obligatory, the indispensable means to it are also lawful and obligatory.'[24]

The Constitution of the United States guarantees the fundamental rights of the individual. If the constitutional provisions are enforced there can be no question of destroying the Union which would endure forever. As Lincoln puts it: 'Continue to execute all the express provisions of our National Constitution, and the Union will endure forever—it being impossible to destroy it except by some action not provided for in the instrument itself.'[25] Civil War would be unnecessary in a State where the fundamental rights of the individual are guaranteed. As Professor H. Lauterpacht has observed: 'It is possible that in the ultimate rational development of the political organisation of mankind rebellion against national authority will appear in an altogether different light. When that happens international law will fulfil functions of a scope infinitely wider than it does at present. It will render unlawful not only international but also civil war in a way comparable to the suppression of civil war within the component territories of the member States of a Federal State as a result of the guarantee, in the Federal Constitution, of the fundamental rights of the individual. The final political organisation of mankind will signify the incorporation of these rights as an organic part of

[24] *Ibid.*, p. 676.
[25] *Ibid.*, p. 649.

the constitution of the international commonwealth in a manner similar to that in which Section 4 of Article IV of the Constitution of the United States provides... In so far as civil war is due to a disregard or suppression of those rights, it will be eliminated as the result of the constitutional guarantees provided by the *civitas maxima* and enforced by judicial review and executive action.'[26]

In Pakistan, there was no constitutional regime with guarantees of fundamental rights of the individual. There was no constitution ordained by the people of Pakistan obligating the government in power, expressly or by implication, to prevent the declaration of independence of East Bengal by the majority people. The argument is available only to a popular government exercising authority under a constitution in which human rights and fundamental freedoms are not only enshrined but also enforced. Such an argument was never available to a military dictator trying to suppress the verdict of the people freely declared for the establishment of a constitutional regime on the basis of the six-point programme.

4.   It is because of the constitutional provisions and their enforcement procedures in the United States, which guaranteed a majority rule with checks and balances and protected the minority rights, that Lincoln had concluded that the idea of secession in the context of the facts before him was of the essence of anarchy. In the first inaugural address he said : 'A *majority* held in restraint by constitutional checks and limitations, and always changing easily with deliberate change of popular opinions and sentiments, is the *only true sovereign of a free people*. Whoever rejects it does, of necessity, fly to anarchy or to despotism. *Unanimity is impossible*; the *rule of a minority*, as a permanent arrangement, is *wholly inadmissible;* so that, *rejecting the majority principle, anarchy* or *despotism* in some form is all that is left.'[27] (emphasis added)

Even in a constitutional regime the minority may acquire a right of revolution if the constitutional guarantees are in practice disregarded by the majority in power. There was no such denial in the United States which could support the secessionist movement. As Lincoln pointed out: "All profess to be content in the Union if all constitutional rights can be maintained. Is it true, then, that any right, plainly written in the Constitution, has been denied? I think not. Happily the human mind is so constituted that no party can reach to the audacity of doing this. Think, if you can, of a single instance in which a plainly written provision of the Constitution has ever been denied. If by the mere force of numbers a *majority should deprive a minority* of any clearly written *constitutional right*, it

    [26] H. Lauterpacht, *Recognition in International Law* (Cambridge, 1947), p. 93.
    [27] *Writings of Lincoln*, op. cit., p. 653.

might, in a moral point of view, *justify revolution*—certainly would if such a right were a vital one. But such is not our case. All the vital rights of minorities and of individuals are so plainly assured to them by affirmations and negations, guarantees and prohibitions, in the Constitution, that controversies never arise concerning them."[28] (emphasis added)

If the above principles are applied to the Pakistani case, the declaration of independence of East Bengal can never be compared with the secessionist movement in the USA for, as Lincoln had shown, it is the rejection of the majority principle, not its acceptance, which results in anarchy or despotism. He had equated the idea of secession by a minority with anarchy. The warning of Lincoln has come true in Pakistan.

Yahya knew that unanimity in the National Assembly was impossible in view of the attitude of Bhutto's PPP. He also knew that 210 out of 300 members were agreeable to the establishment of an interim government headed by Sheikh Mujib. He was further aware that a minority government under the leadership of Mr Bhutto as a permanent arrangement was 'wholly inadmissible.' Had he permitted the National Assembly to meet and discuss the constitutional framework on the basis of the six-point programme, perhaps there could have been some kind of workable agreement. Instead of following the normal constitutional procedure, he summarily rejected the majority principle and unleashed a reign of terror to upset the verdict of the people. Following Lincoln's logic, the inference is unavoidable that by rejecting the majority principle, the military ruler only promoted anarchy and despotism in Pakistan.

5. When a majority is denied its democratic right of framing a popular constitution or is prevented from exercising its constitutional right of amending the constitution, the revolutionary right of the majority to dismember the country as a means of implementing self-determination, can never be in dispute. This is the inherent right of the people themselves. A military dictator has no say in the matter. As Lincoln had expressed the idea in his first inaugural address: "This country, with its institutions, belongs to the *people* who *inhabit* it. Whenever they shall grow weary of the existing government, they can exercise their constitutional right of amending it, or their *revolutionary right to dismember* or overthrow it... The chief magistrate derives all his authority from the people, and they have conferred none upon him to fix *terms for the separation of the States. The people themselves can do this also if they choose*; but the executive, as such, has nothing to do with it."[29] (emphasis added)

[28] *Ibid.*, p. 652.
[29] *Ibid.*, pp. 655, 656.

If one considers the principles so enunciated by Lincoln in the context of Pakistan, the majority Awami League had four clear alternatives after the elections in December 1970:

(i) On the floor of the National Assembly, to introduce a national constitution based on the six-point programme which provided for a federal structure with maximum autonomy for the provinces, adequate powers for the federal government and the removal of economic and all other disparities between the provinces. Since unanimity is impossible, the framing of such a constitution would have been fully in conformity with democratic principles, even if the minority were in disagreement. If such a constitution were permitted to be framed and enforced, perhaps in course of time there would have emerged a strong and united Pakistan without discrimination between its two wings.

(ii) It was not improbable that on the floor of the National Assembly the majority party as a measure of accommodation to the minority would have agreed to some modifications of the six-point programme. Since the majority had won the elections on a mandate from the people to implement a particular programme, any such modification could only become effective if it were acceptable to the majority people voting in its favour.

(iii) Instead of employing democratic compulsion and forcing the six-point programme upon the minority parties, the Awami League could have lawfully announced on the floor of the National Assembly its decision to separate and establish an independent State of Bangladesh in a peaceful manner. Such a step could not have been compared with the secessionist movement in the USA. No one acquainted with the history of Pakistan will doubt for a moment that such a step would have been fully in conformity with the will of the majority people of Pakistan who resided in East Bengal. It will have been observed that early in March 1971 Sheikh Mujib had staked his political future in trying to persuade his people to exercise restraint and not to press forward the demand for an independent State of Bangladesh. This he did only with a view to preserving the integrity of Pakistan and its eroding image as one nation.

(iv) Since it became impossible to implement the will of the people in a constitutional manner and in accordance with the established democratic principles due to the refusal of the military ruler to convene the National Assembly and his subsequent armed action in East Bengal, the majority had the undoubted revolutionary right to establish a separate and independent State of Bangladesh in exercise of its recognized right of self-determination. The resultant dismemberment of Pakistan is fully permissible in international law. Such a step could not have been considered a secession for, as Sheikh Mujib had observed: 'We are the majority so we cannot secede. They, the Westerners, are the minority, and it is up to them to secede.'[30]

By no stretch of imagination can a military oligarchy without any popular base claim lawful authority to suppress the electoral verdict for a federal structure on the basis of six-point programme or the revolutionary right of the majority to establish a sovereign and independent State of Bangladesh—both being considered as permissible modes for implementing self-determination. A dictator or a tyrant has no right to resist such a movement for, as Professor Lauterpacht pointed out, 'there is no self-determination and no independence under the rule of a tyranny.'[31]

6. The geographical position of the States provided another important reason against separation of the southern States. As Lincoln pointed out: "*Physically speaking, we cannot separate.* We cannot remove our respective sections from each other, nor build an impassable wall between them. A husband and wife may be divorced, and go out of the presence and beyond the reach of each other; but the different parts of our country cannot do this. They cannot but remain face to face, and intercourse, either amicable or hostile, must continue between them. Is it possible, then, to make that intercourse more advantageous or more satisfactory after separation than before? Can aliens make treaties easier than friends can make laws? Can treaties be more faithfully enforced between aliens than laws can among friends? Suppose you go to war, you cannot fight always; and when, after much loss on both sides, and no gain on either, you cease fighting, the identical old question as to terms of intercourse are again upon you.'[32] (emphasis added)

No one would seriously suggest that the above reasoning had any application to Pakistan—described as 'a geographical curiosity and, as it sadly proved, a political absurdity'[33]—with its two wings separated by 1,200 miles of Indian territory, 2,450 miles away by sea from each other, without any direct land communication.

7. Finally, the issues involved in the two situations were fundamentally different. In the United States the issues were:

(i) Should the institution of slavery be strengthened, perpetuated and extended?

(ii) Was there any basis for the apprehension among some people in the South that the installation of the first Republican President in the USA would endanger their peace and personal security?

In Pakistan, the issues were:

[30] *Newsweek*, 5 April 1971, p. 11.
[31] Lauterpacht, *Recognition in International Law* (Cambridge, 1947), p. 173.
[32] Writings of Lincoln, op. cit., pp. 654, 655.
[33] *Time*, 2 August 1971, p. 30.

28

(i) Can a military dictator by taking recourse to bullets replace the authority of the ballots for a constitutional regime?

(ii) When the majority is deprived of its democratic right to establish a constitutional regime, is it permissible for the majority to declare independence as a mode of implementing self-determination in respect of the geographically separated territory in which they reside?

Pakistan's Plea of Internal Public Order

Pakistan claimed immunity from international scrutiny on the ground that the impugned acts were matters essentially within her domestic jurisdiction and accordingly Article 2(7) of the Charter precluded UN intervention. Since value deprivations of individuals had always been sought to be justified by the deprivers in the name of the familiar strategy of internal public order, it will be pertinent to examine briefly the legal status of such an argument in the context of the events in Pakistan.

Even under the customary law before the Charter regime, every State was under a legal duty to treat its population humanely. 'Each State has a legal duty to see that conditions prevailing within its own territory do not menace international peace and order, and to this end it must treat its own population in a way which will not violate the dictates of humanity and justice or shock the conscience of the mankind.'[34]

In fact, the *magna carta* of mankind or the Universal Declaration of 1948 became necessary because the disregard of human rights 'have resulted in barbarous acts which have outraged the conscience of mankind.' The law of the Charter regime has made matters of human rights *ipso facto* matters of international concern. The concern for human rights has been thoroughly internationalized even where no element of violence is involved. The reason is that in an intensely interdependent world in which 'peoples interact not merely through the modalities of collaborative or combative operations but also through shared subjectivities',[35] systematic suppression of human rights by any government produces deprivatory effects not only upon its own people but also upon peoples beyond the border. The position has been admirably summed up by McDougal and Reisman: 'Hence, domestic jurisdiction means little more than a general community concession of primary, but not exclusive, competence over matters arising and intimately concerned with aspects of the internal public order of states. Where such acts precipitate major inclusive deprivations,

[34] 'The International Law of the Future' (1944), 38 AJIL Supp., p. 55.

[35] McDougal and Reisman, 'Rhodesia and the United Nations: The Lawfulness of International Concern' (1968), 62 AJIL, pp. 1, 12.

jurisdiction is internationalized and inclusive concern and measures become permissible.'[36] Much earlier, Professor Lauterpacht had said: '... human rights and freedoms having become the subject of a solemn international obligation and of one of the fundamental purposes of the Charter, are no longer a matter which is essentially within the domestic jurisdiction of the Members of the United Nations.'[37]

Any serious breach of human rights obligations in a particular State is therefore bound to disturb the conditions of stability without which peaceful and friendly relations among nations cannot be maintained. It is because of this close correlation between the observance of human rights and the fundamental freedoms on the one hand and the maintenance of international peace and security on the other that Article 2(7) of the Charter itself contemplates that the domestic jurisdiction clause 'shall not prejudice the application of enforcement measures under Chapter VII.'

The Rhodesian Precedent and Default of UN in Pakistan

An important precedent in United Nations practice can be found on this point in the Rhodesian case. It will be recalled that the main contention of Ian Smith's regime against United Nations intervention in connection with the Unilateral Declaration of Independence (UDI) was that the matter was essentially within the domestic jurisdiction of Rhodesia and no element of coercion or aggression was involved. This contention was rejected by the United Nations on the main ground that any attempt to perpetuate minority rule amounts to a denial of the right of the majority to self-determination and as such the matter becomes one of serious international concern calling for the application of appropriate international prescriptions—both persuasive and coercive. It will be pertinent to refer to Resolution 2012 (XX) of 12 October 1965, 2022 (XX) of 5 November 1965 and 2024 (XX) of 11 November 1965 of the General Assembly, and also Resolutions 216 of 12 November 1965, 217 of 20 November 1965 and 221 of 9 April 1966, of the Security Council.[38]

The impact of the resolutions is not confined to the Rhodesian situation and the general principles laid down there are fully applicable to the Pakistani context. The resolutions are of universal application because in terms their source of authority was traced to the Universal Declaration and the Colonial Resolution 1514(XX) which, we have already submitted, are not confined to a trust or non-self governing territory but apply to every territory where the right of self-determination has been denied to the people. Three important

---

[36] *Ibid.*, p. 15.

[37] Lauterpacht, *International Law and Human Rights* (1950), p. 178.

[38] For texts, see (1966), 60 AJIL, pp. 921-6.

general principles emerge from the aforesaid United Nations resolutions on Rhodesia.

First, the right of the people to self-determination will be considered to have been denied if the principle of majority rule through appropriate constitutional process is not introduced. Accordingly, the United Nations 'recognizes the legitimacy of their (i.e. the majority of the people) struggle for the enjoyment of their right.' Having so recognized the principle of majority rule as a vehicle for the expression of self-determination, it was provided that 'the perpetuation of such minority rule (i.e., white minority regime of Ian Smith) would be incompatible with the principle of equal rights and self-determination of peoples.' Accordingly the United Nations emphasized the duty of non-recognition of 'illegal racist minority' regime which had usurped power in Rhodesia.

Second, where a majority has been deprived of the right to self-determination, the deprivatory measures are no longer a matter of internal public order of the State concerned. In Rhodesia, the constitutional system of enfranchisement was largely based on wealth criteria which could only be understood in the light of the Land Apportionment Act, 1943, under which half of the best land was allocated for white use, i.e. for less than 6% of the population. Industry was being controlled by the whites and the African workers received one-twelfth of the wages compared to a European for the same work. The application of the Preventive Detention Act of 1959, the Vagrancy Act, the notorious Law and Order (Maintenance) Act of 1960 and the Emergency Powers (Maintenance of Law and Order) Regulations, permitting, *inter alia,* detention of opponents of the minority rule, were considered by the international community to have had enormously deprivatory effects upon the majority of the population.[39] Not only was the legitimacy of such deprivatory measures on the pretext of internal public order rejected by the world body, it recommended appropriate constitutional measures for the effective transfer of power 'to a representative government in keeping with the aspirations of the majority of the people.' The United Nations recommended that constitutional arrangements on the basis of universal adult suffrage should not only be made but must be preceded by: (a) repeal of all repressive and discriminatory municipal legislations; (b) release of all political prisoners, political detainees and restrictees; (c) removal of all restrictions on the political activities of the majority of the people, and (d) the establishment of full democratic freedom and equality of political rights.

Third, the United Nations also pointed out the consequences of an attempt to perpetuate minority rule by the denial of majority rights

[39] McDougal and Reisman, op. cit., p. 4.

to political freedom and independence. The nature of sanctions recommended by the international community is also significant. The United Nations recognized that such a deprivation could easily create 'an explosive situation' within the State 'which threatens international peace and security' calling for urgent action by the Security Council under Chapter VII. The Council accordingly called upon all States not to entertain any diplomatic or other relations with the illegal minority regime and to refrain from any action which would assist or encourage the illegal regime and in particular desist from providing the illegal regime with arms, equipment and military materials, and to do their utmost to break off economic relations and to impose an embargo on vital supplies like oil and petroleum products. Should it so appear that supplies of any vital products from the outside world 'will afford great assistance and encouragement to the illegal regime in Southern Rhodesia, thereby enabling it to remain longer in being', the resultant situation would constitute a threat to peace. When the situation developed into a threat to peace, the Council called upon all States to ensure 'the diversion of any of their vessels reasonably believed to be carrying' such vital products and 'destined for Rhodesia.' The Council called upon the United Kingdom 'to prevent by the use of force, if necessary' the arrival of any such vessel and 'to arrest and detain' any tanker carrying such supplies for the illegal regime.

A pertinent question arises: did the international community make any attempt to discharge its responsibility for promoting self-determination in Pakistan as it did in Rhodesia? If the United Nations could emphasize the duty of non-recognition of the minority regime of Ian Smith, why did it not recommend to the international community the duty of non-recognition of the military dictator in Pakistan who did not even have that much of a popular base which Ian Smith's minority government had in Rhodesia? If the United Nations could consider the enforcement of repressive laws in Rhodesia a matter of international concern and recommend their repeal, why did it not consider the repressive laws in Pakistan, equally if not more pernicious, during the last 24 years, a matter of international concern? If the United Nations could recommend the release of all political prisoners and removal of all restrictions on the political activities of the majority people in Rhodesia, why did it not recommend similar measures for the enforcement of the legitimate rights of the majority people in Pakistan with a view to promoting self-determination? Denial of the majority principle even without any element of violence was considered by the world body to have created an 'explosive situation' in Rhodesia threatening international peace and security, but the persistent refusal for a period of 24 years to transfer power to the majority in Pakistan was completely ignored by the international community. To help implement majority rule, the United Nations not only directed severance of diplomatic and economic relations with the minority regime, but called upon its members to desist from providing it with arms, equipment and military materials and any other products which would enable the illegal regime 'to remain longer in being.' Is it not surprising that in Pakistan, far from exercising any of its persuasive and coercive power, the United Nations by its conspicuous silence proved its acquiescence in the supply of sophisticated weapons by some of the great powers to the army of occupation enabling the latter 'to remain longer in being' by committing crimes against humanity?

The United Nations has condemned the racism of Ian Smith, but in spite of its precepts in Resolution 1904 (XVIII) the United Nations made no protest against the promotion and practice of racial discrimination in East Bengal by the Punjabi-dominated West. Racial discrimination in contemporary international law means 'any distinction, exclusion, restriction or preference based on race, colour, descent, or national or ethnic origin which has the purpose or effect of nullifying or impairing the recognition, enjoyment or exercise, on an equal footing, of human rights and fundamental freedoms in the political, economic, social, cultural or any other field of public life.'[40] If one were to apply this definition to Pakistan, racial discrimination against the Bengalis becomes patent in every field of governmental and public activity—political, cultural, economic and administrative. The racial chauvinism in Pakistan led to a war of genocide. Yet the world body made no effort to condemn or stop this pernicious racist trend.

Biggest Exodus in History and Threat to the Peace in South Asia

The failure of the international community to prevent in time the massive violation of human rights in East Bengal resulted in a most formidable threat to the peace in South Asia. In Rhodesia the United Nations acted promptly on a constructive threat to the peace, in this subcontinent nothing was done even after the consummation of an unprecedented tragedy.

As a direct result of the sanguinary deeds of the army of occupation, the military rulers of Pakistan adroitly saddled India with eight million refugees from East Bengal by the third week of August 1971. Mrs Indira Gandhi, Prime Minister of India, has described the exodus as 'history's biggest and cruellest migration',[41] while Senator Edward Kennedy characterized it as the 'greatest human tragedy in modern

[40] Article 1 of International Convention on the Elimination of All Forms of Racial Discrimination (1966), 60 AJIL, p. 650.
[41] *The Evening Standard*, London, 7 June 1971.

times.'[42]   This mass exodus has no parallel in modern history. In 19 years, between 1948 and 1967, the total number of Arab refugees from Israel amounted to only 1,350,000;[43] the entire population of Laos is three million of which only 700,000 were displaced since 1962;[44] the total number of refugees in South Vietnam, according to Senator Edward Kennedy's Judicial Sub-Committee on Refugees,[45] amounted to six million during the longest war in America's history.   In India, however, within two and a half months the figure of six million was reached; by August 21, 1971 it went up to eight million, and by 27 September it was well over nine million.   On 14 August Senator Edward Kennedy said in Delhi that 'he thought that a total of 12 million during the next few weeks' was not an unreasonable estimate.[46]   The break-up of the arrival of refugees from East Bengal is as follows:[47]

Up to 17 April 1971	...	119,565
Up to 24 April 1971	...	655,874
Up to 1 May 1971	...	867,428
Up to 8 May 1971	...	1,572,220
Up to 15 May 1971	...	2,399,667
Up to 22 May 1971	...	3,371,931
Up to 29 May 1971	...	3,688,350
Up to 5 June 1971	...	4,982,792
Up to 12 June 1971	...	5,522,563
Up to 15 June 1971	...	5,985,342
By 28 July 1971	...	7,098,809
By 21 August 1971	..	8,018,743
By 27 September 1971	...	9,065,835
By November 1971	...	9,800,000

As on 21 August, besides other areas, there were 6,109,000 refugees in West Bengal, 1,260,000 in Tripura 340,000 in Meghalaya, 244,000 in Assam. As on 27 September, there were 9,056,620 refugees in the aforesaid border areas of India.

[42] *The Statesman*, Calcutta, 15 August 1971.

[43] Quincy Wright, *The Middle Eastern Crisis* (1970), 64 No. 4, AJIL. pp. 71, 82.

[44] *Time*, 10 May, 1971, p. 18.

[45] *Ibid.*

[46] *The Statesman*, 15 August 1971.   On 25 October 1971, *Time* magazine wrote: 'It is now officially estimated that refugees will swell to 12 million by the end of the year.'

[47] *The Statesman*, 19 June, 1 August; *Amrita Bazar Patrika*, 22 August 1971; *Bangla Desh Documents* (External Affairs Ministry, New Delhi, September, 1971), p. 446; S. P. Jagota and I. C. Jain, *The Current Refugee Situation in India and International Law*: Paper read before the Annual Seminar of the International Law Association, Indian Branch, New Delhi on 10 October 1971. *Time*, 6 December 1971.

The tragic irony of the situation was revealed by Mr James Cameron in his article 'Catastrophe Unlimited' published in *The Evening Standard*, London, on 7 June 1971:

> It is presumably irrelevant now—since the Powers considered it irrelevant at the time—to consider the wholly outrageous origin of this tragedy which has sent millions of people into exile, destitution and death.   If the UN chose to condone them there is no more to say, except that it is condoning the administration of the world's largest Islamic State on the political principles of the late Al Capone... It has taken us some time to appreciate that in Bengal the Indian Raj is faced with something that is probably going to be far too big to contain—physically, medically and politically, perhaps even militarily... The fact is that the typhoon got the ratings, the Purge of Bengal didn't. Presumably it is easier to feel the impulse of outrage at an act of nature, which however awful has no special political implications or strings.   God sends the typhoons but God is not, as far as we know, a member of SEATO nor a debtor to the World Bank... If, as I believe likely, this month will end with some ten million refugees in West Bengal territory, the military government of Pakistan will have achieved a remarkable thing. It will have... adroitly saddled India with an almost insuperable problem at her most vulnerable and dangerous place. Bengal—tense, overcrowded, desperately poor, politically hysterical, forever on the verge of some disaster or another, cannot cope with the situation. There is no hope whatever of absorbing the refugees.

Infringement of India's Legal Rights

India's early reaction to this problem of unprecedented magnitude can be assessed from, among others, three speeches of Prime Minister Mrs Indira Gandhi on 24 May, 26 May and 15 June 1971.[48] She made three main points.   First, that India was disappointed at the unconscionably long time the world had taken to react to the tragedy of East Bengal. The great powers had a special responsibility to prevent the continued suppression of human rights and the uprooting of millions in East Bengal thereby rendering them homeless. Mrs Gandhi said: 'We have heard much talk of democracy.   The Allies claimed that World War II was fought to save democracy. But when democracy is being so flagrantly and ruthlessly destroyed, we do not hear much.   Could there be a greater and clearer expression of democracy than what we have witnessed in the elections in Pakistan—in Bangladesh, under a military regime?' Second, Mrs Gandhi,

48 *The Statesman*, Calcutta, 25 May, 27 May, 16 June 1971.

in tune with the enlightened public opinion throughout the world, protested against the 'wanton destruction of peace, good neighbourliness and the elementary principles of humanity by the insensible action of the military rulers of Pakistan.' The refugee influx and other developments caused by Pakistan's calculated genocide in Bangladesh 'threatens the peace and security of India, and indeed of South-East Asia.' While warning the rulers of Pakistan that they could no longer seek a solution to their political problems at the cost of India on India's soil, by causing millions of their citizens to flee from their homes, she asked the world community to recognize the serious threat to the peace and stability of the subcontinent directly caused by the massive influx of refugees from East Bengal. Its many-sided repercussions on India's internal affairs precluded the matter from being considered an internal problem of Pakistan. The relief given by India to the refugees on humanitarian grounds was not to be used as an excuse to push more and more people across the border. The problems of providing relief to the refugees imposed a 'tremendous burden' on 'a country which is one of the poorest in the world.' For India this was an 'intolerable situation.' The response of the international community was 'pitiable.' What had been promised was only one-tenth of what was actually needed. Mrs Gandhi is reported to have told a Swiss news agency on 20 August that the total foreign assistance received by that time 'adds up to one week's requirement' and that Indian Parliament's allocation of Rs. 260 crores for refugee relief would help the arrangements to continue until the end of December.[49] Senator Kennedy shared the view that international assistance had been hopelessly inadequate. An AP report from Washington on 26 August states that the Senator realized how little the outside world had done and how paultry the American contribution (Rs. 60 crores funnelled through UN) looked when contrasted to the prospect of an Indian budget for Rs. 375 to Rs. 750 crores for refugee relief in the new year alone.[50]

Third, that in these circumstances India could only grant temporary refuge to the millions who had fled from the reign of terror. While 'we will do our best' to look after the refugees on a 'temporary basis', 'even if we have to go hungry', Mrs Gandhi added 'we have no intention of sending the refugees back merely to be butchered.' The Indian people were asked to be prepared for heavier burdens so that India could discharge her responsibilities not only to her own people but also 'to the million who have fled from the reign of terror to take temporary refuge here.' Should the world community fail to pay heed, India would be constrained to take all necessary measures

[49] *The Hindusthan Standard*, 21 August 1971.
[50] *Amrita Bazar Patrika*, 27 August 1971.

to ensure her security and preservation. Unless conditions were created for the early return of the refugees 'under credible guarantees' for their safety and well-being, there could be no lasting stability or peace in the subcontinent. There had to be a political settlement and not a military solution. A political settlement could only mean an agreement with Sheikh Mujibur Rahman and his Awami League colleagues who had won the recent elections: 'What they wanted was for them to decide.'

India's disappointment at the failure of the United Nations to deal with the most fundamental issues in the Bangladesh crisis was again expressed by Mrs Gandhi on 20 August. She said: 'I am afraid the UN has not done much. It has ignored the basic question of why these people have come. They would not have left their homes unless there were compelling reasons. The UN should see why these people are coming and create conditions by which this exodus will stop.'[51] On 30 August, addressing the evacuees from East Bengal, the Prime Minister repeated the assurance that unless conditions were created for their safe return they would not be pushed back to their country. Mrs Gandhi again deplored that foreign assistance received so far was only enough to meet barely a week's expenditure on refugees.[52]

Time magazine of 2 August 1971 comments: 'Mrs. Gandhi is faced both with mounting pressure for military action, and an awesome cost that could set her own economy back years. India is feeding the refugees for a mere 1·10 rupees (15 ¢) per person per day, but even that amounts to more than $ 1,000,000 a day. The first six months alone, Indian officials say, will cost $ 400 million. Contributions pledged by other countries (the US leads with $ 73 million) equal barely one-third of that—and much of that money has not yet actually been paid... For all of India's commitment "to Bangla Desh democracy and those who are fighting for their rights", in the words of Mrs Gandhi, New Delhi is not at all interested in taking on the burden of East Bengal's problems. The only answer, as New Delhi sees it, is a political solution that would enable refugees to return to their homes.' Again, on 25 October 1971 *Time* wrote: 'The current dispute has grown out of the Pakistani army's harsh repression of a Bengali movement demanding greater autonomy for the much-exploited eastern sector of the divided nation. The resulting flood of impoverished East Pakistani refugees has placed an intolerable strain on India's already overburdened economy. New Delhi has insisted from the first that the refugees, who now number well over 9,000,000 by official estimates, must be allowed to return to their homes in East Pakistan. Before that is possible, however, a political

[51] *The Hindusthan Standard*, 21 August 1971.
[52] *The Statesman*, Calcutta, 31 August 1971.

solution must be found that would end the Pakistani army's reign of terror, wanton destruction and pogroms... The cost (of relief) to the Indian government for the fiscal year ending next March 31 may run as high as $ 830 million. The US has supplied so far $ 83·2 million for the refugees...'[53]

By November the social strains and the staggering burden on India became unbearable. *Newsweek* of 6 December 1971 stated: 'These social strains and staggering financial burden of refugees' relief seem more than India can possibly bear. Estimates indicate that the program will have cost $ 900 million by next March, of which only $ 250 million has been offset by donations and pledges from abroad. Fully 16 percent of India's current national budget is now eaten up in refugee relief, and the country's food stocks, painstakingly built up over two good crop years as a cushion against leaner times, are fast dwindling. Special taxes have been levied, and the government has cut back drastically all other pending arrears even to the extent of shelving long-planned development programs. "We cannot even reckon how much the refugees will cost us in '72", an Indian official told *Newsweek's* Arnaud de Borchgrave, "because the prospect is also too horrendous to contemplate".'

The conflict between India's national interest of protecting her security and her economy and her humanitarian duty to grant asylum to the victims of genocidal acts placed India in an almost impossible position. As Mrs Gandhi had explained: 'We are simply telling the world what the Pakistani Army is doing inside Bangladesh. Killing thousands and thousands of human beings might not be of any concern to the world but India is worried and this is the reason which prompted India in allowing refugees to come to our soil.' The influx of refugees gave rise to a host of financial, administrative, social and political problems. Yet people inside Bangladesh were still being killed and women raped. Mrs Gandhi asked: 'How can we ask the

---

[53] As at the end of August 1971, the total estimated expenditure for 8 million refugees for 6 months at Rs. 3/- per day per person was Rs. 432 crores or US $ 576 million; but the total amount of assistance received/promised from abroad was only $ 146.576 million: *Bangla Desh Documents*, p. 447. On 16 October the Governor of Reserve Bank of India estimated the cost of refugee burden on India at Rs. 500 crores during the then financial year: *The Times of India* (Delhi) 17 October 1971. At the meeting of the Aid India Consortium in Paris in October 1971, it was noticed that out of the World Bank's assessment of the cost of refugee relief at $ 700 million for the financial year 1971-72, only about $ 200 million had been pledged to date through worldwide contributions. Again, at the end of September the deficit in India had reached Rs. 350 crores of which less than Rs. 30 crores was expected to be raised during the rest of the financial year by the new taxes levied in October. *The Statesman*, Calcutta, 26, 28 October 1971. These were indicative of the intolerable burden on India's economy arising out of the massive refugee influx.

refugees to go back at this stage, although, their staying in India is a burden on us and we are a poor nation.' Although the whole world had witnessed the plight of the refugees and had seen the results of the reign of terror unleashed by the Pakistani Army on the people of Bangladesh yet nothing had been done to solve the problem and none of the big nations asked Pakistan to stop the genocide of the people of Bangladesh. 'It has been said of me that I am rather obstinate. But to stop the genocide in East Bengal is not a matter of my obstinacy. It is in our national interest to save the 75 million people of Bangladesh from being decimated. It is certainly in the interest of Bangladesh also.' 'The problem of Bangladesh', Mrs Gandhi said, 'could be solved only by asking the Pakistani Army to vacate Bangladesh so that these millions of people who left their homes and hearths could go back and pursue their lives peacefully.'[54]

India's restraint is without precedent and perhaps no other country would have waited so patiently for a political and peaceful solution of the problem. As Mr John Grigg pointed out in *The Sunday Times*, London (reproduced in *The Statesman*, Calcutta, 9 December 1971) :

> Apart from the financial cost involved—quite staggering for a poor country—the social tensions have been almost unbearable, and it is doubtful if any other country in the world would have borne them so patiently for so long. We in Britain have only to recall the outcry that there was here when it was suggested that 200,000 East African Asians (fellow citizens incidentally) might descend upon us. Yet, what would 200,000 have been among 50 million, compared with seven million refugees (citizens of another State) in West Bengal alone, among a local population of 40 million, or the 1·3 million refugees in Tripura alongside a local population of 1·5 million? And yet, after all, we are a rich nation.

The Indian policy was fully in conformity with the relevant norms of international law, particularly with the recent developments in the law of refugees. Even under customary law there was a right of remonstrance and protest in the name of humanity if arbitrary or harsh treatment by a state of its nationals affected the well-defined interests of another state. For instance, when certain rigorous measures were applied by Rumania against her Jewish nationals, forcing many of them to emigrate to the United States, Secretary Hay declared on 17 July 1902: 'The right of remonstrance against the acts of the Roumanian government is clearly established in favour

---

[54] See *The Statesman*, Calcutta, 1, 3, 4 December 1971 for Mrs. Indira Gandhi's speeches before the Rajya Sabha, the meeting of the Congress workers in New Delhi and the public meeting in Calcutta.

of this government. Whether consciously and of purpose or not, these helpless people, burdened and spurned by their native land, are forced by the sovereign power of Roumania upon the charity of the United States. This government cannot be a tacit party to such an international wrong. It is constrained to protest against the treatment to which the Jews of Roumania are subjected, not alone because it has unimpeachable ground to remonstrate against the resultant injury to itself, but in the name of humanity.'[55]

Apart from the general principle, the matter ceased to be one of Pakistan's internal public order because by the failure of her government to secure the life, property and personal honour of the minorities, a serious breach of the Indo-Pakistani Agreement of 8 April 1950 (popularly known as the Nehru-Liaquat Ali Agreement) was committed. It is an acknowledged fact that the Hindu minority of East Bengal has been one of the special targets of the army of occupation, and millions of them have fled to India in terror and panic. The agreement of 1950 was meant for their protection in East Bengal. In paragraph 'A' the agreement provides, *inter alia*: 'The Governments of India and Pakistan solemnly agree that each shall ensure, to the minorities throughout its territory, complete equality of citizenship, irrespective of religion, a full sense of security in respect of life, culture, property and personal honour, freedom of movement within each country and freedom of occupation, speech and worship, subject to law and morality... Both Governments declare these rights to be fundamental and undertake to enforce them effectively.'

This is similar to other international agreements providing for the protection of racial, linguistic and religious minorities, e.g. peace treaties concluded after the First World War and the supplementary conventions. In connexion with such international agreements, Hyde observed: "The harsh treatment of a national may, however, be indissolubly associated with a violation of some obligation towards a foreign State. When it is, the matter ceases to be one of domestic concern."[56]

Pakistan's right to political independence is limited by her obligations not only to treat her own nationals humanely but also not to interfere with the territorial integrity or political independence of India. The formulation of the right to political independence in the Draft Declaration on the Rights and Duties of States is subject to the proviso that, in providing for its own well-being, a state 'shall not impair or violate the legitimate rights of other states.' The comment

---

[55] Communication to American Minister of Roumania, 17 July 1962, Moore, *Digest of International Law*, VI, p. 364; Hyde, *International Law* (2nd revised ed.), Vol. I, p. 210, f.n. 6.

[56] Hyde, *Ibid*.

of the United Kingdom on Article 4 of the Draft indicated certain exceptions to the right to political independence, such as, 'instances of a state acting with utmost barbarity and inhumanity to its own nationals, or making preparations which appear to foreshadow a policy of aggression, or again of pursuing a course which leads to the economic strangulation of another state.'[57]   Again, Fitzmaurice, the UK delegate to the 6th Committee of the General Assembly, thought of a case where state 'A' sends 'several million unarmed men' into the neighbouring sate 'B', affecting the nerve centres of state 'B' and weakening it; in such a case state 'A' is to be considered an aggressor, entitling state 'B' to exercise its right of self-defence against state 'A'.[58]

The mass exodus of Pakistani nationals to India was the result of a deliberate policy executed with cruel efficiency.   It had all the elements of an assault and therefore amounted to an infringement of India's territorial integrity in a manner inconsistent with the purposes of the United Nations within the meaning of Article 2(4) of the Charter.   Further, even assuming that there was no violation of India's territorial integrity, there had been undoubtedly a serious breach of India's right to political independence which means the right to maintain both internal and external sovereignty.   The need to protect the national economy of a country is no less important than the need to protect her territorial integrity.   The 'unilateral action' of Pakistan which had 'endangered' 'the basic economy' of India and 'thus jeopardized the security' of India, can and should be considered an act of aggression—as would appear from the Bolivian draft defining 'aggression' submitted to the 6th Committee of the General Assembly on 11 January 1952.[59]   According to Bowett,[60] there is logically no reason why the right to self-defence should not be admitted when a State's economic interests are violated.

Even when faced with the intolerable burden of maintaining 9 million evacuees from Pakistan, and threatened with another 3 million in the near future, and despite overwhelming popular pressure, and at the cost of her vital national interests, India displayed the utmost restraint in refraining from taking military action in self-defence under Article 51 of the Charter.   Since the United Nations did not act, India would have been within her legitimate rights to proceed under Article 51, not for the purpose of annexing any part of Pakis-

[57] Quoted by Bowett, *Self-Defence in International Law* (Manchester 1958), p. 51.
[58] Off. Rec. G. A. 6th Sess. 6th Committee, 292nd meeting, para 40.
[59] A/C 6/L. 211, cited in Report by the Secy. Gen. on the Question of Defining Aggression, A/2111, 3 Oct. 1952, p. 58.
[60] Bowett, op. cit., p. 107.

tani territory, but for ensuring that her own territory and political independence were not invaded by atrocious crimes against humanity committed by the army of occupation against the people of East Bengal. India's obligation not to use force under Article 2(4) has to be read along with her right under Article 51.

India's exemplary restraint in refraining from immediate military action in self-defence received wide international acclaim. This no doubt avoided an immediate war but unfortunately it did not help the restoration of international peace and stability in the subcontinent. To use Rabindranath Tagore's expression, India's restraint only imposed 'quiet' but did not bring about 'peace' in the subcontinent. The ultimate wisdom of this policy was to be judged by the degree and effectiveness of international response to the freedom movement in East Bengal.

Apart from giving shetlter to 10 million terror-stricken refugees, India, in partial fulfilment of her obligations under the Charter and the contemporary law of self-determination, expressed her unqualified moral support to the people of East Bengal struggling for their independence from an exploitative tyranny. Does that amount to intervention? It would be a gross abuse of the term to call it 'intervention'; for, as Professor Lauterpacht pointed out: 'There is no self-determination and no independence under the rule of tyranny, and there is no intervention except in a sense dangerously approaching an abuse of language, when, by means of procedure which is international and disinterested in character, safeguards are provided for ensuring freedom from a rule of violence which may be more destructive than any foreign intervention.'[61]

Since every state is under a duty to assist the people of another state in their struggle for self-determination and in their resistance to any illegal use of force by a government without popular base, moral, material and military support to the people of East Bengal would have been in compliance with the contemporary norms of international law. This obligation to help and assist, emanating as it does from the Charter provisions of human rights and fundamental freedoms, of equal rights and self-determination, does not become inoperative simply because the supposedly self-propelled UN machinery has been rendered ineffective owing to the great-power chess game, at the expense of millions of East Bengalis. No country except China publicly supported Yahya's government for suppressing the freely declared verdict of the people by force. Many condemned Yahya's actions but did not extend any moral or material help to the struggle for freedom of the people of East Bengal. Reasons other than moral

[61] H. Lauterpacht, *Recognition in International Law* (Cambridge, 1947), p. 173.

or legal must explain such inaction, but it would indeed be surprising if one who came forward with moderate help was accused of subversive intervention.

In an ordinary civil strife the duty of non-intervention normally arises because it is not clear which of the two sides represents the will of the people; the object being to ensure that the will of the people is not subverted. This appears from a careful scrutiny of the General Assembly resolutions of 1 December 1949 (Essentials of Peace) and 17 November 1950 (Peace Through Deeds). The purpose of these resolutions is to prohibit such intervention as would have the effect of 'subverting the will of the people in any state' having a 'legally established government' understood in the light of Article 21 of the Universal Declaration viz. the will of the people shall be the basis of the authority of the government as expressed through periodic and genuine elections by universal and equal suffrage. But where, as in Pakistan, the will of the people was unmistakably declared, only those who helped Yahya in subverting the popular will can be accused of illegal intervention, not those who helped its implementation.

Any other interpretation will defeat the fundamental Charter obligation of promoting self-determination by perpetuating tyranny and dictatorship. A successful revolution against tyranny requires not only moral but material support from the international community. As Quincy Wright had said: 'Furthermore, the right of revolution, recognised by international law, would be interfered with by a rule which forbade all outside communication, travel, trade and financial assistance intended to help revolutionists. Successful revolutions have usually depended to some extent upon such outside contacts and assistance.'[62]

India's Duty Towards the Refugees and the Obligations of the International Community

The humanitarian impulse to protect political refugees or victims of persecution, known in international law since the seventeenth century, has now become a pertinent international community standard. Grotius, Suarez and Wolff believed in certain natural and inalienable rights of the individual, and that their protection was vested in human society. The grant of asylum by a sovereign state was the performance of a humanitarian duty on behalf of the human society. In the nineteenth century the grant of asylum to political offenders was linked up with the growth of democratic institutions. There is a common belief that the institution of asylum, if properly developed, can help promote democracy against totalitarianism. In the twentieth century, with the development of human rights and

[62] Q. Wright, *Subversive Intervention* (1960), 54 AJIL, pp. 521, 530.

fundamental freedoms, the emphasis has shifted to the right of the individual refugee. He has been given the right to *seek and enjoy* asylum in a foreign state. There is as yet no legal duty cast upon a state to grant asylum to a refugee, and correspondingly, the refugee has no right to *receive* asylum in a foreign state. This is because the grant or refusal of asylum is still considered permissive in nature, and an attribute of sovereignty.

Since 1946, however, there have been some important developments in the international law of refugees. As a result, certain legal norms in the developing system of international rule of law have emerged. These norms can be deduced, *inter alia*, from: (a) Articles 13 and 14 of the Universal Declaration of Human Rights of 6 Decemer 1948; the European Convention for Protection of Human Rights, 1950; the International Covenant on Civil and Political Rights adopted by the General Assembly on 16 December 1966; and the American Convention on Human Rights, 1969; (b) the Geneva Convention relating to the Status of the Refugees of 28 July 1951, entered into force on 22 April 1954, read with the Protocol which entered into force on 4 October 1967; (c) the Principles concerning the Treatment of Refugees adopted by the Asian-African Legal Consultative Committee at Bangkok in 1966 (hereafter referred to as the Bangkok Principles); (d) the Draft Declaration on the Right of Asylum (1960) of the Commission on Human Rights; and the Declaration on Territorial Asylum adopted by the General Assembly on 14 December 1967 by Resolution 2312 (XXII).[63]

It will be my endeavour to consider briefly some of the relevant legal

[63] For texts of Universal Declaration, *International Organisation*, 1949, Vol. III, p. 202; *European Convention of 1950, Collection of International Conventions, Agreements and other Texts concerning Refugees,* published by the Office of the UN High Commissioner for Refugees, 1971, *UNHCR Collection,* p. 149; American Convention of 1969, *UNHCR Collection,* p. 263; International Covenant on Civil and Political Rights of 16 December 1966 (1967) 61 AJIL, p. 870; Geneva Convention of 28 July 1951, *189 UN Treaty Series,* p. 137; and for the Protocol of 1967, *UNHCR Collection,* p. 53; Bangkok Principles, Annexure I to the Paper by Jagota and Jain mentioned hereafter; Draft Declaration on the Right of Asylum (1960), *UN Yearbook,* 1960, p. 341; United Nations Declaration on Territorial Asylum, *UN Yearbook* 1967, p. 760. Also see Ian Brownlie, *Basic Documents on Human Rights* (Oxford University Press, London, 1971); P. Weis, 'The United Nations Declaration on Territorial Asylum', the *Canadian Yearbook of International Law,* 1969, p. 92. Two papers read before the Annual Seminar of the International Law Association, Indian Branch, New Delhi, on 10 October 1971 made important contributions to the subject under discussion; (i) Dr. S. P. Jagota and Mr. J. C. Jain; 'The Current Refugee Situation in India and International Law'; (ii) Miss Basanti Mitra, M. A. (Columbia): The Practice of Asylum in International Law. Readers interested in a more comprehensive study of the refugee situation in India will find the above source materials useful.

norms which seem applicable to the refugee situation in India. Early in 1946 the General Assembly of the United Nations recognized that refugees or displaced persons who expressed their reluctance to return to their country of origin should not be forced to do so.[64] The right of a person to leave, and to return, to his country, and his right to seek and enjoy asylum, were thereafter incorporated in the Universal Declaration of Human Rights of 6 December 1948:

Article 13.
> (1) Everyone has the right to freedom of movement and residence within the borders of each State.
> (2) Everyone has the right to leave any country, including his own, and to return to his country.

Article 14.
> (1) Everyone has the right to seek and to enjoy in other countries asylum from persecution.
> (2) This right may not be invoked in the case of prosecutions genuinely arising from non-political crimes or from acts contrary to the purposes and principles of the United Nations.

The International Covenant on Civil and Political Rights provides:

Article 12.
> (2) Everyone shall be free to leave any country, including his own.
> (4) No one shall be arbitrarily deprived of the right to enter his own country.

Thus, while the International Covenant on Civil and Political Rights conceded the right of the individual to leave, enter or return, to his own country, it did not recognize the right of a refugee to seek and enjoy asylum as provided in Article 14(1) of the Universal Declaration. Even the more comprehensive European Convention on Human Rights gives no direct right of asylum or non-refoulement to political or other refugees. Although the possibility of embodying a right of asylum in a Protocol to the Convention has been discussed in the Council of Europe, no way has yet been discussed in the Council of Europe, no way has yet been found of overcoming the difficulties of formulating such a right.[65] Indeed, the huge influx of refugees from East Bengal suggests that the formulation and enforcement of a right of asylum without any corresponding measure to ensure implementa-

---

[64] Basanti Mitra, *Ibid.*, p. 25.

[65] J. E. S. Fawcett, *The Application of the European Convention on Human Rights* (Oxford University Press, London, 1969), p. 59.

tion of self-determination in the country of origin, may, in conceivable circumstances, induce a military dictator or a non-representative ruler to drive out with impunity on a massive scale all political non-conformists, and thereby ensure the perpetuation of a totalitarian regime.

The following points seem relevant in the context of the refugee situation in India. First, the evacuees from East Bengal are 'refugees' as defined in contemporary international law. A refugee is a person who, owing to persecution or well-founded fear of persecution, for reasons of race, colour, religion, political belief or membership of a particular social group, leaves the state of his nationality or habitual residence, or being outside such state, is unwilling to return to it or to avail himself of its protection.[66] There can be no controversy that massive migrations from East Bengal took place owing to actual persecution of the Bengalis by the military regime of Pakistan for reasons of race, religion and political belief. Accordingly, the refugees from East Bengal are entitled to the protection of the international law of refugees.

Second, the right of the refugees to *seek and enjoy* asylum is well established. This is, however, a nebulous right. It does not confer a right of entry nor a duty to admit a refugee. As Fawcett points out in the context of the European Convention on Human Rights, there are two distinct elements, a right of entry as a refugee from political and other persecution, and a right not to be expelled after lawful entry. Few if any states are prepared to grant the first, at least in an unqualified form. The Status of Refugees Convention 1951, as amended, to which all the contracting states to the European Convention are parties, gives a limited right of non-refoulement to victims of persecution. Further, the constitutions, laws or practice of some of the contracting states give in varying degrees a right of asylum; for example, the Federal Republic of Germany. While no alien has a legal right to enter British territory, in practice asylum may be granted if there are good grounds for thinking that his life or liberty would be endangered because of his political opinions if he were required to leave the United Kingdom, and there are no positive grounds for considering him undesirable.[67] The humanitarian impulse to protect a victim of persecution is therefore clearly discernible in state practice.

Subsequent efforts of the international community have succeeded

---

[66] This definition is in conformity with Article I of the Bangkok Principles read with Article I of the 1951 Convention.

[67] Secretary of State for Home Department (written reply) : *Commons Debates*, vol. 583, cols. 1422-35 & col. 135: cited in *Contemporary Survey* (July 1959), p. 553-5. Fawcett, op. cit., p. 59.

in providing important guidelines with a view to conferring better rights on the refugees who are victims of persecution. Some of these guidelines can be found in Articles III and VIII of the Bangkok Principles and Article III of the United Nations Declaration on Territorial Asylum 1967.

Bangkok Principles
Article III

1. A State has the sovereign right to grant or refuse asylum in its territory to a refugee.

2. The exercise of the right to grant such asylum to a refugee shall be respected by all other States and shall not be regarded as an unfriendly act.

3. No one seeking asylum in accordance with these principles should, except for overriding reasons of national security or safeguarding the populations, be subjected to measures such as rejection at the frontier, return or expulsion which would result in compelling him to return to or remain in a territory if there is a well-founded fear of persecution endangering his life, physical integrity or liberty in that territory.

4. In cases where a State decides to apply any of the above-mentioned measures to a person seeking asylum, it should grant provisional asylum under such conditions as it may deem appropriate, to enable the person thus endangered to seek asylum in another country.

Article VIII, Paragraph 3

A refugee shall not be deported or returned to a State or Country where his life or liberty would be threatened for reasons of race, colour, religion, political belief or membership of a particular group.

United Nations Declaration (1967)
Article 3

1. No person referred to in article 1, paragraph 1, shall be subjected to measures such as rejection at the frontier or, if he has already entered the territory in which he seeks asylum, expulsion or compulsory return to any State where he may be subjected to persecution.

2. Exception may be made to the foregoing principle only for overriding reasons of national security or in order to safeguard the population, as in the case of a mass influx of persons.

3. Should a State decide in any case that exception to the principle stated in paragraph 1 of this article would be justified,

it shall consider the possibility of granting to the person concerned, under such conditions as it may deem appropriate, an opportunity, whether by way of provisional asylum or, otherwise, of going to another State.

While the sovereign right to grant or refuse asylum in exercise of the discretionary power of the state of asylum is acknowledged, the discretion is controlled by the principle of non-refoulement in cases where rejection at the frontier or return after admission of a refugee will endanger his life or liberty. Exceptions to the obligation of non-refoulement are operative where overriding reasons of national security or safeguarding the population are involved. To meet an exceptional situation of this nature, the institution of provisional asylum has been introduced.

Relying upon the exceptions to the principle of non-refoulement mentioned above, it was suggested[68] that the refugee situation in India being quantitatively and qualitatively different from the situation arising from a few individuals seeking asylum, the refugee law would have allowed India to close its borders with East Bengal and not to permit entry to the millions escaping from persecution in that country. It is undoubtedly true that for safeguarding the population of India and the economic security of the country, if India had decided to close its frontiers to prevent the massive influx of refugees, no technical objection could have been raised. If, however, the aforesaid provisioins of the Bangkok Principles and the United Nations Declaration are read as a whole, and if they are considered in the light of the humanitarian principle of non-refoulement embodied therein, it seems to us that the better view would be, in the case of a massive influx of refugees as in the situation under consideration, that there is a humanitarian obligation to grant provisional or temporary asylum on such conditions as India considers appropriate, and not to compel them to return to a reign of terror and persecution.

The question whether India was under a legal duty to grant asylum to the ten million refugees is now only of academic importance. In fact, at a considerable risk to her national security, national economy and the interest of the population, India gave shelter to the refugees as a provisional or temporary measure in fulfilment of the principle of non-refoulement. To use the expression of the international instruments, the grant of provisional asylum by India can only be characterized as 'a peaceful and humanitarian act' and

---

[68] S. P. Jagota and J. C. Jain, 'The Current Refugee Situation in India and International Law' (Paper read before the Annual Seminar of the International Law Association, Indian Branch, New Delhi, 10 December 1971), para 21.

'shall be respected by all other states' and 'cannot be regarded as un-friendly by any other state.'

Third, there is the question of the status of asylum granted by India to the refugees from East Bengal. As will have been observed, it was the declared policy of the Government of India that the asylum was of a temporary nature. The refugees could not be assimilated in India and they were to return as soon as conditions permitted. Accordingly, the refugees were being sheltered and maintained in appropriate camps located within states on the borders of East Bengal. It was suggested that there were three conditions of provisional asylum in the current situation:[69] (a) the refugees from East Bengal would be on Indian soil for as short a period as necessary; (b) as soon as the situation in East Bengal which led to the flight of refugees reverted to peace and normalcy, as a consequence of which the refugees would be in a position to return to their homeland in safety, honour and freedom, they should do so *en bloc*; (c) with the restoration of such normalcy in East Bengal, the legal status of the refugees in India would terminate.

Article II, paragraph 2, of the Bangkok Principles provides:

> A refugee shall lose his status as a refugee if he does not return to the State of which he is a national, or to the Country of his nationality, or, if he has no nationality, to the State or Country of which he was a habitual resident, or if he fails to avail himself of the protection of such State or Country after the *circumstances in which he became a refugee have ceased to exist.*
>
> *Explanation*: It would be for the *State of asylum* of the refugee to *decide* whether the *circumstances* in which he became a refugee have *ceased to exist*. (emphasis added)

Accordingly, before the termination of the status of the refugees, India had to assess objectively whether the circumstances which compelled the refugees to flee the country of origin (Pakistan) did in fact cease to exist. It is in this context that the duty of Pakistan as the state of origin, and the obligation of the international community, assumed great importance.

Fourth, the paramount duty of Pakistan was to bring to an end the circumstances in which nearly 10 million East Bengalis became refugees. The fulfilment of this duty would have facilitated the exercise of the right of the refugees to return home. Under Article V of the Bangkok Principles, it was the further duty of Pakistan to compensate the refugee for such loss as bodily injury, deprivation of personal liberty in denial of human rights, death of dependents of

[69] *Ibid.*, para 25.

the refugee or of the person whose dependent the refugee was, and destruction of or damage to the property and assets of the refugee caused by the military rulers or public officials or mob violence.

The fulfilment of this immediate duty was linked with the more fundamental duty of the military rulers to implement self-determination in Pakistan. On any rational perspective, the massive migrations were caused by the refusal of the military rulers to transfer power to the elected representatives of the people, and the suppression of self-determination by a war of genocide and a reign of terror. It was therefore impossible to expect that the circumstances which made them refugees could possibly cease to exist in the absence of an unconditional transfer of power by the military rulers to the elected leaders of the people. The modality of transfer of power was a matter for negotiation between the leaders of the Awami League and the military junta. This is what was meant by a political solution of the crisis in Pakistan. Without such a solution, India could not have taken a decision under Article II, paragraph 2, of the Bangkok Principles, that effective conditions were created for the safe return of the refugees.

Finally the members of the United Nations had certain clear obligations in dealing with the refugee situation in India which was a matter of 'concern to the international community.' Article II, paragraph 2, of the United Nations Declaration (1967) provides: 'Where a State finds difficulty in granting or continuing to grant asylum, States individually or jointly or through the United Nations shall consider, in a spirit of international solidarity, appropriate measures to lighten the burden on that State.' In order to lighten the burden on India the international community had two obligations: (a) to provide adequate financial assistance for the relief and maintenance of the refugees in India, and (b) to compel Pakistan to create conditions in East Bengal making it possible for the refugees to return home safe and secure, and with dignity and honour, in exercise of their inalienable human rights. In other words, it was the duty of the international community to see to the fulfilment of the conditions on which provisional asylum was granted by India on humanitarian grounds.

The deliberations of the Economic and Social Council at its 50th session in New York in May 1971 and at its 51st session in Geneva in July 1971, the efforts of the United Nations High Commissioner for Refugees, the disbursement of financial assistance, the efforts of the Aid India Consortium in Paris in October 1971, and similar other steps were indicative of a common consciousness of the immense financial burden on India in meeting the refugee situation; but the financial assistance provided or promised was hopelessly inadequate and did not prevent a serious disruption of the Indian economy.

But the more fundamental default lay in the failure of the international community to provide an effective political solution of the crisis in Pakistan. Nothing was done for the fulfilment of the conditions of provisional asylum. The matter was not even placed in the agenda of the Security Council or the General Assembly in its 26th session. In the absence of a political reconciliation between the leaders of the Awami League and the military rulers of Pakistan, the circumstances which created the refugee situation could not be eliminated. The obligation of the world body to help promote self-determination in Pakistan and its further obligation to lighten the burden of the refugee situation in India, operated concurrently to make it incumbent upon the United Nations to persuade or coerce the military rulers of Pakistan to agree to a political solution acceptable to the leaders of the Awami League.

Arab Refugees : East Bengal Refugees—UN Precedent Ignored

On the theoretical aspect, the UN precedent in the Middle East is instructive. The response of the United Nations to the situation in the Middle East will appear from the Security Council resolution 237 (1967) adopted on 14 June 1967, the General Assembly resolution 2252 (ES-V) adopted on 4 July 1967, resolution VI (XXIV) of the Commission on Human Rights and the resolution adopted by the United Nations Conference on Human Rights at its 23rd plenary meeting held at Teheran on 7 May 1968.[70] Three principles emerge from these resolutions :

(1) The international community affirmed the inalienable rights of all inhabitants who had left their homes as a result of hostilities in the Middle East to return, resume normal life, recover their properties and homes, and rejoin their families according to the provisions of the Universal Declaration.

(2) The Government of Israel was called upon: (i) to desist forthwith from acts of destroying homes of Arab civilian population inhabiting areas occupied by Israel and to respect and implement the Universal Declaration as well as the Geneva Convention of 12 August 1949 relating to the treatment of prisoners of war and the protection of civilian persons; (ii) to ensure the safety, welfare and security of the inhabitants of the areas where military operations had taken place and to facilitate the return of those inhabitants who had fled the areas.

(3) It was the duty of all governments, organizations and individuals to make special contributions with a view to enabling

[70] (1968) 62 AJIL, p. 305; (1969) 63 AJIL, p. 677.

the United Nations agencies and other international organizations to provide humanitarian assistance, particularly to the displaced persons, on an emergency basis and as a temporary measure. The General Assembly, the Secretary-General and the Commission on Human Rights were required to see to the implementation of the policy of the world body and to keep the matter under constant review.

Although the problem of the refugees from East Bengal was much worse, and without any parallel in history, it was not unreasonable to hope that the United Nations, following its own precedent, would at least declare categorically the inalienable rights of the East Bengal refugees, and call upon the Government of Pakistan to create suitable conditions with credible guarantees to facilitate their return home.   This was not done.   The international response was confined to providing some hopelessly inadequate relief measures.

Since it was impossible for India to maintain millions of refugees on a permanent basis, and since it was also impossible for the United Nations agencies to do so, as the Director-General of the FAO frankly admitted[71] that to provide emergency food aid was beyond the resources of FAO and the World Food Programme, how did the United Nations propose to solve the problem? Unless the immediate and root causes were totally eliminated, it was futile to expect the refugees to return.   Unless the refugees were persuaded to return home voluntarily, it was again futile to expect peace and stability in the subcontinent.

Real Causes of Mass Exodus

The immediate cause of the mass exodus was to be found in the genocidal acts, ghastly tortures, unbridled cruelties and other sanguinary deeds of Yahya's army of occupation in East Bengal.   And the root cause was the denial of the principle of self-determination for a period of 24 years.   From the very beginning it was clear that unless the international community could help the elimination of both the immediate and the root causes, it could never hope to preserve international peace and stability in this sensitive area of South Asia. Unfortunately, the United Nations' efforts were directed throughout towards the symptoms, rather than the causes, of the disease.   Such proposals as the posting of UN observers on both sides of the border for the ostensible purpose of supervising the return of the refugees, and the posting of a 150-strong observer team with 'communication experts' in East Bengal, were politically motivated suggestions with

---

[71] *The Times*, London, 8 June 1971.

sinister implications and were in complete disregard of the interests of the refugees and the people of East Bengal.

A total withdrawal of Yahya's army of occupation from the entire territory of East Bengal was the minimum requirement for the removal of the immediate cause of the trouble. It was not enough to withdraw the troops to the barracks in East Bengal and to provide a puppet civil administration nominated by the military rulers of Pakistan. There could be no credible guarantee for the safety of the evacuees until and unless the army was withdrawn, the organization of the Razakars disbanded, and the 'Peace Committees' dissolved.

The hollowness of Yahya's assurances to the evacuees from East Bengal have been exposed time and again by impartial international observers. On 26 May 1971, *The Times*, London, carried a report of its correspondent, Peter Hazelhurst, stating that President Yahya's promise that he would hand over power in East Pakistan to the repentant members of the Awami League and take back millions of refugees who had crossed into India was received 'as a cruel joke by homeless Bengalis'. This was indeed a cruel joke for, as Hazelhurst states: 'While President Yahya was issuing his bland assurance in West Pakistan yesterday, I heard his troops machine-gunning defenceless women and children who were trying to flee to India across the River Ichamati in small boats.'

Six weeks later, the claim of the military rulers that East Bengal was rapidly returning to normalcy and the way was open for refugees to return and resume normal lives, was tested by Murray Sayle, another British correspondent, in his article 'A Regime of Thugs and Bigots' published in *The Sunday Times* of 11 July 1971. After a week's tour of some of the areas in East Bengal from which many thousands of refugees fled, Sayle found that not only was the claim of the military regime untrue, 'in fact a repulsive political system is rapidly taking shape which may well make it impossible for them (refugees) to return.' The political system consisted of an ineffective civil administration and a parallel government run by 5,000 Razakars and members of the 'Peace Committees' selected by the military authorities. The Razakars were provided with rifles. Sayle observed: "Their work consists of 'security checks'—guiding the West Pakistani troops to the homes of supporters of the Awami League. They are supposed to be under the orders of local 'Peace Committees' which are selected by the military authorities on a similar basis of 'loyalty to Pakistan'. These people are, in fact, representatives of the political parties who were routed at the last elections, with an admixture of men with criminal records and bigoted Muslims... The work of the local Peace Committee and Razakar high command could hardly be said to have achieved 'normalcy' either." In fact, according to Sayle, there was a reign of terror in East Bengal; many civilians were killed and murdered by the army and the Razakars in 'security operations' and the police was helpless because of a military directive that complaints against Razakars were to be investigated only by the military authority.

There were formidable material obstacles which made it difficult for the refugees to return. Landed property of the evacuees normally worth Rs. 3,000 an acre had been sold by the martial law administration for one and a half rupees an acre in auctions held in the absence of the owners. As Sayle points out: "Lotapaharpur summarised for me the true position about the refugees. No one here really expects them to return in any numbers, because there is an atmosphere of terror in East Pakistan, because the material difficulties in the way of their return are almost insuperable, and their homes, farms, crops, small businesses, and other assets are being transferred under paper-thin legal devices to people who have strong motives to make sure they never come back—in fact, to their political and religious enemies. But the military administration has indeed opened 'reception centres' and 'transit camps.' I drove up to Benapole close to the Indian border to inspect these preparations... The entire population of Benapole reception centre was five forlorn dogs." At another reception centre at Sathkhira, Sayle found that it was guarded by two Razakars, armed with shotguns, helping with 'security checks' and 'asking about people's political views.' Sayle concludes: "On the refugees issue, it is clear that only a very brave or very foolish refugee would even try to return as things are, and that his welcome would be very doubtful if he did... Even more alarming is the development, with the 'Peace Committees' and Razakars, of two parallel governments in East Pakistan, one the normal civil administration, which is well-intentioned, reasonably efficient, but now speedily approaching complete impotence; the other a regime of paid informers, bigots and thugs answerable to no one and apparently above whatever law is left in East Pakistan. The pacification methods used on the North-West Frontier by the British of long ago, burning villages and gunning down their inhabitants, are bad enough when imported into a heavily populated and peaceful place like East Pakistan. The introduction of political methods of Hitler and Mussolini is even less defensible."

Even in late October the position had not changed much. On 25 October 1971 *Time* magazine recorded: 'Though Islamabad has ordered the military command to ease off on its repressive tactics, refugees are still trekking into India at the rate of about 30,000 a day, telling of villages burned, residents shot, and prominent figures carried off and never heard of again.'

It was therefore difficult for the refugees to take seriously the assurances of the military regime. Superficial changes like the transfer of the military governor, the appointment of a civilian as governor, the establishment of a civilian administration consisting of collaborators of the military regime, serving voluntarily or under coercion, and similar measures, were of no avail. These measures were not enough to restore the confidence of the refugees so long as Yahya's troops remained in East Bengal and the Razakars and members of the peace committees were at large.

Pattern of Political Solution : International Response—Unofficial

The more fundametal issue was the question of a political solution of the crisis, without which the root cause of the mass exodus could not have been eliminated. *The Sunday Times* of 11 July 1971 carried an article, 'The Repression in Bengal: What We must Do' written by Mr Reginald Prentice, a former Minister of Overseas Development and a member of the British Parliamentary delegation that visited East Bengal and West Pakistan. Mr Prentice gave his assessment of the pattern of political solution which alone could have solved the crisis in Pakistan. He said: "This downward spiral can only be reversed by a political solution acceptable to the people of East Pakistan. In practice this must mean a political solution acceptable to Sheikh Mujibur Rahman and the Awami League. The pattern is the familiar one of a colonial situation breaking up, in which the only people who can make an effective settlement are the leaders of the political party which has the confidence of the population. Yahya Khan must either accept this or continue with his policy of suppression—a policy which is bound to fail sooner or later. Supposing that Sheikh Mujib was released from prison, the Awami League recognized again and genuine discussions were held, what could be the outcome? The six-point programme on which the Awami League won the election last autumn provided for East Bengal to be self-governing for most purposes, but with the Central Government controlling foreign affairs and defence. The idea of one Pakistan would be preserved, but the provincial Government in the East would have effective control over its own destiny. It is doubtful whether this solution is still possible. There has been too much bloodshed and bitterness in recent months. The essential point is surely this: whether the settlement is to be some kind of loose federation, or whether (more probably) it is to be complete independence for Bangladesh will have to be decided by the Awami League, as the only credible representatives of the people of East Bengal. They must make the decision and the military rulers of West Pakistan must accept that

decision. At present the military rulers are in no mood to do anything of the kind."

Mr Prentice suggested three ways in which pressure could have
been maintained in favour of a political solution. First, that the
Western Powers should have stood firmly by their decision not to
renew economic aid (apart from relief aid, properly supervised by
the UN for the victims of the likely famine in East Pakistan)...
'Speaking from my experience as a former Minister of Overaseas
Development, I believe it is wrong to attach political conditions to
aid in 99 cases out of a 100—but this is the 100th case' Second,
that 'there should be an immediate end to the shipment of arms from
the USA to Pakistan. World opinion should back those Senators
and Congressmen in Washington who have urged the Administration
to reverse its policy. That the United States should line up with
China in supplying the armed forces of Pakistan at the moment is
something that defies any rational explanation.' Third, that 'there
should be the most explicit condemnation from governments, parlia-
ments and influential commentators of all kinds. It must be made
clear that the governments and peoples of the world identify themselves with the aspirations of the people of Bangladesh, and that we
are united in demanding a shift of policy by the Government of West
Pakistan.'

It is interesting to note the unofficial view of an eminent American,
Professor J. K. Galbraith. According to him[72] a peaceful political
solution recognizing the right of the people of East Bengal to govern
themselves was the only way out of the crisis. The right of the
people of Bangladesh to govern themselves meant the right to have a
government of their choice regardless of whether it was good, moderate or extreme. The sense of security necessary to persuade the
refugees to return could arise if the people of Bangladesh were put
in charge of their own security with Sheikh Mujibur Rahman at the
helm of affairs. The people of Bangladesh had to be in charge of
their destiny, of their own lives, their politics and their polity. A
solution could not be one that involved rule by and from West Pakistan.
Only if the West Pakistanis showed the wisdom called for would the
ultimate catastrophe be avoided. In such a situation it was quite
likely that history would repeat itself and a situation emerge in which
West Pakistan and Bangladesh might live as friends the same way
as India, and her former colonial ruler, Britain, were doing.

From an early stage of the crisis, the only reasonable political
solution appeared to be to accept the inevitable fact of the separation
of the two wings of Pakistan and the birth of a new state in East
Bengal. There was no possibility of the restoration of the *status*

[72] *The Statesman*, Calcutta, 15 September 1971.

quo ante. The military crackdown on 25 March sealed off the chances of a negotiated settlement within the framework of a united Pakistan. What happened since then clinched the issue. Even those who did not consider the division of Pakistan as the best solution or a desirable one were constrained to admit that it was the only possible solution. For instance, Mr Mitchell Sharp, the Canadian Foreign Minister in a letter to *The Globe and Mail* (10 July 1971), Ottawa, wrote: 'It would be irresponsible to recommend the division of Pakistan, a country already in dire economic strains, into two separate and weaker States. It may be that this will turn out to be the only solution: whether it would be the best solution is another matter.'[73] Mr Peter Shore, Labour MP and former British Minister, told newsmen in New Delhi on 2 September that what was happening in Bangladesh was the 'death throes of old Pakistan and the birth pangs of what, I am sure, will be a new nation.' The issue before the world, he said, was whether the new, infant nation was to be mutilated by immense suffering or some arrangement should be made for its development.[74]

The inevitability of separation, sooner or later, was generally accepted by the international community. Extracts from two popular American magazines are set out chronologically as indicative of the trend of the world opinon.

Time, 5 April 1971: 'Pakistan: Toppling Over the Brink':

> With the awesome fury of a cyclone off the Bay of Bengal, civil war swept across East Pakistan last week. In city after crowded, dusty city the army turned its guns on mobs of rioting civilians. Casualties mounted into the thousands. Though the full toll remained uncertain because of censorship and disorganization in the world's most densely populated corner (1,400 people per sq. mi.), at week's end some estimates had 2,000 dead. Even if President Agha Mohammed Yahya Khan is prepared to accept casualties of a geometrically greater magnitude, the outcome is likely to be the final breakup of East and West Pakistan and the painful birth of a new nation named Bangla Desh (Bengal State).

Newsweek, 5 April 1971:

> In branding Mujib an outlaw, Yahya slammed shut the door to further negotiations and opted instead for a military solution to his dilemma ... 'for the short term', said a US analyst,

---

[73] Reported in *The Statesman,* Calcutta, 14 July 1971.
[74] *The Hindusthan Standard,* 2 September 1971.

'Pakistan's army should be able to tear hell out of the Bengali landscape. But for the long term, they have a terrible logistics problem.' But no matter how harsh the federal crackdown, Bengali resistance—whether in the form of civil disobedience or Viet Cong-style guerrilla struggle—appeared likely to continue. Yahya, in fact, was seemingly faced with the ugly prospect of being a colonial ruler in his own country. For when the federal Army opened up with tanks and automatic weapons in Dacca last week, it mortally wounded any remaining chance that the two disparate wings of Pakistan could ever live in harmony again.

Time, 26 April 1971:

The Bangla Desh forces are critically short of gasoline and diesel fuel and lack of field-communication equipment necessary for organized military activity. They have avoided any full-scale engagements, in which they would undoubtedly sustain heavy losses. Some observers believe, in fact, that the long guerrilla phase of the civil war has already begun, with the army holding most of the towns and the rebels controlling much of the country-side. Despite the apparent determination of the Pakistan government to maintain its hold on East Bengal, the sheer human arithmetic of the situation seemed to indicate that the Bengalis would ultimately win freedom or at least some form of regional autonomy. At the present time, the East Bengalis outnumber the West Pakistani soldiers in their midst by about 1,000 to 1.

Time, 3 May 1971:

Still, everywhere I visited on the journey to Dacca, I found astonishing unanimity on the Bengali desire for independence and a determination to resist the Pakistani army with whatever means available. 'We will not be slaves', said one resistance officer, 'so there is no choice but to fight until we win.' The oncoming monsoon rains and the Islamabad government's financial problems will also work in favour of Bangla Desh. As the months pass and such hardships increase, Islamabad may have to face the fact that unity by force of arms is not exactly the Pakistan that Jinnah had in mind.

Newsweek, 28 June 1971:

All this savagery suggests that the Pakistani Army either is crazed by blood lust or, more likely, is carrying out a calculated policy of terror amounting to genocide against the whole Bengali population. The architect appears to be Lt.-Gen. Tikka Khan, the military governor of East Pakistan. Presumably, Pakistan's President knows something about what is going on, but he may not realise that babies are being burned alive, girls sold into virtual slavery and whole families murdered. He told the mili-- tary governor to put down a rebellion, and Tikka Khan has done it—efficiently and ruthlessly. As a result, East Pakistan is still nominally a part of Pakistan. But brutality inflicted by West on East in the last three months has made it certain that it will only be a matter of time before Pakistan becomes two countries. And those two countries will be irreparably split—at least until the last of today's maimed and brutalized children grow old and die with their memories of what happened when Yahya Khan decided to preserve their country.

Time, 2 August 1971:

Fear and deep sullen hatred are everywhere evident among the Bengalis. Few will talk to reporters in public, but letters telling of atrocities and destroyed villages are stuck in journalists' mail- boxes at Dacca's Hotel Intercontinental. In the privacy of his home one night, a senior Bengali bureaucrat declared: 'This will be a bitter protracted struggle, may be worse than Vietnam. But we will win in the end.' Estimates of the death toll in the army crackdown range from 200,000 all the way up to a million. The lower figure is more widely accepted, but the number may never be known. For one thing, countless corpses have been dumped in rivers, wells and mass graves... Half of the Mukti Bahini's reported 50,000 fighters come from the East Bengal Regiment, the para-military East Bengal Rifles, and the Bengali police, who defected in the early days of the fighting. Young recruits, many of them students, are being trained to blend in with the peasants, who feed them, and serve as lookouts, scouts and hit-and-run saboteurs. Twice guerrillas have knocked out power in Dacca, and they have kept the Dacca-Chittagong rail- way line severed for weeks. Wherever possible they raise the green, red and gold Bangla Desh flag. They claim to have killed 25,000 Pakistani troops though the figure may well be closer to 2,500 plus 10,000 wounded (according to a reliable estimate). Resistance fighters already control the countryside at night and much of it in the daytime.. Embroiled in a developing, if still disorganized, guerrilla war, Pakistan faces ever bleaker prospects as the conflict spreads. By now, in fact, chances of ever recover- ing voluntary national unity seem nil. But to Yahya Khan and the other tough West Pakistani generals who rule the world's fifth largest nation, an East-West parting is out of the question. For the sake of Pakistan's unity, Yahya declared last month, "no sacrifice is too great." The unity he envisions, however, might well leave East Pakistan a cringing colony. In an effort to stamp out Bengali culture, even street names are being changed. Shakari Bazar Road in Dacca is now called Tikka Khan Road after the hard-as-nails commander who now rules East Pakistan under martial rule.   The proud Bengalis are unlikely to give in. A warm and friendly but volatile people whose twin passions are politics and poetry, they have nurtured a gentle and distinctive culture of their own. . . There is a case for Yahya's Lincolnesque attempt to hold the Pakistani house together; there is none for his methods.   He might have succeeded had he tried to accommodate the East's justifiable demands for greater autonomy. But his tough crackdown virtually guarantees that the country's two halves, which have precious little in common, will never be successfully reunited.

Newsweek, 2 August 1971:

But in the end, the greatest threat to Pakistan is the flaring hatreds that Yahya's army has spawned.   "Pakistan died in March", says a Karachi editor.   'The only way this land can be held together is by the bayonet and the torch.   But that is not unity, that is slavery.   There can never be one nation in the future, only two enemies.'

Time, 25 October 1971:

Observers doubt that the situation would ease even if Yahya were to release Mujib and lift a ban on the Awami League. Where the Bengalis once were merely demanding greater autonomy, they now seem determined to fight for outright independence.

In a paper mentioned before,[75] as early as on 1 April 1971, Professors Mason, Dorfman and Marglin had said: "The independence of East Pakistan is inevitable." *The New Statesman,* London, of 16 April 1971, under the caption 'Blood of Bangla Desh' in red type commented: "If blood is the price of a people's right to independence, Bangla Desh has overpaid.   Of all the recent struggles to bring down governments and change frontiers in the name of national freedom, the war in East Bengal may prove the bloodiest and briefest.   On this level alone, East Pakistanis have achieved a record of suffering. But

---

[75] *Harvard Paper,* op. cit.

even if their movement is destroyed within a few days or weeks, it may only be a temporary defeat in a war of liberation which will eventually be recognized as just." *The Washington Daily News* of 30 June 1971 said: "History suggested, however, that West Pakistan from 1,000 miles away cannot for ever subjugate the Bengali people. What we are doing by sending arms to Pakistan is to make sure that Bengalis will remember that American weapons murdered them during the birth pang of their beloved Bangla Desh (Bengali nation)."

Professor Louis Dumont, a director at the Institute of Higher Studies in Paris, in an article in *Le Monde* on 6 August 1971 pointed out that East Bengal was virtually independent and the time she would take to be fully independent would depend to a great extent on the international community. This was because West Pakistan could not maintain its "policy of occupation" of East Bengal without considerable international assistance. The Government of Pakistan had lost its legitimacy by going to war against a majority of its citizens. In his view, the killings in East Bengal by West Pakistan army were in vain because "the Pakistan of yesterday is dead." Professor Dumont suggested that all military assistance to Pakistan must be stopped and no aid of any kind should go there until the evacuation of the Army from East Bengal.

International Response—Official

Official international response in suggesting a pattern of solution to the crisis in Pakistan was far from uniform or adequate. In so far as the problem related to the ten million refugees from East Bengal, there was a general consensus that the situation had imposed an intolerable burden on India and that an atmosphere should have been created in East Bengal to make it possible for the refugees to return home safely. But there was no consensus whatsoever with regard to the conditions which were a prerequisite for the return of the refugees.

On the merit of the question of self-determination of the people of Bangladesh, two trends were discernible: (a) It was an internal matter of Pakistan and there was no warrant for the international community even to discuss it; (b) It was not a matter solely within the domestic jurisdiction of Pakistan, and the situation called for a political solution.

The two different approaches were broadly represented by Mr Adam Malik, President of the 26th session of the United Nations General Assembly, and by U Thant, the Secretary-General, respectively. On 22 September 1971,[76] Mr Malik ruled out even the possibility of a debate on the East Bengal situation in the General Assembly on the

[76] *The Hindusthan Standard*, 24 September 1971.

ground that it was an internal political matter and, as such, should not be discussed in the world forum. The other trend could be seen in U Thant's introductory note to the Secretary-General's report on work of the United Nations.[77] The basic problem of East Bengal, according to him, could have been solved only "if a political solution based on reconciliation and the respect of humanitarian principles was achieved... Equally serious is the undoubted fact that reconciliation and improved political atmosphere and the success of relief efforts are indispensable prerequisites for the return of any of the refugees now in India."

On 29 September, the Soviet Foreign Minister, Mr Gromyko, told the General Assembly[78] that the grave situation obtaining in East Bengal was not an internal problem of Pakistan and that "we are convinced that a relaxation of tension in the area can be achieved only through a political settlement to the questions that have arisen in Pakistan." The Soviet-Indian joint statement issued from Moscow on 29 September 1971 *inter alia* states: "Taking note of the developments in East Bengal since March 25, 1971, both sides consider that the interests of the preservation of peace demand that urgent measures should be taken to reach a political solution to the problems which have arisen there, paying regard to the wishes, the inalienable rights and lawful interests of the people of East Bengal as well as the speediest and safe return of the refugees to their homeland in conditions safeguarding their honour and dignity." Again on 1 October, the Soviet President, Mr Nikolai Podgorny, called for an "equitable political settlement of the Bangladesh issue with due regard shown for the legitimate rights and interests of the people in that region."[79]

Towards the end of October, the Prime Minister, Mrs Indira Gandhi, went on a tour to western Europe and the USA 'in quest of peace' with a view to presenting the realities of the situation to some of the leaders of the world. According to informed sources, Belgium was in agreement with the Indian view that there should be a political solution of the Bangladesh problem with a guarantee for safe return of the refugees.[80] The British view reportedly preferred a political solution within the broad framework of Pakistan.[81] The French President, M Georges Pompidou, said that the East Bengal crisis was of a political nature and, therefore, there should have been a political solution; otherwise, he added, the whole of Indian subconti-

---

[77] *The Hindusthan Standard*, 20 September 1971.
[78] *The Statesman*, Calcutta, 30 September 1971.
[79] *Ibid.*
[80] *The Statesman*, Calcutta, 26 October 1971.
[81] *The Statesman*, Calcutta, 1 November 1971.

nent would be swept off in a storm with consequences hard to predict.[82] The West German declaration stated: "The Federal Government is ready to support to the best of its ability all measures which would help in promoting a political solution of the problem. The Federal Government is convinced that for the sake of maintaining peace and stability in that region, a political solution to the problem of East Pakistan must be found that will eliminate the existing situation of strife and ultimately enable the refugees to return home."[83]

In her letter of 15 December 1971 to President Nixon, Mrs Gandhi had it publicly recorded:

> The tragic war which is continuing could have been averted if during the nine months prior to Pakistan's attack on us on December 3, great leaders of the world had paid some attention to the fact of revolt, tried to see the reality of the situation and searched for a genuine attempt for reconciliation. I wrote letters along these lines. I undertook a tour in quest of peace at a time when it was extremely difficult to leave the country in the hope of presenting to some of the leaders of the world the situation as I saw it. It was heart-breaking to find that while there was sympathy for poor refugees, the disease itself was ignored. War could also have been avoided if the power, influence and the authority of all the States and, above all, of the USA had got Sheikh Mujibur Rahman released. Instead, we were told that a civilian administration was being installed. Everyone knows that this civilian administration was a farce. Today, the farce has turned into a tragedy. Lip service was paid to the need for a political solution, but not a single worthwhile step was taken to bring this about. Instead, the rulers of West Pakistan went ahead holding farcical elections to seats which had been arbitrarily declared vacant. There was not even a whisper that anyone from the outside world had tried to have contact with Mujibur Rahman.[84]

While the fate of 75 million people of Bangladesh was being perfunctorily dealt with in superficial attempts for a political solution, the only solution that was acceptable to the people of Bangladesh was clearly stated by their leaders. Mr Abu Sayeed Chowdhury, leader of the 16-member Bangladesh delegation to the UN, on 1 October said that no solution would be acceptable to the people of Bangladesh unless three conditions were fulfilled: (i) the recogni-

[82] *The Statesman*, Calcutta, 9 November 1971.
[83] *The Statesman*, Calcutta, 12 November 1971.
[84] *The Statesman*, Calcutta, 17 December 1971.

tion of Bangladesh as an independent state, (ii) immediate and un-conditional release of Sheikh Mujibur Rahman, and (iii) the with-drawal of the occupation forces of President Yahya Khan. The Bangladesh Cabinet fully shared this view.[85]

The demand for total independence was reiterated by the Bangla-desh Cabinet in a public statement: "The joint statement of the Indian Prime Minister, Mrs Gandhi, and Soviet leaders reflects a deep understanding of the Bangladesh issue in the Kremlin. While suggesting a political solution of the problem, the joint statement advocates 'urgent measures paying regard to the wishes, the inalien-able rights and lawful interests of the people of East Bengal.' These three basic principles can only lead to the support of total indepen-dence of Bangladesh for which the 75 million people of Bangladesh are shedding blood every moment. Due importance has been given in the joint statement with regard to 'speediest return of refugees to their homes with honour and dignity.' This can happen only if the refugees are enabled to return in freedom which is the avowed policy of the Government of Bangladesh. At a time when the destiny of 75 million struggling people of Bangladesh is being discussed all over the world and in the UN, we wish to reiterate and re-emphasize that total independence is our goal. We urge all the powers of the world to support this goal. The people of Bangladesh and their elected representatives have given irrevocable verdict on this issue."[86]

UN's Perfidious Role : Stifling a liberation movement and giving succour to a military junta

On 27 December 1971, *Time* magazine wrote:

The Losers. Islamabad, of course, was the principal loser in the outcome of the war. But there were two others as well. One was the United Nations. The Security Council last week groped desperately toward trying to achieve an international consensus on what to do about the struggle, and ended up with seven cease-fire resolutions that were never acted upon at all. The other loser was Washington, which had tried to bring about a political settlement, but from the New Delhi viewpoint—and to other observers as well—appeared wholeheartedly committed to the support of Pakistan's military dictatorship.

If the United Nations were a loser in the outcome of the war, the real victor was the Charter of the United Nations. The United

[85] *The Statesman*, Calcutta, 2 October 1971, PTI report from New York. Also see *The Statesman*, Calcutta, 4 October 1971.
[86] *The Statesman*, Calcutta, 4 October 1971.

Nations became a loser not because it failed to secure a consensus on cease-fire with the two-fold objective of defeating the war of self-determination of the Bengali people and perpetuating the oppressive rule of a military dictator. The United Nations became a loser because of its failure to reconcile the Charter principles of human rights and self-determination with the principle of territorial integrity. The failure of the United Nations to prevent the outbreak of war by the removal of its root cause and again, after the outbreak of war, its attempt to mobilize international assistance in support of General Yahya Khan were responsible for reducing the credibility of the world body to a vanishing point.

When the General Assembly of the United Nations met at its 26th session in September 1971, all its members were fully aware of the realities of the situation in the subcontinent and the real causes of the tension. They were aware that unless the 10 million refugees returned to Bangladesh safe and secure, there was no possibility of maintaining peace in the subcontinent. They were also aware that it was impossible to expect the refugees to return home so long Yahya's army of occupation remained in Bangladesh. The progress of events between March and September was notoriously well known: the ruthless war of genocide by the military regime, the increasing achievements of the Mukti Bahini supported by the entire nation in Bangladesh, the certainty of the ultimate defeat of the Pakistani army in spite of military and economic assistance provided by some of the big powers, and mounting pressures on India's economic, political and territorial security as a result of Pakistan's acts of aggression. By September, it was known to the world that separation between the two wings of Pakistan was inevitable and the only political solution which could have saved the situation was for the world community to assist the two wings of Pakistan to fix amicably what Abraham Lincoln would have described as "terms for the separation." This would have not only helped the realization of self-determination of the people of Bangladesh but would have immediately restored peace and stability in the subcontinent by the voluntary return of the refugees to their own country. Yet one finds that although in the general debate in the 26th session of the General Assembly 47 speakers called for a political reconciliation in Pakistan, no action whatsoever was taken by the world body to initiate moves for a political solution.

On the contrary, prior to the outbreak of war, steps were taken for salvaging the dwindling strength and eroding image of the army of occupation. Several moves were initiated at the international level with a view to involving the United Nations in favour of Yahya's army of occupation in Bangladesh. In June 1971, there was a US sponsored move to send a team of Vietnam-style communications experts to East Bengal ostensibly to help in relief operations. The attempt did not succeed. Later, a proposal was initiated by some Western countries with a view to posting UN observers on both sides of the Indo-Pakistan borders. This fell through because India declined to accept any foreign observers on her soil. The third attempt was made on 1 December when the UN Secretary-General sent Pakistan's request for the posting of UN observers on the East Bengal border to the Security Council for debate. The obvious object of such a move was to hamper the increasingly successful operations of the liberation forces and to assist the military junta to retain its control over a hostile population in Bangladesh. The purpose was to divert the attention from the war of self-determination of the Bengali people and to internationalize the issue by projecting the problem as an Indo-Pakistani dispute. Each one of these attempts was opposed not only by India but by the leaders and freedom fighters of Bangladesh who found it difficult to guarantee the security of the UN observers during the final phase of the war of liberation and unsettled conditions inside Bangladesh.[87]

Prior to the outbreak of war on 3 December, Pakistan moved its army to Indian borders in the western sector in preparation of a regular war. There was not a whisper of protest from any of the big nations. Yet, India did not move its army for 10 days after Pakistani Army had occupied forward positions. Mrs Gandhi said on 2 December: "We went to the UN observers and protested to them that Pakistan should not be allowed to bring her forces to the forward areas. After enquiries, the UN observers told us that the Pakistanis were carrying military exercises and would withdraw after 10 days. Are the 10 days not yet over?"[88] There was another

---

[87] The then Foreign Minister of Bangladesh said on 2 December that UN observers of any description would be regarded as 'messengers and protectors of imperialist and colonial interests' and the Mukti Bahini would treat them 'as unwelcome guests' in the same way as Yahya's occupation army was being treated: *The Statesman*, 3 December 1971. Mrs Gandhi said that the attempts to bring the UN observers were part of the game of confusing the realities of the situation and those who made such attempts 'cannot but be suspect in the eyes of the people'. She gave three reasons why such proposals were not acceptable. First, the basic objective of posting such observers in East Bengal was to check the activities of the Mukti Bahini, but the effort would have been futile since all the checks and controls in Vietnam failed to stop the guerrilla activities there. Second, it was impossible for the observers to function since the Bangladesh Government made it plain that it could not guarantee their safety. Third, the observers would not be in a position to ensure the return of the refugees since the refugees said that they would go back only when Bangladesh was free and there was peace. *The Statesman*, 1, 3, 4 December 1971.

[88] *The Statesman*, Calcutta, 3 December 1971.

strong reason why the Indian troops could not be withdrawn from the forward areas. India was thrice attacked by Pakistan in the past and no responsible Government could take the risk of leaving the border unguarded at a critical juncture. Unlike Pakistan, India's cantonments were far from the borders and, accordingly, it was not possible for India to bring her troops back quickly to the forward areas in the case of a sudden Pakistani attack. Thirdly, those who asked India to withdraw her troops from the border were not prepared to give a guarantee to India that Pakistan would vacate the areas she occupied in the event of a war against India.[89]

Thereafter a full-scale war broke out in the subcontinent on 3 December 1971, when Pakistan launched its aerial attacks simultaneously on several Indian airfields (Amritsar, Srinagar, Pathankot, Abantipur, Uttarlai, Jodhpur, Agra and Ambala) in the western sector and also opened fire on India's defensive positions in Sulenanki, Khem Karan, Poonch and other areas. This was followed by Pakistan's formal declaration of war against India. The Prime Minister, Mrs Indira Gandhi, told the nation in a broadcast shortly after midnight: "At 5-30 p.m. today, Pakistan launched a full-scale war against us. We have no option but to put our country on a war-footing." She declared that "wanton and unprovoked aggression of Pakistan would be decisively and timely repelled. Today the war in Bangladesh has become a war on India. Peace cannot last if we cannot guard our freedom, our democracy and our way of life. So, today we fight not merly for territorial integrity but for the basic ideals which have given strength to this country and on which alone we can progress to a better future."[90] On 6 December, the Prime Minister declared in Parliament India's decision to grant recognition to the Peoples Republic of Bangladesh. Within a few hours, Islamabad broke off diplomatic relations with New Delhi. On 16 December, the Pakistani army surrendered unconditionally in Bangladesh and India announced a unilateral cease-fire on the western front from 8 p.m. on 17 December. The official spokesman in New Delhi stated:[91] "We have repeatedly declared that India has no territorial ambitions. Now that Pakistani armed forces have surrendered in Bangladesh and Bangladesh is free, it is pointless, in our view, to continue the present conflict. Therefore, in order to stop bloodshed and unnecessary loss of life, we have ordered our armed forces to cease-fire everywhere in western front with effect from 20·00 hours IST on Friday, December 17, 1971. It is our earnest hope that there will

[89] *The Statesman*, Calcutta, 1, 2, 3 and 4 December, 1971 for Mrs. Gandhi's speeches.
[90] *The Statesman*, Calcutta, 4 December 1971.
[91] *The Statesman*, Calcutta, 17 December 1971.

be corresponding immediate response from the Government of Pakistan." On 17 December, President Yahya Khan accepted India's offer and thus the 14-day war came to an end.

After nine months of silence, the United Nations all of a sudden became busy in the month of December. On 5 December, the United States moved a resolution before the Security Council which called upon India and Pakistan for cessation of hostilities, withdrawal of armed forces and authorized the UN Secretary-General to place observers along the India-Pakistan borders. The resolution also called upon India, Pakistan and others 'to exert their best efforts towards the creation of a climate conducive to the voluntary return of the refugees to East Pakistan' and asked India and Pakistan to respond affirmatively to the Secretary-General's offer and good offices.[92] The resolution which was vetoed by the Soviet Union received the support of 11 members, including China. It was opposed by the Soviet Union and Poland, while Britain and France abstained from voting. On 6 December, another resolution[93] was moved by eight members before the Security Council calling for a Indo-Pakistani cease-fire and military withdrawal. The resolution was supported by China and the USA and nine other members. The Soviet Union and Poland opposed it. Britain and France abstained from voting. Earlier, the Security Council had rejected a Soviet resolution which called for a 'political settlement in East Pakistan which would inevitably result in the cessation of hostilities.'

Thereafter, the General Assembly in exercise of its jurisdiction under the controversial Uniting for Peace resolution took cognizance of the situation. On 8 December, the Assembly adopted the following resolution by a 104-11 vote:[94]

The General Assembly noting the reports of the Secretary-General of December 3 and 4, 1971, and the letter from the President of the Security Council transmitting the text of Council resolution 3039 (1971) of December 6, 1971.

Gravely concerned that hostilities have broken out between India and Pakistan which constitute an immediate threat to international peace and security.

Recognizing the need to deal appropriately at a subsequent stage within the framework of the Charter of the U.N. with the issues which have given rise to the hostilities.

Convinced that an early political solution would be necessary

[92] *The Statesman*, Calcutta, 6 December 1971.
[93] *The Statesman*, Calcutta, 7 December 1971.
[94] *The Statesman*, Calcutta, 9 December 1971.

for the restoration of conditions of normalcy in the area of conflict and for the return of the refugees to their homes.

Mindful of the provisions of the Charter, in particular of Article 2 Paragraph 4 of the U.N. Charter.

Recalling the declaration on the strengthening of international security, particularly Paragraphs 4, 5 and 6.

Recognizing further the need to take immediate measures to bring about an immediate cessation of hostilities between India and Pakistan and effect a withdrawal of their armed forces quickly to their own side of the India-Pakistan borders.

Mindful of the purposes and principles of the Charter and of the General Assembly's responsibilities under the relevant provisions of the Charter and of Assembly resolution 377A (V) of November 3, 1950.

1. Calls upon the Governments of India and Pakistan to take forthwith all measures for an immediate cease-fire and withdrawal of their armed forces on the territory of the other to their own side of the India-Pakistan borders;

2. Urges that efforts be intensified in order to bring about, speedily and in accordance with the purposes and principles of the Charter of the U.N., conditions necessary for the voluntary return of the East Pakistani refugees to their homes;

3. Calls for the full cooperation of all States with the Secretary-General for rendering assistance to and relieving the distress of those refugees;

4. Urges that every effort be made to safeguard the lives and well-being of the civilian population in the area of conflict;

5. Requests the Secretary-General to keep the General Assembly and the Security Council promptly and currently informed on the implementation of the present resolution;

6. Decides to follow the question closely and to meet again should the situation so demand;

7. Calls upon the Security Council to take appropriate action in the light of the present resolution.

In view of the acceptance of the above resolution, the Soviet resolution, which called upon the Pakistan Government to take effective action for a political settlement simultaneously with cease-fire and cessation of hostilities, was not taken up by the Assembly. The Soviet resolution reads:[95] The General Assembly gravely concerned

---

[95] *Ibid.*

that hostilities have broken out between India and Pakistan which constitute an immediate threat to international peace and security.

1. Calls upon all parties concerned forthwith, as a first step, for an immediate cease-fire and cessation of all hostilities.

2. Calls upon the Government of Pakistan simultaneously to take effective action towards a political settlement in East Pakistan, giving immediate recognition to the will of the East Pakistan population as expressed in the elections of December 1970.

3. Declares that the provisions of operative Paragraphs 1 and 2 of this resolution constitute a single whole.

4. Requests the Secretary-General to keep the Security Council and the General Assembly promptly and currently informed on the implementation of the present resolution.

5. Calls upon the Security Council to take appropriate measures in the light of the present resolution.

In a letter addressed by the Prime Minister of India to the UN Secretary-General[96] and read out before the Security Council, Mrs Gandhi stated that "there can be a cease-fire and withdrawal of Indian armed forces" if the Pakistani rulers withdrew their own forces from Bangladesh and reached a peaceful settlement with the leaders of Bangladesh. "Given an assurance of a desire to examine these basic causes with objectivity, India will not be found wanting in offering its utmost cooperation." Referring to the Bangladesh liberation movement, Mrs Gandhi said: "The armed forces of the new State have long been engaged in a struggle against the forces of West Pakistan in Bangladesh. In the circumstances, is it realistic to call upon India to cease-fire without at the same time giving a hearing to the representatives of Bangladesh whose armed forces are engaged against the forces of West Pakistan?"

On 14 December, another United States resolution before the Security Council seeking a cease-fire without any reference to the causes of the conflict was vetoed by the Soviet Union. It received the support of eleven members, was opposed by the Soviet Union and Poland, Britain and France abstaining.

On 15 December, Britain proposed[97] that the Council be reconvened when the President felt that sufficient progress had been made to warrant a meeting. The proposal was approved by a 11-0 vote with four abstentions.

[96] *The Statesman*, Calcutta, 14 December 1971.
[97] *The Statesman*, Calcutta, 16 December 1971.

After Pakistan's acceptance of India's unilateral declaration of cease-fire, the Security Council on 21 December approved a resolution (by 11-0 vote with 4 abstentions) which in its operative part provided *inter alia*: "Demands that a durable cease-fire and cessation of all hostilities in all areas of conflict be strictly observed and remain in effect until withdrawals take place, as soon as practicable, of all armed forces to their respective territories and to positions which fully respect the cease-fire line in Jammu and Kashmir supervised by the UN Military Observation Groups for India and Pakistan."[98]

An analysis of the resolution adopted by the General Assembly in the context of the situation in Bangladesh will not only expose its fundamental weakness and unworkability but would also expose an international attempt to stifle the movement for self-determination and to prolong the repressive rule of the military junta in Bangladesh. Besides, the resolution in its operative part is self-destructive, and again the recitals and the operative part are mutually conflicting. First, although for the first time the United Nations took notice of the fact that there were certain "issues which have given rise to the hostilities", such issues were to be dealt with appropriately "at a subsequent stage within the framework of the Charter." In other words, cease-fire was to become effective at once, but the settlement of the issues which gave rise to the hostilities was to be negotiated at an uncertain future date. By its failure to categorize the issues and linking up the solution thereof with an effective cease-fire and withdrawal of troops, a settlement was proposed which was impossible of achievement. The seven issues were: (a) The denial of self-determination to the majority people of Pakistan residing in Bangladesh for a period of eleven years by the West Pakistanis and for a further period of thirteen years by the military junta of West Pakistan whose title to governmental authority was illegal and *ultra vires* the Charter of the United Nations, the Universal Declaration of Human Rights and the international law of the Charter regime as elaborated in 1970 Declaration; (b) the commencement of a war of genocide and the continuation of the genocidal acts by West Pakistan's army of occupation in Bangladesh resulting in the death of a million Bengalis, rendering another two million homeless destitutes inside Bangladesh, and forcing a further ten million to seek asylum in India; (c) the failure of the world body to persuade or coerce the military junta to stop its genocidal acts, to release Sheikh Mujibur Rahman and to reach a political reconciliation with the majority leaders represented by the Awami League; (d) the failure of the world body to recognize that without a political solution indicated above, it was impossible for the refugees to return home safe and

[98] *The Statesman*, Calcutta, 23 December 1971.

secure; (e) the failure of the international community to appreciate the reality of the fact that 75 million people for a period of nine months were engaged in a bitter struggle against the forces of West Pakistan for achieving self-determination in Bangladesh; (f) the failure of the world body to recognize the factum of independence of the people of Bangladesh and the reality of the existence of Bangladesh as an independent sovereign state internationally recognized by India and Bhutan; (g) the failure of the world body to characterize Pakistan's actions in sending ten million Bengalis to India and its subsequent aerial attacks on 3 December as acts of aggression committed by Pakistan and to appreciate that India's response was in self-defence. The nature of all the seven issues was such that it was impossible to deal with them compartmentally or piecemeal and no solution could become workable unless all the issues in their entirety were effectively dealt with.

Second, so far as the eastern sector was concerned, the resolution in its operative part contemplated immediate cease-fire and withdrawal of armed forces of India from Bangladesh but not the withdrawal of armed forces of West Pakistan from Bangladesh. It totally ignored the stark reality of a well-organized cohesive force of a 100,000-strong Mukti Bahini engaged in a bitter war with the Pakistani forces. Since the Government of Bangladesh was not taken into confidence nor even granted a hearing in spite of the requests of the Soviet Union and India, the new nation or its Government was under no obligation nor was called upon to stop fighting with the Pakistani forces. Accordingly, even if India accepted the resolution, the objective set forth could not have been realised.[99]

Third, in its operative part, the resolution *assumed* that voluntary return of the refugees from India to Bangladesh was consistent with the continuation of the occupation forces of West Pakistan in Bangladesh. The assumption was wholly unfounded. Incontrovertible evidence collected since 25 March 1971 clearly established that the 10 million people, who came to India to escape the genocidal acts of the Pakistani troops, were not willing to go back to the clutches of the same oppressors. As Mr John Grigg wrote in *The Sunday Times*: "It has been glaringly obvious to her (Mrs Gandhi) and to anyone with first-hand knowledge of the situation that the refugees would return only if and when the military regime in East Bengal was

---

[99] About the resolution, India's representative, Mr Samar Sen, told the General Assembly: "It is unrealistic because there are two kinds of battle in the area—one between the Indian and Pakistani troops and another between the Pakistani troops and the Mukti Bahini. The resolution leaves out one and therefore it will not work". *The Statesman*, 9 December 1971.

liquidated and power transferred to the people's elect, more specially to Sheikh Mujib (I talked to hundreds of refugees in early October and can testify that they would not dream of going back on any other terms)."[100]

Fourth, the objective of the operative part to protect the interest of West Pakistan's occupation forces in Bangladesh was destructive of the purpose of the recitals to achieve "an early political solution" necessary for the restoration of "condition of normalcy." There was a total failure on the part of the United Nations to reconcile the concurrent need of a political solution and cease-fire.

Fifth, the General Assembly in its anxiety to postpone the inevitable disintegration of Pakistan referred only to Article 2(4) of the Charter in the context of territorial integrity of Pakistan, but completely ignored the rights of the people of Bangladesh, the principle of equal rights and self-determination and human rights and fundamental freedoms in accordance with the Articles 1(2), (3) and 56, and the right of the Bengali people not only to resist the illegal use of force but to receive international assistance in their struggle as elaborated in the 1970 Declaration.

Sixth, a criticism more fundamental is to be found in the objective the resolution sought to achieve. It was the first attempt in the history of the United Nations to make a concerted international move to stifle a war of liberation in which an entire nation of 75 million people was fighting for freedom against the oppressive rule of a military dictator. The intended effect of the resolution was to make the territory of Bangladesh safe for the occupation forces of West Pakistan threatened with certain defeat, and to promote the intransigence of the military junta by removing the compulsion of a democratic and peaceful solution. After the recognition of Bangladesh by India on 6 December, the people of India and Bangladesh became joint partisans in the war of liberation. The resolution intended that India should withdraw its military assistance to its ally, Bangladesh, and desist from performing its international duty of assisting a people struggling for freedom, thereby delaying the liberation of Bangladesh about to be achieved. The purpose of the resolution was to further promote the tension in the subcontinent by prolonging the agony of the war between the Mukti Bahini and the Pakistani forces.

In striking contrast, the Soviet resolution by providing simultaneously for cease-fire and effective action towards a political settlement in the operative part took cognizance of the realities of the situation, the causes of origin of the conflict, and recommended reme-

---

[100] "India's Just Cause—Victory to Benefit Subcontinent" by John Grigg, *The Sunday Times*, London, reproduced in the Statesman, 9 December 1971.

dial measures fully in consonance with the international law of the Charter regime.

The fact that three permanent members of the Security Council had dissociated themselves from the resolutions vetoed by the Soviet Union indicated the weakness of a cease-fire resolution unless unanimity was reached. International consensus was reached in respect of the Security Council resolution of 21 December 1971 because it took into account the reality of the situation, viz., the liberation of Bangladesh and the withdrawal of the Pakistani army of occupation from the territory of the new State. Accordingly, the resolution contemplated a durable cease-fire and subsequent withdrawals of Pakistani and Indian troops in the western sector only.

The basic cause of the tension was the presence of the Pakistani army in Bangladesh. The tension was removed as soon as the Pakistani troops unconditionally surrendered in Bangladesh. The people of Bangladesh achieved their self-determination and the refugees of their own accord started returning to Bangladesh safe and secure.

The Soviet View

The Soviet view of the real cause of the tension was expressed in a statement issued from Moscow on 5 December 1971 by the official Agency, Tass (reproduced in *The Statesman*, Calcutta, 6 December 1971), which states *inter alia*:

"It is well known that the situation created in East Pakistan as a result of the Pakistan Government's action against the population of the part of the country was the main cause of the tension that mounted lately in relations between Pakistan and India. A mass movement for autonomy, for elementary civil rights and freedom developed in East Pakistan in recent years. The Awami League headed by Sheikh Mujibur Rahman received the unanimous support of the East Pakistan population at elections to legislative bodies in December 1970. After the election, talks began between the President of Pakistan and the leader of the Awami League on the question of the future State organization that envisaged an autonomy for East Pakistan. But, evidently not desiring to bring matters to an agreement, the Government of Pakistan suddenly broke off the talks on March 25, 1971. Mr Mujibur Rahman and other leaders of the Awami League were arrested and thrown into prison. Started immediately were cruel repressions against the population, thousands of people were killed and many million East Pakistani citizens had to flee to neighbouring India for their life.

"An atmosphere of mass terror and lawlessness set in in East Pakistan. On encountering a growing resistance by the East Pakistani population to the mass repression and persecutions, the Government of Pakistan tried to put the blame for the situation on India and embarked on a course of aggravating relations with her. Proceeding from a concern for the preservation of peace, the Soviet Government repeatedly expressed to President Yahya Khan and the Government of Pakistan its concern over the situation in the Hindusthan Peninsula in connection with the events in East Pakistan. Condemning the policy of repression and persecution as a method of solving political questions, it drew the Pakistani Government's attention to the need of a political settlement in East Pakistan. Expressed from the Soviet side was the conviction that the renunciation of the policy of repression, the release of Mr Rahman and the immediate resumption of talks with the aim of finding such a solution that would accord with the will expressed by the population of East Pakistan at the elections of December 1970 can be the only realistic road. This would ensure conditions also for the return to their home of millions of East Pakistani refugees who found refuge in India. Approaching the Government of Pakistan with these considerations, the Soviet Government acted in accordance with the principles of humaneness and wishing the Pakistani people well in the solution, in a democratic manner, of the complex problems facing the country. Since the Pakistani Government did not take measures for a political settlement in East Pakistan and continued to build up military preparations against India, the Soviet leaders informed President Yahya Khan that Pakistan's armed attack against India under whatever pretext would evoke the most resolute condemnation in the Soviet Union... In the face of the military threat now hanging over Hindusthan, the Soviet Union comes for the speediest ending of the bloodshed and for a political settlement in East Pakistan on the basis of respect for the lawful rights and interests of its people. The Soviet Government also believe that the Governments of all countries should refrain from steps signifying in this or that way their involvement in the conflict and leading to a further aggravation of the situation in the Hindusthan Peninsula."

Two Americas : Involvement in Pakistan's Crisis

Inside East Bengal, the Associated Press correspondent, Arnold Zeitlin, was once told by a Bengali doctor: "The U.S. Government sends us food to keep us alive and bullets to kill us."[101] This is one aspect of the nature of American involvement in the Pakistani crisis.

One is reminded of the Senator William Fulbright's assessment of his own people:

There are two Americas. One is the America of Lincoln and

---

[101] *The Statesman*, Calcutta, 2 August 1971.

Adlai Stevenson; the other is the America of Teddy Roosevelt and the modern superpatriots. One is generous and humane, the other narrowly egotistical; one is self-critical, the other self-righteous; one is sensible, the other romantic; one is good-humored, the other solemn; one is inquiring, the other pontificating; one is moderate, the other filled with passionate intensity; one is judicious and the other arrogant in the use of great power.[102]

The distinguished Senator pointed out that after 25 years of world power, the United States must decide 'which of the two sides of its national character is to predominate—the humanism of Lincoln or the arrogance of those who would make America the world's policeman. One or the other will help shape the spirit of the age—unless of course we refuse to choose, in which case America may come to play a less important role in the world, leaving the great decisions to others.'[103] The Senator, however, regretted: "The current tendency is toward a more strident and aggressive American foreign policy, which is to say, toward a policy closer to the spirit of Theodore Roosevelt than of Lincoln."[104]

Both the Americas were involved in the East Bengal tragedy—the arrogant America that sent the bullets which killed the Bengalis and Lincoln's America that called for an immediate suspension of all aid to the military rulers of Pakistan; the arrogant America that helped the perpetuation of the exploitative tyranny of West Pakistan, and Lincoln's America that supported the struggle of the Bengali people for freedom from colonial exploitation. For the world's most resourceful nation, East Bengal might have been a small issue, but it was nonetheless a fundamental one, involving human values, and throwing a big challenge to the American people to decide which of the two sides of its national character was to predominate.

The quantum of the United States military aid to Pakistan is classified figure, but two estimates put it between $ 1·5 to $ 2 billion for the period between 1954 and 1965.[105] The Indian Minister for Defence Production told the Rajya Sabha on 4 August 1971 that both China and the USA supplied Pakistan with arms at concessional rates or 'throw-away prices', and the French sold them against hard cash 'with no concession'; and the Government of India's estimate of the

---

[102] Fulbright: *The Arrogance of Power* (Vintage Books, New York, January 1967), p. 245.

[103] *Ibid.*, p. 246.

[104] *Ibid.*

[105] *The New York Times*, 28 September 1964; Frank N. Trager, 'United States and Pakistan', *Orbis* Vol. IX, Fall 1965, No. 3.

value of US arms shipments to Pakistan since the pact of 1954 was $ 2 billion.[106]

The military assistance to Pakistan included F-104 Starfighters, Patton tanks, armoured personnel carriers, and automatic and recoilless infantry weapons. Pakistan has been an early member of SEATO and CENTO. The purpose of this military aid was to bolster the armed containment of the Communist bloc in the Dulles era of U.S. foreign policy; but apart from wars against India and the Mukti Bahini in the recent war of liberation, the only active use of these weapons had occurred against the unarmed and defenceless civilian population of East Bengal.[107] Although Washington stopped arms deliveries to both India and Pakistan when the war broke out in 1965, the United States in October 1970 made an exception to its embargo on military sales to Pakistan. Available information disclosed that the United States offered to supply to Pakistan 300 armoured personnel carriers, four maritime reconnaissance aircraft, six F-104 jet fighters and seven B-57 bombers.[108] Still later, *Time* of 25 October 1971, wrote: "Senator Edward Kennedy charges that the U.S. is sending another sort of aid to the subcontinent as well. In spite of a State Department freeze on new military aid shipments to Pakistan, says Kennedy, the Pentagon has signed new defence contracts totalling nearly $10 million with the Pakistan Government within the past five months. Kennedy's investigation also revealed that U.S. firms have received State Department licences to ship to Pakistan arms and ammunition purchased from the Soviet Union and in Eastern Europe."

What happened after 25 March 1971 was summed up in *Time* magazine of 23 August 1971:

> After the shooting started last March, the U.S. Consul-General in Dacca, Archer K. Blood, asked Washington for a quick, forthright condemnation of the Central Government's brutal crackdown. But Joseph S. Farland, the U.S. Ambassador to Pakistan and a Nixon political appointee, argued that the U.S. should do

---

[106] *The Statesman*, Calcutta, 5 August 1971.

[107] *The Washington Post* 30 March 1971, *The New York Times* 29 and 30 March 1971, for eye-witness accounts by correspondents of use of US supplied tanks; also see *Conflict in East Pakistan: Background and Prospects* by Professors Edward S. Mason, Robert Dorfman and Stephen A. Martin, reproduced by the Department of Information, Government of Bangladesh, Mujibnagar and reprinted by Calcutta University Bagladesh Sahayak Samity (hereafter referred to as the *Harvard Paper*). For a summary of the paper, see *Bangla Desh Documents*, op. cit., pp. 9-15.

[108] *Harvard Paper*, op. cit.

nothing to displease Yahya and thereby drive him into Peking's arms. In Washington, Farland's pleas for 'quiet diplomacy' won out. The official policy was deliberately ambiguous. There was no condemnation, no reproach, only a promise to stop military sales and hold economic aid 'in abeyance' for fiscal year 1972 (the House rejected the Administration's $ 132 million Pakistan aid request outright and the Senate is expected to follow suit). In New Delhi, again Ambassador Kenneth Keating, 71, protested that quiet diplomacy was having no appreciable effect on Yahya and was confusing the Indians. Keating, who is said to be in deep despair, was ignored, and Blood was transferred to the State's personnel office in Washington. Soon word went out that the policy of not being beastly to Yahya had been personally endorsed by President Nixon. In India's view, U.S. diplomacy was not quiet but downright deceitful. When Swaran Singh visited Washington last June, he was assured by Administration officials that no US arms would flow to Pakistan. Singh returned home just as the news came out that some arms shipments were being made after all. Washington clumsily explained that there had been an 'administrative oversight' involving sales licensed before the embargo was imposed. Last week, the State conceded that $ 4,000,000 in Pakistan-bound arms remains 'in the pipeline'.

The real value of the US military assistance has to be measured in terms of its power and ability to help the perpetuation of military oligarchies by suppressing popular national movements. When so viewed, it will appear that in a poor country even a small amount of US arms aid can produce a devastating effect. Mr. John Duncan Powell had studied the impact of the US military assistance in Latin America.[109] He has shown that the smallness of the sums involved was deceptive, and measured in terms of their effect on the ability of the military forces to apply violence against civilian groups, American arms played a very significant role. In poor countries with low *per capita* income and fragile political institutions, even a small amount of military assistance could give a soldier an overwhelming advantage over an ordinary civilian in a conflict between them. Taking into consideration AID figures on cumulative assistance per soldier as of 1962, and matching them against *per capita* income, Mr. Powell has shown that each member of Nicaragua's armed forces represented $ 930 worth of US arms and training, and available for use against poor civilians with a total *per capita* income of only $ 205,

---

[109] Powell, 'Military Assistance and Militarism in Latin America' *Western Political Quarterly*, June 1965, pp. 382-92.

the corresponding figures in Guatemala being $ 538 worth of US arms and training as against a total *per capita* income of $ 185.

In the context of Powell's study, Senator Fulbright had said:[110] "America's modest military aid in Latin America is decidedly more effective than its mercenary forces in Europe and Asia, not, however, in holding back communists but in holding *up* military oligarchies... Viewed in the physical and economic context of a poor country in Central America, United States military assistance no longer appears small and innocent; it contributes in an important way to the perpetuation of military oligarchies." Senator Fulbright's view of the final outcome of US military assistance to Latin America has proved almost prophetic in other areas of the world. He said:

> On an evening in the summer of 1966, an American journalist's interview with rebels in the Guatemalan jungle was shown on television. A young rebel leader said he was a Marxist because Marxism, as he understood it, called for giving the land to the peasants; he thought of the United States as an enemy, because, he thought, American arms and powers were always placed at the disposal of the oppressors of his people. This view of America is not unknown in other parts of the world; it is one of the rewards of the 'forward strategy' of American military assistance.[111]

This view of America was confirmed in East Bengal with tragic consequences. Innocent Bengali civilians of all ages were the worst victims of the US military assistance to Pakistan. If one applies Powell's formula to Pakistan, it would appear that as of 1970 $ 2 billion was the amount of US arms aid to Pakistan. The total strength of the three services in Pakistan is 324,500 men.[112] If one takes into account the cumulative effect of US military assistance per soldier and contrasts it with the *per capita* income of an average Bengali, the result is a staggering one, namely, each West Pakistani soldier in East Bengal represented $ 6163 worth of US arms as against a total *per capita* income of $ 30 in East Bengal.

In other words, to produce an identical havoc on civilian population, it would cost the USA a unit of arms aid worth $ 34·38 at Guatemala, $ 22·04 in Nicaragua and only 48 cents in East Bengal. To put it differently, if only a dollar worth of US arms is needed to produce a particular impact in East Bengal, it would cost the USA

---

[110] Fulbright, op. cit., pp. 230-31.

[111] *Ibid.*, p. 232.

[112] Jay Inder Singh, 'Pakistan's Military Strength', *The Illustrated Weekly of India*, 15 August 1971, pp. 13-15.

$ 46 in Nicaragua and $ 78 in Guatemala to produce an identical impact. The argument that the US arms already supplied to Pakistan or those which were 'in the pipeline' involved only small sums therefore appears to be dangerously deceptive in the context of East Bengal.

The sophisticated American weapons were used by the Yahya regime for killing and torturing innocent Bengalis of all ages, for destroying universities and students' dormitories, for bombing defenceless towns, cities and villages. The American weapons had helped Yahya in his war crimes and crimes against humanity, including genocide. One recalls what Bertrand Russell had said about the supply of a phosphorous explosive by the USA for use in the Vietnam war early in 1964. He said:[113] "I am reminded of the argument of an eminent Nazi that he did not kill a single Jew; he provided the lorries."

The American weapons were used not only for suppressing the struggle for freedom of 75 million Bengalis but also on several occasions against India, including the war in the first week of December 1971.

The question, therefore, arises: "Was the American military assistance used for the purpose for which it was furnished?" On 19 May 1954, the United States and Pakistan signed the Mutual Defence Assistance Agreement at Karachi.[114] Articles 1 and 2 of the agreement provide as follows:

"1. The Government of the United States will make available to the Government of Pakistan such equipment, materials, services or other assistance as the Government of the United States may authorise in accordance with such terms and conditions as may be agreed. The furnishing and use of such assistance shall be consistent with the Charter of the United Nations. Such assistance as may be made available by the Government of the United States pursuant to this Agreement will be furnished under the provisions and subject to all the terms, conditions and termination provisions of the Mutual Defence Assistance Act of 1949 and the Mutual Security Act of 1951, acts amendatory or supplementary thereto, appropriation acts thereunder, or any other applicable legislative provisions. The two Governments will, from time to time, negotiate detailed arrangements necessary to carry out the provisions of this paragraph.

"2. The Government of Pakistan will use this assistance exclusively to maintain its internal security, its legitimate self-defence, or to

---

[113] B. Russell, *War Crimes in Vietnam* (Allen & Unwin, 1967), p. 62.
[114] *Documents on American Foreign Relations, 1954* (Harper, New York, 1954), pp. 379-83, for text of the agreement; also see, Roy Chowdhury, *Military Alliances and Neutrality in War and Peace* (Orient Longmans, 1966), pp. 47-8.

permit it to participate in the defence of the area, or in United Nations collective security arrangements and measures, and Pakistan will not undertake any act of aggression against any other nation. The Government of Pakistan will not, without the prior agreement of the Government of the United States, devote such assistance to purposes other than those for which it was furnished."

Both the 'furnishing' and the 'use' of such assistance should be (a) consistent with the Charter of the United Nations, and (b) subject to all the terms, conditions and termination provisions of the Mutual Defence Assistance Act, 1949, and the Mutual Security Act, 1951.   The Mutual Defence Assistance Act of 1949 (Public Law 329, 81st Congress, 1st session) provided in the declaration of its policy: "These measures include the furnishing of military assistance essential to enable the United States and other nations dedicated to the purpose and principles of the United Nations Charter to participate effectively in arrangements for individual and collective self-defence in support of those purposes and principles."

The impressive array of modern weaponry was given expressly for defensive purposes.   Since the weapons were not used in East Bengal for defensive purposes, the question arises whether the use of such assistance in East Bengal can be legally justified on the ground of 'internal security of Pakistan.'   The test is: Was it the intention of the parties that the American weapons could be used upon unarmed civilians of Pakistan by a military junta for suppressing the return to a constitutional regime on the basis of the will of the majority freely declared in the first national elections?

It would be unfair to impute any such intention to either Pakistan or the United States.   At the time of the agreement, Pakistan was under a civilian administration with the parliamentary form of government and a military regime was not even remotely in contemplation.   So far as the United States is concerned, there are several reasons why such an intention cannot be imputed.   First, one-sided treaties 'permitting foreign military assistance against internal revolt' have been discounted in modern times since they are considered as 'manifestations of imperialism.'[115] It will be particularly difficult to impute such an intention to the United States, 'the foremost advocate of colonial liberation after World War II, who set an example by liberating its own Philippine colony in 1946.'[116] It was the United States which had denied the claim of autocratic monarchs of Europe after the Napoleonic period to assist each other by military aid when menaced by popular revolt. The United States 'has often asserted the

[115] Quincy Wright, 'Intervention on Invitation' (1959), 53 AJIL, p. 119.
[116] Fulbright, op. cit., p. 115.

right of revolution against tyrannical governments and has supported the principle of self-determination of peoples during World Wars I and II and in the United Nations.'[117]

Second, the use of such assistance for the purpose for which it was, in fact, used in East Bengal would be contrary to the letter and spirit of the Mutual Defence Assistance Act of 1949 and the Mutual Security Act of 1951.

Third, the 'furnishing' and the 'use' of such assistance must be in conformity with the Charter of the United Nations; the Charter and the contemporary law of self-determination prohibit both the furnishing of such assistance by the USA and the use thereof by the military regime of Pakistan, for suppressing the will of the elected majority for a democratic government.

Finally, the expression 'internal security' must mean the security of a government based on the will of the people since the Universal Declaration clearly contemplates that the only basis of governmental authority is the consent of the people freely expressed in periodic and genuine elections. International law does not permit a non-representative government to suppress by force the movement for self-determination even by a dismemberment of the country. The expression 'internal security' must therefore mean the security of a fully representative government, and not the security of a military junta against a popular movement for self-determination. Even in a case where assistance is provided on the invitation of another government, faced with internal revolt, as in the case of US intervention in the Lebanon on the invitation of President Chamoun, it is the legal duty of the invitee state to ascertain objectively whether the inviting government is a popular government, 'in a position to represent the state'. American international lawyers criticized the US intervention in Lebanon on the ground that the popular base of the Chamoun government was not proved.[118]

In construing Articles 1 and 2 of the 1954 agreement, it is therefore impossible to impute an intention to the United States which would permit the use of the assistance in the manner in which it was made by the Yahya Government. It will follow that the US military assistance had been used for 'purposes other than those for which it was furnished'. Accordingly, in terms of Article 2, 'prior agreement' of the US Government was necessary before the Government of Pakistan could use it on its unarmed civilian population in East Bengal. It will be reasonable to assume that the consent of the US Government was neither sought for nor given. It, therefore, seems strange that even after the US arms had been used contrary to the

[117] Quincy Wright, 'Intervention on Invitation', op. cit., p. 122.
[118] *Ibid.*

terms of the agreement, instead of terminating the assistance forth-with, the US administration openly agreed to send another $ 4 million worth of arms to the Pakistan Government.

In the context of Vietnam, where the Secretary of State had referred 'on no fewer than three occasions' to the Congressional approval of aid programmes 'as a basis of authority for the American military involvement in Vietnam', Senator Fulbright pointed out:[119] "I very much doubt that any member of the Senate ever supposed that by voting for foreign aid, the Senate was authorizing or com-mitting the United States to use its armed forces to sustain the ruling government of any recipient country against foreign attack, much less against internal insurrection. I rather doubt, too, that those who cited such a connection thought of it *before* the United States took over the Vietnamese War."

The clearest proof of the illegal use of the US military assistance by the Yahya Government is that early in August, the House of Representatives voted for suspension of aid to Pakistan. The House amended the Act relating to foreign assistance programme for the fiscal year to include a specific ban on the grant of further military and economic assistance (except for food and medicines) to Pakistan until a political settlement was reached. The Senate approved the amendment after the summer recess.[120]

It is possible to assess the popular reaction in the USA against the continuance of arms shipments to the Pakistan Government. For instance, the *New York Times* of 6 August 1971 pointed out that the Administration's continuing support of the Pakistani Government had not served to moderate Islamabad's policies but rather it had put the USA in a 'position of subsidizing, and thus seeming to condone, crimes against humanity unequalled since Hitler's time... America's self-respect as well as its interest in genuine stability on the sub-continent calls for the immediate suspension of aid to Pakistan... There is no need for the Senate's return from recess next month before ending this unconscionable support for repression.'

Senator Kennedy said in Washington on 6 August 1971: "It makes no sense to provide the West Pakistan Government with military supplies which help create refugees while spending millions of dollars to aid those refugees."[121] After his extensive tour of the refugee camps

---

[119] Fulbright, op. cit., pp. 233-4.

[120] Mr Chester Bowles' letter to the *Times of India*, 24 August 1971. On 14 October 1971 the U.S. Senate Foreign Relations Committee voted to ban all forms of foreign aid to Pakistan until the President informed Congress that the situation in East Bengal was reasonably stable and refugees were allowed to return. Reuter report in *The Statesman* (New Delhi), 16 October 1971.

[121] *The Statesman*, Calcutta, 7 August 1971.

in India, when he had seen the tragic results of the use of American military assistance upon civilians, Senator Kennedy observed on 16 August 1971 in New Delhi that, speaking for himself, he found the US Administration's reasoning singularly unpersuasive. 'I find continuingly difficult to understand it.'[122] On his return to Washington, Senator Kennedy said on 26 August: "We must end immediately all further U.S. arms shipments to West Pakistan" along with "all other economic support to a regime that continues to violate the most basic principles of humanity. We demonstrate to the generals of West Pakistan and to the people of the world that the United States has a deep and abiding revulsion of the monumental slaughter that has ravaged East Bengal."[123]

Earlier, on 31 July, *The Washington Post,* in an editorial said that in Pakistan the world was witnessing a holocaust unmatched since Hitler. The great nations with an interest in the subcontinent had been unwilling to halt their separate routine quests for national advantage merely for the sake of reducing the toll of human lives. The editorial criticized the major Powers, particularly those who did not hesitate to grant aids to Pakistan even after the genocide. The Soviet Union 'is perhaps the least to blame', for 'the Russians did not have an important position in Pakistan and they have used East Bengal's agony only to consolidate their position in India.' About the Chinese policy, it said: "They have rejected the Bengalis' cause of popular Government and fight against tyranny and they have encouraged the wrath of the Martial Law regime against the freedom-seeking East Bengalis, and have gone even to the point of offering to defend Pakistan against outside (meaning Indian) intervention." But the *Post* was most critical of the American action or inaction, and condemned it in one terse sentence: "American policy is, for Americans, even more regrettable."

The reaction of the outside world to American policy can be seen from an editorial in the *Guardian* of London of 30 August 1971: "Mr Nixon, presumably, will do nothing either until a full-fledged war broke out. And yet for any democratic country, professing to hold the ideals of democracy, East Pakistan presents straightforward gut issues... America's reaction oscillates between the malevolent and chillingly naive: a big Power play divorced, however sincerely, from the littlemen—the millions of them—who will eventually mould events."

What was the real purpose of the US military assistance to Pakistan? If the purpose was to assist the US policy of the containment of the Soviet Union in South Asia, it seems irrational and

[122] *The Statesman,* Calcutta, 17 August 1971.
[123] AP report in the *Amrita Bazar Patrika,* 27 August 1971.

35

unrealistic, for, as Chester Bowels puts it: "For the U.S. to spend more than 800 million dollars to build up West Pakistan's military capacity against USSR is about as rational as if the Soviets were to arm Mexico to counter-balance the United States."[124] If the purpose were to promote the US foreign policy of the Dulles era through mutual defence organisations like the SEATO, it again proved a failure. When the council of ministers representing SEATO countries in their Manila communique of 3 July 1970 announced their support for the US foreign policy in Vietnam, Laos and Cambodia, the Pakistani delegate promptly dissociated himself from it.[125] If the purpose of US assistance were to play Pakistan against China, it certainly has not succeeded. The governments of Pakistan and China have come closer together, and ironically enough, Pakistan is the beneficiary of both Chinese and American weapons. With reference to the current argument of the Pentagon and the State Department that if the USA did not continue its arms aid to Pakistan, China would do so, Chester Bowles observed: "This argument could be used with equal validity by a dope peddler to justify selling heroin."[126]

Pakistan has, in fact, used US military assistance only for two purposes. Apart from employing US arms against her own nationals, Pakistan has used them against India. Before the conclusion of the 1954 agreement, President Eisenhower in his letter of 24 February 1954 to Prime Minister Nehru gave a categorical assurace:[127] "What we are proposing to do, and what Pakistan is agreeing to do, is not directed in any way against India. And I am confirming publicly that if our aid to any country, including Pakistan, is used and directed against another in aggression, I will undertake immediately, in accordance with my constitutional authority, appropriate action both within and without the U.N. to thwart such aggression." This assurance was repeated time and again by official spokesmen of the US Government.[128] But the assurance did not prevent Pakistan from using the arms against India in 1965 nor in 1971. In fact, the 1965 war was caused *because* of the American military assistance to Pakistan. As Senator Fulbright had pointed out:

Former Ambassador John Kenneth Galbraith believes that

[124] Chester Bowles, 'US Arms to Pakistan: A Tragedy of Errors', *The Washington Post*, 15 August 1971; reproduced under the caption 'War Clouds over South Asia' in *The Hindusthan Standard*, 26 August 1971.

[125] United States Foreign Policy, 1969-1970 (Department of State Publication 8575, March 1971), Report of the Secretary of State, pp. 506-519.

[126] Chester Bowles, op. cit.

[127] Documents on American Foreign Relations, 1954 (Harper, New York, 1955), pp. 374-5.

[128] Roy Chowdhury *Military Alliances*, op. cit.

American military aid to Pakistan actually *caused* the war between India and Pakistan in 1965, simply because, quite apart from the merits of the Kashmir dispute, if the United States had not provided the arms, Pakistan would not have been able to seek a military solution.

These arms of course were meant to be used for defence against China and the Soviet Union, not against India. The trouble was that Pakistan did not and does not share the American view of Kashmir as a secondary issue and therefore regards India, not China or Russia, as her principal enemy. American military assistance had been provided on the condition and in the expectation that it would be used against only communist aggression, but as might have been expected these pledges were cast aside in the summer of 1965.

Should this have come as a great surprise? I do not think so. President Ayub Khan said with perfect candor in 1961 that the United States should be 'mindful of the fact that if our territory was violated, we would spend our time dealing with the enemy rather than putting the American weapons in cotton wool'.[129]

History was repeating itself. Emboldened by the continuance of arms shipments from the USA, President Yahya on 4 August 1971 threatened India with 'an overall war.'[130] Henry Kissinger is reported to have told officials in New Delhi that 'if China entered the fray between India and Pakistan, India must not expect any help from the U.S.'[131] India was constrained to protest to USA on 7 August 1971 that she considered military and diplomatic support by USA to Pakistan as 'hostile acts.'[132] Thereafter, the Indo-Soviet Friendship Treaty was signed on 9 August 1971. On 23 August *Time* magazine comments: "But there was no disguising that Washington was wounded and that the wound was largely self-inflicted." When *Newsweek* on 2 August 1971 commented that should two communist superpowers become involved in a war between India and Pakistan it would be 'agonizing' for the US to choose between the two, the answer came from a simple American lady, Catherine G. Kelley of the American Embassy—USAID, Islamabad. In a letter to *Newsweek* on 30 August 1971 she wrote: "But I wonder how you can suggest that there should be an 'agonizing choice' between supporting India

---

[129] Fulbright, op. cit., p. 229.
[130] *The Statesman*, Calcutta, 5 August 1971.
[131] *Time*, 23 August 1971, p. 7.
[132] *The Statesman*, Calcutta, 8 August 1971.

or Pakistan if it came to a crunch. If the U.S. has to agonize over the question of supporting a democracy as opposed to a military suppressionist regime that has murdered a million of its own citizens and driven more than 6 million from their homes and country, then the United States has forfeited the right to ever again purport to exercise moral leadership or promote democracy."

In the same vein, the *Washington Post* in an editorial 'War Threat on the Sub-Continent' ridiculed the State Department's call for restraint on both Pakistan and India. "It was an appeal rendered grotesque by the twin facts that one side, Pakistan, is almost entirely responsible for the threat to the peace, and the USA is a partisan of that side... India, the victim of the Pakistani military regime's excesses against its own people, has incurred the burden of ten million or more refugees." About the inaction of the international community, the *Post* said that an "unconscionable element of hypocrisy smirks beneath the international flare of concern over the possible outbreak of war between India and Pakistan. It is not just that war has been possible for months, and will remain possible so long as Pakistan baulks the return of normal conditions in its Eastern Wing. It is that the international community, as represented at the U.N., has resolutely refused to do what is manifestly required... Forty-seven speakers in the general debate (in the UN General Assembly) called for a political reconciliation in Pakistan but none took the implementing step—inscribing the issue on the agenda of the General Assembly or the Security Council—that might have led to action. By action, we mean tough pressure on Pakistan." The American position was characterised as 'disgraceful.'[133]

The US arms aid to Pakistan, therefore, not only helped a military oligarchy in its war against 75 million Bengalis struggling for liberation, it promoted the gloomy prospect of a war against India which ultimately broke out on 3 December 1971 after Pakistan's aerial attacks on India.

The subsequent policy of the US Administration in the South Asian conflict appeared incredible not only to the people of Bangladesh and India but to a significant section of the American public opinion. Having condoned genocide and aligned itself with a discredited military junta since 25 March, the Nixon Administration, while publicly pretending to be neutral, pursued systematically an anti-Bangladesh and anti-Indian policy with a view to salvaging the military regime of Yahya Khan. The intensity of this policy was not fully known until the disclosures of the secret proceedings of Pentagon, State Department, and National Security Council by Jack Anderson, the

---

[133] Reproduced in *The Statesman*, Calcutta, 25 October 1971.

well-known American columnist (hereafter referred to as the *Anderson Papers*).[134]

The information now available establishes several points.

First, the Nixon Administration was never serious about any genuine political accommodation in Bangladesh and did nothing worthwhile to persuade General Yahya Khan to release Sheikh Mujibur Rahman. Mrs Indira Gandhi's version of the US efforts in the matter stood confirmed. Mrs Gandhi in her letter of 15 December 1971[135] to President Nixon had pointed out that the war could have been avoided if the USA had used its influence to have Mujibur Rahman released. She said:

> "Our earnest plea that Sheikh Mujibur Rahman should be released, or that, even if he were to be kept under detention, contact with him might be established, was not considered practi-

[134] The documents represent Pentagon, State Department and National Security Council summaries of five meetings of the top-level Washington Special Action Group (WASAG) in White House's super-secret situation room on December 3, 4, 5, 6 and 8, 1971 as well as an assortment of incoming ambassadorial cables. They appeared in eight separate articles by the well-known columnist Jack Anderson, and three of the Pentagon summaries appeared in the *Washington Post* of 5 January 1972. The relevant extracts were carried by *The Statesman* of 7 January 1972 in a report from its Washington correspondent, Warren W. Unna. *The Statesman* of 7 January 1972 also carried reports showing that Mr. Kenneth B. Keating, US Ambassador to India, challenged the statement made by the Nixon Administration to justify its pro-Pakistani policy during the war in December 1971, and observed that it detracted from American credibility. For the Anderson revelations also see 'The Kissinger Tilt', *Time*, 17 January 1972. President Nixon's public stance of neutrality was further exposed in his subsequent message to the Congress on 9 February 1972 (as reported in *The Statesman*, Calcutta, 10 February 1972): "During the week beginning December 6, we received convincing evidence that India was seriously contemplating the seizure of Pakistan-held portions of Kashmir and the destruction of Pakistan's military forces in the west. We could not ignore this evidence; neither could we ignore the fact that when we repeatedly asked India and its supporters for clean assurances to the contrary, we did not receive them. We had to take action to prevent a wide war". Neither the source nor the nature of the evidence was disclosed. In the same message, President Nixon made another fantastic claim: "We obtained assurance from President Yahya Khan that Sheikh Mujibur Rahman would not be executed". There now seems to be two contenders for the humanitarian action, for it is Mr Bhutto's claim that it was he who saved the life of Sheikh Mujibur Rahman despite President Yahya Khan's order for his execution. The odds are, however, in President Bhutto's favour for Sheikh Mujibur Rahman, after his release, gave details of Yahya's plan to have him executed before handing over power to President Bhutto. Sheikh Mujibur Rahman has made this revelation several times after his release, notably at the ITA interview with Mr David Frost on 16 January 1972.

[135] *The Statesman*, Calcutta, 17 December 1971.

cal on the ground that the USA could not urge policies which might lead to the overthrow of President Yahya Khan. While the United States recognized that Mujib was a core factor in the situation and unquestionably in the long run Pakistan must acquiesce in the direction of greater autonomy for East Pakistan, arguments were advanced to demonstrate the fragility of the situation and of Yahya Khan's difficulty. Mr President, may I ask you in all sincerity: Was the release or even secret negotiations with a single human being, namely, Sheikh Mujibur Rahman, more disastrous than the waging of a war?"

Even after the war broke out, and while a cease-fire move was being initiated by the US Government, there was no place for a genuine political accommodation in Bangladesh or for the release of Sheikh Mujib in the US policy. The Anderson Papers had revealed that while Mr Samuel De Palma, the Assistant Secretary of State for International Organization Affairs, pointed out the difficulty of persuading the UN in accepting the pro-Pakistani US policy "because most of the countries who might go with us did not want to tilt toward Pakistan to the extent we did", Dr Kissinger replied, "We have told the Paks we would make our statement. Let's go ahead put in our statement any way, regardless of what other countries want to do. We need now to make our stand clear even though it has taken us two weeks of fiddling... we can say that we favour political accommodation, but the real job of the Security Council is to prevent military action... *we will go along in general terms* with reference to *political accommodations* in East Pakistan, *but* we will *certainly not imply or suggest any specifics such as the release of Mujib.*" (emphasis added.)

The earnest plea of Ambassador Keating that the USA should follow its historic policy of supporting people who wanted their independence, that the Bengalis clearly wanted to shake off their Pakistani shackles, and that the advancing Indian troops were being greeted in East Pakistan truly as liberators had no impact on the Nixon Administration. It even appeared that those professional diplomats in the State Department, who pleaded for a measure of autonomy for the Bengalis or wanted the USA to remain neutral in the Indo-Pakistani conflict, were provoking, according to Dr Kissinger, "Presidential wrath".

Second, although it was known that the aerial attacks on 3 December by Pakistan took India by surprise,[136] and India's response was

---

[136] *Time,* 13 December 1971 : 'It did appear that India was taken by surprise: nearly every senior cabinet official was out of the capital at the time, including Mrs Gandhi, who was in Calcutta. During the night, Pakistani planes repeatedly

in self-defence, yet the "US Ambassador to the United Nations, George Bush, branded the Indian action as 'aggression'—a word that Washington subsequently but lamely explained had not been authorised."[137]   No reference was made by the USA to Pakistan's first attack.   Jack Anderson has shown that although the Presidential Adviser had assured Washington's reporters during a non-attributable background session on 7 December that it was "totally inaccurate" to call the Nixon Administration anti-Indian, the secret summaries of the WASAG meetings told a different story.   At the 3 December meeting, Dr Kissinger is quoted as telling high officials: "I'm getting hell every half hour from the President that we're not being tough enough on India.   He has just called me again.   He does not believe we are carrying out his wishes. *He wants to tilt in favour of Pakistan.*   He feels everything we do comes out otherwise..." Dr Kissinger was again quoted as saying: *"The President does not want to be even-handed.*   The President believes that *India* is the attacker."* (emphasis added)

Third, the policy of the Administration was definitely directed towards protecting the disintegrating authority of the military junta. With this object in view, the Administration contemplated three steps: (a) Plans to send arms to Pakistan: At the December 6 WASAG meeting, Dr Kissinger had been quoted as saying: "The President may *want to honour those* (Pakistan) requests (for arms). *He isn't inclined to let the Pakistanis be defeated."* One of the Pentagon summaries published in the *Washington Post* of 5 January 1972 continues: "Dr Kissinger asked whether we have the right to authorize Jordan or Saudi Arabia to transfer military equipment to Pakistan.   Mr Christopher Van Hollen, the Deputy Secretary of State for South Asian Affairs, declared this third-country method of furnishing arms was illegal.   Then his boss, Assistant Secretary Joseph Sisco, said the matter should be explored 'very quietly'."   According to *Newsweek* of 27 December 1971: "At one point early in the war, the Administration considered asking Iran, Jordan and Turkey,— all Moslem countries like Pakistan—to serve as conduits for the shipment of U.S. arms to Pakistan.   But the Soviet Union learned of the plan and quickly told the three nations that it would consider any such gun-running an aggressive act." (b) One finds from the Anderson Papers that at the December 3 WASAG meeting, Assistant Secretary of State Sisco "suggested that economic steps could be taken against India but that similar moves against Pakistan should be

---

attacked twelve Indian airfields.   On the grounds, Pakistan launched attacks along the western border.'

[137] *Time,* 20 December 1971.

announced as 'under review'.'" The next day, Dr Kissinger instructed the WASAG: "On aid matters, the President wants to proceed against India only." (c) Having failed to secure cease-fire through the United Nations, and when the liberation struggle in Bangladesh was about to be successful, Dr Kissinger was quoted as saying: "If the U.N. can't operate in this kind of situation effectively, its utility has come to an end... we have to take action. The President is blaming me..."

The action that Washington took was a resort to gunboat diplomacy. *Newsweek* of 27 December 1971 states: "Then, last week, in a seeming reversion to gunboat diplomacy, Washington ordered an eight-ship task force—spearheaded by the nuclear-armed aircraft carrier *Enterprise*—to sail from Vietnam into the Bay of Bengal. While the possible need to evacuate Americans from East Pakistan was cited as a reason for the ship's mission, many Indians saw the naval force as a brazen attempt to pressure New Delhi into backing down."

The Indian assessment of the purpose of the despatch of the task force was fully corroborated by columnist Jack Anderson, who, on the basis of the official documents disclosed, said: "This provocative naval deployment was intended (a) to compel India to divert both ships and planes to shadow the task force; (b) to weaken India's blockade against East Pakistan; (c) possibly to divert the Indian aircraft carrier Vikrant from its military mission and (d) to force India to keep planes on defence alert, thus reducing their operations against Pakistani ground troops." Anderson further said that "provocative leaks were arranged regarding the task force's approach from such places as Djkarta, Manila and Singapore, all to make both India and Soviet Union readily aware of the US show of force."

Had the United States policy in the Security Council and the General Assembly succeeded, the three results would have been: First, strengthening the military dictatorship both in Bangladesh and in West Pakistan; second, prolonging the agony of the 75 million people struggling for liberation; and third, making it impossible for the 10 million Bengali refugees to return home, thereby causing irreparable damage to India's national interests and her security.

On the other hand, the successful outcome of the war of liberation has prepared the foundation for the peace in the subcontinent by the removal of the root causes of the tension. The three visible benefits are:

First, the implementation of the principle of self-determination in Bangladesh—the eighth largest nation in the world in terms of population—and the consequential stoppage of the genocidal acts committed for nine months by the West Pakistani army of occupation.

Second, it has facilitated the return of 10 million refugees from

India to Bangladesh and thus removed the most serious cause of the tension in the subcontinent.

Third, the liberation of Bangladesh would also prove as a blessing in disguise for the people of West Pakistan. *Time* magazine of 20 December 1971 pointed out that the Islamabad regime, shorn of a region that was politically, logistically and militarily difficult to manage, might "prove a much more homogeneous unit" and in that sense "the breakup could prove to be a blessing in disguise." John Grigg wrote in *The Sunday Times*, London:[138] "She (Mrs Gandhi) deserves our unqualified backing... Above all, we ought to reflect that India's cause is, in the broadest sense, our cause, for India is the only country in the Third World which has preserved and cherished our legacy of democracy... Indira Gandhi is too far-sighted a statesman to have any expansionist aims. Her sole desire is to say goodbye to the refugees. But it is also true that, if she wins the war, it is not only India that will benefit. For one result of India's victory would be the collapse of a military rule and the triumph of democracy in both parts of Pakistan. It is no paradox, therefore, to say that India is fighting to bring freedom to all the people of the subcontinent, who are, in the eye of God, one people." One prediction of John Grigg has been fulfilled, namely, the immediate collapse of Yahya's power. But the triumph of democracy still remained to be fulfilled by the end of the year because there were no indications that President Bhutto, who had derived his title from Yahya Khan's martial law, was inclined to establish his authority democratically after revoking the martial law.

The charge of the Nixon Administration that India had committed aggression against Pakistan was thoroughly disproved by (a) India's recognition of Bangladesh as an independent sovereign state and (b) by the declaration of a unilateral cease-fire at a point of time when in the western sector Pakistani forces were in considerable difficulty. The unilateral cease-fire was India's independent decision and not the result of any Soviet pressure alleged to have been influenced by the Nixon Administration.[139] India, time and again, had publicly declared that she never had any intention of annexing any Pakistani territory. No one seriously believed that India had any such design. The *Newsweek* of 8 December 1971 pointed out: "Nonetheless, no one was suggesting that India had any ideas of annexing the territory." India's objective was fulfilled when Bangladesh became free. As *Time* magazine of 20 December 1971 pointed out: "In New Delhi, the mood is not so much of jingoism as jubilation that India's main goal—the establishment of a government in East Bengal

[138] Reproduced in *The Statesman*, Calcutta, 9 December 1971.
[139] *Time* and *Newsweek* of 3 January 1972, for Mrs. Gandhi's statements.

that would ensure the return of the refugees—was accomplished so quickly." As the Indian Army, in collaboration with the Mukti Bahini, was proceeding from one liberated area to another, the American journalists are on record to prove that they were universally acclaimed as liberators, and not as colonisers or occupiers. One Bengali journalist told the *Time* correspondent, Dan Coggin: "Now we know how the Parisians felt when the Allies were approaching." Again, Dan Coggin wrote from Dacca: "It was a liberation day. Dacca exploded in ecstasy of hard-won happiness."[140] Earlier, as the Allied troops of India and Bangladesh were advancing first to Jessore and then to Comilla and finally to the outskirts of Dacca, everywhere the people of Bangladesh cheered and greeted the Indian soldiers as liberators.[141] The charge of the Nixon Administration that India had aggressive intentions was, therefore, proved completely unfounded.

The people of Bangladesh and India became painfully aware in the crucial year of 1971 of the existence of the two Americas— Nixon's America and Lincoln's America. In spite of the hostility of Nixon's America, the undoubted sympathy of Lincoln's America was expressed in unmistakable terms. The perplexed Acting President Syed Nazrul Islam of Bangladesh asked *Newsweek* representative: "The US press has spelled out the basic issues. The story is now known. As a result, your Congress is supporting us, too. We cannot understand why the US Government is against us."[142]

In one of the biggest moral issues of the Charter regime, the two Americas moved in completely different lines, one supporting a ruthless military dictator, the other supporting the cause of a poor people struggling for liberation. *Time* magazine of 20 December stated:

"Senator Kennedy declared that the Administration had turned a deaf ear for eight months to the brutal and systematic repression of East Bengal by the Pakistani army; and now was condemning the response of India toward an increasingly desperate situation on its eastern borders." Senators Edmund Muskie and Hubert Humphrey echoed Kennedy's charges. The critics were by no means limited to ambitious politicians. In the *New York Times*, John P. Lewis, onetime U.S.A.I.D. director in India (1964-69) and now dean of the Woodrow Wilson School of Public and International Affairs at Princeton, wrote: "We have managed to align ourselves with the wrong side of about as big and simple a moral issue as the world has seen lately; and we have sided with a minor military dictatorship against the world's second largest nation." In Britain, the conservative

---

[140] *Time*, 27 December 1971.
[141] *Time*, 20 December 1971.
[142] *Newsweek*, 6 December 1971.

London *Daily Telegraph* accused Washington of "a blundering diplomatic performance which can have few parallels. . ." It is true that the new US policy toward China has further restricted Washington's room for manoeuvre with the Indians, but this hardly explains or excuses the Administration's handling of recent affairs on the Indian subcontinent. Because of blunders in both substance and tone, the USA has (1) destroyed whatever chance it had to be neutral in the East Asian conflict; (2) tended to reinforce the Russia-India, China-Pakistan lineup; (3) seemingly placed itself morally and politically on the side of a particularly brutal regime, which, moreover, is an almost certain loser; and (4) made a shambles of its position on the subcontinent."

Among the numerous American citizens who had publicly dissociated themselves from the policy of the Nixon Administration, one can perhaps refer to Anthony Lewis who wrote in *The New York Times* of 7 December 1971:

> Suppose that Britain in the 1930s had responded to Hitler's savagery by the early threat or use of military force instead of appeasement, if the Nixon Administration had been in power in Washington at the time, it would presumably... charge Britain with 'major responsibility for the broader hostilities which have ensued.' So one must think after the American statement over the weekend blaming India for the hostilities with Pakistan. Few things said in the name of the United States lately have been quite so indecent. The anonymous State Department official who made the comment matched Uriah Heep in sheer oleaginous cynicism about the facts of the situation and about our own moral position.

The USA is the richest nation on earth. Bertrand Russell pointed out in January 1966 that sixty per cent of the world's resources were owned by the USA with six per cent of the world's population. The arms expenditure of the USA exceeded the entire national income of all developing countries. It exceeded the world's annual exports of all commodities. It exceeded the national income of Africa, Asia and Latin America. The US military budget then was $ 60,000 million per year.[143] At present the USA has 375 major foreign military bases and 3,000 minor ones all over the world. The security treaties and agreements bind the USA to more than 40 countries.[144] The vast resources of the USA can be employed either to promote or to impede the realisation of human rights and fundamental free-

---

[143] Bertrand Russell, op. cit., p. 94.
[144] *Time*, 31 May 1971, p. 21.

doms, of equal rights and self-determination, throughout the world. One should never forget that it was at the initiative of the USA that the human rights provisions were included in the Charter of the United Nations.[145] It is, therefore, most unfortunate that during the Charter regime, many undemocratic puppet governments, right-wing dictatorships and military juntas received the blessings and support of the US administration. Like Pakistan, the army officers in Greece overthrew a constitutional government in 1967. The Nixon Administration reversed the earlier policy of the Johnson administration, lifted the embargo, and commenced military assistance to the junta hoping that it would hasten the day of liberalization in Greece. Recently, while agreeing to provide additional military supplies worth $ 56 million, the State Department announced that 'the trend toward a constitutional order is established.' But Premier Papadopoulos promptly declared that he would not permit a return to normal political life until he considered it possible and beneficial. As a result, America forfeited the affection of the Greek people from every walk of life.[146] The pattern was the same in Greece and Pakistan. Like Yahya, Papadopoulos did not believe in 'reinstituting democratic elections in the near future.'[147]

The military generals of Turkey, another recipient of US aid, overthrew an elected Government in 1960 and hanged Premier Menderes. The soldiers framed a new constitution and permitted a civilian government to come into nominal power. But in March 1971 the military officers gave an ultimatum to Premier Demirel, 'who was fond of saying that only a parliamentary majority could depose him,' and he had no option left but to resign.[148] No civilian government can survive in Turkey unless it is acceptable to the army.

About the successive puppet governments in Vietnam, Bertrand Russel has said: "But you American soldiers have seen for yourselves what kind of governments have existed in Saigon. They are brutal, corrupt, dictatorial and completely despised by the people. Why is it that these governments have been able to continue, one after another, in Saigon, despite the fact that the students, the women, the villagers, everyone risks life itself to overthrow them? The sole answer is that the United States is using its enormous military force to impose on the people of Vietnam puppet governments which do not represent them."[149]

Even with all her resources and direct involvement in the Vietnam

---

[145] Goodrich, Hambro & Simons, 'Charter of the UN' (3rd. ed.), p. 372.
[146] Newsweek, 3 May 1971.
[147] Time, 6 September, 1971.
[148] Time, 22 March, 1971.
[149] Bertrand Russell, op. cit., pp. 107-8.

war, the USA could not win it. The lesson of the Vietnam war, according to *Time* magazine, is: "Vietnam should teach us—as it did the French—that modern armies and industrial strength are not effective in all regions of the world or the automatic answer to wars of 'national liberation' (even those backed by other nations)... The Vietnam has done more than any other factor in recent years to reduce US global influence."[150]

Senator Fulbright had said: "The American view of revolution is thus shaped by a simple but so far insuperable dilemma: we are simultaneously hostile to communism and sympathetic to nationalism, and when the two become closely associated, we become agitated, frustrated, angry, precipitate, and inconstant. Or, to make the point by simple metaphor: loving corn and hating lima beans, we simply cannot make up our minds about succotash."[151]

This view of American policy is understandable in Vietnam but remains completely inexplicable in Pakistan. The US policy in Vietnam was an expression of the then anti-communist puritanism; but the US policy in Pakistan was a total negation of both nationalism and democracy. Where the movement for freedom is a nationalist movement of a democratic and peaceful people, and no communism is involved, why should there be any dilemma? The succotash in such a case represents the ideal political society of which America has been the foremost champion.

East Bengal presented a perfectly straightforward problem to the people of America. Has the historic document of 1776 no extra-territorial application? Are the precepts of Abraham Lincoln confined to the American people? If the answer to both be in the negative, as it must be, Yahya never had any answer to the claim of the Bengali people for independence. The document of 1776 with unmistakable clarity points out the situation when it becomes necessary for two peoples to separate and dissolve the political bonds that bind them. Lincoln has indicated situations when separation is permissible, and when it is not. Public opinion in America accepted the fact that there was colonial exploitation of the East by the West for 24 years, and that the separation between the two wings of Pakistan was inevitable. If one should compare the facts presented to the world by Jefferson to prove the repeated injuries and usurpations by George III with those showing injuries and usurpations by the military rulers of Pakistan, could there be any doubt that legally and morally the case for independence of East Bengal was even stronger than that of the American colonies? If on those facts Jefferson could declare in 1776 that George III was unfit to be the ruler of the

[150] *Time*, 31 May 1971.
[151] Fulbright, op. cit., p. 77.

American people, could anyone have seriously suggested in 1971, after all his sanguinary deeds, that Yahya could still remain the ruler of the people of East Bengal? To secure the inalienable rights of the people of America it was declared to be their duty to provide new guards. This is exactly what the Bengali people did with a view to securing their inalienable rights. Again, should anyone contrast the precepts of the first Republican President with the action of the thirteenth Republican President, can there be any doubt that American idealism and American democracy had suffered by default in East Bengal?

In championing the cause of the freedom of the Indian people during the last war, President Franklin Roosevelt pointed out to Prime Minister Winston Churchill the adverse effect the denial of Indian freedom was having on the public opinion in the USA. True to the American tradition, the President referred to the facts of American history, the struggle for independence from colonial rule, and the constitutional experiments from 1775 to 1787. The President was not impressed by the argument of Mr Churchill that the transfer of power to the majority in India would amount to a negation of minority rights of Moslem India, particularly the Punjabi Moslems. On being informed of the breakdown of the Cripps mission, the President wrote to Mr Churchill: "I regret to say that I am unable to agree with the point of view contained in your message to me, that public opinion in the United States believes that negotiations have broken down on general broad issues. Here the general impression is quite the contrary. The feeling is held almost universally that the deadlock has been due to the British Government's unwillingness to concede the right of self-government to the Indian notwithstanding the willingness of the Indians to entrust to the competent British authorities technical military and naval defence control."[152]

Mr Churchill later recorded: "I was thankful that events had already made such an act of madness impossible. The human race cannot make progress without idealism, but idealism at other peoples' expense and without regard to the consequences of ruin and slaughter which fall upon millions of humble homes cannot be considered as its highest or noblest form. The President's mind was back in the American War of Independence and he thought of the Indian problem in terms of the thirteen colonies fighting George III at the end of the eighteenth century. I, on the other hand, was responsible for preserving the peace and safety of the Indian continent, sheltering nearly a fifth of the population of the globe."[153]

[152] Winston S. Churchill, The *Second World War* (Cartwell Edition), Vol. IV, Chapter XII, p. 167.
[153] *Ibid.*, p. 168.

This is reminiscent of General Yahya's attitude while resisting the transfer of power to the representatives of the majority. Both invested themselves with the responsibility of 'preserving the peace and safety' of the territory and for 'sheltering' the population. The idealism that Mr Churchill condemned is the idealism of championing the cause of freedom of the oppressed people, the idealism that represents the true American tradition, the Lincolnian humanism 'that mankind can hold to.' The only difference between the two situations is to be found in the difference of attitude between President Roosevelt and President Nixon.

In 1965, Archibald MacLeish had noticed that faith in 'the idea of America' had been shaken for the world and, what was more important, for the American people. Much of the idealism and inspiration were disappearing from American policy. But he was not pessimistic. He was still hopeful that the position was retrievable. Why? Because still 'there is a human warmth, a human meaning which nothing has killed in almost twenty years and which nothing is likely to kill... What has always held this country together is an idea—a dream if you will—a large and abstract thought of the sort the realistic and the sophisticated may reject but mankind can hold to.'[154] It was this 'dream' of MacLeish that Fulbright wanted to project by a reappraisal of the American foreign policy, with a view to changing 'the feel of America in the world's mind.' Fulbright said:[155]

> The foremost need of American foreign policy is a renewal of dedication to 'an idea that mankind can hold to'—not a missionary idea full of pretensions about being the world's policemen but a Lincolnian idea expressing that powerful strand of decency and humanity which is the true source of America's greatness.

The small problem of East Bengal was a big challenge to the conscience of America. The militarism of Yahya was equated with Nazism of Hitler. Both were psychotic aberrations. Could American idealism co-exist with a violent and degenerate militarism supported by American resources?

---

[154] Archibald MacLeish, Address to the Congress of the International Publishers Association, 31 May 1965.
[155] Fulbright, op. cit., p. 247.

CHAPTER SIX

RECOGNITION IN INTERNATIONAL LAW: INDIA'S APPLICATION OF THE JEFFERSONIAN NORM

India's Recognition of Bangladesh

It will have been observed that the Proclamation of Independence Order of the People's Republic of Bangladesh was made operative retroactively from 26 March 1971 when Bangabandhu Sheikh Mujibur Rahman duly made a declaration of independence in Dacca, which was later confirmed by the elected representatives of the people of Bangladesh. Since then, on several occasions, the Government of Bangladesh made appeals to the nations of the world for recognition and assistance. On 17 April 1971, the Prime Minister of Bangladesh said: "Every day this (recognition) is delayed a thousand lives are lost and most of Bangladesh's vital assets are destroyed."[1]

The Indian people and their Government had consistently expressed their sympathy with the people of Bangladesh in their struggle for liberation and a democratic way of life. In a resolution moved by the Prime Minister of India in the Parliament on 31 March 1971, and adopted unanimously, it was stated:[2]

> Instead of respecting the will of the people so unmistakably expressed through the election in Pakistan in December 1970, the Government of Pakistan has chosen to flout the mandate of the people. The Government of Pakistan has not only refused to transfer power to the legally elected representatives but has

[1] See Chapter IV.

[2] For text of the resolution, see *Bangla Desh Documents* (External Affairs Ministry, New Delhi, September 1971), p. 672. Also see pp. 672-713 *inter alia* for India's sympathy with the struggle for liberation of the Bengali people and her cautious approach to the question of recognition. Throughout the country there was a popular demand for immediate recognition of the Government of Bangladesh. Legal arguments in support of recognition were advanced, among others: 'Legal Aspects' by Rahmatullah Khan, *Bangla Desh* (Vikas, 1971); V. K. Krishna Menon, M. C. Chagla, M. C. Setalvad and C. K. Dapthari in *Bangla Desh—Background and Perspectives* (National 1971); S. K. Mukherjee, *Bangla Desh and International Law* (WBPSA, Calcutta, 1971); *Mainstream,,* 17 July 1971.

arbitrarily prevented the National Assembly from assuming its rightful and sovereign role. The people of East Bengal are being sought to be suppressed by the naked use of force, by bayonets, machine-guns, tanks, artillery and aircraft... Throughout the length and breadth of our land, our people have condemned, in unmistakable terms, the atrocities now being perpetrated on an unprecedented scale and upon an unarmed and innocent people. This House expresses its profound sympathy for and solidarity with the people of East Bengal in their struggle for a democratic way of life. Bearing in mind the permanent interests which India has in peace, and committed as we are to uphold and defend human rights, this House demands immediate cessation of the use of force and the massacre of defenceless people. This House calls upon all peoples and Governments of the world to take urgent and constructive steps to prevail upon the Government of Pakistan to put an end immediately to the systematic decimation of people which amounts to genocide. This House records its profound conviction that the historic upsurge of the 75 million people of East Bengal will triumph. The House wishes to assure them that their struggle and sacrifices will receive the wholehearted sympathy and support of the people of India.

In spite of tremendous national pressure, India delayed her recognition of Bangladesh till 6 December 1971. On 6 December, Prime Minister Mrs Indira Gandhi told the Parliament that her Government did not act precipitately in the matter of recognition and the eventual decision was not guided merely by emotion but 'by an assessment of prevailing and future realities.'[3] It will appear that an objective assessment of three factors persuaded the Government of India to extend recognition to Bangladesh on 6 December 1971. These are:

First, with the unanimous revolt of the entire people of Bangladesh, and the success of their struggle, it did become increasingly apparent that the so-called *mother State of Pakistan* was totally incapable of bringing the people of Bangladesh back under its control.
Second, as for the *legitimacy of the Bangladesh Government,* the whole world was by that time aware that it reflected the *will of the overwhelming majority of the people,* which not many Governments could claim to represent. In Jefferson's famous

[3] See *The Statesman,* 7 December 1971 for the speech of the Prime Minister announcing the recognition of Bangladesh.

words, the Government of Bangladesh was supported by the *will of the nation, substantially declared.* Applying Jefferson's criterion, the *military regime* in Pakistan was *hardly representative* of its people.

Third, since West Pakistan was waging war against India since 3 December, 'the people of Bangladesh battling for their very existence, and the people of India fighting to defeat aggression' found themselves 'partisans in the same cause'. After the commencement of the war, India's 'normal hesitation' to grant recognition 'which could come in the way of a peaceful solution or which might be construed as intervention' lost its significance.

New Bearings on the Traditional Norms

The first ground of recognition mentioned above was obviously India's objective assessment of the ultimate result of the struggle for liberation and was in compliance with the traditional norms of recognition in a situation of colonial war. Mrs Gandhi's first ground is reminiscent of what Canning had said in the context of the recognition of the Latin American colonies: "No man will say that there is a reasonable hope of her (Spain) recovering that jurisdiction. No man will say that in such circumstances our Recognition of those States can be indefinitely postponed."[4] Canning was also in agreement with the view: "we have no pretence to be so difficult and so scrupulous as to insist that a new government shall have all the stability of an old one before we acknowledge its independence."[5]

It is the second ground, namely, the judgment on the legitimacy of the two rival claimants—West Pakistan and Bangladesh—and its impact on the traditional norms of recognition that has a significance perhaps much more profound than hitherto realized. It emphasizes the importance of reconciling the traditional norms of recognition and the contemporary norms of self-determination. From a slightly different angle, it emphasizes the need for reconciling the principle of Article 2(4), namely, the territorial integrity of Pakistan, with the principle of Article 1(2) of the Charter, namely, the principle of equal rights and self-determination of the people residing in Pakistan. Neither the known current views of the declaratory theory nor of the constitutive theory of the law of recognition meets the situation. Both the declaratory theory providing that irrespective of recognition a State comes into existence as soon as the objective tests are

---

[4] Canning's memorandum to the Cabinet of 15 November 1822: Webster, *Britain and the Independence of Latin America 1812-1830*, Vol. II, p. 393: H. Lauterpacht, *Recognition in International Law* (Cambridge, 1947), p. 14.

[5] *The Speeches of the Right Hon'ble George Canning*, edited by Therry (second ed. 1830), Vol V, p. 302; Lauterpacht, *Ibid.*, p. 15.

satisfied and that recognition is merely declaratory of the existence of that fact, and the Hegelian positivism of the constitutive theory, making the unfettered will of the recognizing State the determining factor, contemplate that the recognition of statehood will depend upon the minimum requirements of the existence of an independent government exercising effective authority within a defined territory. According to the declaratory view such requirements, for instance, would be considered as fulfilled in the two Germanys, the two Koreas, the two Vietnams and the two Chinas and their existence as States did not depend upon recognition by others. This theory finds support from the award of the Arbitrator Taft in the well-known case *Tinoco Concessions Arbitration*.[6] The reasoning is considered applicable to recognition of States and further there is a substantial state practice behind this view.[7] On the other hand, the constitutive theory would permit a discretion in the recognizing State even if the objective tests are satisfied. With a view to removing the possibility of an arbitrary exercise of discretion, Professor Lauterpacht urged the duty of recognition under the constitutive theory when the objective tests are satisfied.[8] In such an event, however, one would not find much difference between the two theories.

But neither of these two reconciles the traditional concept of effectiveness of governmental authority with the contemporary norms of self-determination. Without such reconciliation, the ultimate place of the law of recognition in the system of jurisprudence would remain uncertain, as visualized by Professor Lauterpacht 25 years ago. The second ground of India's recognition as a legal principle was anticipated, but not developed, by Dr Ian Brownlie when he said: "The principle of self-determination will today be set against the concept of effective government, more particularly when the latter is used in arguments for continuation of colonial rule. The relevant question may now be: 'in whose interest and for what legal purpose is government 'effective'?"[9]

It is of great juridical significance that India took into account the democratic legitimacy of the Bangladesh Government and the unrepresentative character of the military regime in Pakistan as one of the principal grounds which prompted her to extend recognition to Bangladesh. At the time when recognition was granted, India did not rely upon the traditional requirement of an independent Bangladesh Government then exercising effective authority within a

[6] L. C. Green: *International Law Through Cases* (second edition), p. 84.

[7] Dr Ian Brownlie: *Principles of Public International Law* (Oxford University Press, London, 1966), pp. 82-4.

[8] See Lauterpacht; *Recognition in International Law*, generally Chapter V.

[9] Brownlie, op. cit., p. 67.

defined territory although she did take into account the certainty of the ultimate victory of the people of Bangladesh in the war of liberation. Such an approach, it is submitted, reconciles the principle of self-determination with the norms of recognition oriented in the light of contemporary juridical developments. If the law of recognition is not to suffer from an agonizing elasticity or elusive variability, and is to be considered a branch of the discipline of international law of the Charter regime, its contents must be in conformity with the contemporary legal norms, particularly the norms of self-determination and the legitimacy of governmental authority having the character of *jus cogens*.

A modest attempt has been made in this chapter to deal generally with one fundamental branch of the law of recognition, namely, the legal test of effectiveness in relation to the governmental authority in Pakistan, arising out of the second ground of India's recognition of Bangladesh. The relevant questions are: What was the status of the military government in Pakistan? What was the status of the People's Republic of Bangladesh and its government?—The position has to be examined particularly in the light of the developments between 26 March 1971, the date from which Bangladesh Government claims its effectiveness, and India's *de jure* recognition of 6 December 1971.

Legitimacy of a Military Junta : Legal Norms and State Practice

The situation in Pakistan put the most important branch of the law of recognition to a crucial test, namely, the effectiveness of a governmental authority. Since the right of man to government by consent has become a part of international law, the problem to be considered is: Was the military junta in Pakistan, from which even President Bhutto derives his authority, in power for 13 years, entitled to be considered the legitimate government of Pakistan?

The present writer would like to disagree with Dr Ian Brownlie[10] that there is in international law no definition of a 'legitimate government.' Irrespective of its status under the national constitution, a particular government can only pass the test of legitimacy in international law if it satisfies the principle of Article 21(3) of the Universal Declaration: "The will of the people shall be the basis of the authority of Government; this will shall be expressed in periodic and genuine elections which shall be by universal and equal suffrage

[10] Brownlie, *International Law and the Use of Force by States* (Oxford 1963), p. 323. "There is in international law no definition of a 'legitimate government'. It will often happen that a government which is constitutional in that it has a legal basis which rests upon a long-accepted state of fact has to use extra-constitutional and probably illegal means to maintain itself."

and shall be held by secret vote or by equivalent free voting procedures." To ignore this test of democratic legitimacy is to substitute
dictatorial or military legitimacy for the discredited doctrine of
monarchic legitimacy. A military junta coming to power by a *coup*—
violent or bloodless—can only claim a temporary, provisional title,
and unless there is subsequent legitimation by free and popular consent within a reasonable period, its title is forfeited in international
law notwithstanding its internal physical effectiveness as a governmental authority.

Twenty-five years ago, Professor Lauterpacht, with a view to
removing the chaotic procedure of individual recognition, recommended the procedure of collective recognition and formulated the
test of effectiveness in the law of recognition in the system of jurisprudence. He said:[11]

> In an international society in which the right of man to political
> freedom and to government by consent will become part of the
> law of nations, *recognition will be denied*—in addition to other
> means of enforcement—*to a dictatorial regime* which has come to
> power by way of revolution and which, even if to all appearances
> effective, *declines to submit* its rule to the test of *clearly
> expressed popular* approval. That consummation may be far off.
> Yet we are not at liberty to regard it as lying in the infinite
> future. In fact, we are entitled to say that in so far as effective-
> ness based on and evidenced by the consent of the governed has
> become part of international practice, the *right of man to govern-
> ment by consent* has, to that extent, become *part of international
> law*. That connection is revealing in its significance inasmuch
> as it brings to mind the ultimate place of the law of recognition
> in the system of jurisprudence. It is independent of the signi-
> ficant, though still indefinite and elastic, acknowledgment of
> 'human rights and fundamental freedoms' in the various provi-
> sions of the Charter of the United Nations. Of these rights and
> freedoms, the right to government by consent is not the least
> fundamental. We are not likely to do justice to a weighty issue
> by the plausible retort that the insistence on an international
> plane and through the medium of the weapon of recognition
> based on the test of democratic legitimacy constitutes interven-
> tion in denial of the self-determination and of the independence
> of nations. There is *no self-determination and no independence
> under the rule of tyranny*, and there is no intervention, except in
> a sense dangerously approaching an abuse of language, when,
> by means of procedure which is international and disinterested

[11] Lauterpacht, *Recognition in International Law* (Cambridge, 1947), pp. 172-3.

in character, safeguards are provided for ensuring freedom from a rule of violence which may be more destructive of national independence than any foreign intervention. (emphasis added)

It is true that Professor Lauterpacht's vision of collective recognition has still not materialized, but the principle of human rights and fundamental freedoms, of equal rights and self-determination, are no more indefinite or elastic. Normative rules have been prescribed. Of these rules, the rule of democratic legitimacy of a governmental authority is the most fundamental. A particular state, in its individual policy of recognition, may still disregard this rule with impunity, for there is as yet no effective machinery to enforce compliance; but the disregard of a rule does not affect its validity nor can the delinquent state claim a legal basis for its action under the rule of international law.

The test of effectiveness as interpreted above, fortified by the legal discipline of the Charter regime, is however not a creature of the UN Charter. The test has been in existence at least since Jefferson's time,[12] and in spite of several deviations, it has been substantially followed in the British and American practice ever since. In British state practice, it was followed with regard to the successive revolutions between 1848 and 1871 in France, between 1868 and 1873 in Spain, and after the revolution in Portugal in 1910, and in China in 1912. Even after the First World War, when the Government of Fan Noli came to power in Albania by violence, and dissolved the Parliament and refused to summon its successor, the British Government refused the request for recognition on the ground that 'the usual practice of His Majesty's Government in these matters is to refuse formal recognition of Governments which have attained power by revolutionary methods until it is clearly demonstrated that these Governments have the support or, at any rate, the consent of the majority of the population.'[13]

Two instances of the American practice may be cited. The US Government refused to recognize the Rivas Government which came to power in Nicaragua in 1855, and was in effective control, because 'it appears to be no more than a violent usurpation of power, brought about by an irregular self-organized military force, as yet un-

---

[12] C. G. Fenwick, editorial comment, *Recognition of De facto Government: Old Guidelines and New Obligations* (1969), 63 AJIL, p. 98: "As early as 1793 Jefferson established for the United States the principle which still holds today, that a new government coming into power by the overthrow of a constitutional government should be recognised if it represents 'the will of the nation, substantially declared'."

[13] Quoted by Lauterpacht, *Recognition*, op. cit., p. 123.

sanctioned by the will or acquiescence of the people of Nicaragua.'[14] (emphasis added)

President Wilson's approach to the military junta in Mexico in 1913-1914 is instructive, particularly in the context of the usurpation of power by the military oligarchy in Pakistan. Madero was elected President of Mexico in October 1911 and entered upon the duties of his office the following month. In February 1913, he was captured and his resignation secured through the revolt of the army. General Huerta thereupon assumed the provisional presidency. On 22 February, Madero was killed while in the custody of the authorities. Declining to recognize Huerta, President Wilson sent John Lind to Mexico City for a satisfactory settlement *inter alia* on the basis of immediate cessation of fighting, an early and free election in which Huerta must agree not to be a candidate, and the agreement of all the parties to abide by the results of the election and to cooperate in organizing and supporting the new administration. The Lind mission proved abortive as Huerta declined to accept the terms. In October 1913, Huerta, who had announced general election to be held later during the month, caused the arrest of numerous deputies attending the session of the National Congress, dissolved that body and assumed the role of a dictator. The election was held and the results showed that Huerta was the choice of the electorate. On 7 November 1913, Secretary Bryan announced that President Wilson deemed it to be 'his immediate duty to require Huerta's retirement from the Mexican Government, and that the Government of the United States must now proceed to employ such means as may be necessary to secure this result.' On 24 November 1913, Secretary Bryan again declared: 'It is the purpose of the United States therefore to *discredit* and defeat *usurpations whenever they occur*. The present policy of the United States is to *isolate* General Huerta entirely; to cut him off from foreign sympathy and aid and from domestic credit, whether moral or material, and to *force him out*. It hopes and believes that isolation will accomplish this end and shall await the results without irritation or impatience.' In his annual message of 2 December 1913, President Wilson declared that there could be no certain prospect of peace in America until Huerta had surrendered 'his usurped authority in Mexico; until it is understood on all hands, indeed, that such *pretended governments* will not be countenanced or dealt with by the Government of the United States.' He added that Mexico had no government, and that a mere *military despotism* had been set up which had hardly more than the semblance of national authority. This, he said, had *originated in the usurpation* of Huerta who, he

[14] Moore, *Digest of International Law*, Vol. I, p. 140.

declared, had, after a brief attempt to play the part of a constitutional President, 'at last cast aside even the pretence of legal right and declared himself dictator.' It was said that in consequence, there existed in Mexico a condition of affairs which rendered it doubtful whether even the most *elementary and fundamental rights of the Mexican people* or of the foreign citizens resident there could long be successfully safeguarded.[15]

President Wilson's policy in Mexico had two aspects: first, refusal to recognize a title originating in military usurpation; second, to act upon an affirmative policy designed to cause General Huerta to resign from the presidency which he did in or about July 1914. While the second part of the policy had been described as 'constituting intervention'[16] the first part of the policy is undoubtedly in consonance with the Jeffersonian tradition that a government entitled to recognition must be a popular government. The present writer disagrees with the view[17] that President Wilson's approach to Huerta's usurpation must be put down as an exception, for three reasons: first, as will have been observed, the elementary and fundamental rights of the Mexican people guided the formulation of the President's policy; second, what appeared repugnant to the President was the origin of title in military usurpation; third, there cannot be two moral standards—one for Latin America and another for the rest of the world. In fact, the same principle was also applied to non-American states by President Wilson's administration.[18]

Between President Wilson and President Kennedy, the principle did not change. The Charter of the Organization of the American States contemplates that the political organizations of its members must be 'on the basis of effective exercise of representative democracy.' The institution of free elections is doubtless the most effective proof of the will of the nation. In the Hemisphere, the American Declaration of Rights and Duties of Man assured free elections in 1948 to some extent. Resolution XXVI of the Second Special Inter-American Conference of 1965 (Informal Procedures on the Recognition of *De Facto* Governments) laid down that after the overthrow of a government and its replacement by a *de facto* government, conditions of recognition would include the test as to whether the *de facto*

[15] Hyde, *International Law*, Vol. I (second revised edition), pp. 166-168.

[16] *Ibid.*

[17] Fenwick, op. cit., pp. 98-9: 'President Wilson's refusal in 1913 to recognize General Huerta in Mexico because of the violation of constitutional provisions and the assassination of President Madero must be put down as an exception, based upon the high moral standards he proclaimed as controlling his relations with Latin America.'

[18] Lauterpacht, *Recognition*, op. cit., p. 128.

government proposed to hold elections within a reasonable period and agreed to fulfil its international obligations under the international instruments and *respect for human rights* as expressed in the American Declaration of Rights and Duties of Man. The insertion of the provision as to the holding of elections was at the instance of the American rapporteur and was considered to be completely in agreement with the US Government's recent state practice.[19]

President Kennedy's policy in Latin America has been summed up by Cochran:[20] 'The late President was so concerned for the development of effective constitutional government that he refused to recognize any *de facto* government in Latin America until it had indicated its intention to hold elections within a reasonable period. This requirement was added to the traditional requirements that a *de facto* government maintain effective control over the territory and exhibit a willingness to comply with the international obligations of the state.' In support of this statement, Cochran has referred to President Kennedy's views with regard to El Salvador (February 1961), the *coup* in Peru (1962) and Guatemala (1963), Ecuador (1963), the Dominican Republic (1963) and Honduras (1963).

The statement issued by the US Department of State on 17 August 1962 regarding the recognition of the military junta in Peru is instructive. The junta was recognized as the 'Provisional Government of Peru.' The statement *inter alia* mentions: 'In considering this action, and our economic assistance programme within the framework of the Charter of Punta del Este, the United States Government notes that *the junta has decreed the restoration of constitutional guarantees of civil liberties* in Peru. It has set the date June 9, 1963, for the holding of *free elections*. Furthermore, it has guaranteed that, under the Constitution, *all political parties* will be accorded full electoral rights and that the *results* of the election, *whatever they may be,* will be *respected and defended* by the junta and the armed forces which it represents. By announcing that on July 28, 1963, power will be turned over to an elected President and Congress, the junta has affirmed the *provisional* nature of its position.' It was also noted that the junta had adopted an open-door policy regarding

---

[19] 62 AJIL 460, 464; also see 63 AJIL 90.

[20] Charles L. Cochran, *The Development of an Inter-American Policy for the Recognition of De Facto Government* (1968), 62 AJIL 460, 463. Cochran seems to have erred on the side of over-simplification in stating that the requirement of holding elections was added by President Kennedy to the traditional requirements. The traditional requirements from Jefferson's time included legitimation by popular consent. The best expression of popular consent is by free election; any deviation in American state practice from this requirement must be considered a departure from the traditional requirements.

elections which would permit international representatives to be present in Peru to observe the carrying out of the electoral process in accordance with the announced terms and conditions. 'Thus, the interim government has taken important steps on the road back to constitutional government in Peru.'[21]   (emphasis added)

The US State practice with regard to the recognition of provisional government of Togo indicates that the requirement of democratic legitimacy as a condition of recognition was not confined to Latin America. The Department of State issued the following press release on 6 June 1963:[22] "The Government of the United States received a request for recognition from the Provisional Government of the Republic of Togo.   In this request, the provisional government stated that its first goal was to '*re-establish legality*' rapidly by organizing *general elections.*   On May 5, the Togolese people adopted a *new constitution,* chose deputies representing all political parties to the National Assembly, and elected a new President and Vice-President. The Togolese Government has also stated that it is prepared to respect its international obligations. Believing that these declarations and events provide a *basis for democratic rule* in Togo and expressing the hope that all the elements in Togo will cooperate toward that end, the United States has decided to recognize the Government of the Republic of Togo." (emphasis added)

It is true that the principle of democratic legitimacy, which occupies an important position in the inter-American law of recognition, is regulated by special instruments.   But the same result will follow from the Charter, the Universal Declaration and the 1970 Declaration on Principles of International Law.   There are no territorial limits to the application of the principle.   It is because of the universal application of the principle that the US Government often advises a friendly military junta, outside Latin America, to return to a constitutional regime, and it feels embarrassed when the advice is disregarded, as in Greece and Pakistan.

The fact that there had been many deviations from the requirement of legitimation by popular consent in both British and American practice does not reduce the importance of the test as a valid legal norm.[23]   After the last war, the position became complicated, particularly the policy of the US Government, owing to the anti-Communist fervour of the cold war era.   This accounts for many departures from the traditional test in the American practice.   The slightest

---

[21] (1963) 57 AJIL, pp. 119-120.

[22] (1963) 57 AJIL 904.

[23] Between the two World Wars, there were many such departures, e.g. Chile (1924), Ecuador (1925), Argentina, Peru and Bolivia (1930), Chile (1932), the Franco Government in Spain (1939).

suspicion of a Communist leaning would persuade the US Government to support a *coup* or a revolution sponsored by a military junta or a right-wing dictatorship. In such cases, legitimation by popular consent was not insisted upon. Such departures took place not only in Latin America but throughout the world. Whether it is the superstitious dictatorship of Haiti or the dictatorial government of South Vietnam, the military oligarchy of the Dominican Republic or Turkey, or the military junta of Greece or Pakistan, the absence of popular base would not prevent the continuing recognition of the government in power. Without a contested election, Thieu would be accepted as the choice of the electorate in South Vietnam. But there would be a complaint about the absence of popular base if a left-wing dictatorship replaced a right-wing dictatorship, as in the case of Fidel Castro, despite the support of the Cuban people. In other cases, recognition would continue on the assurance of the men in power to return to a constitutional regime in due course—an assurance hardly meant to be fulfilled—as in the case of the military junta in Pakistan or Greece.

It was in the context of these departures from the traditional rule that the doctrine of effectiveness through popular consent was considered to have been replaced by the doctrine of stability or effectiveness through acquiescence. This is, however, not the effectiveness by popular consent as contemplated in the law of recognition by the Jeffersonian norm; for, as Professor Lauterpacht had said:[24]

"A tyrannical and despotic regime may be—and usually is—effective so long as it lasts. The obedience which it enjoys may be imposed, passive and resentful. But there is no sufficient warrant for maintaining that an authority based on that kind of obedience is necessarily short-lived and therefore not 'effective' from the point of view of permanence and stability. Moreover, there is substance in the suggestion that a government wielding absolute powers may be based on the acquiescence of the majority of the population, although the constitution of the State and its political system do not allow of an unhampered and truly free expression of the approval of the nation. Also, when it is said that the consent of the population must be given in accordance with the provisions of the constitution, do we mean the constitution of the old or of the new regime? It is not practicable to insist on an expression of popular approval in forms provided for by the constitution which has been overthrown. A revolutionary dictatorship will not be easily persuaded to allow the will of the people to be ascertained in a way prescribed by the constitution which it has supplanted. If, on the other hand, we mean

---

[24] Lauterpacht, *Recognition*, op. cit., p. 137.

the constitution enacted by the new regime, what guarantee is there that its provisions render possible a truly free popular verdict?"

Legal Status of the Military Junta in Pakistan

Responsible international opinion expressed the view that the military junta in Pakistan had long forfeited any moral claim to international support or recognition.[25] We now propose to consider whether the military government of Yahya forfeited its legal claim to continued recognition as a legitimate government in Pakistan. In view of the status of the military junta in the law of recognition and international practice discussed above, the initial recognition of the military junta in Pakistan in October 1958 by the world states, including the USA and Great Britain, must be considered to be of a provisional and interim nature. The law of recognition requires that the provisional status should terminate within a reasonable time either by a transfer of power to a popular government freely elected or by the legitimation of the title of the junta by freely expressed popular consent. In Pakistan, there was no question of the confirmation of the title of the military junta and the people expressed their verdict in favour of a constitutional regime to be led by Sheikh Mujib. The popular verdict was suppressed by the junta by military force.

That a return to the democratic rule was the basis of the continued recognition of the military junta by the USA, in accordance with the traditional policy, is implicit in the Foreign Policy Report (1969-1970) of the US Secretary of State:[26] "Three events overshadowed others in Pakistan during 1969 and 1970: the disturbance in early 1969 resulting in the resignation of President Ayub Khan and the succession of President Yahya Khan, the massive cyclonic storm disaster in East Pakistan in November 1970, and the *first direct national elections in the country's history* in December. Following

---

[25] The *New York Post* commented editorially: 'Yahya Government has long since forfeited any claim to US support, financial or moral'. Quoted in the Statesman, 4 September 1971. Also the Statesman, 29 September 1971, for the opinion of an American architect, Mr. Stanley Tigerman from Chicago, who resigned from his World Bank assignment in East Bengal. He said: 'My moral judgment forbids me to continue my association with the Fascist army rule in East Bengal. I have no intention of working for a military government with its implication. Moreover, I will never again travel to East Pakistan. Lastly, when the country is free and achieves rights of self-determination I would wish to visit and work in Bangladesh for I have come to love these people and their country very much,'

[26] United States Foreign Policy, 1969-70, A Report of the Secretary of State: Department of State Publication 8575, General Foreign Policy Series 254, released March 1971, Washington, p, 93.

his assumption of office, President Yahya proclaimed martial law. At the same time, he announced his *intention* to return Pakistan to *civilian, democratic rule as quickly as possible.* During the next year, he moved steadily in that direction, and in the middle of 1970 called for national elections in December 1970 to choose a constitution-making body. The elections resulted in heavy victories for two parties, the Awami League in East Pakistan and the People's Party in West Pakistan." (emphasis added)

The report of Mr. William P. Rogers did not significantly mention an important fact, namely, that the Awami League had an absolute majority in the National Assembly. Following the Lincolnian principle that the rejection of the majority rule means either anarchy or despotism in some form or other, Sheikh Mujib, as of right, was entitled to form a government and implement the six-point pro-gramme, despite the opposition of one of the minority parties led by Z. A. Bhutto. As subsequent events showed, a contemptuous disregard by Yahya of the Lincolnian warning was responsible for a crisis of unprecedented magnitude.

We have already mentioned that the efforts of General Yahya to impose a constitution on the people of Pakistan were indicative of a design to perpetuate the effective control of the military junta and, as such, the efforts amounted to a total denial of the principle of self-determination. These efforts are reminiscent of General Huerta's attempt in Mexico to hold elections and to play the role of a constitu-tional ruler which President Wilson had condemned as a denial of the elementary and fundamental rights of the Mexican people. The elementary democratic safeguards for a constitutional regime which President Wilson, through the Lind Mission, demanded from Huerta, or which President Kennedy expected from the military junta in Peru through the Note of 17 August 1962, were conspicuously left out of the constitutional reforms of Yahya. Yet, between March and December 1971, the Nixon Administration became completely aligned with the discredited military regime of Pakistan and made desperate efforts, both within and outside the United Nations, to rescue the Yahya regime from the inevitable disaster that followed. The US policy also became conspicuous for its failure to take any worthwhile steps for political reconciliation between the elected majo-rity represented by the Awami League and the military junta of West Pakistan.

It will, therefore, seem to follow that neither the military junta in Pakistan during the period of 13 years did, nor the government contemplated under the proposed constitution of General Yahya could, satisfy the test of effectiveness of governmental authority through popular consent. Accordingly, such a junta could not claim democratic legitimacy which is the foundation of the contemporary law of recognition. The provisional title of the military junta to governmental authority, therefore, stood forfeited.

Two additional facts arising out of the contemporary law of self-determination as elaborated in the 1970 Declaration, and relevant to the question of the recognition of a legitimate government in Pakistan, must not be ignored by the international community. First, it was the duty of the international community to assist the majority people of Pakistan residing in East Bengal to achieve self-determination in whatever legally permissible form they chose to adopt; second, it was not only the duty of the Government of Pakistan to promote self-determination but also to refrain from forcible suppression thereof. Following the Rhodesian precedent, there arose a clear duty of non-recognition, and not merely a moral obligation of condemnation of the military junta which, instead of promoting, had been continuously denying the majority rule in Pakistan during the last 13 years. Just as the denial of majority rule through appropriate constitutional process by the minority regime of Ian Smith was considered to have been a denial of the right of self-determination, and accordingly the duty of non-recognition of the illegal minority regime arose in Rhodesia, so also the principle would apply *mutatis mutandis* in still greater force to the situation in Pakistan.

The use of force by the Yahya regime since 25 March imposed an additional duty on the international community in relation to the status of the junta. In accordance with Principle (e) of the 1970 Declaration, the use of force by the military junta in East Bengal was unlawful, and the resistance by the people was not only lawful but deserved international assistance. The situation which was created by the illegal use of force in East Bengal should have been legally condemned and correspondingly there was the duty not to recognize such a situation created for the benefit of the wrong-doer. This is really an application in the domestic field of the established principle in international relations that 'there is a legal duty or obligation not to recognize any situation resulting from the illegal use of force which rests on state practice, general principles and considerations of policy.'[27] The origin of the principle is founded on a fundamental maxim of jurisprudence: *ex injuria jus non oritur.* An illegality cannot, as a rule, become a source of legal right to the wrong-doer.

---

[27] Brownlie, op. cit., p. 423; also see generally, Brownlie Chapter XXV: Lauterpacht, *Recognition,* Chapter XXI. The principle was developed in the field of international relations from Article 10 of the Convenant of the League of Nations, the Pact of Paris, Stimson Note of 1932, resolution of the Assembly of the League of 11 March 1932. Saavedra Lamas Treaty of 10 October 1933 and other similar instruments.

The application of the principle to a situation created by forcible suppression of self-determination in Pakistan during the Charter regime is additionally supported by the Charter of the United Nations, the Universal Declaration, Resolutions 1514 (XV), 1541 (XV), 1904 (XVIII) and 2200 (XXI), the Rhodesian precedent and the 1970 Declaration on Principles of International Law. To recognize the title of the military junta and its right to hold East Bengal by use of force would amount to a contravention by the international community of its imperative obligations under the aforesaid international instruments.

This writer is fully aware that he will be met with the plausible accusation of ignoring the operation and effect of the rival maxim: *ex facits jus oritur*. Law is a product of social reality. It will be argued that international law, conceived as an enforceable rule of conduct, is determined to a considerable extent by social realities, social feasibility and practicability. Military governments are in power in a number of countries. They are physically effective. They provide apparent stability. In some countries, military oligarchies are in effective control exercised through nominal or puppet civilian governments. Not only is the recognition of these non-representative governments continuing, but the international community maintains social, cultural, economic and political intercourse with them. It may even be argued that in Pakistan there was an additional fact to be reckoned with, namely, that the existence of the military regime for a long period of 13 years had probably confirmed its title by acquisitive prescription.

To such arguments the present writer will answer as follows: First, law is a discipline. Law prescribes norms to be observed. There are certain fundamental legal norms which are not variable. Effectiveness of a governmental authority based on popular consent expressed in the manner prescribed in Article 21 of the Universal Declaration is one of those fundamental norms. Second, the application of the above principle must necessarily postulate that the recognition of a military government, however expedient it might appear to the recognizing state from the point of view of its national policy, must be considered as of a provisional and interim nature, to be replaced by the recognition of a popular government within a reasonable period. Any departure from this norm must be considered in law to be 'a temporary adaptation to a transient period of political retrogression.'[28] Third, it is submitted that in contemporary law,

---

[28] The principle, formulated by Professor Lauterpacht with regard to the departure from the traditional norm between the two world wars by the USA and Britain, seems to be applicable with greater force today because of the development and the formulation of the principle of human rights and funda-

the refusal of a military regime either to prove its own effectiveness through popular consent or to transfer power to a popular government amounts to a forfeiture of title. The principle operates retrospectively and makes the initial title of the military junta a nullity. Acquiescence cannot and does not confer title on the military junta, or make legal an illegal act. It is a negative posture of 'see-no-evil, hear-no-evil.' Such acquiescence is merely indicative of a desire on the part of the recognizing state to disregard, as a matter of expediency, the effects of the illegal act of the military junta. But in contemporary law, such a situation may involve the recognizing state in a breach of its own duty to help the promotion of self-determination in the country where the military junta is in power. Fourth, it is submitted that the principle of confirmation of a title by acquisitive prescription, where such title is claimed by a non-representative government, is wholly repugnant to the contemporary law of self-determination. Besides, acquisitive prescription presupposes uninterrupted enjoyment of governmental power, and not a situation where such power is being continuously challenged by massive popular movements, as happened in East Bengal.

Legal Status of the Peoples Republic of Bangladesh and its Government : Democratic Legitimacy

The form of self-determination in East Bengal ultimately depended upon the will of the people freely expressed. Implementation of the principle of the majority rule and a constitutional regime in Pakistan on the basis of the six-point programme after the December elections would have been in compliance with the principle of self-determination. But the restoration of *status quo anti bellum* was ruled out after March 1970. At the commencement of the war of genocide, the *New York Times* of 31 March 1971 commented: "The brutality of Western troops towards their 'Moslem brothers' in the East tends only to confirm the argument of the outright secessionists in Bengal who argue that differences between East and West are irreconcilable." Yet in theory a federation of autonomous units of East Bengal and West Pakistan or a confederation of two independent states of West Pakistan and Bangladesh was not inconceivable. But this could have

---

mental freedoms, of equal rights and self-determination, during the last 24 years. Professor Lauterpacht had said: 'There is no compelling reason to assume that its abandonment after the First World War was more than a temporary adaptation to a transient period of political retrogression. Its re-emergence, when accompanied by appropriate international safeguards, must be regarded as a rational development deeply rooted in history.' Lauterpacht, *Recognition*, op. cit., p. 139.

materialized only with the consent of the Awami League, not by the decree of Yahya Khan or Z. A. Bhutto.

Bangladesh presents a unique problem. In the normal course of democratic process, the Awami League should have formed a government for the whole of Pakistan with Sheikh Mujibur Rahman as Prime Minister. Disregard of this procedure and subsequent military operations by the Yahya regime compelled the majority of the people of Pakistan residing in East Bengal to declare the independence of their own territory and to separate from Pakistan. The idea of the division of a country as a mode of implementing self-determination at the instance of the majority is perhaps without precedent. It is unfortunate that the separation did not take place peacfully as in the case of Singapore.[29] On the other hand, to maintain the independence so declared, the people of East Bengal became engaged in a defensive war of liberation against the Pakistani army of occupation. This was really a struggle for freedom from a status of subordination or colonial status by the people of East Bengal against a different racial and cultural group administering the territory from a geographically separated area. In considering the question of recognition of Bangladesh during the period of the war of liberation, emphasis should therefore have been given to the norms of self-determination relevant to a colonized people reduced to a subordinate status; and not the normal tests of recognition applicable to a civil war for acquisition of power between two political groups within a state, as in the case of the Spanish Civil War.

In the Pakistani context, U Thant had said[30] that the conflict between the principles of territorial integrity of states and self-determination had often before in history given rise to fratricidal strife and in recent years has provoked highly emotional reactions in the international community. While one can fully appreciate the emotional reactions both in favour of territorial integrity and its dismemberment, the legal reaction can only be in conformity with two accepted principles: first, the division of a country is a perfectly permissible mode for achieving self-determination; second, the defence that self-determination does not permit the dismemberment of a country is not open to a military dictator in a regime without a popular constitution. The legal perspective in respect of the situation in Pakistan should therefore be oriented accordingly.

If the contemporary law of self-determination is to become an

---

[29] The US Recognition of Singapore as a sovereign and independent state was on the basis that the division of Malaysia represented "the authoritative decision of the people of Singapore and the people of Malaysia..." Note of 11 August 1965 from Mr Dean Rusk (1966). 60 AJIL. p. 96.

[30] *Hindusthan Standard*, 20 September 1971.

effective branch of international law, then either the machinery tests of the law of recognition have to readjust themselves to the former or one must accept the inevitable inference that the two are not reconcilable. The present writer submits that there is a common denominator of fundamental importance applicable to both branches: the only test of effectiveness of a governmental organisation is democratic legitimacy or popular support. The other tests in the law of recognition are machinery provisions which must be reconciled with the common denominator.

Mujib's Awami League : Proof of Effectiveness in Three Stages

In East Bengal, within a year, the test of effectiveness through popular support was met by the Awami League in three different stages. The first was the overwhelming electoral support in favour of the Awami League in December 1970. There is no precedent in modern history that in an admittedly free and fair election on the basis of adult suffrage a particular political party could command cent per cent popular support.

Second, the Awami League which, in the normal course, should have formed the government both at the Centre and in East Bengal, proved its effectiveness although it was not formally in power during the non-violent non-cooperation movement between 1 and 25 March 1971. The success of the movement is again without precedent in history. Sheikh Mujib's directives to the people of East Bengal were carried out in a highly disciplined manner by the entire people.[31] The economy and the administration were run on the basis of Sheikh Mujib's directives with overwhelming support from the people of East Bengal. President Yahya was a mute spectator to the total failure of his effectiveness as a governmental authority during this period. One can well anticipate the argument that the success of the movement did not prove the effectiveness of an independent government asking for recognition, because East Bengal had not then declared her independence. But this is merely a technical argument. If without being in power, the Awami League could prove its effectiveness, it would be absurd to suggest that being in power it would have been any the less effective. Again, no one would seriously suggest that the people of East Bengal would have been less responsive to Sheikh Mujib's directives had he asked them to follow the direc-

---

[31] An American observer, giving a list of the harsh martial law orders of General Tikka Khan, said that these were "in sharp contrast with the tranquillity and self-imposed discipline under which the people of Bangladesh governed themselves during the three weeks' rule of the Awami League. I have never seen such proof of ability for self-government." *The Statesman*, Calcutta, 21 July 1971.

tives in aid of a movement for independence of East Bengal. It is well known that Sheikh Mujib even staked his political career by restraining his people from pressing for complete independence, and to seek a political solution within the framework of a united Pakistan. Further, there can be no two opinions that if normal conditions were restored (namely, the withdrawal of the Pakistani troops from East Bengal, the release of Sheikh Mujib and the Awami League leaders from prison, and the return of the refugees from India to East Bengal), and a referendum held on the question of separation of East Bengal from Pakistan, the people of East Bengal would have overwhelmingly voted for independence.

Third, the effectiveness of the Awami League was again proved between March and December 1971 during the progressively successful operations of the Mukti Bahini and the popular support behind them. Readers will have noticed from Chapter IV that after the initial setback during the first period (26 March to end of May), the diminishing control of the military regime of Pakistan during the second period (June-July) was evident from the fact that its authority was confined only to the main cities, while the writ of Bangladesh Government ran throughout the countryside. During the third period (August and September) vast areas were liberated from the army of occupation and were being administered with as much effectiveness as one could expect in the abnormal situation of a war of liberation. By the end of the fourth period (October to 3 December), the eventual victory of the Bangladesh forces and the ultimate defeat of the forces of West Pakistan became a virtual certainty although the war might have been somewhat prolonged had the Indian and the Mukti Bahini forces not become partisans in the same cause during the last phase (3 December to 16 December).

Consequences of Delayed Recognition

Failure to reconcile the norms of recognition with the norms of self-determination in a situation like Bangladesh may present formidable problems. Let us take one instance. Professor Lauterpacht has said:[32] "Undoubtedly, a government which has ceased to be effective has no claim to recognition. However, so long as the party or parties which challenge its authority have not asserted themselves to the point of being themselves entitled to recognition, the established government, however weakened, is entitled to continued recognition. Effectiveness is presumed to exist so long as the lawful government has not been definitely displaced by a rival authority."

One can conceive of many situations in which the test will be

---

[32] Lauterpacht, *Recognition*, op. cit., 354.

properly operative in contemporary law. But in a situation like that of Bangladesh conflicting problems may arise. First, if the effectiveness contemplated is the effectiveness through popular consent, then physical effectiveness of firepower must be eliminated as a relevant consideration. But if an effectiveness of the latter kind is contemplated, then it will conflict with several norms of self-determination, particularly in the case of the struggle for freedom of a subdued or colonial people.

Second, the theory of displacement of a government in the law of recognition may become incongruous with the contemporary law of self-determination. The law of self-determination contemplates displacement through ballots; if, however, the law of recognition contemplates displacement through firepower, reconciliation becomes difficult. Such incongruity becomes patent in Bangladesh. A military dictator, completely oblivious of his legal obligations to promote self-determination and not to use force for suppressing it, ignored the verdict of the people and attempted to maintain his physical effectiveness by a war of genocide and a reign of terror and persecution. The people of East Bengal had the moral will to displace the violator of their democratic rights and to defend their independence. But they were denied the physical means to stop such violations. How did one expect the ordinary people of East Bengal in such a situation to displace physically the Yahya regime?

Third, in his efforts to suppress the popular verdict and self-determination, the military dictator was furnished with arms and ammunition, and was given economic assistance by some powerful nations, "thereby enabling it to remain longer in being", contrary to the spirit of the Rhodesian precedent. This involved a breach not only of the contemporary law of self-determination, which forbids such assistance to a non-representative ruler, but it also involved a breach of the customary law of non-intervention. "Supposing it (foreign intervention) on the other hand to be directed against rebels, the fact that it has become necessary to call in foreign help is enough to show that the issue of the conflict would without it be uncertain, and consequently that there is doubt as to which side would ultimately establish itself as the legal representative of the state."[33]

Fourth, under the law of self-determination as elaborated in the 1970 Declaration, the people of East Bengal during their struggle for independence were entitled to claim international assistance. As Brownlie points out, one of the corollaries of the legal principle of self-determination is that "intervention against a liberation movement may be unlawful and assistance to the movement may be law-

---

[33] Hall, *International Law* (6th ed.), p. 287.

ful."[34] Yet one finds that during the war of liberation, not only some of the big powers like the USA and China gave moral and material support to the discredited military regime of Yahya but, in fact, the forum of the United Nations was sought to be used for sanctioning a scheme which, had it succeeded, would have hampered the struggle of the liberation forces and temporarily saved the military junta.   Again when by the fortuitous circumstance of Pakistani attack on India on 3 December, Indian assistance in aid of the liberation forces became inevitable, two big powers, the USA and China, tried to characterize it as 'aggression' by India against Pakistan. Apart from India's legal rights in self-defence against Pakistan's aggression resulting in 10 million refugees, it would have been perfectly legitimate, and indeed it was India's duty, in response to the request of the Bangladesh Government and as a member of the international community, to provide substantial material and military assistance to the liberation forces at a much earlier stage, in view of the default of the world body to respond to its own duty to help self-determination in Bangladesh.

When one finds that instead of providing assistance to the people who could lawfully claim it, such assistance was given to a military usurper to maintain its physical effectiveness, how can one reconcile the norms of self-determination with the technical norms of recognition? On a proper reconciliation of the relevant norms and reorientation of the concept of effectiveness, Bangladesh and its government were justified in their claim for international recognition with effect from 26 March 1971. The result, it is submitted, would not have been affected even on the assumption that during the early period of the struggle the Government of Bangladesh did not succeed in demonstrating the existence of 'a coercive, relatively centralized legal order'[35] or by the possibility that liberated zones might have been re-occupied by the Pakistani forces.   Under a rule of law where the principles of democratic legitimacy and self-determination have received due priorities, the caution against premature recognition needs to be balanced against the dangers of belated recognition. Although the recognition of Panama by the USA was characterized

[34] Brownlie, op. cit., p. 483. Also see Rupert Emerson, "The United Nations and Colonialism", *International Relations*, November 1970, p. 773; "The legitimacy of colonial struggle for self-determination and independence was recognized and all states were invited to provide material and moral assistance to such national liberation movement, i.e., UN members were overtly invited to enlist in armed struggle to overthrow colonial and racial discriminatory regimes". Also quoted by Rahamatullah Khan, *Bangla Desh* (Vikas, 1971), p. 99.

[35] Hans Kelsen, 'Recognition in International Law—Theoretical Observations, *International Law in the Twentieth Century*, American Society of International Law (1969), p. 591.

as intervention in a *laissez faire* international society, one of the principles behind such recognition was stated to be: "And if in the present instance, the powers of the world gave their recognition with unwonted promptitude, it is only because they entertained the common conviction that *interests of vast importance to the whole civilized world were at stake* which would by any other course be put in peril."[36] (emphasis added)

As early as on 17 April 1971, when the Prime Minister of Bangladesh appealed to the nations of the world for recognition and assistance, both material and moral, in their struggle for freedom, he said: "Every day this is delayed, a thousand lives are lost and most of Bangladesh's vital assets are destroyed." Refusal to provide recognition and assistance by the international community when requested has had devastating consequences, viz., an estimated death toll of 3 million, forcing 10 million into exile and rendering homeless another 2 million. A more poignant instance of permissive conscience of the international community is difficult to conceive.

---

[36] Moore on *Digest of International Law*, Vol. III, pp. 90-91; Lauterpacht. *Recognition*, op. cit., p. 22. Also see Hyde. *International Law* (2nd revised ed.), Vol. I, p. 153, f.n. 5.

BIBLIOGRAPHY

The following list contains an essential bibliography on the issues discussed in my book although it does not necessarily mean that they have been referred to in the book :

I. BOOKS

1. Ali, T. *Military Rule or People's Power* (London, Jonathan Cape, 1970)

2. Ahmed, Mustaq *Government & Politics in Pakistan* (Second Edition, Karachi)

3. Ayoob, M., Gupta, A., Khan, R., Deshpande, G. P., Narayan, R., Gupta, S. *Bangla Desh—A Struggle for Nationhood* (Vikas Publications, New Delhi, 1971)

4. Ahmad, Manzooruddin *Pakistan: The Emerging Islamic State* (Karachi, Allies Book Co., 1966)

5. Ali, Choudhury Mohammad *Emergence of Pakistan* (New York, Columbia University Press, 1967)

6. Ali, S. and Gable, R. W. *Pakistan: A Selected Bibliography* (Los Angeles, International Publication Administration Centre, University of Southern California, 1966. International Public Admistration Series, 7)

7. Ambedkar, B. R. *Pakistan or Partition of India* (2nd ed. Bombay, Thacker & Co., 1945)

8. Aziz, K. K. *The Making of Pakistan* (London, 1967)

9. Bowett, D. W. *Self-Defence in International Law* (Manchester, 1958)

10. Brownlie, Ian *International Law and the Use of Force by States* (Oxford University Press, London, 1963)

11. Brownlie, Ian

Principles of Public International Law (Oxford University Press, London, 1966)

12. Brownlie, Ian

Basic Documents on Human Rights (Oxford University Press, London, 1971)

13. Basu, D.

Constitutional Documents, Vol. I, British Constitutional Documents Relating to India. (S. C. Sarkar & Sons, Calcutta, 1969)

14. Banerjee, D. N.

East Pakistan: A Case-Study in Muslim Politics (Vikas, New Delhi, 1969)

15. Bhargava, G. S.

Pakistan in Crisis (Vikas, New Delhi, 1969)

16. Bhutto, Zulfikar Ali

The Myth of Independence (London, Oxford University Press, 1969)

17. Basler, Roy P. (editor)

Collected Works of Abraham Lincoln 9 Vols (Rutgers University Press, USA. 1953)

18. Briggs, H. W.

The Law of Nations (Stevens, 1953)

19. *Bangla Desh Documents*

Published by Ministry of External Affairs, Government of India (New Delhi, September 1971)

20. Broomfield, J. H.

Elite Conflict in a Plural Society (University of California Press, 1968)

21. Churchill, Winston.

The Second World War Chartwell ed. Vol. IV

22. Coupland, R.

Constitutional Development in British India (1942)

23. Callard, Keith

Pakistan: A Political Study (London, George Allen and Unwin, 1957)

24. *Constitutions of Asian Countries*

Prepared by the Secretariat of the Asian-African Legal Consultative Committee, New Delhi (N. M. Tripathi, Bombay, 1968)

25. *Case for Bangladesh* — Published by the Communist Party of India (New Delhi, May 1971)

26. Commager, Henry Steele (editor) — *Living Ideas in America* (Harper, New York 1951)

27. Commager, Henry Steele (editor) — *Documents of American History* (New York, Appleton-Century-Crofts, Inc., 1950)

28. Fawcett, J. E. S. — *The Application of the European Convention on Human Rights* (Oxford University Press, London 1969)

29. Fulbright, J. William — *The Arrogance of Power* (Vintage Books, New York, January 1967)

30. *First Five-Year Plan* — Vols. 1 & 2 (Karachi, Government of Pakistan Press, 1956)

31. Gankovsky, Y. V. & L. R. Gordon-Polonskay — *A History of Pakistan 1947-1958* (U.S.S.R., Academy of Sciences, Institute of Asia, 'Nauka' Publishing House, Moscow, 1964)

32. Goodnow, H. F. — *The Civil Services of Pakistan* (New Haven, 1964)

33. Goodrich, Hambro & Simons — *Charter of the United Nations* (3rd revised ed., Columbia University Press, New York, 1969)

34. Green, L. C. — *International Law Through Cases* (Stevens, 2nd ed.)

35. Gross, Leo (editor) — *International Law in the Twentieth Century* (The American Society of International Law, USA, 1969)

36. Hyde — *International Law, 3 Vols (2nd revised ed. 1945)

40

37. Hall   *A Treatise on International Law*
                                  (8th ed. 1924)

38. Haq Mahbubul   *The Strategy of Economic Plan-*
                                  ning : A Case Study of Pakistan
                                  (Lahore, 1963)

39. Hussain, Arif   *Pakistan : Its Ideology and*
                                  Foreign Policy (London, Frank
                                  Cass & Co., 1966)

40. Henry David Thoreau   Civil Disobedience (1849)
                                  The Writings of Henry David
                                  Thoreau (Cambridge, 1893,
                                  IV)

41. *The Writings of Thomas*   New York (G. P. Putnam &
    Jefferson   Sons, 1894)

42. Jennings, Ivor   *Constitutional Problems in Pakis-*
                                  tan (Cambridge University
                                  Press, 1957)

43. Kashyap S. C. (editor)   *BANGLA DESH — Background*
                                  and Perspectives (Institute of
                                  Constitutional and Parliamen-
                                  tary Studies, New Delhi,
                                  National, 1971)

44. Khan, Mohammed Ayub   *Friends Not Masters—A Political*
                                  Autobiography (Oxford Uni-
                                  versity Press, Pakistan Branch,
                                  1967)

45. Kamal, K. A.   *Sheikh Mujibur Rahman : Man*
                                  and Politician (2nd ed. Dacca,
                                  1970)

46. Lauterpacht, H.   *Recognition in International Law*
                                  (Cambridge, Cambridge Uni-
                                  versity Press, 1947)

47. Lauterpacht, H.   *International Law and Human*
                                  Rights (1950)

48. Mascarenhas, Anthony   *The Rape of Bangla Desh* (Vikas
                                  Publications, Delhi, 1971)

49. Montesquieu   *The Spirit of the Laws*, Book XI,
                                  Chapter VI

50. Mukherjea, S. K.   *Bangladesh and International Law* (Calcutta, 1971)

51. Lauterpacht, H. (editor)   *Oppenheim's International Law* Vol. I, Vol. II

52. O'Connell, D. P.   *International Law* 2 Vols. (Stevens, 2nd edition, London 1970)

53. Phillips, C. H.   *The Evolution of India and Pakistan 1858-1947, Selected Documents* (Oxford University Press, London)

54. Russell, Bertrand   *War Crimes in Vietnam* (Allen & Unwin 1967)

55. Roy Chowdhury, Subrata   *Military Alliances And Neutrality In War And Peace* (Orient Longmans, 1966)

56. Rushbrook, Williams L.F.R.   *The State of Pakistan* (London, Faber and Faber, 1962)

57. Syeed Khalid Bin   *The Political System of Pakistan* (Oxford University Press, Pakistan Branch, 1967)

58. Sengupta, J.   *Eclipse of East Pakistan* (Calcutta, 1963)

59. Swisher, Carl Brent   *The Theory And Practice of American National Government* (Houghton Mifflin Co., U.S.A. 1951)

60. Stern, Philip van Doren   *The Life and Writings of Abraham Lincoln* (Modern Library, New York, 1950)

61. Therry (editor)   *The Speeches of the Right Hon'ble George Canning* Vol V (2nd edition 1830)

62. Webster   *Britain and the Independence of Latin America* 1812-1830 Vol II (1938)

II. CONSTITUTIONAL DOCUMENTS, INTERNATIONAL CONVENTIONS AND AGREEMENTS, U. N. RESOLUTIONS AND DOCUMENTS

1. The Government of India Act, 1858 (21 & 22 Vict. C. 106)
2. The Indian Councils Act, 1861 (24 & 25 Vict., C. 67)
3. The Bengal Local Self-Government Act, 1885
4. The Reform Proposals of 1908 (Morley-Minto Reforms)
5. The Indian Councils Act, 1909 (9 Edward VII, C. 4)
6. The Declaration of the British Government of 20 August 1919
7. The Montagu-Chelmsford Report of 1918
8. The Government of India Act 1919 (9 & 10 Geo. V, C. 101)
9. The Royal Proclamation of 1919
10. The Simon Commission's Report of 1930
11. The Government of India Act, 1935 (26 Geo. V, C. 2)
12. The Mountbatten Plan and the Statement of the British Government of 3 June 1947
13. *The Transfer of Power 1942-47*:
    Vol. I—The Cripps Mission (1970, H. M. S. O. London)
    Vol. II—Quit India (1971, H. M. S. O. London)
14. The Indian Independence Act, 1947 (10 & 11, Geo. VI, C. 30)
15. Resolution of the Muslim League at Lahore, 24 March 1940 (Parl. Papers, X, India and the War (1939-40), Cmd. 6196
16. Objectives Resolution adopted by the Constituent Assembly of Pakistan on 12 March, 1949, Karachi, Constituent Assembly 1949
17. The Constitution of the Islamic Republic of Pakistan, 1956 (Produced by the Department of Advertising, Films and Publications, Government of Pakistan, Karachi March 1956)
18. The Constitution of the Republic of Pakistan, 1962: inclusive of insertions up to and by the Constitution (Fourth Amendment) Act, 1965: Constitutions of Asian Countries, N. M. Tripathi Private Ltd., Bombay, 1968
19. Constituent Assembly Debates, Official Reports (Karachi: Government of Pakistan Press, 1947-56)
20. The Interim Report of the Basic Principles Committee (Karachi: Government of Pakistan Press, 1950)
21. The Final Report of the Basic Principles Committee (Karachi: Government of Pakistan Press, 1952)
22. The Report of the Basic Principles Committee (as adopted by the Constituent Assembly, 1954, Karachi: Government of Pakistan Press, 1954)
23. *One Unit—Historical Constitutional and Administrative Perspective* (Lahore: Government of the Punjab Press, 1955)

24. Basic Democracies, Rules and Ordinances 1959-60. (Karachi, Government of Pakistan Press)

25. Report of the Constitution Commission, 1961 (Karachi, Manager of Publications, 1962)

26. Franchise Commission Report. The Gazette of Pakistan Extraordinary, Karachi, 23 August 1963

27. Presidential Election Results, 1965. Rawalpindi, Election Commission, Pakistan, 1965

28. Election Laws Manual with Electoral Rolls Order and Rules. 1969, and Provisional Constitution Order, 1969: Lahore, Lahore Law Times Publications, 1969

29. Supplementary to Election Laws Manual ; containing: I. Provisional Constitution Order, 1969 ; II. Electoral Rolls Order, 1969 ; III. Electoral Rolls Rules, 1969 ; IV. Legal Framework Order, 1970 ; V. National Assembly Rules of Procedure, 1970 ; VI. Province of West Pakistan (Dissolution) Order, 1970. Lahore, Lahore Law Times Publications 1970.

30. Legal Framework Order (President's Order No. 2 of 1970) of 30 March 1970 (Press release, March 30, 1970, by Government of Pakistan, Press Information Department, Rawalpindi)

31. The Bangladesh Proclamation of Independence Order of 10 April 1971 (effective from 26 March 1971) Bangla Desh Documents (External Affairs Ministry, New Delhi, September 1971) pp. 281-282

32. Nehru-Liaquat Ali Agreement of 8 April 1950

33. The Hague Convention (IV) Respecting the Laws and Customs of War on Land of 18 October 1907. J. B. Scott, *The Hague Conventions and Declarations of 1899 and 1907*. H. W. Briggs, *The Law of Nations* (2nd ed.)

34. The Geneva Protocol of 17 June 1925

35. Geneva Convention of 27 July 1929 for the Relief of the Wounded and Sick in Armies in the Field
Geneva Convention of 27 July 1929 Relative to the Treatment of Prisoners of War

36. American Declaration of the Rights and Duties of Man, 1948 Brownlie, *Basic Documents on Human Rights* (Oxford, 1971) p. 389

37. Convention on the Prevention and Punishment of the Crime of Genocide, 1948
(1949) Vol. III International Organization p. 206
Brownlie, *Basic Documents* p. 116

38. The Universal Declaration of Human Rights of 6 December 1948
(1949) Vol. III, International Organization p. 202
Brownlie, *Basic Documents on Human Rights* (1971) p. 106

39. Four Geneva Conventions of 12 August 1949:
(i) For the Amelioration of the Condition of the Wounded and Sick in Armed Forces in the Field

(ii) For the Amelioration of the Condition of the Wounded, Sick and Shipwrecked Members of Armed Forces

(iii) Relative to the Treatment of Prisoners of War

(iv) Relative to the Protection of Civilian Persons in Time of War

(1950) Vol. 75 United Nations Treaty Series, I.   Nos. 970-973

40. European Convention on Human Rights, 1950 and its Five Protocols.
Collection of International Conventions, Agreements and other Texts Concerning Refugees, published by the Office of the UN High Commissioner for Refugees, 1971 (UNHCR Collection) p. 149
Brownlie, *Basic Documents* p. 338

41. Geneva Convention Relating to the Status of Refugees of 28 July 1951, entered into force on 22 April 1954
189 UN Treaty Series p. 137
Brownlie, *Basic Documents*, p. 135
Protocol Relating to the Status of Refugees adopted by the General Assembly on 16 December 1966
(1967) 42 British Yearbook p. 67
UNHCR Collection p. 53.

42. The Declaration on the Granting of Independence to Colonial Countries and Peoples—General Assembly Resolution 1514 (XV) of 14 December 1960
UN Yearbook 1960 p. 49
Brownlie, *Basic Documents* p. 113

43. General Assembly Resolution 1541 (XV) of 15 December 1960 on the Transmission of Information under Article 73(e) of the Charter.
UN Yearbook p. 509

44. Draft Declaration on the Right of Asylum of the Commission on Human Rights 1960
(1960) UN Yearbook p. 341

45. The Declaration on the Elimination of All Forms of Racial Discrimination: General Assembly Resolution of 1904 (XVIII) of 20 November 1963
(1964) 58 American Journal of International Law (AJIL) p. 1081

46. United Nations Resolutions on Rhodesia:
General Assembly Resolution: 2012(XX) of 12 October 1965
General Assembly Resolution: 2022(XX) of 5 November 1965
General Assembly Resolution: 2024(XX) of 11 November 1965
Security Council Resolutions:
216 of 12 November 1965
217 of 20 November 1965
221 of 9 April 1966
(1966) 60 AJIL pp. 291-296

47. International Convention on the Elimination of All Forms of Racial Discrimination, 1966 adopted by the General Assembly on 21 December 1965
(1966) 60 AJIL p. 650
Brownlie, *Basic Documents* p. 237

48. International Covenant on Economic, Social and Cultural Rights And International Covenant on Civil and Political Rights (approved by the General Assembly by Resolution 2200 (XXI)
(1967) 61 AJIL pp. 861-890

49. Principles Concerning the Treatment of Refugees adopted by the Asian-African Legal Consultative Committee at Bangkok in 1966
Annexure I to the Paper 'The Current Refugees Situation in India and International Law' by S. P. Jogota and J. C. Jain

50. United Nations Declaration on Territorial Asylum, 1967 adopted by the General Assembly on 14 December 1967 by Resolution 2312 (XXII)
UN Yearbook 1967 p. 760

51. UN Resolution on Arab Refugees:
Security Council Resolution 237 (1967) of 14 June 1967
General Assembly Resolution 2252 (ES-V) of 4 July 1967
Resolution VI (XXIV) of Commission on Human Rights
Resolution adopted by the United Nations Conference on Human Rights at its 23rd plenary meeting at Tehran on 7 May 1968
(1968) 62 AJIL p. 305
(1969) 63 AJIL p. 677

52. The Proclamation of Tehran, 1968
(1969) 63 AJIL p. 674
Brownlie, *Basic Documents* p. 253

53. Convention on Non-Applicability of Statutory Limitations to War Crimes and Crimes against Humanity (adopted by the General Assembly on 26 November 1968, and entered into force on 11 November 1970)
Keesings Contemporary Archives, 1969-70 p. 23196

54. American Convention on Human Rights, 1969
UNHCR Collection, p. 263
Brownlie, *Basic Documents,* p. 399

55. Draft Resolution L. 489 adopted by the General Assembly as Resolution 2603A (XXIV) on 16 December 1969 on Question of Chemical and Bacteriological (Biological) Weapons
(1970) 64 AJIL 393

56. Declaration on Principles of International Law Concerning Friendly Relations and Co-operation Among States in Accordance with the Charter of the United Nations, 1970 (adopted by the General Assembly by Resolution 2625 (XXV) of 24 October 1970)

International Legal Materials, Vol. IX. No. 6, November 1970 pp. 1292-1297

57. UN Resolutions on Human Rights in Armed Conflicts: General Assembly Resolutions 2675 (XXV), 2676 (XXV) and 2677 (XXV) of 9 December 1970
United Nations Press Services, N. Y. Resolutions of Legal Interest, 15 September—17 December, 1970, p. 49-56

58. UN Resolution on Punishment for War Crimes and Crimes against Humanity: Resolution 2712 (XXV) of 15 December 1970
United Nations Press Services, N. Y. Resolutions of Legal Interest 15 September—17 December, 1970, p. 57

59. U.N. General Assembly Resolution No.   377A(V)   of   3-11-50
    ,,   ,,   ,,   ,,   478(V)   ,, 16-12-50
    ,,   ,,   ,,   ,,   598(VI)   ,, 12- 1-52
    ,,   ,,   ,,   ,,   1514(XV)   ,, 14-12-60
    ,,   ,,   ,,   ,,   1541(XV)   ,, 15-12-60
    ,,   ,,   ,,   ,,   1904(XVIII) ,, 20-11-63
    ,,   ,,   ,,   ,,   2012(XX)   ,, 12-10-65
    ,,   ,,   ,,   ,,   2022(XX)   ,,   5-11-65
    ,,   ,,   ,,   ,,   2024(XX)   ,, 11-11-65
    ,,   ,,   ,,   ,,   2200(XXI)   ,, 16-12-66
    ,,   ,,   ,,   ,,   2252(ES-V)   ,,   4- 7-67
    ,,   ,,   ,,   ,,   2312(XXII)   ,, 14-12-67
    ,,   ,,   ,,   ,,   2603A(XXIV) ,, 16-12-69
    ,,   ,,   ,,   ,,   2625(XXV)   ,, 24-10-70
    ,,   ,,   ,,   ,,   2675(XXV)   ,,   9-12-70
    ,,   ,,   ,,   ,,   2676(XXV)   ,,   9-12-70
    ,,   ,,   ,,   ,,   2677(XXV)   ,,   9-12-70
    ,,   ,,   ,,   ,,   2712(XXV)   ,, 15-12-70
    ,,   ,,   ,,   ,,   ————   ,,   8-12-71

60. Security Council Resolution   216 of 12-11-65
    ,,   ,,   217 ,, 20-11-65
    ,,   ,,   221 ,, 9- 4-66
    ,,   ,,   237 ,, 4- 6-67
    ,,   ,,   3039 ,, 6-12-71
    ,,   ,,   ———— ,, 15-12-71
    ,,   ,,   ———— ,, 21-12-71

61. Official Records, General Assembly, 6th Session, 6th Committee, 292nd meeting, para 40

62. Report by the Secretary-General on the Question of Defining Aggression, A/2111, 3 October 1952 p. 58

63. UN Report on Economic and Social Council (16.8.64—31.7.65) Chapter XIII, Sec. VI

64. Deliberations of the Economic and Social Council at its 50th Session in New York in May 1971 and 51st Session in Geneva in July 1971

III. REPORTS, JOURNALS, PAMPHLETS, PAPERS, NEWSPAPERS, PRESS RELEASES ETC.

1. Judgement of the Nuremberg Tribunal of 30 September 1946
   6964 (1946) Command Papers, (1947) 41 AJIL p. 172-333

2. Judgement of the International Military Tribunal of the Far East of November 4, 1948
   Annual Digest and Reports of Public International Law, 1948

3. *Dissentient Judgement of Justice R. B. Pal of International Military Tribunal for the Far East* (Sanyal & Co. Calcutta 1953)

4. Law Reports of Trials of War Criminals, 15 Vols. Selected and prepared by the United Nations War Crimes Commission and Published for it by His Majesty's Stationery Office (1946-1949)

5. International Court of Justice Reports (1951)
   (Advisory Opinion on reservation to the Genocide Convention)

6. Judgement of the Pakistan Federal Court in Federation of Pakistan *vs* Moulivi Tamizuddin Khan, Lahore, Government Printing, 1955.

7. *Ex parte Yamashita*:
   (1946) 327 U. S. Supreme Court Reports p. 1-90 Lawyers ed. p. 499

8. History of the United Nations War Crimes Commission 1948

9. International Organization (1949) Vol. III pp. 202, 206, 499

10. International Relations, November 1970

11. International Conciliation, November 1961.

12. U. N. Yearbook, 1960 pp. 49, 341, 509

13. U. N. Yearbook 1967, p. 760

14. The Canadian Yearbook on International Law 1969 p. 92

15. Report of the World Bank Mission to East Pakistan 1971

16. 33 California Law Review pp. 177-218

17. American Journal of International Law: (1944) Vol. 38 Supp ; (1945) Vol. 39 Supp ; (1947) Vol. 41 ; (1948) Vol. 42 ; (1960) Vol. 54 ; (1963) Vol. 57 ; (1964) Vol. 58 ; (1966) Vol. 60 ; (1967) Vol. 61 ; (1968) Vol. 62 ; (1969) Vol. 63 ; (1970) Vol. 64 ; (NB : Page references in the footnotes)

18. Cambridge Review—28 May 1971

19. Pakistan Development Review—Volume 8, 1968 pp. 452-88

20. Asian Review—Vol. 2, No. 2 (January 1909) pp. 136-47

21. The New Republic—19 March 1956.

22. 6668 (1945) Command Papers (Great Britain)
    The Nuremberg Charter
    6696 (1945) Command Papers (Great Britain)
    The Indictment of 18 October 1945

6964 (1946) Command Papers (Great Britain)
The Nuremberg Judgement

23. Keesings Contemporary Archives 1954, p. 13746
Keesings Contemporary Archives January 30—February 6, 1971-72 p. 24413
Keesings Contemporary Archives 1969-70, p. 23196

24. War Bulletins of Bangladesh Forces HQ, Public Relations Department, Bangladesh Government, various issues between June and November 1971.

25. *Conflict in East Pakistan Background and Prospects*   By Professors Edward S. Mason, Robert Dorfman, and Stephen A Marglin. Reproduced by the Department of Information, Government of Bangladesh, Mujibnagar ; reprinted by Calcutta University Bangladesh Sahayak Samity.

26. *History of Economic and Political Domination of East Pakistan*   A Paper reviewed for the Ripon Society by J. Lee Auspitz, President, Ripon Society—Stephen A. Marglin, Professor of Economics, Harvard University ; and Gustav F. Papenek, Lecturer in Economics and former Director, Development Advisory Service, Harvard University. Bangla Desh Documents, External Affairs Ministry, Government of India, New Delhi, September 1971, p. 5.

27. Documents on American Foreign Relations, 1954 (Harper, New York, 1954)

28. United States Foreign Policy, 1969-70, Report of the Secretary of State. Department of State Publication, General Foreign Policy Series 254, released March 1971, Washington.

29. Statement before Special Tribunal in Agartala Conspiracy Case by Mujibur Rahman

30. *6-Point Formula—Our Right to Live*, Sheikh Mujibur Rahman (23 March 1966)

31. Report of Advisory Panel for the Fourth Five Year Plan, Planning Commission, Government of Pakistan, July 1970.

32. Who Should be in the Dock: A Talk by Subrata Roy Chowdhury, All India Radio, Calcutta, Hindusthan Standard, 14 July 1971.

33. Press Information Department, Government of Pakistan, Handout E, No. 684-R, Rawalpindi, 28.3.1970,

34. Press Release, March 30, 1970, by Government of Pakistan, Press Information Department, Rawalpindi.

35. Press Note issued by the Dacca University on 23 December 1971

36. 'The Current Refugee Situation in India and International Law' by S. P. Jagota & J. C. Jain ; 'The Practice of Asylum in International Law' by Miss Basanti Mitra: Papers read before the Annual Seminar of the International Law Association, Indian Branch, New Delhi, on 10 October 1971.

37. Time Magazine, 30 November, 7 and 21 December 1970 ; 15 March, 5, 26 April, 3 May, 21 June, 2 and 23 August, 25 October, 6, 20 and 27 December 1971 ; 3 January 1972.

38. Newsweek, 5, 26 April, 3 May, 28 June, 2 August, 22 November, 6, 27 December 1971 ; 3 January 1972.

39. Times, London, 2 January 1965 ; 22 March 3, 5 and 26 April, 3 and 31 May, 2, 5, 8, 11 and 21 June, 33 August, 6 September, 25 October, 13, 20 and 27 December 1971.

40. New York Times, 5 January 1965 ; 7, 28, 29, 30, 31 March, 7 April, 14 July, 5 and 6 August, 28 September and 7 December 1971.

41. The Guardian, London, 31 March, 27 May, 5 June, 6 and 30 August 1971

42. The Daily Telegraph, London, 3, 30 March, 6 August, 1971.

43. Sunday Telegraph, London, 1 August 1971.

44. Daily Mirror, London, 16 June 1971.

45. Daily Mail, London, 7 June 1971.

46. Observer, London, 6 July 1968.

47. The Sunday Times, London, 6, 13, 20 June, 11 July, 9 December 1971.

48. Evening Standard, London, 7 June 1971.

49. The Statesman, Calcutta 1, 4, 7, 8, 9, 10, 14, 15, 20, 21, 26, 27 April, 6, 13, 20, 23, 25 27 May, 12, 16 June, 4, 9, 14, 21, 22, 23 and 24 July, 2, 5, 6, 8, 9, 15, 17, 19 August, 1, 4, 6, 11, 15, 18, 19, 21, 28 and 30 September ; 2, 4, 20, 25, 26 October, 1, 2, 20, 25, 26, 28 October, 1, 2, 9, 10, 12, 13, 27, 28 29 30 November, 1, 2, 3, 4, ,6, 7, 8, 9, 10, 11, 14, 16, 17, 18, 19, 20, 21, 23, 24 25, 27, 28, 29, 30, 31 December 1971 ; 1, 4, 18, 23, 25, January 1972.

50. The Sunday Statesman, New Delhi, 18 April 1971.

51. The Statesman, New Delhi, 16 October 1971.

52. Dawn (Karachi), 26 November 1951 ; 4 April 1957 ; 17 and 21 March 1966 ; 14 March 1969 ; 29 October, 20, 28 December 1970; 12 January, 4, 5, 6, 7, 8, 11, 12, 13, 14, 15, 16, 17, 18, 23, 25, 26, 27 and 28 March 1971.

53. The Pakistan Times (Lahore), 17 and 19 March, 3 April 1954 ;

1 May 1964 ; 26 March 1969 ; 22 December 1970 ; 20 and 31 January, 1, 23, and 26 March 1971.

54. Morning News (Karachi & Dacca), 26 and 28 October, 26, 27 and 28 November 1970 ; 2, 7 and 25 March 1971.

55. Pakistan Observer, 19, 22 December 1970 ; 4 and 15 January 1971.

56. Hindusthan Standard, Calcutta, 14 and 30 July, 26 August, 2, 20 September, 17, 20, 24, 25, 26, 27, 30 and 31 December 1971 ; 5, 7, 8 January 1972.

57. The Sunday Standard, 18 April 1971.

58. Amrita Bazar Patrika, Calcutta, 5 and 23 June, 4, 10 July, 22 & 27 August 1971.

59. Ananda Bazar Patrika, 8 January 1972.

60. The People (Dacca), 10, 11, 12, 18, 20 and 21 October, 1, 6, 10, 13, 14, 15, 16, 19 November 1970 ; 2 & 3 March 1971.

61. The Manila Chronicle, 5 July 1971.

62. The Baltimore Sun, 14 May 1971.

63. Times of India, 2 May 1971, 24.8.1971. 17 October 1971.

64. The Hong Kong Standard, 25 June 1971.

65. Dagena Nyheter, Stockholm, 27 June 1971.

66. Vecenje Novesty, Yugoslavia, 8 July 1971.

67. The Saturday Review (U.S.A.), 22 May 1971.

68. Washington Daily News, 30 June 1971.

69. Palaver Weekly, Ghana, 8 July 1971.

70. Illustrated Weekly of India, Bombay, 15 August, 19 December 1971 ; 16 January 1972.

71. Joi Bangla, 24 September 1971.

72. Western Political Quarterly, June 1965 pp. 382-92.

73. Mainstream, 17 July 1971.

74. Religion, Caracas (Venezuela), 3 July 1971.

75. Washington Post, 31 July 1971, 15 August 1971.

76. Wall Street, Journal, New York, 23 July 1971.

77. The Christian Science Monitor, 31 July 1971.

78. Globe And Mail, Ottawa, Canada, 10 July 1971.

INDEX

This Index has been very kindly prepared by
Mr Nandadulal Mukherjee